Jewish Arguments and Counterarguments

Jewish Arguments and Counterarguments

ESSAYS AND ADDRESSES

STEVEN BAYME

KTAV PUBLISHING HOUSE, INC.
in association with
THE AMERICAN JEWISH COMMITTEE

Library of Congress Cataloging-in-Publication Data

Bayme, Steven
   Jewish arguments and counterarguments: essays and addresses / Steven Bayme.
      p. cm.
   ISBN 0-88125-738-9
   1. Jews--United States--Identity. 2. Jews--United States--Social conditions. 3. Jewish
families--United States. 4. Orthodox Judaism--Relations--Nontraditional Jews. 5.
Judaism--United States. 8. Israel and the Diaspora. I.Title.

e184.36.e84 b385 2002
305.892'4073--dc21

                                                                        2002023826

Distributed by
Ktav Publishing House, Inc.
900 Jefferson Street
Hoboken, NJ 07030
201-963-9524 FAX 201-963-0102
Email orders@ktav.com
Web www.ktav.com

To Jack and Susan Lapin, two leaders of the American Jewish Committee whose tireless commitment, personal friendship, and unstinting support for ensuring the future continuity of Jewish life have and always will inspire my efforts.

CONTENTS

Contents / viii

JEWISH FAMILY POLICY

INTERMARRIAGE, JEWISH CONTINUITY, AND OUTREACH

Contents / ix

LETTERS TO THE EDITOR

Publication of this volume was made possible in part by a grant from the Susan and Jack Lapin Fund for Jewish Continuity.

FOREWORD

In *Ethics of the Fathers,* Hillel states: "An ignorant person cannot be pious; the timid cannot learn; nor can the quick-tempered teach."

Dr. Steven Bayme is unquestionably a pious individual, a learned man, and a gifted teacher. If proof were needed, this book provides it in abundance.

A deeply committed Jew, Steve has devoted his entire professional life to enhancing the ties that bind Jews to their heritage and to one another.

In the pursuit of his noble mission, he brings an extraordinary breadth and depth of knowledge that comes from an insatiable thirst for study and exploration of the world of ideas. Steve is seldom without a book in hand—on topics ranging from politics and history to theology and sociology—and he approaches each new volume as a reader with inexhaustible curiosity and well-honed critical instincts. Best of all, because of an enviably retentive memory, he seems to have instant recall of everything he has ever read.

Steve is a gifted teacher, a skill he has used to great effect not only in the university classroom but also in the meeting rooms of the American Jewish Committee and other American Jewish religious and secular institutions.

Drawing upon his vast storehouse of knowledge, infectious enthusiasm for his chosen topic, and engaging demeanor, he has opened up the treasure trove of Jewish civilization in its wide array of hues and forms—and in its interaction with Western civilization more broadly—for countless admiring students. In the process, he has contributed to the education of generations of Jews about the joys and riches of their identity, as well as helped shape the communal debate on such pressing issues as Jewish demography, literacy, intra-Jewish relations, and Israel-Diaspora ties.

Like Steve's previous book, *Understanding Jewish History,* which met with critical acclaim for its comprehensive, erudite, and accessible approach to Jewish history, the present volume is also certain to garner much attention and wide readership. Touching on contemporary—and, in some cases, highly controversial—themes of vital importance to the Jewish people, and written with passion, honesty, and intellectual rigor, this collection of essays, speeches, and published articles will surely become an invaluable reference tool for the Jewish community for many years to come.

At our regular American Jewish Committee staff meetings, Steve often begins his comments by saying that he has "three points" to make, perhaps because Jews from an early age have been taught that so much of our identity is based on the principle of three. In that spirit, let me conclude with my bottom-line "three points" about Steve: he has been a cherished colleague of mine for two decades, an invaluable asset to the American Jewish Committee, and an eloquent voice in any and all discussions about the Jewish condition.

David A. Harris
Executive Director, American Jewish Committee
November 2001

INTRODUCTION

The present volume, consisting of my published writings over the past two decades, spans three thematic clusters: American Jewry and Judaism, Israel and Jewish peoplehood, and the claims of Jewish tradition in the modern world. These three areas have defined my professional responsibilities at the American Jewish Committee of monitoring the condition of American Jewry and finding ways to enhance it, strengthening ties among Jews worldwide and especially with Israel, the most critical expression of Jewish peoplehood today, and demonstrating the salience of Jewish heritage and values in a modern culture that glorifies individual conscience and freedom of behavior.

Given that context, the ideas expressed in this volume have all emanated from my professional responsibilities at the American Jewish Committee. Family policy, intermarriage, and Jewish education have been central themes within AJC's overall mandate of enhancing Jewish continuity and countering assimilation. In fact, the AJC was the first of the national civic agencies to create a commission and department devoted to strengthening Jewish life, on the assumption that the Jewish community's human relations efforts made sense only if there existed a critical mass of Jews interested in leading a creative Jewish life. Similarly, the AJC was the first American Jewish organization to open an office in Israel and subsequently to establish the Dorothy and Julius Koppelman Institute on American Jewish-Israeli Relations to address questions of Jewish peoplehood and to build bridges between Israel and Diaspora Jewry. Lastly, in recent years the AJC has devoted attention to intra-Jewish tensions, even while acknowledging that internal Jewish challenges and dangers are quite likely to prove divisive if not insoluble within the Jewish community.

Professionally, then, this volume is an outgrowth of my responsibilities as a communal servant and spokesperson at the AJC. Yet there is also a personal dimension to this work. Friends and acquaintances often tease me by saying that I earn a living off their dinnertime conversations. In truth, I am fortunate in that my personal and professional interests often do converge, and work becomes a "labor of love" of monitoring, analyzing, and disseminating information on the Jewish condition. For the past 20 years, the American Jewish Committee has been the setting of this convergence of my passionately held interests and my professional responsibilities. Of that more later, but first, where did this journey begin?

The Boston, Massachusetts, of the 1950s and 1960s in which I was raised was hardly the "Athens of America" made famous by Harvard University and the Massachusetts Institute of Technology. Rather, the Boston that I knew and loved resembled more a Jewish shtetl than a cultural mecca. In this shtetl the ties of Jewish peoplehood were paramount. The "Jewish street" consisted of many types of Jews—learned and unlearned, affluent and poor, religious and secular. Uniting them was the common bond of knowing that there were too few of us and therefore Jews were responsible for one another.

In retrospect, I am struck by how marginal anti-Semitism was to this sense of Jewish identity. To be sure, there were tensions with gentiles. I lived in a changing Jewish neighborhood, and anti-Jewish slurs and even violence against Jewish institutions and individuals were by no means uncommon occurrences. Moreover, while the Holocaust as an event was mentioned only rarely, there was hardly a Jewish family untouched by it. Yet these memories, and, in some cases, more recent brushes with anti-Semitism, were not central to defining my Jewishness, much less comprise a reason for remaining a Jew. Rather my identity lay more in appreciation of Judaism and Jewish peoplehood than in fear of gentile society. The imagery of the sukkah captures my childhood experience. Although the sukkah offered poor physical protection against the elements, the sounds and smells of Jewish song, learning, food, and family within the humble hut seemed far more compelling than the chilly weather of Boston Octobers (or, for that matter, the yearly gloom that set in with the annual collapse of the Red Sox).

For these reasons, I continue to register some discomfort at the growth of Holocaust consciousness in contemporary America. One prominent Hillel director reports that more students on his campus are taking the course on the Holocaust than are enrolled in all other Jewish studies courses combined. Although the Holocaust occupies a rightful place as a dominant historical event of our time (my initial university teaching experience, in fact, was a course on the Holocaust), I cannot see constructing a Jewish identity upon a narrative of Jewish destruction—much less do I perceive the Holocaust as the primary statement of who and what the Jews are as a people.

Moreover, the Jewish day school that I attended for 13 years in Boston, the Maimonides School founded in 1938 by Rabbi Joseph B. Soloveitchik, provided a marvelous social and intellectual setting for my Jewish identity to grow and develop. Discovering history at a very early age, I quickly started reading Jewish history voraciously. The Hebrew language, Bible, and Talmud became as familiar to me as American history, politics, and sports—although, to be sure, math and physics remained impenetrable to a mind focused upon the humanities and social sciences.

These interests began to acquire intellectual substance during my high school years. The Maimonides Day School proudly defined itself as Modern Orthodox. Rabbi Soloveitchik, its intellectual dean, prided himself on being rooted in both the world of Torah and that of general philosophy, and he constructed a school in which commitment to excellence in secular studies matched the dedication to excellence in Judaic studies. Rabbi Soloveitchik's weekly Saturday night public lectures articulated a vision of Judaism that was intellectually demanding and encouraged doubt and the search for answers rather than the certainty offered by simplistic solutions.

Moreover, the opportunities available to me in high school multiplied. High school debates on public policy issues with both public and parochial schools in the Boston area exposed me to contemporaries with other world views, lifestyles, and even religious beliefs, while providing wonderful training in research and advocacy. These skills served well my later enthusiasm for participation in the staff and lay leadership debates within the American Jewish Committee. A high school history teacher who questioned the historicity of the splitting of the Red Sea in biblical times exposed me to a world of skepticism and doubt about the very traditions I cherished and demonstrated that Orthodox Jewish education need not be equated with dogmatism and intolerance of dissenting opinion. Perhaps most gratifying and inspirational was an East European rabbi, a teacher of Talmud and Bible to the junior and senior classes, who assigned a series of research papers. These required us to compare and contrast the accounts of creation in traditional commentaries with the views of modern science, the varying ethical sensibilities of the stories of the patriarchs, and, most surprisingly, the Joseph narrative in traditional commentaries with Thomas Mann's *Joseph and His Brothers.* The excitement of sustained research and writing on two very different types of source materials provided a capstone for 13 years of Jewish day school education. In short, I am convinced that I was blessed in receiving a Jewish education at its finest in its demand of student achievement in both Judaic and secular realms and in its willingness to address the tensions between those two realms.

By the time I graduated high school in June 1967—a significant date as I will note later—I was convinced of the salience of Modern Orthodoxy. Modern Orthodoxy's vision of living in two worlds, carefully weighing the ties and tensions between them, suggested an intellectual adventure that I found compelling and which, I was sure, would prove to be the wave of the future. As one Jewish communal professional would comment to me decades later, "The image of Modern Orthodoxy conveyed is so attractive that anyone in their right mind would want to be part of it." Of course, she was correct in perceiving that Modern Orthodoxy had by no means triumphed and that my personal vision of it did not always match its reality.

Nevertheless, I entered university study in September 1967, determined to explore higher education at the flagship institution of Modern Orthodoxy, Yeshiva University in New York. Yeshiva in the 1960s was, indeed, an exciting place. Like other campuses, it experienced its own upheavals concerning Vietnam, civil rights, and campus governance. Yet this was student activism filtered through the confrontation between Jewish tradition and modern culture. Dr. Irving (Yitz) Greenberg, then a professor of history at Yeshiva and the most controversial, and, for some, the most influential member of the faculty of that era, brilliantly articulated the challenge of creating a distinctive synthesis of Judaism and Western culture intended to transform both in exciting ways. To his right, Yeshiva's Talmud faculty criticized Greenberg's openness to biblical criticism, his dialogue with Conservative and Reform rabbis and theologians, and his indebtedness to Christian sources and thinkers. Over time, these isolationist forces triumphed, as Yeshiva and American Orthodoxy moved steadily rightward. For me, however, participation in those debates in the late 1960s existentially defined my Jewish identity and convinced me that study of Judaic heritage could be both challenging and fulfilling intellectually and religiously, while laying the groundwork for a life-long labor of love in Jewish public affairs.

Simultaneously, the Jewish world in which I had been nurtured changed profoundly after my high school years. In May 1967, three Arab armies stood poised on Israel's borders calling for her destruction as a nation-state. The call for "evenhandedness" articulated in European capitals, the Vatican, and even in some Washington circles echoed an earlier period of Jewish history in which the world had, in fact, abandoned the Jews. When one television commentator predicted an Israeli victory, I was baffled. Jews were not supposed to win wars, or so I thought. The only hope lay in continued diplomacy to avert an Arab attack—a view shared at the time by representatives of Israel's National Religious Party, to which I nominally owed allegiance.

The events of June 1967 changed those perceptions. Israel's dramatic victory not only rescued the Jewish State from national tragedy; it fundamentally altered the self-perception of Jewish peoplehood. Here was a different Jew—one who was capable of defending himself and therefore merited universal admiration rather than pity.

Moreover, Israel now assumed center stage on the Jewish agenda. Hardly a conversation between committed Jews could pass without some reference to Israel's international context. The desire to visit Israel and to study there entered Jewish aspirations. Whereas prior to 1967, Israel had occupied a distant albeit desirable place on my radar screen, after the Six-Day War I would have to give serious and sustained thought to the relationship of Diaspora Jewry to Israel and how the return of Jewish sovereignty had altered irrevocably the meaning of

Jewish identity and membership in the Jewish people. These questions would stay with me for decades. For now, I felt intense pride in my Jewishness and in the Jews as a people of achievement, rather than as perpetual victims.

Yet despite the ongoing influence of Israel and recurring pulls of potential aliya, Diaspora Jewishness also placed claims upon me. I was living in the United States, a society which had welcomed Jews more thoroughly and provided greater opportunities for Jewish participation than had any society in Diaspora Jewish history. Moreover, Jewish history itself was proving to be the centerpiece of my academic interests. As I contemplated graduate school and doctoral work, I saw a natural match between my personal interest in history and professional work in the academic study of Jewish historical experience.

In that spirit, I entered a doctoral program in Jewish history at Columbia University in September 1971. Notwithstanding its reputation as a great secular university, Columbia at that time hosted an incredibly diverse and rich Jewish life. My roommate was Daniel Kurtzer, an Orthodox Jew and friend from undergraduate days, who would distinguish himself subsequently as a State Department officer and as U.S. ambassador to both Egypt and Israel. Adjacent to Columbia, the Jewish Theological Seminary, the premier institution of Conservative Judaism, not only enhanced my choice of course offerings, but provided a rich presence of Jewish traditionalism socially and religiously. Most importantly, Columbia's Jewish community operated on the principles of pluralism and inclusivity. Different types of Jews required different avenues for Judaic expression. The interaction of Jews of differing ideologies, it was believed, would create a stronger and more vibrant Jewish community.

Moreover, the Columbia faculty in Jewish history underscored the importance of Diaspora Jewry. Although Arthur Hertzberg then qualified as historian of Zionism par excellence, he and his colleagues, all disciples of Salo Baron, the dean of modern Jewish historians, decried the lachrymose conception of Jewish history as comprising a tale of unmitigated woe and repression. Their narration of Jewish history comprised a narrative that was far richer than anti-Semitism. Jewish history was about building community, religious life, accommodation with gentile society, the history of Jewish ideas, and social and economic behaviors. The Holocaust years, to be sure, comprised an important exception, but they provided a poor prism through which to view the entire Jewish experience. Ismar Schorsch, later Chancellor at the Jewish Theological Seminary, taught the history of the Holocaust, but he too underscored the importance of Jewish communal and religious institutions and the capacity of Jewish leaders to meet the challenges embedded in Jewish modernity. To be sure, anti-Semitism was latent in every society in which Jews had lived. However, what made the Jews interesting as a people was their successful adaptation to the surrounding society rather than their isolation from it.

Professionally, I discovered the joy of teaching. Dr. Norman Lamm, a former professor with whom I had studied Jewish philosophy and mysticism, became president of Yeshiva University and tendered me my first teaching appointment in Jewish and general history. Nervous at first, I was soon completely hooked on the "drug" of teaching. A long day of classes left me only exhilarated and eager to return for more. For one thing, Yeshiva University undergraduates were superb and a joy to teach. Products of intensive Jewish education, they provided a natural forum to explore Jewish ideas and their intersection with Western culture. The excellence of Yeshiva's student body remains to this day. One of my greatest professional joys occurred in the late 1990s when Yeshiva College Dean Norman Adler invited me to teach an honors seminar on the American Jewish community. But in the 1970s, my conversations with students, participation in campus politics, and ongoing preparation for classes convinced me that I was blessed with a wonderful opportunity to help shape the Jewish community and to articulate a distinctive vision of what it meant to be a Jew in the modern world.

Yet, by the late 1970s, Yeshiva and Modern Orthodoxy had changed profoundly. Students seemed increasingly preoccupied with Talmudic study and were limiting their secular pursuits to preprofessional rather than liberal arts concerns. American Orthodoxy had developed a new norm of following high school education with a year of study at an Israeli yeshiva, signaling the ascendancy of the world of Torah at the expense of secular learning. The once-marginal view within Orthodoxy that restricted secular study strictly to purposes of earning a living had now become much more mainstream. Increasingly I encountered opposition to my teaching style that encouraged questioning and doubt. Moreover, my publicly stated concerns about the religious messianism of Jewish settlers on the West Bank often put me at odds with political groupings on campus, e.g., the Jewish Defense League, which opposed any territorial compromise whatsoever. I wondered aloud to students why Rabbi Meir Kahane remained a featured speaker on campus, long after Kahane himself had been ostracized by the general Jewish community and despite his message of hatred and racism toward Arabs, which sounded chillingly reminiscent of the Nuremberg legislation of the 1930s.

Nevertheless, I was eager for intellectual combat and probably would have continued at Yeshiva had pragmatic considerations not intruded and new opportunities beckoned. For one thing, my 1973 marriage had resulted in the birth of our first child in 1977, and I was beginning to worry about a financial squeeze. The rabbi of my synagogue cautioned me that I would never afford day school tuition on my existing salary. Even more importantly, I discovered that I was not personally suited to a lifetime of archival research. Although I completed my doctoral dissertation satisfactorily in 1977, I questioned whether I had the passion for original research into relatively esoteric historical questions. I wondered whether I might be more suited temperamentally for more popular research and writing on contemporary topics than to publishing articles of interest primarily to other researchers and historians. At the same time, I well recognized that the financial and professional rewards of academia would fall to those who authored precisely the types of research for which I was increasingly questioning my capacities.

Marriage and parenting affected me in other ways as well. Quickly I discovered that these were two experiences that placed maximal demands and expectations, yet for which little or no training had been provided. Responsibility for the development of infants into Jewish adults would prove especially humbling. Once again, however, I discovered the riches of Jewish tradition and its power to enhance family life. At my Orthodox high school, I recalled how I had first been exposed to the beautiful writings on the Sabbath by the premiere theologian of Conservative Judaism, Abraham Joshua Heschel. Heschel had defined Judaism as "sacred time" and portrayed the Shabbat as a marvelous Jewish institution providing a 25-hour retreat from mundane concerns and an opportunity for families to be together around the common Jewish table. Once again, I was convinced of the power of Jewish tradition. Shabbat provided precious family time, while giving Jews a distinctive character and institution found nowhere else in the ancient world. The historian in me began to identify family as an arena to explore the relationship between tradition and modern culture—a subject that would preoccupy me increasingly in the years ahead. More immediately, especially given my concerns about Orthodoxy's rightward drift, I wondered whether my experience with Heschel suggested that Jewish religious leaders might better cooperate with one another in articulating the beauties of Judaism and Jewish tradition than in casting stones at each other's doctrines.

My practical concerns of family and career ultimately prevailed, and I began to look outside academia for employment. Answering a blind ad in the *New York Jewish Week,* I came to Hadassah, the premiere Jewish women's organization. I learned that Henrietta Szold, legendary founder of Hadassah, had built an organization based on practical projects to benefit the Jewish settlement in pre-state Palestine and the creation of Hadassah study circles to provide Jewish education for American Jewish women. Hadassah presented me with the opportunity to direct its adult education program targeted to 375,000 women and 25,000 Hadassah activists. The experience was rewarding in several senses: First, it stimulated my thinking about adult education and the possibilities and challenges it poses to the Jewish community. Secondly, as a grassroots organization, Hadassah offered a critical window onto American Jewish life in local communities, far removed from major academic centers and the critical mass of New York Jewry. Lastly, as a women's Zionist organization, Hadassah persuaded me again of the centrality of Israel to the contemporary Jewish world. These were all themes that I would return to in writings over the subsequent decades.

If Hadassah provided a transition from academic to communal work, my career took its most fundamental and enduring turn in the early 1980s. Yehuda Rosenman, the long-time director of the American Jewish Committee's Jewish Communal Affairs Department, whom I had met while at Hadassah, invited me to join the AJC as assistant director of the department he headed. The American Jewish Committee, I quickly discovered, was a unique organization, in many ways ideally suited to my talents and interests. For one thing, the AJC was headed by superb professionals—Bert Gold, David Gordis, the late Ira Silverman, and, for the past decade, David Harris, all of whom valued my work and stimulated its growth. More generally, the AJC operates on the principle that ideas do matter and that Jewish agencies need to engage on the battleground of ideas in order to influence and shape the overall climate of opinion. In such an environment, what many communal professionals and lay leaders liked to term the "Harvard of Jewish agencies," I could devote myself to thinking, teaching, and writing about contemporary Jewish issues.

Moreover, a natural synergy existed between AJC's agenda and my own intellectual and professional interests. I hoped to supply AJC with some programmatic substance, and AJC would provide the appropriate forum for my ideas to be heard. Indeed, the range of issues AJC encouraged me to address—intermarriage, Jewish education, Jewish peoplehood, religious pluralism, and Israel-Diaspora relations, among many others—seemed to comprise an ideal fit between my own persona and the vital questions on the cutting edge of Jewish life. Yehuda Rosenman, my first supervisor at AJC and a wonderful mentor in Jewish communal work, promised me that I would have the opportunity to provide leadership and direction to the Jewish community. He was not wrong, either in his prediction, or in his diagnosis that the opportunity to work with him and AJC would shape my career.

Yehuda also predicted that AJC would undergo a gradual but significant transformation as a Jewish agency. In particular, during the last decade, under the professional leadership of David Harris and Shula Bahat, working together with AJC lay leadership, the American Jewish Committee has become much more unambiguous in its Jewishness and firmly anchored in its relationship with Israel. David Harris, in particular, underscored the responsibility of Jewish leadership to defend the collective welfare of the Jewish people and to translate Israel's concerns on matters of foreign policy and security to elite and influential

Jewish and non-Jewish audiences. Moreover, at a time of growing concern for Jewish continuity, David and Shula encouraged my efforts to infuse the AJC with Judaic content and to bring Jewish identity and education into the front lines of AJC culture and policy debates. A decade later, the transformation of AJC as a Jewish agency continues, but few question the centrality of internal Jewish communal concerns to AJC's mission. I hope I have played a small role in that transformation, but none of it would have been possible without the support of AJC's superb professional and volunteer leadership.

Lastly, the AJC constituency proved a natural setting for my teaching and writing. Often AJC meetings resembled those of the Council on Foreign Relations—well-educated and accomplished individuals with a passion for public policy gathering to discuss the major issues of the day. I wondered why we could not muster the same level of expertise expended on general public policy concerns to internal Jewish matters. At root, if the Jews define themselves as people of the book, why should that book remain closed to all but a tiny minority of Jews? These were some of the objectives I set for myself in undertaking the challenges so vitally posed by the American Jewish Committee.

In short, the AJC has provided me a home for the past two decades—a place to teach, uniting my academic interests with my commitment to activism on the front lines of Jewish communal life. In many ways, the present volume is an outgrowth and a statement of that 20-year marriage between myself and AJC. Publication of this volume represents an important milestone in our ongoing relationship and what, for me, has been a true labor of love.

More specifically, the organization of this book, drawn from two decades of writing and speaking, reflects the diversity of the AJC agenda, my own personal and intellectual development, and the match between those elements. The opening section reflects my historical training—providing historical perspective on critical events and trends in the Jewish experience. More recently I have become very interested in questions of historical memory—how events are remembered and the transmittal of historical memory to current consciousness. In this area, I have increasingly been convinced of the power of Jewish tradition to enhance our personal and collective communal lives. Yet tradition and modernity do not coexist all that easily. As mentioned earlier, I had been struggling with the relationship of tradition to modern culture since high school days. At the AJC, I defined the areas of the contemporary Jewish family, modern Jewish identity, and mixed marriage as ideal laboratories to test the interplay of Jewish tradition and modern values. The third, fourth, and fifth sections of this volume reflect these concerns respectively. Lastly, as noted, in recent years I have focused on issues of Jewish peoplehood, intra-Jewish tensions, and Israel-Diaspora relations. These are treated in the concluding sections of the volume.

The volume is not organized chronologically, except where appropriate within sections. Rather, the essays have been grouped topically and are reprinted without alterations except for needless repetitions and occasional corrections of style. In reviewing these essays, I am struck by how many have been stimulated or occasioned by the reading of books. Indeed, reading books continues to be my primary vice—at the price of an overcrowded residence and office. But no apologies, for books form a wonderful statement of what is a Jewish home and provide substance to our self-definition as "people of the book." Reading books and writing critical reviews have shaped many of my ideas that dot the pages of this volume.

Aside from the stimulation of books, the primary influence for me, as for most people I know, has been other people. Indeed this volume is an outgrowth of the wonderful personal and professional relationships that I have been blessed with over many years. Many of these have already been noted. The idea for the book originated in discussions with Shula Bahat, the AJC associate executive director, who has been a close friend and colleague throughout my years at AJC. It has been a joy to work with David Harris, AJC executive director. One fairly well-kept secret of my success has been that the best ideas originated in David's office by my presenting a suggestion, David countering with another, and, like the true Hegelian he often resembles, David helping me to shape these ideas into an effective synthesis and program. AJC's dedicated and talented professional staff—too numerous to name individually—have been a joy to work with, both personally and professionally.

I have also been privileged to work with wonderful lay leaders at

AJC. E. Robert Goodkind, Robert S. Rifkind, Howard Gilbert, Charlotte Holstein, Jack Lapin, Mimi Alperin, and Lynn Kroll have each chaired the AJC Commission that supervises my work. Each in his or her own way has uniquely enhanced our program. In 1980 Charles and Elaine Petschek established the William Petschek National Jewish Family Center, which would sponsor our work on family issues and has since been ably chaired by E. Robert Goodkind, the late Rita Greenland, Marcia Burnam, Jerry Bubis, and Blu Greenberg. In 1982 Bert Gold and Selma Hirsch established the very first institute dedicated to building ties between Israel and American Jewry and which would house my activities, programs, and writings on Israel-Diaspora relations. I have been privileged to work with Undersecretary Stuart Eisenstadt, Ambassador Alfred Moses, Robert S. Rifkind, Mort Kornreich, and Ambassador Peter Rosenblatt, each of whom chaired the Institute, which in 2000 was renamed the Dorothy and Julius Koppelman Institute on American Jewish-Israeli Relations. AJC presidents—Maynard Wishner, Howard Friedman, Ted Ellenoff, Alfred Moses, Sholom Comay, Robert S. Rifkind, Bruce Ramer, and Harold Tanner—each provided both models of Jewish leadership and personal support for my professional work.

In the broader Jewish community, many professional colleagues have greatly enhanced my work through ongoing contact, discussion, frequent alliances, and more than occasional disagreements. Jack Wertheimer, Jack Ukeles, Sylvia Fishman, Gary Rosenblatt, Charles Liebman, Jerry Bubis, Alan Silverstein, Richard Joel, Blu Greenberg, Sam Heilman, Jerome Chanes, Francine Klagsbrun, Chaim Waxman, and Steven M. Cohen have all regularly stimulated my thinking, both orally and in print. For many years I was privileged to participate in the deliberations of the Wexner Foundation Fellowship Committee. These four days annually for twelve years provided a continuing seminar on American Jewish life, Israel-Diaspora relations, and the Jewish communal future. I thank the other members of the committee—Robert Chazan, Sara Lee, Sam Klagsbrun, Bernard Reisman, Jonathan Woocher, and John Ruskay—and Wexner Foundation officers Maurice Corson, Larry Moses, and Cindy Chazan for providing that first-hand education on the Jewish community. For the past five years, I have been privileged to serve on the faculty of the Wexner Heritage Foundation for future Jewish communal leaders and the Nahum Goldmann Fellowship for international Jewish leaders. The students in these classes—men and women dedicated to building a positive Jewish future—have all stimulated my thinking and served as a corrective to some of my pessimism about the Jewish future. I thank Nathan Laufer and Shoshana Gelfand of the Wexner Heritage Foundation and Jerry Hochbaum and Marc Brandriss of the Memorial Foundation for Jewish Culture for inviting my participation in these fellowship programs.

Roselyn Bell, AJC's writer/editor, graciously agreed to serve as my editor and help bring this volume to fruition. Florina Jenkins, my loyal and dedicated secretary at AJC for many years, typed the final manuscript. It has been my pleasure to work again with Bernard Scharfstein of the KTAV Publishing House.

Some of the best discussions of contemporary Jewish life have occurred around my dining room table and on social occasions with friends. Harvey and Hadassah Bennett, Harvey and Helene Benovitz, Joe and Erica Brodie, Sorie and Ed Goldstein, Bob and Tobie Goodman, Sidney and Yonina Langer, Ezra and Batya Levin, Lenore and Bernie Malina, Josh and Niti Minkove, David and Esther Muller, Charles and Judy Sheer, Alan and Rita Silverstein, Ina and David Tropper, Jack and Mierle Ukeles have all been regular social companions for many years. Our ongoing discussions have not only enriched my family life but also my thinking. Their influence has been felt on virtually every one of these pages, while teaching me that Jewish life is best lived in a strong and vibrant Jewish community.

My greatest debt and source of pleasure, of course, comes from my immediate family. My wife, Edith, has been a true partner in building a Jewish life. Our children, Ilana, Eytan, and Yehuda, have demonstrated to their father both the joys of Jewish parenting and how wrongheaded his thinking can be. Our son-in-law, Ari, has enriched all of our lives while demonstrating to us that one can enjoy life as well. Ari's parents, Albert and Judy Milstein, have given new meaning to the word family. It is my hope that this volume will be not only in memory of what has been, but also a taste of what is yet to come.

Steven Bayme, October 2001

JEWISH HISTORY AND JEWISH HISTORICAL MEMORY

As mentioned in the introductory essay, my initial training was as a Jewish historian, and historical interests continue to permeate much of my work. In recent years, however, I have become fascinated by questions of historical memory—what claims our images of the past exert upon our present-day mindset. Therefore the essays in this section embody a dual aim—to correct stereotypes and misrepresentations that Jews have about their past, e.g., that Jews have always been a persecuted people, and to explore what particular historical memories might communicate to contemporary Jews, e.g., the meaning of Passover today.

Conflicting Jewish Responses to Modernity

Although historians past and present have differed as to the exact origins of Jewish modernity, the consensus is that the onset of modernity posed definite challenges to the existence and self-identity of the Jew. Modernity connoted the acceptance of Western categories as criteria by which Judaism could be evaluated. In this sense Benedict Spinoza weighed Judaism by the category of universal reason and found it wanting. Haskalah, as will be demonstrated, attempted to interpret Judaism by the standards of Western cultural norms. In other words, the medieval Jew perceived himself as superior to the external culture. In contrast, the modern Jewish temper demanded acceptance by the standards of the external culture and began to acknowledge the greatness of Gentile society.

Unquestionably certain medieval Jews, notably Maimonides, appreciated the value of secular learning. Yet modernity meant the collapse of the traditional medieval synthesis of faith and reason. Where Maimonides had supremacized faith over reason, modern culture demanded that reason evaluate items of faith. In this sense the European Enlightenment markedly differed from medieval rationalism much as the Jewish Haskalah deviated from the paths of medieval Jewish philosophy.[1]

For Ashkenazic Jews, modernity also meant a departure from the medieval educational curriculum. As will be seen, efforts were made to transform the medieval *ḥeder* into an institution that emphasized both Judaic and secular instruction.

Finally, modernity brought the collapse of the traditional Jewish communal structure. Autonomy and corporate status disintegrated as emancipation came in stages to the various Jewish communities of

Reprinted from Stanley Wagner and Raphael Jospe, eds., *Great Schisms in Jewish History* (Hoboken, NJ: KTAV, 1981).

3

Western Europe. The rise of modern nation-states meant that members of separate, private autonomous corporations such as the medieval Jewish community had to be either integrated into the nation-state body politic, i.e., as citizens, or expelled from the body politic altogether. In this sense the emancipation of the Jew became a necessity for the modern nation-state.[2]

These changes did not occur overnight. Their origins may be traced to the first stirrings of discussion regarding Jewish emancipation in the seventeenth century. For Sephardic Jewry many of these trends can be traced even earlier.[3] Yet the thrust of these changes challenged the very self-identity of the modern Jew. His dilemma became one of rationalizing his own continued separate existence in a world in which medieval religious differentiations had been blurred.

These challenges to Jewish identity spawned a variety of ideologies propounding change and adjustment in Jewish life. Perhaps the first such ideology was that of the Haskalah, or Jewish enlightenment. Haskalah, a word derived from the Hebrew *hiph'il,* or causative form, aimed at both the introduction of secular culture into Jewish life and an effort to enlighten the Jews themselves. In other words, the Haskalah, as will be seen, constituted an effort to transform the Jews socially, culturally, and economically.

For example, Naftali Herz Wessely (1725–1803), a Haskalah poet and biblical exegete, published in 1782 his *Divrei Shalom Ve'emet* in response to Joseph II's Edict of Toleration, which granted the Jews limited freedoms of occupation and residence.[4] Wessely's pamphlet advocated educational reform in the Jewish schools. The author perceived the dispersion as an opportunity rather than a punishment and urged the Jews to abandon national redemptive hopes and instead to participate fully in the modern culture. Such participation necessitated fundamental changes in Jewish education. A graded curriculum and greater emphasis upon secular and extratalmudic content would mark a significant departure from the traditional *heder* program. For Wessely, secular education, or *Torat Ha-Adam,* chronologically preceded the Torah of God and assumed the stature of a religious command.[5]

Wessely's pamphlet by no means comprised the entire thrust of the Haskalah. The movement contained different intellectual currents and varied according to both geography and chronology. In Western Europe the Haskalah of Moses Mendelssohn and the *Meassefim,* the group of Mendelssohn's disciples who published the educational and literary journal of the Haskalah, was generally quite conservative. In Eastern Europe, where Enlightenment was to arrive a half-century later, the Haskalah became less religiously oriented and more overtly polemical against the established Orthodoxy.

These differences in both tone and content can be explained in terms of varying social contexts. In Western Europe Jewry received emancipation on the condition that the Jews become men of enlightenment. The Haskalah originated as an ideology for change within the Jewish world and for Jewry's acceptance within the Gentile environment. The conditional grant of emancipation to the "enlightened" Jew created new options of Jewish identity for acculturated Jewish intellectuals. Such individuals now sought to encounter the Gentile upon territory in which religion constituted a negligible difference between them. In such a context Moses Mendelssohn, the "exception Jew" par excellence, attempted to interpret Judaism for enlightenment circles.[6]

This grant of emancipation followed a general secularization of society. The modern capitalist economy, with its stress on individual wealth and worldliness, permitted the Jew to be evaluated as an individual rather than as a member of a group. Even more importantly, the modern nation-state simply could not allow private corporations, e.g., the Jewish *kehillah,* to remain as a "state within a state" and thereby attenuate the centralized nation-state. Finally, the emerging secular culture, with its emphasis upon universal reason, theoretically held little room for religious bigotry and intolerance.

Yet this very grant of emancipation posed new problems of Jewish identity and continued existence. Jewish identity as defined by membership in the community was now placed upon a voluntaristic basis. The very continuation of communal group life was questioned by the proponents of emancipation. Similarly the challenge of modern secularism and its attacks upon religious culture extended to modern Judaism and questioned the necessity for continued religious differentiation between Jew and Christian.[7]

Internal changes paralleled the threats to Jewish identity from without. Rabbinic authority, the traditional power center of Jewry, began to wane. Accusations of closet Sabbetianism, reciprocal bans of excommunication, and widespread envy of rabbinical positions, culminating in the infamous Emden-Eybeschuetz controversy of the 1750s, all contributed to a general decline of prestige for the organized rabbinate. In such a context, advocates of changes within Jewish life that necessitated diminished rabbinic authority found a ready audience.[8]

The world-view of Moses Mendelssohn, most renowned of the Western *Maskilim,* may be understood as a response to these challenges to Jewish identity. In general Mendelssohn's theories epitomized the ideology of the Haskalah in the West. For Mendelssohn Judaism equaled the religion of pure reason. Whereas Christianity demanded belief in irrational doctrines, e.g., Incarnation, Virgin Birth, and Resurrection, Judaism allegedly knew of no dogmas. The truths of Judaism consisted of purely rational propositions discoverable by anyone who reflected upon religious matters. Revelation for the Jew consisted of a corpus of legislation binding upon every Jew as a member of God's Chosen People. Philosophically Judaism stood united with rational religion. The two differed solely in the realm of religious ritual.

The validity of Mendelssohn's position depends upon the definition of dogma. Obviously belief in the revelation of law constituted belief in a truth accessible only through faith. Moreover, the very concept of a Chosen People defied rational analysis. Similarly Mendelssohn's explanation of miracles as a realm of physical fact, i.e., events which historically occurred, yet upon which the truths of religion do not depend, failed to satisfy the test of reason.

Yet Mendelssohn did not regard these areas as "dogmas" in the salvational sense. He argued, following Joseph Albo, the fifteenth-century Spanish-Jewish philosopher and communal leader, that Judaism contains many truths, which the individual ought to accept, yet one's personal salvation does not depend upon belief in such doctrines. In that sense Mendelssohn portrayed Judaism as less "dogmatic" than Christianity. This reading of Judaism certainly approximated the standard of rational religion first adumbrated by Tillotson and Locke.[9]

Mendelssohn's somewhat questionable formulation of Judaism did not comprise the core of his significance. Rather he contributed primarily toward the formulation of a defensive Jewish ideology. The presuppositions of a modern culture questioned the necessity for continued Jewish separateness. Challenged by the question of the compatibility of Judaism and its legalistic system with a modern system of democracy, Mendelssohn responded in *Jerusalem* that the two were indeed compatible.

The problem of compatibility had been first raised in the seventeenth century by Benedict Spinoza. In his *Theological-Political Treatise,* the Dutch-Jewish philosopher portrayed Judaism as a system of law applicable solely to a political nation-state. The implication for Spinoza was clear. Judaism and modernity could not coexist, and therefore Jewry constituted an anachronism in the modern world.[10]

Ironically the ultra-Orthodox Moses Sofer, better known as the Hatam Sofer, adopted a similar line of reasoning in the nineteenth century. Sofer agreed that Judaism and modernity were in mutual contradiction. In consequence, he and his community waged bitter war against modernism on the slogal "*Hadash 'asur min ha-Torah*" ("Innovations are prohibited scripturally").[11]

Mendelssohn attempted to refute these assumptions. The very title of *Jerusalem* signified that the holiest Jewish city continued to symbolize the eternality of Judaism and traditional observance even though the city itself had lost its earthly splendor and political power.

The analysis of Jerusalem as a spiritual force rather than a political power lay at the base of Mendelssohn's philosophical originality. For reasons totally alien to the thought of Montesquieu and Jefferson, Mendelssohn advocated separation of church and state. The political Jerusalem had been historically unique; the spiritual Jerusalem continued as a religious model more rational and inspiring than that of Christianity. In other words, whereas Christianity possessed dogmas and potentially idolatrous symbols. Judaism knew of no dogmas and possessed only *mitzvot,* i.e. commands to action.

This social theory rested upon a somewhat odd reading of history. For Mendelssohn, as for Hobbes and Locke, the State of Nature had evolved into a social contract. The terms of that social contract, however, dictated that men had duties to the state but none to the church. The church could advise and teach but possessed no compulsive power.

Similarly the Jewish institution of the *ḥerem,* or ban of excommunication, constituted at best an anachronism and at worst a fundamental infringement upon the political rights of freedom of expression. Moreover, by denying the individual religious instruction to remedy his disbelief, excommunication would be religiously incorrect.

Mendelssohn's desire to abolish the *ḥerem* must be understood within an historical context. Generally his political theory was quietist. He believed, following Liebniz, that whatever unfolded represented the divine will and should therefore be accepted. Men ought to attempt little by themselves although certain modest steps might be taken. Mendelssohn here took such a modest step. He pleaded for full equality and emancipation for the Jews. Whereas earlier *shtadlanim,* or court Jews, e.g., Menasseh ben Israel, had requested tolerance for the Jews, Mendelssohn demanded full emancipation.

Yet Mendelssohn realized that emancipation carried a heavy price. Wilhelm Döhm, who had earlier argued for improvement in Jewish civil status at Mendelssohn's bequest, had urged temporary retention of the *ḥerem* until the Jews fully entered general culture. Mendelssohn wished immediate entry. The secular authorities clearly did not desire the retention of corporate powers or a "state within a state." Therefore although Mendelssohn did advocate the retention of certain Jewish courts, the *ḥerem* had to be rejected.

In most other respects Mendelssohn remained remarkably conservative in his call for change within the Jewish community. Medieval Jewish philosophy had already portrayed Judaism as essentially rationalist, and the aforementioned Joseph Albo had reduced the number of dogmas within Judaism to three. Although disagreeing on the presence of any dogmas within Judaism, Mendelssohn perceived himself as the heir of Maimonides, one who straddled both the world of Judaism and that of secular culture, wishing to introduce general trends into Jewish life.[12]

In sharp contrast with Mendelssohn's Western version of Haskalah stood the later East European wing of the Jewish enlightenment, epitomized by men such as Abraham Mapu, Isaac Erter, and Joseph Perl.[13] Where Mendelssohn had defended traditional Judaism, these Eastern *maskilim* bitterly attacked the rabbinical establishment for its conservatism and obscurantism. For example, Mapu, the father of the modern Hebrew novel, utilized the medium of historical fiction to mock the bosses of the contemporary Russian *kahal.* By romanticizing biblical heroes as *maskilim,* Mapu characterized the younger intellectuals of his own day as giants towering above the contemporary rabbis of Eastern Europe. Allied authors singled out Hasidism for abuse. *Maskilim* such as Erter and Perl utilized the short story for satirizing the alleged primitivism and backwardness of Hasidim in Eastern Europe.

Yehuda Leib Gordon, pioneer of modern Hebrew poetry, epitomized the polemical thrust of the East Europeah Haskalah. Moreover, Gordon represented the shift in the mood of Haskalah from one of optimism to one of despair. Gordon had hoped to implement Haskalah education through government-sponsored schools. Yet as the dean of such an institution, he quickly encountered opposition and even persecution. As a means of counterattack, Gordon turned to poetry. In one of his most famous poems, Gordon ridiculed rabbinical divorce procedures by illustrating how an incomplete *yod* in a bill of divorce could result in the tragedy of an *agunah,* a woman forbidden from remarrying because her former husband could not be found.[14] Like Mapu, Gordon turned to history as a medium for expressing contemporary social criticism. In discussing the rebellion against Rome, Gordon mocked the rabbis for failing to fulfill the injunction of "teach the sons of Judah the martial arts." On the contrary the rabbis of Roman times had been too preoccupied with the minutiae of halakhic discourse to confront pragmatic questions of self-defense. Prophetic political theory suffered the same abuse. Gordon's Jeremiah personified a defeatist who consistently counseled quietistic surrender rather than self-defense.[15]

The historical portraits may not be taken uncritically. Modern research points to the full participation in the Great Revolt against Rome on the part of most Pharisaic teachers. Rabbi Yoḥanan ben Zakkai at most represented a minority view among the rabbis. Moreover Gordon obscured the political wisdom inherent in the approaches of Jeremiah and Yoḥanan ben Zakkai. To suggest that the Jews make peace with ancient empires rather than continue to fight on to the last man may well have been prudence rather than defeatism. In the final analysis the political theory of Yavneh triumphed over that of Jerusalem.[16]

Distortion of historical fact results, for Gordon, in distortion of contemporary reality. Behind the poems lay a critique of the rabbis for failure to organize Jewish self-defense units against the Russian *pogromchiks*. Gordon rightly despaired of the failure to resist, a despair that permeated the entire Russian-Jewish community and led to organized self-defense, primarily by the Bund, during the next round of pogroms in 1904–1905, seven years following Gordon's death. Yet one must question whether the rabbis were solely to blame for this failure.

Jewish revolutionaries, eager to minimize the divergence between themselves and their colleagues in the revolutionary movement, some of whom greeted the outbreaks as healthy albeit unfortunate indications that the Russian peasants had begun to concentrate upon their real social and economic difficulties, similarly muted their responses to the pogroms or minimized their anti-Jewish aspects. One could hardly expect a stranger rendition of the phrase "Anti-Semitism is the socialism of fools."[17]

To replace traditional rabbinism Gordon advocated numerous reforms within Jewish life. He urged that the Jew learn Russian and love the Gentile in the hope that Jew and Russian would socialize one with another. In the economic sphere Gordon urged that the Jews abandon mercantile occupations for "productive" labor. In particular farming appealed to him. Much as Tolstoy had idealized man's attachments to the soil, so Gordon extolled farming as that occupation which would root the Jew in soil and nature as well as solidify the Jewish presence in Russia. Politically the Jew ought to demonstrate his civic virtue through service in the army and prompt payment of taxes. Finally the Jew ought to relegate religious distinctiveness to his home life and become indistinguishable from the Gentile in public.[18]

Certain common themes permeated the writings of Mendelssohn and Gordon. In particular they both stressed the virtues of good citizenship. However, the differences in terms of Gordon's satirical and anti-Orthodox style and rhetoric outweighed these similarities. Such variations must be understood as consequences of the differing social context in which East European Haskalah flourished. Although the questions of emancipation in Eastern Europe resembled those of Western Europe, the order of prospective change was reversed. In other words, emancipation in Eastern Europe meant that the Jews would first have to transform themselves, and only then would they receive their civic rights. Consequently East European *maskilim,* as proponents of change, bitterly attacked the Orthodox, who resisted such change on the grounds that it would ultimately mean the disappearance of the Jew. Haskalah polemics and sharp-edged satire only reflected the bitterness of the underlying struggle for control of the dynamics of the Jewish community.

These differing ideologies varied greatly in the degree of their successes. In Western Europe the Haskalah generally recorded success. Jewry attained complete emancipation by the mid-nineteenth century, and virtually every country established a non-sectarian school system in which Jews participated. The Western Jew, whether Orthodox or assimilationist, reflected the impact of modern culture.

As a consequence the traditional communal or *kehillah* structure of medieval Jewry disintegrated. Although the processes of decline of the *kehillah* had antedated the development of Haskalah, e.g., through the rise of Hasidic communities,[19] Haskalah itself functioned as an ideology for change in Jewish communal organization. The *maskilim* attacked rabbinical authority in general and the institution of the *herem* in particular. At least one historian has noted their class orientation as spokesmen of the rising Jewish middle classes and thus in opposition to the aristocratic leaders of the *kehillah.*[20] Through their emphasis on the Bible, e.g., in the curriculum of the Haskalah *Freischule* at Berlin, Hinukh Nearim, the *maskilim* implicitly attacked the Talmud, whose values formed the crux of rabbinic Judaism.[21] The postemancipation Jew no longer viewed his life-style as sharply restricted by synagogal legislation.

In contrast, Haskalah in Eastern Europe failed on most counts. Acts of apparent enlightenment and liberalism, e.g., the Crown School system, which promised Jewry secular education but in actuality furthered conversionist purposes, only masked far more reactionary policies.[22] So long as the Czar remained in power, Russian Jewry never attained the grant of political emancipation. On the contrary, the false dawn of enlightenment quickly gave way to the onset of terrible pogroms. By the close of the nineteenth century, Haskalah in Russia had virtually expired. The Russian-Jewish youth and intelligentsia had generally drifted into alternative movements, such as Zionism and the revolutionary Left, or had abandoned Russia for the more liberal shores of America. These alternatives signified an exasperation with remaking Russian Jewry internally. Only fundamental changes in Russian society could make Haskalah viable. Rooted in the assumption that Russia could evolve peacefully into a modern constitutional and democratic state, Haskalah waned as the revolutionary movement strengthened. Even Y. L. Gordon himself questioned to whom he might address his poems if the best of the youth had already chosen the path of revolution over that of reform.[23]

Yet Haskalah—both in Western and in Eastern Europe—created certain changes in Jewish life. Certainly a new attitude toward the value of secular learning developed. Even the traditionalist camp of the Gaon of Vilna to some extent incorporated the new intellectual currents.[24] Similarly the rabbinic *ḥeder* gave way to the new broadly-based curriculum envisioned by the *maskilim*.

These changes did not come easily. Tensions between the *maskilim* and the defenders of the status quo often erupted into full-scale warfare. Similarly the Hasidim, right-wing critics of the established Orthodoxy, soon joined forces with their erstwhile opponents to combat the new currents of Enlightenment. As Kabbalists the Hasidim defended the irrational and the mythic against the strictures of rationalism. Moreover, they criticized the Mendelssohnian conception of a purely transcendental deity. Such a Deity could never satisfy the religious needs of the common people, who needed to sense God in the here and now. Clearly the Hasidic emphasis upon an immanent deity who permeates this world directly contradicted the deity Mendelssohn portrayed.

The *mitnagdim* also opposed the new currents of enlightenment and secularization. In their eyes the *maskilim* were at best naive and at worst destructive. Although the *maskilim* had hoped for an alliance with the *mitnagdim* against the Hasidim, the rise of Haskalah and its arrival in Eastern Europe signaled the close of the Hasidic-mitnagdic rivalry and the forging of new bonds between Hasidim and *mitnagdim*. Thus, Haskalah, through its attacks against Orthodoxy, ironically helped repair a major rift within the Orthodox camp.

In particular the *mitnagdim* opposed emancipation and defended rabbinic education. Perhaps their greatest victory lay in their opposition to the Crown Schools, theoretically institutions of Enlightenment and therefore enthusiastically supported by the *maskilim,* but in reality conversionist agencies. The naivete of the *maskilim* in their unqualified enthusiasm for the Czarist-backed project confirmed the *mitnagdim's* suspicions of the new currents.

These conflicts between the *maskilim* and their opponents frequently assumed ugly forms. Bans were issued against the reading of Haskalah literature and occasional book-burnings occurred. At times the secular government received requests for intervention and responded by censoring a number of works of the Haskalah.[25]

In Western Europe the mitnagdic rabbis were more restrained in their opposition to Haskalah, and some even agreed on the desirability of emancipation. Yet Haskalah and its ideals struck a sensitive chord. Mendelssohn's expressed wish for an end to the use of the *ḥerem* implied the surrender of traditional rabbinic authority. Wessely's educational reforms aroused a storm of controversy although the proposals for secular education and a graded curriculum were not terribly far removed from the desires of the renowned Gaon of Vilna. Yet whereas Wessely's earlier works had received wide-ranging *haskamot,*[26] or approvals, his pamphlet on education seemed so widely at variance with contemporary practice that his erstwhile friends among the rabbis were the quickest to attack his theories.

Fortunately such conflicts eventually subsided. Even Wessely ultimately regained the approval of the rabbinic world. In this sense West European Haskalah could succeed as even the rabbis became enamored of emancipation. Secular education became a desirable endeavor for most Western Jews.

In a wider scope Haskalah signified another in a series of periods in Jewish intellectual history in which Jewish thought and culture partially integrated with general culture. Obviously the political condition of Jewry had to stabilize as a prerequisite for such integration to take place. Yet given a period of tranquility in Jewish-Gentile relations. Haskalah could and did interact with the European Enlightenment. Haskalah shared the Enlightenment's desire to create a religion devoid of superstition and solidly rooted in principles accessible through reason alone. Little differentiated Mendelssohn's religion of reason from that of Tillotson or Locke. Similarly the *maskilim* shared the general veneration of the Bible common to Herder and Lessing.

Yet the Haskalah never endorsed the openly anti-religious polemic of Voltaire and Bayle. For the *philosophes,* organized religion remained the stronghold of superstition and even immorality. Mendelssohn and the early *maskilim* argued that Judaism as it existed equaled the religion of reason. Thus Solomon Maimon defended even the Talmud against those who argued that it consisted of the Jewish equivalent to *l'infâme.* In this respect the Haskalah approximated the German Enlightenment in contrast to the openly anti-religious French Enlightenment.[27]

In other words the *maskilim* were also apologists for Judaism to the world of Enlightenment. Yet their apologetics frequently had deleterious effects. The *maskilim* created an image of Judaism as a compilation of rational and universal truths coupled with a corpus of legislation mysteriously commanded to the Jews alone. Liberal Protestant circles, particularly Kant, Hegel, Schleiermacher, and Harnack, quickly caricatured contemporary Judaism in the original language of the Gospels. Borrowing the Mendelssohnian image of Judaism, these men understood Judaism as strictly legislative and devoid of mysticism. Jesus for them represented the reformer who wished to restore ethical autonomy into a religion badly encumbered by a list of do's and don'ts.[28]

In assessing the impact of Haskalah on modern Jewish history, both a positive and a negative legacy emerge. Certainly the Haskalah signified the revival of the Hebrew language and the renaissance of Hebrew literature.[29] Moreover the new relationship to secular culture captured the hearts of all but the most extreme elements within Jewish life. Finally the spirit of rebellion against rabbinic and *kehillah* authority did produce positive changes in the social, communal, and economic structures of nineteenth-century European Jewry.[30]

Yet these accomplishments must be weighted in conjunction with the negative side-effects of the Haskalah's legacy. Undoubtedly many quickly leaped from Haskalah to total assimilation. David Friedlander in Germany, a disciple of Mendelssohn, contemplated total conversion to Christianity upon deistic principles until rebuffed by a more devout Lutheran pastor.[31] Similarly Y. L. Gordon bewailed the nearly complete assimilation of Russian-Jewish youth so that few still bothered to read his Hebrew poems.[32] In other words, the assimilatory motif in the sense of a desire to join the modern world, common to both West European and East European Haskalah, succeeded in weaning many completely away from any semblance of Jewish identity or wish for Jewish survival. Occasionally this process could even evolve into Jewish self-hatred.[33]

Moreover Haskalah polemics shattered the cohesiveness of European Jewry. The critiques of the Talmud, the Polish *melamdim*, the *kehillah* leadership, and Hasidism all signified the creation of rigid barriers between the enlightened West Europeans and the seemingly backward *Ostjuden*. German Jewry's rediscovery of the *Ostjuden* during World War I indicated how a century of polemical battles had in reality created two separate Jewries with few bridges between them.[34]

Finally, the religion of reason preached by the *maskilim* could not ensure the survival of Judaism. Ultimately rationalist theology failed to convey much meaning to men in need of faith. The religion of reason suited an age of optimism and hope in a better world. The resurgence of modern anti-Semitism and the rise of global warfare shattered this optimistic reading of history and evoked "theologies of crisis" with much more personal and demanding forms.

In this respect, perhaps the greatest failure of the Haskalah was that it quickly became outdated. One might go further and suggest that other modern Jewish ideologies similarly fell "behind the times." Much as Jewish Enlightenment arose in the final stages of the general European Enlightenment, so the Jewish Kantianism of Hermann Cohen and Leo Baeck arose only during the final stages of Kant's sway over European philosophy. More tellingly the modern political Zionism of Pinsker and Herzl postdated the heyday of European nationalism.

In effect Haskalah represented an early effort by the Jews to join modernity. Subsequent ideologies, e.g., religious movements, *Wissenschaft des Judentums,* and political Zionism, similarly represented attempts by the Jews to integrate themselves into the idiom of the modern world. In the case of the latter, the Haskalah's program for the economic regeneration of Jewry was co-opted and transformed in locales from Eastern Europe to Palestine. In this sense the Haskalah did not influence these ideologies directly but rather initiated such an effort and set the groundwork for subsequent attempts to define the identity of the Jew in the modern world.

In particular the Haskalah failed to exert a direct influence upon *Wissenschaft des Judentums,* a movement to initiate the academic study of Jews and Judaism. The *maskilim* wrote biographies of great personalities in Jewish history whom they envisioned as role-models and proto-*maskilim.* For them, history served to edify and inspire its student. The men of *Wissenschaft* attempted something far different. They wished to integrate the study of Jewish history into general history and to legitimize Jewish scholarship as respectable academic work. For them the act of scholarship itself became the medium of expressing Jewish identity and translating Jewish culture to the outside world rather than a search for historical role-models and edification.[35]

The connection between Haskalah and modern Zionism was perhaps more direct. Certainly the Zionists co-opted many of the themes of the Haskalah, e.g., the use of Hebrew, the need for productive labor, particularly farming, and the development of a Jewish identity built upon the acceptance of secular norms and criteria of evaluation.[36] More important, Zionism arose only after emancipation had failed to solve the problem of anti-Semitism. As a result Pinsker entitled his work *Auto-Emancipation,* namely that the Jews must now emancipate themselves through normalizing themselves as a people.[37] In other words the ideology of the Haskalah pointed to the need for changes in Jewish life. If those changes could not be secured in the Gentile world, i.e., through emancipation, then they had to be secured elsewhere, e.g., Palestine. In this sense Y. L. Gordon, as noted earlier, symbolized the shift in the mood of Haskalah from one of optimism that the necessary changes might be secured in the Gentile world to one of despair and disappointment in Gentile society. Political Zionism arose on the base of such despair and disappointment.

More generally, study of the Haskalah suggests certain thoughts concerning the general significance of ideological conflicts in modern Jewish history. Ideological conflicts, whether between *maskilim* and

Hasidim, reformers and Orthodox, or Zionists and anti-Zionists, shared a universal preoccupation with the problem of modern Jewish identity. Ideological content often became the central component of Jewish identity. For example, the commitment to *Jewish* scholarship at times became the medium for expressing Jewish identity for the practitioners of *Wissenschaft des Judentums.* Similarly the conflicts of the *maskilim* centered around the question of the Jew's relationship to the culture of the Enlightenment. For Mendelssohn and Wessely, Jewish identity necessitated immersion into the general culture. Their opponents, particularly in Eastern Europe, feared that the general culture negated Jewish identity. Yet both sides shared a commitment to continued Jewish presence and identity.

In this sense one can appreciate the reasons for the vigor with which the conflict was waged. The ideological protagonists and antagonists were not merely splitting hairs over fine points of theory. Their real question was the forms which Jewish identity would assume after undergoing (or in some cases without undergoing) the experience of modernity. The very future of Jewish civilization seemingly rested upon the outcome of the ideological polemic.

The immediate outcome, of course, did not have such far-reaching effects. Modern Jewish history has witnessed the emergence of pluralistic forms of Jewish identity. In that sense modern Jewish ideologies and the conflicts between them helped create the pluralism that is the hallmark of Jewish identity today.

The legacy of ideological conflict in modern Jewish history does not point to the victory of any particular ideology. Rather the various ideologies themselves suggest variant formulations of modern Jewish identity. Haskalah and the conflict it engendered constituted ideological expressions of those differing and pluralistic formulations.

Notes

1. Carl Becker has attempted to demonstrate continuity between thirteenth-century medieval rationalism and the eighteenth-century Enlightenment. See his *The Heavenly Gift of the Eighteenth-Century Philosophers* (New Haven: Yale University Press, 1932), passim. This view has been refuted conclusively by Peter Gay, *The Party of Humanity* (New York: North Books, 1971), pp. 188–210. See also idem, *The Enlightenment: An Interpretation,* vol. 1, *The Rise of Modern Paganism* (New York: Vintage

Books, 1967), passim. Gay argues that the Enlightenment was an age of criticism, a spirit of critical reasoning rather than rational thought developed on the basis of authoritative scripture, which had characterized medieval rationalism. A similar distinction can be drawn between the rationalism of Saadia and the critical analysis of Spinoza. The *maskilim* generally rejected the critical spirit in terms of the Bible, but they certainly subjected Jewish life, thought, and institutions to critical analysis.

2. Salo W. Baron, *A Social and Religious History of the Jews,* (New York: Columbia University Press, 1937), vol. II, pp. 224–229.

3. Frances Malino, *The Sephardic Jews of Bordeaux* (University, Ala.: University of Alabama Press, 1978), p. 25. Yosef Yerushalmi detected similar trends among the Marrano population during its reentry into the Jewish world. See his *From Spanish Court to Italian Ghetto* (New York: Columbia University Press, 1971), pp. 44–50, and more generally throughout the biography.

4. For the terms of the edict, see Raphael Mahler, *A History of Modern Jewry, 1780–1815* (New York: Schocken Books, 1971), pp. 253–255. Although the edict did grant the Jews entry into a variety of professions heretofore restricted, special taxation on Jews remained, and numerous clauses restricted their actual entry into many of these professions. Moreover, the Jews, as will be seen, were now required to either enter the general school system or build such schools for themselves.

5. Naftali Herz Wessely, "Words of Peace and Truth," *Various Letters* (Hebrew), (Vienna: Anton Edlin Schmid, 1827), chap. 1. The term *Torat Ha-adam* has been variously interpreted as secular education, natural religion, and natural law. By all accounts, however, it is clear that Wessely placed the learning of *Torat Ha-adam* as prior to the learning of the Torah of God in terms of educational sequence. See Moshe Pelli, "The Impact of Deism on the Hebrew Literature of the Enlightenment in Germany," *Eighteenth-Century Studies.* VI (1972), pp. 51–52.

6. Jacob Katz first developed this theme in a number of studies. See his *Exclusiveness and Tolerance* (New York: Schocken Books, 1962), chap. 24; idem, *Tradition and Crisis* (New York: Schocken Books, 1971), p. 255, and most recently idem, *Out of the Ghetto* (Cambridge: Harvard University Press, 1973), chap. 4, wherein he modified the term to "semineutral society."

7. Salo W. Baron, "Modern Capitalism and Jewish Fate," reprinted in Baron, *History and Jewish Historians* (Philadelphia: Jewish Publication Society, 1964), pp. 52–56.

8. See in general the final chapters of Katz, *Tradition and Crisis.* In 1751 Jacob Emden accused Jonathan Eybeschuetz of closet Sabbetianism, an accusation which shook the entire communal establishment of Central European Jewry as it initiated a bitter controversy between the partisans of both sides. See Gershom Scholem, *Kabbalah* (New York: Quadrangle Books, 1974), pp. 405–408, and bibliography cited therein.

9. Moshe Pelli correctly drew the distinctions between Mendelssohn's theology and that of the Deists, which rejected historical revelation. See Pelli, pp. 45–51. For the distinctions between Deism and rational religion, e.g., the theologies of Locke and Tillotson, see Peter Gay, ed., *Deism: An Anthology* (Princeton: D. Van Nostrand Co., 1968), pp. 25–26, 52–53.

10. See *Works of Spinoza,* trans. R. A. Elwes (New York: Dover Publications, 1951), p. 195. Julius Guttmann suggested that Mendelssohn, in *Jerusalem,* was replying virtually directly to Spinoza's political theory and its challenge to Judaism. See Guttmann, "Yerushalayim le-Mendelsohnn veha-masekhet hateologit ha-medinit le-Spinoza," *Dat U-Mada'* (Jerusalem: Magnes Press, 1965), pp. 192–195.

11. The Ḥatam Sofer opposed Mendelssohn specifically on the grounds that reason could not be utilized to evaluate Judaism. See Jacob Katz, "Kavim La-Biographia shel Ḥatam Sofer," in E. E. Urbach, ed., *Studies in Mysticism and Religion Presented to Gershom Scholem* (Jerusalem: Magnes Press, 1967), Hebrew sec., pp. 140–142.

12. The best study of Mendelssohn is the recent comprehensive biography by Alexander Altmann, *Moses Mendelssohn: A Biographical Study* (Philadelphia: Jewish Publication Society, 1973), which brilliantly places Mendelssohn within the context of the German Enlightenment. On the imagery of Mendelssohn as a second Maimonides, see James Lehmann, "Maimonides, Mendelssohn and the Me'asfim: Philosophy and the Biographical Imagination of the Early Haskalah," *LBIYB,* 1976, pp. 87–94.

13. Abraham Mapu (1808–1867) was best known for his historical novels, especially *'Ahavat Ẓiyyon* and *'Ayit Ẓavu'a.* See David Patterson, *Abraham Mapu* (London: East and West Library, 1964). Isaac Erter (1791–1851) was known primarily as a satrinist, especially in his book *Ha-Ẓofeh Le-Veit Yisrael.* He also participated in the founding of *He-Ḥaluẓ,* a Hebrew periodical dedicated to religious reform. Joseph Perl (1773–1839), a Galician *maskil,* was most famous for his satires against Hasidism, especially in his *Megaleh Temirin.*

14. See Y. L. Gordon, "Koẓo shel Yud," *Writings* (Tel-Avid: Dvir, 1959), pp. 129–140.

15. "Zedkiyahu Be-veit Ha-Pequdot," ibid., pp. 98–101, on Jeremiah. See also "Bein Shetei Ariot," ibid., pp. 103–107, for the critique of the rabbis for failure to teach self-defense against the Roman Empire.

16. On the victory of the political theory of Yohanan ben Zakkai over that of Masada, see the stimulating essay by Ismar Schorsch. "On the Political Judgement of the Jew," *Leo Baeck Memorial Lecture,* 1977, pp. 9–10.

17. Robert Wistrich, *Revolutionary Jews from Marx to Trotsky* (New York: Harper & Row, 1976), pp. 12–13. See also ibid., pp. 85–86, for a comparison with the very similar reaction of Rosa Luxemburg to later pogroms. See also Lucy Dawidowicz, ed., *The Golden Tradition* (Boston: Beacon Press, 1967), pp. 405–411, and Salo W. Baron, *The Russian Jew under Tsars and Soviets,* 2d ed. (New York: Macmillan Co., 1976), pp. 138–139.

18. Gordon, "Ha-Qiẓah Ami," *Writings,* p. 17.

19. See the final chapter of Katz, *Tradition and Crisis.*

20. Mahler, p. 228, and more generally chap. 13.

21. Ibid., pp. 224–225.

22. In 1844 the Russian government offered the Jews the right to set up their own schools in which both religious and secular subjects would be taught with Jewish teachers responsible for instruction in religion. Dr. Max Lilienthal, a young German Jew, was imported to direct the project. Although the *maskilim* eagerly supported the project, it failed because the Orthodox remained suspicious. In reality Lilienthal soon

recognized that the project was indeed conversionist in intent and abandoned Russia for America. See Louis Greenberg, *The Jews in Russia* (New York: Schocken Books, 1976), I, pp. 33–37.

23. Gordon, "Le-Mi Ani 'Amel," *Writings*, p. 27.

24. Mahler, pp. 540–543.

25. See Moshe Carmilly-Weinberger, *Censorship in Jewish History* (New York: Hermon Press, 1977), pp. 111, 117–122. See also Greenberg, I, pp. 28, 67.

26. See Altmann, pp. 356–357, on the *haskamot* given Wessely.

27. Altmann in particular, as noted above, placed Mendelssohn within the context of the German Enlightenment. See especially pp. 25–50 and more generally throughout the work. See also ibid., pp. 477–487, for the controversy over Wessely. On the anti-Judaism and anti-Semitism of the French Enlightenment, see Arthur Hertzberg, *The French Enlightenment and the Jews* (New York: Schocken Books, 1970), especially chap. 9.

28. On Kant and Hegel's image of Judaism, see Nathan Rotenstreich, *The Recurring Pattern* (New York: Horizon Books, 1964), and more recently Emil Fackenheim, *Encounters Between Judaism and Modern Philosophy* (Philadelphia: Jewish Publication Society, 1973). On Harnack, see his *What Is Christianity?* (New York: Harper & Row, 1957), pp. 47–48, 91–92, 103. On Schleiermacher, see Michael Meyer, *Origins of the Modern Jew* (Detroit: Wayne State University Press, 1967), pp. 104–105.

29. Shalom Spiegel, *Hebrew Reborn* (Philadelphia: Jewish Publication Society, 1962), pp. 20–24. Spiegel suggests that the Haskalah's role in the revival of Hebrew was an unintentional one.

30. Obviously here the Haskalah may not be taken out of context. It is closely interconnected with a wide variety of political, social, economic, and cultural factors, which taken together transformed the modern Jewish community. Certainly one might ascribe to the Haskalah the role of ideological social protest.

31. See Mahler, pp. 207–209, Altmann, pp. 350–352, and the full chapter on Friedlander in Meyer, *Origins of the Modern Jew*.

32. Gordon, "Le-Mi Ani'Amel," *Writings*, p. 27.

33. Perhaps the most telling example is that of Karl Marx, especially in his "On the Jewish Question," reprinted in Ellis Rivkin, ed., *Readings in Modern Jewish History* (Cincinnati, Hebrew Union College, 1957), a work which has attracted great attention. See in particular Solomon Bloom, "Karl Marx and the Jews," *JSS*, 1942, pp. 3–16, Edmund Silberner, "Was Marx an Anti-Semite?" *Historia Judaica*, XI (April 1949), pp. 3–52, and Nathan Rotenstreich, "For and Against Emancipation: The Bruno Bauer Controversy," *LBIYB*, IV (1959), pp. 23–27. Interestingly, Rotenstreich suggests that Marx's conception of Judaism as egoism derived from Mendelssohn's definition of Judaism and in turn was developed by Kant and Feuerbach, ibid., pp. 25–26. See also more generally the biography by Sir Isaiah Berlin, *Karl Marx* (New York: Oxford University Press, 1963), pp. 25–27. Berlin suggests that Marx's hostility toward religion generally and Judaism in particular flowed from the unnatural position of German-Jewish converts to Christianity in the early nineteenth century. This conversion movement, as noted earlier, was to some the logical culmination point of Haskalah ideology.

34. Franz Rosenzweig brilliantly portrayed this rediscovery of East European Jewry

as an encounter with "authentic" Jews. See Nahum Glatzer, ed., *Franz Rosenzweig: His Life and Thought* (New York: Schocken Books, 1958), pp. 74–78.

35. On the aims of *Wissenschaft,* see Ismar Schorsch, "Ideology and History in an Age of Emancipation," in Heinrich Graetz, *The Structure of Jewish History and Other Essays* (New York: Jewish Theological Seminary, 1975), pp. 4–9. A good example of the difference between Haskalah historical writing and that of the men of *Wissenschaft* is the treatment of Rashi. Leopold Zunz, an archetype of *Wissenschaft,* insisted on placing Rashi with a medieval context and ridiculed those who wished to portray him as a modern man. See Michael Meyer, *Ideas of Jewish History* (New York: Behrman House, 1974), pp. 23–25. On the search for role-models in Haskalah biographies, see Lehman, pp. 94–108.

36. See the introduction to Arthur Hertzberg, *The Zionist Idea* (New York: Atheneum, 1969), pp. 15–100, especially the section on Ahad Ha-'Am, pp. 63–72.

37. Ibid., pp. 43–45. See also my M.A. essay, "Conceptions of History in Zionist Thought" (Columbia University, 1973), pp. 3–9.

Selected Bibliography

Altmann, Alexander. *Moses Mendelssohn: A Biographical Study.* Philadelphia Jewish Publication Society, 1973.

Baron, Salo W. *The Russian under Tsars and Soviets.* 2d ed., rev. New York: Macmillan Co., 1976.

Barzillay, Isaac. "The Ideology of the Berlin Haskalah." *PAAJR.* XXV (1956), 1–37.

———. "The Italian and Berlin Haskalah." *PAAJR.* XXIX (1960–61), 17–54.

———. "National and Anti-National Trends in the Berlin Haskalah." *JSS* XXI (1959), 165–192.

Dubnow, Simon. *History of the Jews in Russia and Poland.* 3 vols. Trans. by I. Friedlander. Philadelphia: Jewish Publication Society, 1916.

Ettinger, Shmuel. "The Beginnings of the Change in the Attitude of European Society towards the Jews." *Scripta Hierosolymitana,* VII (1961), 193–219.

Fackenheim, Emil. *Encounters Between Judaism and Modern Philosophy.* Philadelphia: Jewish Publication Society, 1973.

Gay, Peter. *The Enlightenment.* 2 vols. New York: Norton Books, 1977.

Greenberg, Louis. *The Jews in Russia.* 2 vols. New Haven: Yale University Press, 1944, 1951. Reprinted New York: Schocken Books, 1976.

Hertzberg, Arthur. *The French Enlightenment and the Jews.* New York: Schocken Books, 1970.

———. *The Zionist Idea.* 1959. Reprinted New York: Atheneum Books, 1969.

Halkin, Simon. *Modern Hebrew Literature.* New York: Schocken Books, 1971.

Katz, Jacob. *Exclusiveness and Tolerance.* New York: Schocken Books, 1962.

———. *Out of the Ghetto.* Cambridge: Harvard University Press, 1973.

———. *Tradition and Crisis.* New York: Schocken Books, 1971.

Krieger, Leonard. *Kings and Philosophers.* New York: Norton Books, 1970.

Levitats, Isaac. *The Jewish Community in Russia.* New York: Columbia University Press, 1943.

Mahler, Raphael. *A History of Modern Jewry: 1780–1815*. New York: Schocken Books, 1971.

Mendelssohn, Moses. *Jerusalem and Other Jewish Writings*. Edited and translated by Alfred Jospe. New York: Schocken Books, 1969.

———. *Moses Mendelssohn: Selections from His Writings*. Edited and translated by Eva Jospe. New York: Viking Books, 1975.

Meyer, Michael. *The Origins of the Modern Jew*. Detroit: Wayne State University Press, 1967.

Patterson, David. *Abraham Mapu*. London: Horowitz Publishing Co., 1954.

Rotenstreich, Nathan. "For and Against Emancipation: The Bruno Bauer Controversy." *LBIYB*. IV (1959), 3–36.

———. "Mendelssohn's Political Philosophy." *LBIYB*. XI (1966), 28–41.

———. *The Recurring Pattern*. New York: Horizon Books, 1964.

Schorsch, Ismar. "Ideology and History in an Age of Emancipation." In Heinrich Graetz, *The Structure of Jewish History and Other Essays*. New York: Jewish Theological Seminary, 1975.

Spiegel, Shalom. *Hebrew Reborn*. Philadelphia: Jewish Publication Society, 1962.

Claude Montefiore, Lily Montagu, and the Origins of the Jewish Religious Union

Numerous religious difficulties afflicted Anglo-Jewry at the turn of the century. Fewer and fewer individuals were attending services regularly. Intellectuals openly doubted God's existence. The challenges of Higher Criticism of the Bible seemingly undermined the authenticity and originality of Judaism as a religious system. These problems were by no means unique to Judaism, for Christianity, too, witnessed a serious decline in the number of worshippers and in the degree of commitment, and Higher Criticism posed as grave a threat to the integrity of the New Testament as it did to the Old Testament. In this setting a number of Jewish intellectuals and communal leaders resolved to stem the tide of growing religious apathy. Generally upper-class British Jews, they agonized over the future of Judaism among the Anglo-Jewish gentry. Convinced that only drastic measures could save their cause, they prepared themselves for a torrent of criticism and abuse.

On 18 October 1902, Claude Montefiore, Lily Montagu, and others with similar concerns, convened the first services of the Jewish Religious Union. To many, the services represented the contrary of the preservation of Judaism. Yet, to its founders, the Union represented an effort to establish a religious Jewish identity and prevent further attrition of the religious community.[1] To comprehend this new phenomenon and the schism it subsequently engendered within the community, we ought to glance at the general religious situation in Britain at the turn of the century. Contemporary observers commented widely on the decline of religious faith among Englishmen of all denominations. The number of churchgoers declined markedly, while fewer and fewer openly proclaimed acceptance of revealed religion.[2] Among Jewry this problem assumed wider parameters. A religious census conducted by the *Daily News* revealed that only 25% attended synagogue even on a day as religiously significant as the first day of Passover. In the East

Reprinted with permission from the Jewish Historical Society of England (London, England, 1982).

End of London 50% attended services. Yet, in West London, where the wealthier and native Jews tended to reside, the percentage of worshippers sharply dropped. In pronounced contrast, on an ordinary Sunday, 20% of Christians attended church.[3] Solomon Schechter, among others, denounced the religious laxity and shallowness of Anglo-Jewry.[4] In addition to poor attendance at services, this decline in religious practice extended to flagrant disregard for the Sabbath and festivals, for the dietary laws, and for the principle of marrying within the faith. Some had gone so far as to abandon Judaism for organizations that espoused universal ethics, as Felix Adler had done in America.[5]

Certain efforts to halt this decline in religiosity antedated the formation of the Jewish Religious Union. Many urged abbreviating the liturgy, the length of which served to bore rather than edify the worshippers. Others complained of the prevalence of Hebrew, a language few understood and which prevented most from participating in the service.[6] The most noteworthy of such early efforts at religious modernization was, of course, the Reform movement. Originating in the 1840s as a schism, partly within the Bevis Marks Congregation and partly within the community as a whole over the question of the struggle for emancipation, the movement had by now expanded to other centres, notably Manchester, Liverpool and Bradford. Its leading congregation remained the original West London Synagogue, which in 1870 had been replaced by the Berkeley Street Synagogue.[7]

Yet by 1900 Reform had ceased to provide a legitimate alternative to British Orthodoxy. Never truly a radical reform as on the continent or in America, British Reform had been outspoken solely on the question of the authority of the Oral Law, leading to the abolition of the second day of festivals. Otherwise, Reform from its inception had retained the use of Hebrew, prayers for the restoration to Palestine, and separate pews.[8] Only recently had petitions for the restoration of sacrifices been deleted from the prayer book. The incumbent minister at Berkeley Street, the Reverend Morris Joseph, although banned by the Chief Rabbi, Dr. Hermann Adler, from the Orthodox ministry in 1890 for challenging the desirability of the restoration of sacrifices, in many ways echoed the feelings of his Orthodox colleagues. Joseph did urge retention of the dietary laws to preserve Jewish separatism and approved of prayers for the political restoration of Palestine. He stressed that Reform and Orthodoxy shared common goals and labored for co-operation and harmony between the two movements.[9] By 1900 the schism appeared to have been largely healed. The *cherem* of Rabbi N. M. Adler had expired quietly, the Reform synagogue had attained representation at the Board of Deputies, and in 1892 the principal Or-thodox congregations sent delegates to celebrate the jubilee of the West London Synagogue.[10]

Yet despite the appearance of external harmony the potential for fur-ther schism had actually increased. Continued religious laxity served as an argument against the status quo. Moreover, new social and intel-lectual currents, notably the problems of Jewish vice and the arrival of radical Biblical criticism from Germany, challenged the religious establishment to make social and religious responses. Modern Biblical scholarship originated largely in Germany in the 19th century. Julius Wellhausen constructed the 'Documentary Hypothesis' to explain the seemingly various sources and strands within the Pentateuch and sub-sequent Biblical works. The critical methodology and the frequently negative conclusions regarding the historicity and moral value of the Bible threatened to undermine traditional faith and replace it with a rather lower estimate of the Bible as suited solely to a long-gone epoch.[11] Among Anglo-Jewry, Bible criticism also attained a certain respectability in the late 19th century. Some of the Orthodox dismissed it by pointing to inconsistencies among the critics themselves.[12] Chief Rabbi Hermann Adler and his successor Dr. J. H. Hertz, as representa-tives of a more moderate brand of Orthodoxy, sought to refute the es-sential challenge of modern criticism while accepting certain of its detailed findings, which in turn might be useful in comprehending Scripture. In this sense, the Orthodox attempted to respond to Biblical criticism by limiting it to a purely scholarly role and excluding it from popular education, such as the pulpit and the Hebrew schools.[13] Sig-nificantly, Morris Joseph here agreed entirely with Adler's approach.[14] Others advocated wider utilization of the new methods. Israel Abra-hams, for instance, viewed historical learning as a tool for religious reform, arguing that prayer without a head-covering or separate seating for the sexes could be perfectly legitimized by critical study of the past.[15]

Of those who embraced the new scholarship, few did so more zealously than Claude Montefiore, who introduced Anglo-Jewry to the critical study of the Old Testament and chided the Orthodox for their rejection of modern scholarship. To the Christian world Montefiore demonstrated the necessity for a similarly critical study of the New Testament.[16] Only with respect to the estimate of Jewish law did Montefiore diverge significantly from Wellhausen. Heavily influenced by his tutor in rabbinics, Solomon Schechter, Montefiore dismissed Wellhausen's estimate of the law as a totally uncritical acceptance of Paul's Epistles, and instead portrayed it sympathetically as a joy and an uplift for those who observed it.[17] More so than others, Montefiore absorbed and pondered the theological implications of Biblical criticism, arguing that if certain rituals had originated in superstition or were now outdated, they ought not to merit observance. Moreover, if modern scholarship demonstrated the inaccuracy of certain historical sections of Scripture, the modern Jew need not accept such occurrences as factual incidents. Miracles in particular could no longer function as stimuli to faith.[18] Yet Montefiore understood Biblical scholarship as undermining only certain details of Judaism, rather than its essence. For him, the authorship of the Pentateuch, its historical accuracy, or the binding nature of certain rituals, constituted at most marginal questions of religious detail. True faith in the Deity and Divine morality did not depend upon the literal accuracy of Scripture. Long before he established the Jewish Religious Union, Montefiore sought a religious movement that would allow him to retain both theism and a critical understanding of Scripture.[19]

If the growth of Biblical science was an intellectual stimulus to forming the Jewish Religious Union, certain social issues constituted a moral stimulus. Two questions of particular concern to women, the suffragette movement and white slavery, aroused frequent discussion within theological circles. As women attained higher levels of education, they naturally demanded greater communal responsibilities, including functions within the synagogue.[20] The United Synagogue had not been oblivious to the demands of the suffragette movement. Certain

ministers had endorsed it, and even wished to extend it to United Synagogue elections.[21] For others, equality in status between men and
women within Judaism was totally unconscionable. Montefiore, however, castigated the Talmud for its conception of women as inferior.
Others noted that while women formed the bulwark of the Anglican
Church, Jewish women found little room for their talents within the
synagogue.[22] The *Westminster Review,* a journal especially concerned
with women's movements, became a quasi-forum for the discussion of
the role of women within Judaism. Some attempted to dignify the conception of women in traditional Judaism while conceding the essential
domesticity of their role.[23] Others called for extensive changes within
the synagogue. Jewish suffragettes expected the Reform synagogues to
abolish women's second-class status and introduce equality in synagogal affairs. Some went so far as to consider the synagogue a testing-
ground for their social programme.[24] Far more tragic than inequality,
the problem of white slavery among Jews demanded Herculean efforts
of reform. As we shall see, the very same elements involved in the formation of the JRU dominated the Jewish Association for the Protection
of Girls and Women. Claude Montefiore in particular devoted great
personal efforts to the Association's Gentleman's Committee and, in
1902, was the second largest single contributor to the Association's
treasury.[25] He explained his activities as motivated by prophetic concepts of social justice. Unlike those who joined universal ethical societies, Montefiore understood moral activity as "distinctively religious."[26]

This combination of increased religious indifference and the emergence of new issues that warranted religious responses formed the
background to the establishment of the JRU in October 1902. The initial
membership hoped to unite all believing Jews, since it incorporated a
number of diverse elements representing different sectors of the community including intellectuals, notably Claude Montefiore and Israel
Abrahams; social workers, notably Basil Henriques, Lily Montagu and
Harry Lewis; lay officers of the United Synagogue, particularly Isidore
Spielmann and Henry Lucas; the Reform minister Morris Joseph; and
leading Orthodox ministers, most notably A. A. Green and Simeon
Singer. Prominently absent, of course, were representatives of East
London and the provinces, emphasizing that the movement was pri-

marily directed towards native Jewry.[27] The diverse nature of the initial membership indicated that the concerns of Montefiore and Montagu were widely shared. Simeon Singer, a staunchly Orthodox minister, delivered one of the earliest sermons and conceded the ineffectiveness of traditionally Orthodox methods.[28] Harry Lewis, a Zionist, noted his agreement with Montefiore's concerns regarding Biblical criticism and the necessity for a primarily English liturgy.[29] Oswald Simon, a communal worker, shared the religio-ethical vision of Montefiore and Montagu.[30] Morris Joseph noted that the most pressing need was the maintenance of Jewish identity while individual forms might remain a matter of personal choice and conscience.[31]

Perhaps most interesting among the initial members was A. A. Green, the Orthodox minister of the Hampstead Synagogue. One of the community's most outstanding ministers, responsible for one of its most prestigious congregations, the community's unofficial ambassador to the Christian world, and a regular contributor to the *Jewish Chronicle* under the pseudonym 'Tatler,' Green had previously demonstrated his independence from Chief Rabbi Adler over the question of Zionism, which Adler had bitterly opposed. On many intellectual questions Green agreed with Montefiore's position, deliberately utilizing the findings of Biblical criticism in his sermons and boldly proclaiming sacrifices as obsolete. Moreover, like Montefiore, he sought to claim Jesus as a Jewish teacher.[32] Although Green resigned from the Union quite early, he continued to campaign for some of his favorite causes. Under his pseudonym he advocated basic reform of the position of women in the synagogue, including their inclusion in the quorum (*minyan*), abrogation of the prayer 'That you have not made me a woman,' mixed pews, and the presence of women in the pulpit, albeit not as readers or cantors. Publicly, he wholeheartedly endorsed the suffragette movement, on religious principle and noted that in time synagogal disabilities would have to disappear as well.[33] Despite these early efforts at religious diversity, there remained at the core of the movement Bible criticism with its consequent radical theology and universal moral ethics. Zionists, such as Harry Lewis, remained anomalies within the movement, while the Orthodox and Reform elements before long dropped out entirely. In this sense the movement continued to center around Montefiore, Montagu and Abrahams.

Claude Montefiore, nephew of Sir Moses, shared his uncle's mixture of piety and worldliness if not his degree of observance. Montefiore studied at Balliol in the 1870s, as one of the first Jews to matriculate at Oxford after it became permitted for them to do so in 1866. Consequently, Montefiore viewed himself as part of a generation of emancipated Jews who might benefit greatly from the influence of the Christian world. He studied under Benjamin Jowett, a liberal theologian, but one who regarded Judaism as "in an intellectual ghetto." Subsequently, Jowett encouraged Montefiore to examine Judaism, and in particular the Old Testament, from a modern and critical perspective.[34] After Oxford, Montefiore went to Berlin where he engaged Solomon Schechter as a tutor in rabbinics and invited the latter to return with him to Britain. In his famous Hibbert Lectures he acknowledged his debt to Schechter: "To Mr. Schechter I owe more than I can adequately express here. My whole conception of the Law and of its place in Jewish religion and life is largely the fruit of his teaching and inspiration." Significantly, Montefiore implicitly criticized Schechter in later years for an unwillingness to apply the findings of critical scholarship to a fundamental revision of the Law and in that sense praised his own Liberal Judaism as far more consistent than American Conservative Judaism. Yet he continually acknowledged his debt to Schechter, much to the latter's regret.[35]

Despite a personal fear of public speaking, Montefiore consented to deliver the 1892 Hibbert Lectures in honor of his mentor, Jowett. Although he devoted the bulk of the lectures to an historical exposition of Judaism, he took the opportunity to define the future direction of Judaism, and set forth what came to be the Liberal program of the breakdown of the Law in light of Pentateuchal criticism, theistic monotheism and willingness to accept certain ideas of Christianity. Through these principles Montefiore articulated the substance of his theology. Later writings embellished but did not substantively change the program of the Hibbert Lectures, with the notable exception of the subsequent emphasis on social ethics.[36] Montefiore's conception of revelation comprised the core of his program. Unlike the Orthodox, Montefiore did not regard revelation as consisting of historical events. Rather, revelation consisted of Divine teachings to be found in both the Old and New Testaments.[37] Historical events possessed theological significance in so far as they pointed in the general direction of spiritual progress. Herein lay the true meaning of the messianic doctrine, namely the culmination of historical progress.[38] For Montefiore, present-day man perceived more of Divine Spirit than his forebears, in that he is the heir to the legacy of the ancient prophets in addition to his own inspiration. To this extent the history of revelation itself is progressive. Obviously, Montefiore here arrogated to his contemporaries the freedom to make extensive religious changes.[39]

In these ideas Montefiore did not diverge noticeably from Geiger and other Reform theologians. Rather, Montefiore's originality lay in his mysticism and his approach to Christianity. He criticized his fellow reformers for their excessive rationalism and intellectualism, which emphasized ethics at the expense of religious experience.[40] Mysticism, for him, when devoid of superstition, constituted a true religious experience in so far as it evoked a God of nearness to man and immanence in human society rather than the remotely transcendent God of the philosophers.[41] Perhaps for this reason Montefiore undertook to translate Schechter's essay "The Chasidim" from German into English as it represented the first sympathetic estimate of the mystic movement by a man of enlightened rationality.[42] If Montefiore's mysticism diverged from the more standard paths of Reform, his approach to Christianity clearly identified him as a radical within the Reform camp. Harry Wolfson once commented that the JRU intended to halt the drift of upper-class Jews into Christianity. Indeed, the people who formed the JRU had been devoting great efforts to counter British conversionists at the turn of the century.[43] Yet Montefiore's concern for Christianity had far deeper roots. He admired its mysticism and faith and felt that Judaism in its desire to distance itself from Christianity had unjustly neglected these positive features of the daughter religion.[44] Montefiore boldly proclaimed a new era of reconciliation between the faiths in which Judaism could incorporate certain features of Christianity and thereby attain the "complete truth."[45]

In particular, Montefiore insisted that the Jew confront the New Tes-

tament both theologically and critically. Critical scholarship again became the *sine qua non* for theological appreciation for Jew and
Christian alike, enabling the Jew to differentiate between truth and
falsehood in the New Testament as in the Old. Moral truth in particular
might be gleaned from the Gospels. For the future, Montefiore anticipated inclusion of portions of the New Testament into Jewish Scripture.[46] Montefiore's portrait of Jesus pointed to a man 'of noble
character' who sought to universalize the ethic of Judaism. In other
words, Montefiore, as did his contemporary Joseph Klausner, but from
a totally different perspective, sought to reclaim Jesus as a Jewish
teacher. To the believing Christian, Montefiore seemingly failed to confront the essential question of the divinity of Jesus, although privately
Montefiore went so far as to concede the possible truth or partial truth
of the doctrine of the Trinity.[47] If Judaism then should imitate the path
of Jesus and universalize its ethics, an insular Jewish ethic represented
a regression. Indeed, Montefiore remained outspokenly anti-Zionist to
the end of his days, even through the onset of the Hitler years. He even
failed to discern any reason for rejuvenating the Hebrew language.[48]
While Montefiore urged a universalist Jewish ethic, and more generally
a *rapprochement* of Jew and Christian, he continued to value specifically Jewish rituals such as the Sabbath and the festivals for their value
as a means of maintaining links with the past, and perhaps more surprisingly as a means of maintaining the cohesiveness of world Jewry.[49]
Certainly he cautioned against excessive legalism, yet he fully endorsed whatever would bind people together. Along these lines he advocated maintenance of at least the Pentateuchal requirements of the
Sabbath and dietary laws, and outspokenly condemned intermarriage
as spelling the end of Jewry, despite the protests of Benjamin Jowett.[50]

Other personalities followed Montefiore's lead and further developed his ideas. Israel Abrahams lent academic stature to the movement
by his position as an authority on medieval Jewish social history. So
great had been Abrahams' academic standing in the Reform camp that
he had even been considered for the presidency of Hebrew Union College shortly after Schechter accepted the Chancellorship of the Jewish
Theological Seminary.[51] Abrahams insisted on the primacy of belief
and dogma over questions of ethics or the technicalities of Biblical

Criticism. He refrained from attacks on Orthodoxy in his sermons and privately lamented Orthodoxy's failure to succeed in Britain. He aimed primarily at restoring religious feeling to a society in which religious indifference had become the rule. Finally, he followed Montefiore in sympathetically explaining rabbinic Judaism to Christian intellectual audiences.[52]

Similarly, Lily Montagu, the devoted communal worker, contributed a slightly different dimension to the movement. The daughter of the staunchly Orthodox Lord Swaythling, she quarrelled bitterly with her father over the ability of Orthodoxy to stem the drift towards religious indifference. In particular, she worried over the effects of conversionist agencies and envisioned Liberal Judaism as a counter-conversionist movement.[53] Yet Montagu's uniqueness lay in her rejection of traditional sex roles within Judaism. As a young woman she had rebelled against women's inability to participate in the service and traditional conceptions of menstruation. As early as 1905, she urged granting women the right to lead the services and preach from the pulpit. Yet even within the Liberal camp these ideas did not reach fruition until after the First World War. Outside, traditional conceptions regarding women continued to prevail. Montagu herself benefited from the traditional value-system in the sense that she never suffered the invective that opponents of the JRU hurled against Montefiore.[54] Yet Montagu herself abstained from the militant feminism of her day. In her autobiography she spoke of traditional conceptions of women's place in communal social welfare institutions rather than in communal politics. Within the JRU she consistently deferred to Montefiore's superior intellect and sought to assist him primarily with the practical work of the JRU. Within the general suffragette movement she possessed virtually no influence.[55]

The presence of such prominent personalities, and the innovative ideas they advocated, did have some effect on the wider Anglo-Jewish community. The existing Reform movement, for example, greeted Montefiore's services with mixed feelings. At least one member of the West London Synagogue publicly called for Montefiore's resignation from the synagogue's Board of Directors. Lily Montagu, in fact, did resign her position as director of the children's services.[56] Montefiore conceded the relative agreement of his views with those of Morris Joseph, yet he chided Joseph for accepting the findings of Biblical scholarship solely with respect to externals and not with respect to more fundamental questions of Pentateuchal authorship and historicity. Joseph responded with a defence of Orthodoxy, arguing that the latter did not demand total literalism, and equated Montefiore's argument for utilizing Biblical criticism as justification for major changes as 'licence' rather than Reform. In light of these differences between the two movements the JRU rejected an offer to use the West London Synagogue for services lest it compromise its independence from the older and more established Reform group.[57]

Yet in response to the growing radicalism of the JRU, British Reform did make certain changes in a 'leftward' direction. Isidore Harris, the prominent editor of the *Jewish Yearbook* and a graduate of Jews' College, urged the West London Synagogue to moderate its controversy with the JRU, and emphasized the need for a liberal interpretation of the *halacha*.[58] In the meantime, attendance at the West London Synagogue remained very meager. Consequently, by 1910, growing pressure for further changes arose which led to the introduction of English and the shortening of services by half an hour. More radical reforms, such as mixed pews, did not gain approval. The proponents of these reforms hoped to halt any drift into the JRU. In 1912, the Reform synagogue extended the use of English to festival as well as Sabbath prayers. Although the Orthodox condemned these changes, some suspected that they secretly desired similar changes.[59] There, the JRU evoked a mixed response, although condemnations clearly dominated. The Chief Rabbi denounced the movement as "revolt" rather than "reform" and mocked the services as "unJewish irreligious disunion" in a classic example of Adler's tart tongue.[60] In particular, he condemned the Union's drift towards Unitarianism, as well as some practices of the JRU such as Sunday services.[61] Hermann Gollancz, the only minister in Britain besides Adler to have been rabbinically ordained, attacked the movement on intellectual grounds, noting in particular the intense interest in the New Testament and radical Biblical criticism.[62]

Significantly, the opposition did not coalesce immediately with the formation of the JRU. Only towards the end of the decade, with the opening of the Liberal Jewish Synagogue, did the uproar ensue. At first the movement, as noted above, did include prominent Orthodox ministers, who subsequently withdrew. And so long as the movement remained a private service, it did not institutionally challenge Anglo-Judaism, although it undoubtedly constituted an intellectual and theological challenge. But, by establishing its own synagogue, the movement broke ranks with the established institutional arrangements and evoked much more intense opposition. Ideological considerations alone could scarcely have provoked the attack.

More importantly, Liberal Judaism struck a responsive chord within the Orthodox camp, for the intellectual and philanthropic prestige of Montefiore himself drew continued respect and deference from Orthodox leaders.[63] Moreover, within Orthodoxy there arose some clamor for changes similar to those instituted by the JRU. Thus, Hermann Gollancz advocated revision in the Sabbath liturgy to relate it to the needs of those who could not follow a Hebrew service. He called for new prayers and a general shortening of the service, and even justified such actions on the Biblical principle of "At a time of necessity for preserving the Law, thy Torah be annulled."[64] Rev. J. F. Stern of East London went so far as to introduce mixed choirs, and claimed to have saved Orthodoxy in Stepney.[65] Others clamoured for the use of the organ in the synagogue, greater use of English, mixed pews, Sunday services and freedom of speech in the pulpit, in many ways a replica of the programme of the JRU.[66] In other ways the JRU acted as a catalyst within Orthodox institutions. Lord Swaythling acknowledged the philanthropic work of the Union in East London and offered to pay the salaries of three additional workers if other sources provided matching funds for three others. Also, the growth of the Union provided a powerful argument for an increase in the financial support given by the United Synagogue lest "we shall be playing into the hands of Radical Reform."[67] In this sense the growth of the JRU forced Orthodoxy to reconsider its own institutions.

In contrast to the Orthodox, the Zionists unequivocally condemned Montefiore and the JRU. Although the Union itself made few pronouncements on the Zionist question, Montefiore's own attitude represented the overwhelmingly predominant opinion.[68] The Union did invite the avowedly Zionist Stephen Wise to address it in 1910, yet Wise tactfully skirted the issue of Zionism, limiting himself to a plea for Jewish unity.[69] Montefiore himself subsequently refused to debate with Wise on the issue of Zionism out of personal affection for Wise and sorrow at the latter's politics.[70] Although Montefiore held Weizmann himself in high esteem, his comments on Zionism at times grew vitriolic: "I cannot tell you the anxiety the Zionists cause me. Sometimes I get so sick . . . that I feel tempted to chuck all Jewish work and retire . . . and live exclusively as an ordinary Englishman among my *English* neighbors—my own *people* as I call them . . . [the triumph of Zionism would be the] ruin of Judaism and the Jews. I mind the latter much less for they will have brought it upon themselves."[71] Little wonder that even the triumph of Hitler failed to sway Montefiore towards a more positive estimate of Zionism.

Naturally, the Zionists counter-attacked. The *Jewish Review,* a Zionist organ edited by Norman Bentwich and Joseph Hockman, proclaimed that Jewish religious law and nationality constituted an 'organic union' that the JRU sought to divide.[72] Ahad Ha-am, the Zionist intellectual resident in London, personally responded to Montefiore's theology, his sole intervention in Anglo-Jewish public life. Specifically, he warned that Montefiore's acceptance of the New Testament would bring about the merging of Judaism with the rest of humanity and the ultimate obliteration of Judaism. Rather, Judaism must continue to remain aloof from the world in order to survive within it. Ahad Ha-am conceded the necessity for a Jewish stance on the New Testament, but not Montefiore's panegyric. He urged Jews to note the innate differences separating Judaism from Christianity, such as Jewish nationhood and the denial of Christian love. Obviously, Ahad Ha-am preferred the works of his Zionist disciple Joseph Klausner on early Christianity to Montefiore's scholarship and the Liberal Judaism it created.[73]

In the Christian world the JRU failed to elicit significant interest. Some compared it to the modernist currents within the Protestant Church, while others cautioned Jews to remain separate from Christianity and speak less about Jesus.[74] In general, although Montefiore continued to address Christian audiences, his movement failed to attract attention beyond the Jewish community.

What estimate can one then make of the formation of the JRU? Certainly the movement owed more to the intellectual leadership of a single man than did its counterparts in Europe and America, and Claude Montefiore uniquely synthesized radical Biblical criticism, genuine mysticism, serious inspection of Christian teachings, and universalist social ethics. In doing so, he gave Liberal Judaism in Britain particular forms not found in any other Reform movement. Yet the origins of Liberal Judaism perhaps indicate even more about the Anglo-Jewish community than about the history of Reform. Anglo-Jewry had developed a complex arrangement for the community, each institution zealously guarding its own prerogatives and functions. So long as Liberal Judaism remained an ideological movement, it incited neither public schism nor communal concern. Yet by entering the communal sphere and challenging the prerogatives of communal organizations and institutions such as the Chief Rabbinate, the Board of Deputies and numerous bodies responsible for Jewish education, Liberal Judaism sparked off a controversy that would affect the subsequent history of the entire Jewish community of Britain.

Notes

1. Jewish Religious Union, *Jewish Addresses* (London 1904), collection of sermons delivered during first year of the Union's existence, vol. 1. See also Lily Montagu, *The Jewish Religious Union and Its Beginnings* (London 1927) p. 1, and Claude Montefiore, *Liberal Judaism* (London 1903) p. 212.

2. A. J. P. Taylor, *English History 1914–1945* (New York 1965) p. 168. See also editorials in *Jewish Chronicle,* 14 Aug. 1908, p. 6, and 20 Oct. 1911, p. 8.

3. Figures cited in *Jewish Chronicle,* 13 Apr. 1906, p. 23.

4. Solomon Schechter, "Four Epistles to the Jews in England," *Studies in Judaism,* 2nd series (Phila. 1908) pp. 192–3. On the widespread religious indifference in Anglo-Judaism, *Jewish Chronicle,* 1 Dec. 1905, p. 16, and 25 March 1910, p. 17, citing *Weekend.* See also Lion Feuchtwanger, "Reflections on Anglo-Jewish History," *Historia Judaica* IX (1947) pp. 133–4.

5. *Jewish Chronicle,* 24 July 1908, p. 25, and Montagu *op. cit.* p. 10. Stephen Sharot has blamed poor synagogal attendance on the high price of seats and the importance of class within the synagogue, "The Social Determinants in the Religious Practices and Organization of English Jewry with Special Reference to the United Synagogue," unpublished Ph.D. thesis (Oxford 1968) pp. 146–7.

6. *Jewish Chronicle,* 5 Jan. 1900, p. 8, and 12 Jan. 1900, p. 18, editorial, 10 May 1901, pp. 18–19. Even Nathan Adler agreed to abolish the *mi sheberech* and to introduce an English sermon in response to the demands of Manchester reformers. *See,* Bill Williams, *The Making of Manchester Jewry* (Manchester 1976) pp. 248–9.

7. On the origins and progress of Reform, Chaim Bermant, *Troubled Eden* (London 1969) pp. 17, 231, and David Philipson, *The Reform Movement in Judaism* (reprint, New York 1967) p. 106. Perhaps the first scholar to detect the link with the battle for emancipation was Jacob Petuchowski, 'Karaite Tendencies in an early Reform Haggadah,' *Hebrew Union College Annual* XXXI (1960) p. 226, a suggestion pursued in Robert Liberles, 'The Origins of the Jewish Reform Movement in England,' *AJS Review* I (1976) pp. 121–50.

8. On the moderation of early Reform in England, Petuchowski *op. cit.* pp. 224–5. See also the dedication sermon of the West London Synagogue by the Rev. David Marks, in Gunther Plaut (ed.) *The Rise of Reform Judaism* (New York 1963) p. 48, and Cecil Roth, *History of the Great Synagogue* (London 1950) p. 258.

9. On Joseph and his views regarding sacrifices, Philipson *op. cit.* pp. 403, 490; Bermant *op. cit.* pp. 185–6, and Albert Hyamson, *History of the Jews in England* (London 1928) p. 289. On the approximation of Joseph to Orthodoxy, see especially Joseph, *Judaism as Creed and Life* (London 1903) pp. 169–72, 182–3, 186; *Jewish Chronicle,* 31 Dec. 1909, p. 9; 5 Dec. 1913, p. 16, and editorial 3 Oct. 1913, pp. 11–12.

10. Albert Hyamson, *The Sephardim of England* (London 1951) p. 295, and Williams *op. cit.* pp. 258–60. Williams argues that Reform, at least in Manchester, emanated more from currents of German thought than the battle for emancipation as suggested earlier by Liberles, see above n. 7.

11. For the impact of historical criticism in Britain, see the *Nation,* 30 Nov. 1907, pp. 295–6.

12. Such for instance was the reaction of Lily Montagu's father, Samuel Montagu, see Lily Montagu, *Samuel Montagu, First Lord Swaythling* (pamphlet, private circulation, 1913, p. 19, British Library).

13. On Adler's attitude towards higher criticism, see *Jewish Chronicle,* 10 Nov. 1905, p. 16, and 21 July 1911, pp. 21–2. On Hertz, see the preface to vol. 3 of his *Sermons, Addresses, Studies* (London 1938) and his commentary on the Pentateuch. The *Jewish Chronicle* agreed with these stalwarts of Orthodoxy that such teachings be kept from children, see *Jewish Chronicle,* 4 Sept. 1908, pp. 5, 15. The Rev. A. A. Green echoed this attitude under his pseudonym 'Tatler,' *ibid.,* p. 9. For the identification of Tatler with A. A. Green, Cecil Roth *et al., The Jewish Chronicle: One Hundred Years of Newspaper History* (London 1949) p. 136.

14. *JQR* XVIII (O.S. 1906) pp. 292–3, symposium on Biblical criticism and the pulpit. See also Raymond Apple, *The Hampstead Synagogue* (London 1967) p. 36.

15. Israel Abrahams, *Jewish Life in the Middle Ages* (reprint, New York 1969) pp. 280–1.

16. *JQR* IX (1897) p. 245, and XIV (1902) pp. 151–2. See also Montefiore, *Liberal Judaism,* pp. 98–9.

17. Claude Montefiore, "Jewish Scholarship and Christian Silence," *Hibbert Journal* 1 (1902–1903) pp. 335–46. See also *idem, Lectures on the Origin and Growth of*

Religion as Illustrated by the Religion of the Ancient Hebrews (London and Edinburgh 1893) pp. 503–7, 542 (hereafter referred to as *Hibbert Lectures*). See also Joshua Stein, *Claude Montefiore on the Ancient Rabbis* (Montana 1977) p. 13. For Schechter's attitude, "The Law and Recent Criticism," *JQR* III (O.S. 1891) pp. 754–66. For Christian scholarly evaluations of the Jewish law, G. F. Moore, "Christian Writers on Judaism," *Harvard Theological Review* XIV (1921) p. 240.

18. Montefiore, *Liberal Judaism*, pp. 20, 124. *Idem. Hibbert Lectures,* pp. 508–9, 531.

19. *Idem,* "Effect of Biblical Criticism upon the Jewish Religion," *JQR* IV (O.S. 1892) pp. 298, 304. *Idem, Liberal Judaism,* pp. 165–6, 290–1. See also Lucy Cohen, *Some Recollections of Claude Montefiore* (London 1939) p. 57.

20. See *Jewish Chronicle,* editorials, 20 Oct. 1899, p. 18; 3 May 1901, pp. 18–19; 15 Nov. 1901, p. 17. The Sephardim had as early as 1892 permitted women to serve as *Yehidim* (communal officials) provided they were married, Neville Laski, *Laws and Charities of the Spanish and Portuguese Jewish Congregation of London* (London 1952) pp. 45–6. Lily Montagu drew a direct connection between changing conceptions of women and her reformist tendencies, *The Faith of a Jewish Woman* (London 1943) p. 13. On the suffragette movement in Britain generally, George Dangerfield, *The Strange Death of Liberal England* (New York 1935) *passim.*

21. Adler tacitly supported the suffragette movement in British politics in a eulogy he delivered for Queen Victoria, in *Anglo-Jewish Memories* (London 1909) pp. 121–2. His brother, Elkan Adler, was known to be interested in extending the franchise to United Synagogue elections, see letter to Elkan Adler, 24 Feb. 1914, Elkan Adler Collection, Jewish Theological Seminary of America. Similarly, Herman Gollancz felt constrained to respond to feminist critiques, see Gollancz, *Sermons and Addresses* (New York 1909) p. 108. Most interestingly Isidore Spielmann, writing in the religiously conservative *Jewish Review,* admitted the inferior position of Jewish women and advocated their greater participation in synagogal affairs, *Jewish Review* IV (1913) pp. 24–6, 35–6.

22. Montefiore, "Dr. Wiener on the Dietary Laws," *JQR* VIII (O.S. 1896) p. 394. *Idem, A Rabbinic Anthology* (Phila. 1936) p. xviii. Benjamin Lewis contrasted the prominence of English women in the Church to the indifference of Jewish women towards the synagogue in "The Passing of the English Jew," *Nineteenth Century* LXXII (July 1912) p. 502. The *Jewish Chronicle* reported that the Rev. Joseph Hockman, an editor of the *Jewish Review* and one of the brightest young and rising figures in the Anglo-Jewish ministry, resigned from his pulpit over the inability of the rabbinate to adjust to the conditions of modernity, e.g., the place of women in the synagogue, see *Jewish Chronicle,* 20 Aug. 1915, p. 12.

23. "Anyone who has knowledge of Jewish History will know that the position accorded to woman among the Jews was lofty and dignified . . . woman was considered an equal to man, certainly as far as mental capacity was concerned." Thus Joseph Strauss, "Women's Position in Ancient and Modern Jewry," *Westminster Review* 174 (1910) p. 620, see also p. 628. Similarly, Percy Cohen pronounced a fundamental antithesis between Judaism and suffragettism, see Cohen, "Judaism and Feminism," *ibid.,* 180 (1913) pp. 453, 458–60.

24. Elizabeth de Bruin, 'Judaism and Womanhood,' *ibid.,* pp. 124, 130–2. Certainly, Lily Montagu's role in the JRU was an attempt to divorce Judaism from traditional conceptions of women, see Philipson *op. cit.* pp. 407–8, and Montagu, *The J.R.U. and Its Beginnings,* pp. 38–9. The Jewish League for Woman Suffrage enjoyed widespread support among the Anglo-Jewish community, including the Orthodox ministers Daiches, Green and Stern, the Reform Joseph and Lewis, the Liberal Montagu and the Zionist Bentwich. See *Jewish Chronicle,* 8 Nov. 1912, p. 19, and extensive objections from Jewish anti-feminists, *ibid.,* 15 Nov. 1912, p. 19.

25. In 1902, Montefiore donated £55 to the Association, making him the second largest single contributor on the basis of the figures in the Jewish Association for the Protection of Girls and Women, *Annual Report,* 1902, pp. 11, 100, 103, 119. The Orthodox Simeon Singer, subsequently an early supporter of the JRU functioned alongside Montefiore on the Gentleman's Committee, *ibid.,* p. 38. In 1910 Oswald Simon, also an early member of the JRU, blamed the White Slavery problem on the Orthodox practice of hastily arranged marriages between young Jews. Simon noted this with due apologies to "Orthodox co-religionists," *International Jewish Conference on Suppression of the White Slave Traffic* (London 1910) p. 187.

26. *Ibid.,* p. 211. Montefiore specifically noted that his ethics in this case were those of the prophets rather than the New Testament, see Montefiore, "Modern Judaism and the Messianic Hope," *Hibbert Journal* XI (1912–1913) pp. 375–6.

27. Special services were held in the East End, but were dissolved in 1906. One year later it was specified that three members of the JRU's Executive Committee had to be residents of the East End, see Montagu, *The J.R.U. and Its Beginnings,* pp. 17–18. Montefiore in particular feared that the children of East End residents could not accept their parents' Judaism and therefore required a Liberal movement, see *Jewish Chronicle,* 4 Dec. 1908, p. 26. Subsequently, he lamented the failure of Liberal Judaism to win an audience among the working classes, see Montefiore, *Liberal Judaism,* pp. 243–4.

28. Jewish Religious Union, *Jewish Addresses,* p. 16.

29. *Ibid.,* pp. 27, 37–8.

30. Montague, *The JRU and Its Beginnings,* p. 23.

31. Jewish Religious Union, *Jewish Addresses,* pp. 116–7. Joseph subsequently resigned as he could not be party to a schism, see Montagu, *The JRU and Its Beginnings,* pp. 20–1.

32. A. A. Green, *Sermons* (London 1935) pp. 128–31. See also *Jewish Chronicle,* 16 Feb. 1906, pp. 28–9. On Green's prominence within the Anglo-Jewish ministry, see Steven Bayme, "Jewish Leadership and Anti-Semitism in Britain, 1898–1918" (unpublished Ph.D. thesis, Columbia University 1977) pp. 40–1.

33. See 'Tatler' in the *Jewish Chronicle,* 10 July 1908, p. 9; 31 July 1908, p. 7; 5 Feb. 1909, p. 9, and 19 Feb. 1909, p. 7. Green resigned as Tatler shortly after the publication of these highly controversial columns. For the public Green, see *ibid.,* 10 Oct. 1913, p. 29. On Green's resignation from the JRU, see Philipson *op. cit.* p. 409, and Montagu, *The JRU and Its Beginnings,* p. 14.

34. Leonard Montefiore to Mrs Sheldon Blank, 3 May 1955, MS. American Jewish Archives, box 625, Cincinnati, Ohio. See also Jowett to Claude Montefiore, 12 Aug.

1899, cited in Lucy Cohen *op. cit.* pp. 52–3, for Jowett's encouragement to Montefiore to examine Judaism critically. See also Norman Bentwich, 'Claude Montefiore and His Tutor in Rabbinics,' *Montefiore Memorial Lecture,* no. 6 (1966) p. 11.

35. Cited in Victor Reichert, "The Contribution of Claude Montefiore to the Advancement of Judaism on the Commemoration of His Seventieth Birthday," *CCAR Journal* XXXVIII (1928) pp. 504–5. On Montefiore's engaging of Schechter, see Alexander Marx, *Essays in Jewish Biography* (Phila. 1947) p. 232. For Montefiore's critique of historical Judaism, see Montefiore, *Outlines of Liberal Judaism* (London 1923) p. 285.

36. Montefiore, *Hibbert Lectures,* pp. 550–2. See also *idem, Truth in Religion* (London 1906) pp. 15–42, which embellishes these themes, and Montefiore and Basil Henriques, *The English Jew and His Religion* (Keighley 1918) pp. 10–19, which stresses the centrality of social ethics. See also Montefiore's sermon of 11 April 1903 to the JRU, in JRU, *Jewish Addresses,* pp. 142–53. For the personal fear of public speaking, see Montefiore to Max Heller, 17 Jan. 1910, American Jewish Archives, box 528.

37. Montefiore, *Outlines of Liberal Judaism,* p. 78. *Idem, Liberal Judaism,* pp. 169–73.

38. *Idem. Outlines of Liberal Judaism,* pp. 148–9, 156.

39. Ibid., p. 183.

40. *Ibid.,* p. 165. See also *Idem,* "The Mystic Element in Religion," *Free Synagogue Pulpit* 11 (June 1910) pp. 110–15, and *idem,* "Modern Judaism and the Messianic Hope," p. 367 for his critique of the rationalism of American Reform. See also *idem, A Laudation of Judaism* (London 1910) p. 11. Perhaps the sole Reform thinker on the Continent to approximate Montefiore's mysticism was the German theologian Ludwig Steinheim, see selections from his works in Gunther Plaut (ed.) *The Rise of Reform Judaism* (New York 1965) pp. 128–32.

41. See Montefiore, *Liberal Judaism,* pp. 9, 17, 84, 85. *Idem, Outlines of Liberal Judaism,* pp. 57–60. See also *idem, Laudation of Judaism,* p. 10.

42. Reprinted in *Studies in Judaism,* (New York 1970) pp. 150–89. For Montefiore as translator, see Marx *op. cit.* pp. 233–4.

43. Thus Wolfson characterized English Reform as more religious than the pragmatist American and intellectualist German varieties, Wolfson, "Jewish Studies in English Universities," *Menorah Journal* I (1915) pp. 27–8. In an interesting example of how missionaries could act as catalysts for the Jewish community, Gaster wrote to Montefiore that to fail to oppose the activities of the missionaries was to play directly into their hands, see Gaster to Montefiore, 8 Aug. 1900, MS Gaster Papers, 1900–1901 file, items 220–1, Mocatta Library, University of London. For the concern about the conversionists among the early members of the JRU, see *Jewish Chronicle,* 10 May 1901, p. 14; 2 May 1902, p. 11 (reprint of Montefiore's letter to *The Times*), and 10 Nov. 1905, pp. 28–9. See also Montefiore, *Liberal Judaism,* p. 83 and N. S. Joseph, "Why I am not a Christian: A Reply to the Conversionists," *Papers for the Jewish People* III (1908) p. 1. An interesting example of the relative indifference of upper-class Jews towards Judaism and Christianity may be seen in the correspondence of Lady Louise Cohen to her nephew Walter, 17 Feb. 1899; "Pour mon compte, tant que les Juifs auront une cause a défendre, je me rangerai avec eux—c'est un sentiment et non une idée,

tu peux m'en croire. Si le sentiment me quitte (ce qui est possible) ce sera peut-être une décheance." Cited in Hannah Cohen, *Changing Faces* (London 1937) pp. 229–30.

44. Montefiore, "The Mystic Element in Religion," pp. 112–3. See also *idem, Laudation of Judaism,* pp. 5–6.

45. *Idem, Outlines of Liberal Judaism,* pp. 320, 169. See also *idem,* "Judaism and Christianity in Their Relation to Each Other," *JQR* IX (O.S. 1897) pp. 240-1, and *idem,* "Modern Judaism," *Hibbert Journal* XVII (1918–1919) pp. 648–50.

46. *Idem, The Synoptic Gospels* (London 1909) pp. cxxviii, xxi. See also Plaut, *The Growth of Reform Judaism* (New York 1965) p. 185. Publicly, Montefiore maintained that Judaism cannot at present incorporate the New Testament into Scripture, but would be able to do so once Jewish monotheism had triumphed and Judaism could then abandon its distinctiveness without loss, see *idem. Outlines of Liberal Judaism,* pp. 335–8. See also W. R. Matthews, "Claude Montefiore: The Man and His Thought," *Montefiore Memorial Lecture* I (1956) pp. 21–2.

47. For Klausner's treatment of Jesus, see his *Jesus of Nazareth* (Boston 1925) *passim.* For Montefiore, see Montefiore, "The Significance of Jesus for His Own Age," *Hibbert Journal* X (1911–1912) pp. 769–73, and *idem, Outlines of Liberal Judaism,* pp. 330–3. Matthews noted that Montefiore refused to confront the essential question of the divinity of Jesus, opting instead to concentrate on the ethic of the Gospels rather than the theology of John, see Matthews *op. cit.* pp. 14–15. Privately, at least, Montefiore was willing to entertain the possibility of the doctrine of the Trinity possessing partial truth, but not complete truth, see Montefiore to Israel Mattuck n.d. (American Jewish Archives, box 2738):

> I call it a beautiful sermon, and in *such excellent taste.* And so much that is true in it. I like it very much. My only doubt is about the single sentence at the end which runs: 'claiming truth for . . . other beliefs'. If e.g. Christianity is 'true' in that part of it which agrees with Judaism, then the remark is obvious. But if it means that there is 'truth' in those teachings of Christianity which are distinctive of it, and which are not held by Judaism then the sentence needs qualification. If put too broadly I could not accept it.
>
> I got into great hot water with the C.R. for something like your sentence, but I was more guarded. The Trinity is a distinctive teaching of Christianity. What I said was that there might be some truth even in a distinctively Christian doctrine—e.g. the Trinity— though as a whole the doctrine is *not true.* The Trinity emphasizes (it may be) an aspect of truth though, as a whole, or taken without qualification, it is untrue.
>
> If your sentence means that, I agree with it. But it is dangerous teaching, for it needs careful guarded qualification.
>
> Perhaps you meant something however, which I have failed to grasp.
>
> With the exception of that one brief sentence of 15 words, it is *tip top;* lucid, brave and in such perfect taste.

48. See Montefiore, *The Old Testament and After* (London 1923) pp. 553–4, and *idem,* "Dr. Wiener on the Dietary Laws," pp. 408-9. For the death sentence for Hebrew, see *idem. Liberal Judaism,* pp. 144–6. See further Montefiore's letters to Lucy Cohen in Cohen *op. cit.* pp. 212, 226–7, and Montefiore, "Nation or Religious Community," *Trans. JHSE* (1899) reprinted in Michael Selzer (ed.) *Zionism Reconsidered* (London 1970) pp. 49–64. See also Bayme *op. cit.* pp. 308–9. A contrary view of

Montefiore is taken by John Rayner who maintains that had Montefiore lived to witness the horrors of Hitlerism, he would have altered his views on Zionism; see Rayner, "Claude Montefiore: His Religious Teachings," *Synagogue Review* 32 (June 1958) pp. 252–60. This view, while based on an argument from silence and, perhaps, a touch of wishful thinking, ignores the reality that Montefiore did live until 1938 and witnessed the dawn of racial legislation.

49. See Montefiore, *Outlines of Liberal Judaism,* pp. 178–80, 242, 256, 262–7. *Idem, The Jewish Religious Union: Its Principles and Its Future* (London 1909) pp. 16–19.

50. *Ibid.,* p. 19. *Idem, Outlines of Liberal Judaism,* pp. 220–4, 252, 298. *Idem, Liberal Judaism,* pp. 130–1, 204–7. For Jowett's exhortations regarding Jewish-Christian intermarriage, see Jowett to Montefiore, 14 Sept. 1884:

> I think it quite right that the wall of distinction between Jew and Christian be broken down . . . Jewish society in England is too narrow to allow of Jews only marrying within limits of their own community and that they would be placed at great disadvantage if such a rule were enforced. All good persons have much more in common than they have of what is different. For these reasons I am not opposed to mixing marriages . . .

Cited in Lucy Cohen *op. cit.* pp. 35–6.

51. Schechter was encouraged by an American colleague to urge Abrahams to consider the HUC post, see Maurice Harris to Schechter, 9 Jan. 1902, MS Schechter Papers, JTSA. Schechter's reply is indicative of his attitude towards Abrahams and the Liberal camp:

> Abrahams considers himself an advance post of radical reform in America and has [expectations] for the great cause which he hopes will pay him one day . . . He is quite worthy of the cause he represents.

Schechter to Harris, March 1902, *ibid.* Michael Meyer noted that Abrahams was considered for the presidency of JIR. See Meyer, "A Centennial History," in Samuel Karff (ed.) *H.U.C.-J.I.R. at 100 Years* (Cincinnati 1976) p. 52.

52. JRU, *Jewish Addresses,* pp. 47–8, 256. Abrahams too was concerned over the problem of Christian missionaries, see Plaut, *Growth of Reform Judaism,* p. 289. Abrahams' efforts to explain rabbinic Judaism to Christian scholars met at least one receptive ear in Father Tyrrell, see Tyrrell to Abrahams, 22 Jan. 1909, noting that Abrahams' portrayal of rabbinic Judaism "represented a very high stage of religious evolution," in M. D. Pettre (ed.) *Father Tyrrell's Letters* (London 1920) pp. 152–3. For Abrahams' private lament over the failure of Orthodoxy, see Abrahams to David Philipson, 1 March 1903, American Jewish Archives, box 2329.

53. Montagu, "The Relation of Faith to Conduct," *Papers for the Jewish People* II (1907) pp. 11–12. See also *Jewish Chronicle,* 30 Sept. 1904, and 25 May 1906, p. 42. A. A. Green responded that religious services, no matter how desirable, would never meet the threat of the conversionists, see *ibid.,* 7 July 1904, p. 17. On Montagu's conflict with her father, see *ibid.,* 8 April 1910, p. 22, and Ellen Umansky, "The Origin of

the Liberal Jewish Movement in England," paper delivered at 10th Annual Association for Jewish Studies Conference, Boston 1978, p. 4.

54. Montagu, *Faith of a Jewish Woman,* pp. 9–10, 22–3, 37. See also *idem, The J.R.U. and Its Beginnings,* p. 27.

55. Montagu, *My Club and I* (London 1954) *passim.* See also *idem, Faith of a Jewish Woman,* p. 28, and Umansky *op. cit.* p. 7.

56. *Jewish Chronicle,* 22 Oct. 1909, pp. 21–3.

57. Philipson *op. cit.* p. 413. *Jewish Chronicle,* 4 March 1910, p. 15. See also the interchange between Montefiore and Joseph in the *JQR* XVIII (O.S. 1906), especially 299, 311, 315.

58. *Jewish Chronicle,* 3 Dec. 1909, pp. 20–1.

59. The changes in Berkeley Street were covered in *The Times;* see the issues for 28 Jan. 1910, p. 4; 31 Jan. 1910, p. 3; 15 Feb. 1910, p. 12; 30 Jan. 1911, p. 4; 20 Feb. 1911, p. 3; 9 Jan. 1912, p. 4. See also the negative editorial in the *Jewish Chronicle,* 28 Jan. 1910, p. 6, and 10 Jan. 1914, p. 15. On the sparse figures of attendance, see Sharot *op. cit.* pp. 241–4.

60. *Jewish Chronicle,* 8 Oct. 1909, p. 16; 28 May 1909, p. 16.

61. *Ibid.,* 5 Nov. 1909, p. 18, and condemned editorially for the blanket denunciation, *ibid.,* 8 Oct. 1909, pp. 5–6. The Conference of Jewish Ministers of the United Kingdom supported Adler in the schism wholeheartedly, see *The Times,* 27 Dec. 1909, p. 6.

62. *Jewish Chronicle,* 18 March 1910, p. 14.

63. Efforts to remove Montefiore from Orthodox institutions, spearheaded by Swaythling (Samuel Montagu), failed because of Montefiore's prestige, see *Jewish Chronicle,* 15 May, 1908, p. 12; 15 Apr. 1910, pp. 23, 27, and 6 May 1910, p. 16.

64. See Gollancz's sermon of 2 May 1908 in Gollancz *op. cit.* pp. 206–8, and editorial support in *Jewish Chronicle,* 15 May 1908, pp. 5–6.

65. *Ibid.,* 19 June 1908, p. 16.

66. *Ibid.,* 4 March 1910, pp. 5–6. See also Aronides (pseudonym), "The Problem Before Anglo-Jewry," *Contemporary Review* (July 1912) pp. 59–60.

67. Historicus, "Ministers in the Making," *Jewish Review* III (1912) p. 26. See also *The Times,* 3 Nov. 1909, p. 14.

68. Montefiore, *The J.R.U.,* pp. 16–17. See also n. 48 above.

69. *The Times,* 5 March 1910, p. 8; 7 March, 1910, p. 4. See also *Jewish Chronicle,* 14 Jan. 1910, p. 20; 8 Apr. 1910, p. 15.

70. Montefiore to Henry Hurvitz (ed.) *Menorah Journal* (2 Feb. 1915) American Jewish Archives, box 2738.

71. Montefiore to Dr J (n.d.), American Jewish Archives, box 625. On Montefiore's esteem for Weizmann, see Montefiore to Israel Mattuck (n.d.), American Jewish Archives, box 2738. Montefiore's total denationalization of Judaism evoked opposition even among those who were "at the other gates of Christianity," cited in Lucy Cohen *op. cit.* p. 280.

72. Editorial, *Jewish Review* I no. 1 (April 1910) pp. 3–7.

73. Ahad Ha-am, "Judaism and the Gospels," *Jewish Review* I (1910) pp. 206–8. See also *Idem, Al Parashat Derachim* [Hebrew] (Berlin 1921) IV pp. 40–5, 55–6. See

also Leon Simon, *Ahad Ha-am* (Phila. 1960) pp. 239–41, and Isaiah Friedman, *The Question of Palestine* (New York 1973) pp. 32, 340n.

74. The *Jewish Chronicle* cited approvingly M. Paul Sebstier: "I know a good many Jews. The Jews nowadays have one great fault. They speak too much about Jesus." *Jewish Chronicle,* 24 June 1910, p. 29, and the column "Culled," 22 Jan. 1909, p. 17; 25 Feb. 1910, p. 17, for further similar Gentile reaction.

The Jewish Community and the Teaching of American Jewish History

Why should the organized Jewish community encourage the teaching of Jewish history, and, more particularly, the teaching of American Jewish history? American Jewish history, after all, is an academic subject. From that perspective, communal involvement might be considered harmful and intrusive. Also, Jewish organizations are primarily oriented toward the present and the future; the past is, at most, ancillary to their agenda. And finally, if the primary concerns of American Jewry today lie in the area of Jewish continuity, the central theme of American Jewish history—successful integration into American society—contradicts the survivalist aims of Jewish organizations today. Why, then, American Jewish history?

Let us be clear about what the organized community does not seek: American Jewry should not invoke history for propagandistic or political ends. Indeed, political considerations clearly underlay much of the early Jewish interest in American Jewish history. The community encouraged research on colonial American Jewry—indeed, even on the earlier age of discovery—to demonstrate that Jews were here from the beginning. Such concerns stimulated the development of many ethnic historical societies, and particularly the American Jewish Historical Society. If Jewry could demonstrate that it had been "present at the creation," it might deflect the criticism of such nativists as Henry Adams who argued that Jewish immigration was transforming America fundamentally and perniciously.[1] Focusing upon Jewish contributions to American society, including the somewhat fatuous question of the alleged Jewish origins of Christopher Columbus, served as a rejoinder to the anti-Semitic concerns raised by Adams and others.

But historical study today is far more sophisticated than it was in

Reprinted from *Moving Beyond Haym Solomon: The Teaching of American Jewish History to Twentieth Century Jews* (Philadelphia: Temple University, Myer and Rosaline Feinstein Center for American Jewish History, and the American Jewish Committee, 1996).

Adams's time. Among scholars, American history cannot be invoked for blatantly defensive or apologetic aims, and no self-respecting historian or history teacher can enter the field primarily for advocacy purposes. Certainly, historical context can help elucidate the complexities behind a contemporary problem, such as the Arab-Israeli conflict. Also, the symbolism of an historical event may carry political connotations—understanding the Holocaust is a good example. Yet the Jewish community today would not encourage the study of American Jewish history in order to refute anti-Semitic canards or demonstrate the loyalty of Jews to America.

Nor is the community interested in American Jewish history for didactic purposes. To be sure, many Jewish leaders might literally quote the old saw, "Those who do not remember the past are doomed to repeat it." Historical process, however, is by no means that facile. Rarely are conditions so similar and human nature so consistent and predictable that specific lessons may be learned about the present from the past. On the contrary, applying particular lessons might well be hazardous, as America discovered in seeking to apply the Munich analogy to Vietnam, or as Israel discovered when Begin equated the PLO with Nazi Germany. Conditions do change, and human beings are remarkably inconsistent in their responses. Applying quick and easy lessons from the past can make for extremely poor statecraft and policy. Contrary to Thucydides, history does not teach, for the course of history is hardly as cyclical and predictable as Thucydides would have it.[2]

Yet studying history does provide good training for leadership. Contemporary issues and problems do not exist in a vacuum. The origins, development, and contemporary context are all rooted in the past. To approach issues from a strictly present-day perspective will often blind us to complexities and limit our understanding. The Middle East conflict is a good case in point. It did not begin with the Intifada nor, for that matter, the 1967 Six-Day War. The root causes of the conflict lie in Arab rejection of Jewish nationalism as an alien and intrusive force within the region. From this historical perspective, statecraft requires recognition that peace will come, not by signing a treaty, but only through fundamental changes in, and perceptions of Zionism in Arab consciousness, underscored by extensive efforts at public education to signal that the Jewish State is now, indeed, welcome in the Middle East.

Why, then, American Jewish history? Communal expectations include attaining Judaic literacy and enhanced identification as a Jew. These expectations demand both cognitive and affective educational experiences. The Jewish heritage warrants attention both as an academic subject to be mastered and as a rich civilization with which the student should identify and, ultimately, help transmit to the next generation.

To be sure, these expectations may often be unrealistic. Attaining Judaic literacy is a life-long task. Many Judaic concepts—mysticism, for example—are inappropriate for the age levels on which formal Jewish education concentrates. More tellingly, Jewish identification is more a function of home environment than the classroom. One cannot expect schools to fulfill functions unsupported and at times contradicted by the culture of the home.

What schools can do, first and foremost, is teach, and, specifically, teach how to learn. There are three ways of teaching a text. We read, first—and too often exclusively—for information, to find what is inside the text. Second, we read for the author's viewpoint and perspective. Historical texts on this level become voices from the past providing us with insight into the nature and mind-set of the culture under review. Last, we read for personal meaning: does this text say anything to my values, outlook, and sense of self? All too often, however, our education halts on the first level of reading. We accumulate data and information but are unable to make much sense of what the data meant in its own time, much less what it might say to us today.

American Jewish history, in this view, ought to transmit the core experiences of American Jews, reconstruct the mind-set of earlier generations—for example, what it was like to be an immigrant—and ask if these experiences say anything to us today as Jews at the close of the 20th century. Since the present is an outgrowth of what went before, who we are as American Jews today is very much a function of where we have been in American society.

The uniqueness of the American Jewish story lies in its spanning—as Mordecai Kaplan taught—two civilizations. American Jewish history is a success story from the perspective of America. No society in Diaspora Jewish history has been as welcoming and as receptive to Jewish participation as has America. For example, when President Clinton nominated a Jew, Justice Stephen Breyer, to a seat on the Supreme Court, the *New York Times* criticized Clinton for opting for a "safe choice." Whether the irony was lost on the *Times* is unclear, but it is a wonderful statement to make about Jewish integration into American society that a Jewish Supreme Court nominee constitutes a "safe choice." In contrast, recall the controversy that erupted nearly seven decades previously over the nomination of Louis Brandeis to the Supreme Court.

The historical perspective can be applied to the current agony over Jewish intermarriage rates. In the context of American society and American history, intermarriage is a marvelous statement of tolerance and acceptance—the Jew has become a desirable in-law. But from the standpoint of preserving a distinctive Jewish ethos and civilization, intermarriage endangers the Jewish future.

This last point poses the challenge of seeing American Jewish history as a story of Jews living in two civilizations. Relations between the two components have at times been synergistic, but more often tense and ambivalent. The outer lives of American Jews have been remarkably successful. Virtually all barriers to Jewish involvement in American society have disappeared, and a Jewish President is a likelihood in the not-too-distant future. Although real tensions persist between Jews and others, anti-Semitism has been largely relegated to the periphery of American society. Yet just as Jews have found American society welcoming and inclusive, they have also discovered that their private lives are woefully deficient Jewishly. Jews feel remarkably self-confident speaking to centers of power and influence about combating anti-Semitism and safeguarding Israel, yet they are at the same time incredibly inept and ill-at-ease in explaining to their own children, in the privacy of their own homes, why it is important for them to lead a Jewish life.[3]

Moreover, American Jewish history represents the struggles of an ethnic-religious minority to integrate into majority society, yet remain distinctive as a group. Today, the boundary between Jews as minority culture, on the one hand, and majority American society, on the other, is quite fluid. There are Jews practicing Judaism; Jews practicing Christianity; Jews practicing both faiths; and Jews practicing no faith at all. Conversely, we have born-Christians practicing Judaism, practicing both Judaism and Christianity, and practicing Christianity while sharing households with Jewish partners. Such a fluid boundary means an inclusive and welcoming majority. For a minority to survive as a distinctive group, that minority will require firmer boundary lines between itself and the majority culture. That minority, in short, must learn to be both inclusive and exclusive simultaneously—despite the unpopularity and political incorrectness of terms like "exclusive."

American Jewish history must aim to articulate this complex vision. It is a story of Jewish achievement, but also a story of erosion and assimilation. Nor does that complete the picture. For we also live in an age of Jewish renewal, with greater opportunities for Judaic enrichment than at virtually any other time in Jewish history. To cite just one manifestation of this, the academic study of the Jewish heritage is available at virtually every major American university. Within each of the Jewish religious movements, one can find Jews more committed to intensive and creative Jewish living than their parents and grandparents ever would have expected them to be. That story of Jewish renewal also needs to be told.

Can American Jewish history also fulfill the affective goals of sustaining Jewish identity and enhancing students' commitment to their people? The challenges here are more problematic, for the goal is no longer strictly academic. Yet historical study generally, and American Jewish history specifically, has the potential to deepen attachments to Judaism and Jewish peoplehood.

How can this be done? First, historical symbols, even myths, do have a considerable hold upon us. Negative myths, such as the Jew as slave-trader, must be carefully exposed for the falsehoods they are. Failure to do so permits anti-Semites to define our identities. Conversely, positive myths and symbols also need to be explored and qualified. The role of Hebrew as a language within the American colonies, the contributions of Jewish immigrants to building American society, the pioneering role of the Jewish community in the civil rights revolution, and the intellectual leadership of Jews in American culture, all must be carefully probed for accuracy, but also invoked as sustaining symbols of the Jewish presence in America. Doubtless, Haym Solomon's role in the American Revolution has been exaggerated. It is also an inappropriate symbol underscoring the role of the Jew as financier. Yet to the extent that we probe symbols in teaching American Jewish history we will be probing the self-identities of our students, their conceptions of themselves, and their membership in the Jewish people today.

The dominant symbol of our time remains the Holocaust. Ironically, the major statement of a Jewish presence in America has become the United States Holocaust Memorial Museum. The symbol should be explored. More specifically, courses in American Jewish history must deal with American rescue and inaction, the role of American Jewry, and the contribution of Holocaust survivors to renewing Jewish life in America.

But the Holocaust should not be allowed to become the prism through which we view the Jewish past. The Holocaust connotes the moment of Jewish powerlessness, while the story of American Jewry remains one of growing Jewish power, influence, and quest for allies and coalitions. To be sure, these themes lapsed during the isolationist 1930s and the war years. Yet the focus upon the Holocaust in teaching American Jewish history is cognitively disproportionate and affectively distorted in that the Jewish presence and self-image in America have not and should not be equated with victimhood.

What, then, should the affective teaching of American Jewish history accomplish? First, we must teach that we are part of a collective Jewish ethos and people. Historically, ties between Jews and Jewish responsibility for one another have been themes that animated the American Jewish experience. To be a Jew today does mean to assume membership within the Jewish people. Teachers of American Jewish history ought to underscore how native American Jewry related to immigrants, protested anti-Semitism at home and abroad, marshalled American Jewish contributions to Israel, and contributed to the success of the Soviet Jewry movement in realizing the possibility of freedom of immigration for over 2,000,000 Soviet Jews. These stories all communicate the unity of the Jewish people and bonds connecting Jews.

Indeed, the immigration experience itself featured cooperation and mutual responsibility—as well as tension—between Uptown and Downtown Jews. By studying these themes we learn the responsibilities of membership in the Jewish people today.[4]

American Jewish identity is also, if not primarily, religious in nature. Some have noted that we are "modern Marranos"—not in the sense of fearing an Inquisition, but, like the Marranos of old, we approach Judaism in highly personal, voluntary, and existential terms, choosing to incorporate those aspects of the Jewish experience that speak to us. Teachers of American Jewish history ought to underscore how Jews have formulated religious identity in a distinctively pluralist America. The stories of Orthodoxy in America as renewal of halachic observance; Reform as religiously-inspired social action; and Conservative and Reconstructionist Judaism as distinctively American religious movements communicate the enduring power of religion in America. Whereas East European rabbis discouraged immigration to America as a secular country, American Jews—in contrast to their Israeli cousins—have demonstrated the capacity of the Jewish religion to sustain Jewish identity. Exactly how seriously the respective religious movements speak to the minds and hearts of their constituents remains unknown. What is unquestionable is that American Jews define their identity in religious terms, and the synagogues of the religious movements reflect that religious expression.[5]

Lastly, Jewish identity in America is distinctively American, forming part of the American mosaic of diversity and pluralism. How Jews have worked for a better America forms a third theme for affective teaching of American Jewish history. Jewish prominence in the civil rights struggle, their role during the Cold War, and, most recently, the neo-conservative movement, all reflect Jewish commitments to work for the improvement of American society. What "*tikkun olam*" should mean is not the expression of politically liberal causes, but rather the Jewish imperative to "repair" the values and institutions of American society. Jews who express their Jewishness as "*tikkun olam*" should be challenged as to whether they are operating from Jewish mandates and imperatives, or from a liberal universalism dressed up in Jewish garb. Study of Jewish political activism might suggest that Jewish tradition by no means translates into either liberal or conservative ideology. Rather the Jewish commitment to *tikkun olam* means balancing the interests of the Jewish community with the general welfare. American pluralism has been most healthy for Jews when that pluralism has promoted a stable and strong America. A disunited and fragmented American society is far less likely to provide the secure structure and stability on which healthy and creative Jewish life depend.[6]

Each of these "affective" components of teaching American Jewish history should not be taught cognitively. No one expects that historical findings be shaped—let alone altered—towards affective ends. History teachers will quickly lose credibility if they permit ideological convictions to drive teaching—although I dare say that much of what passes for Jewish history on the secondary-school level today is indeed driven by ideology. Rather, what is suggested here is teaching that begins with the cognitive and empirical, demonstrates to students how findings and conclusions are reached, but then invokes those conclusions in answering contemporary dilemmas, particularly the problem of Jewish identity.

That problem, as noted earlier, is primarily personal and existential, even religious. Absent history, we invoke personal memories in asking what being Jewish means. For example, one widely utilized pedagogical exercise asks participants to pick up an object from a grab-bag of Jewish artifacts and associate it with personal Jewish memories. Yet these personal memories and stories are ultimately insufficient. The challenge to educators is to bring those personal stories into contact with the collective experiences of the Jewish people. History serves as such a bridging vehicle—an opportunity to look at the story of the Jewish people and ask: What is my place within that story? The study of the Jewish past, in turn, will enable us to keep one eye on the past and the other on the present and future.

Nor should this plea for the teaching of Jewish history be equated with the contemporary drive for ethnic studies or multiculturalism. Jews are justifiably concerned about multiculturalism's tendency to exclude Judaic culture as white and Eurocentric—an ironic reflection on the acceptability of Jews in mainstream America. Also, multiculturalism has often come to mean a form of intellectual separatism—the study of minority culture in isolation from mainstream culture—as in the Afrocentrist movement.[7] Third, on a philosophical level, multiculturalism suggests cultural relativism—the view that no single value system is inherently better than another. This is a "Star Trek" vision of the future—although in practice Federation officers frequently violated their "Prime Directive" to avoid interference in the internal development of native cultures. Last and by no means least, multiculturalism carries with it a political agenda, with each minority claiming its role as oppressed victim.[8]

Teaching American Jewish history ought to part company with multiculturalism on precisely these points. Jewish history, while concerning itself with a minority, is studied, not in isolation, but within the context of the mainstream culture. The success story of the Jews is precisely their having bought into American culture rather than segregating themselves from it. Nor may Jews blithely accept the relativism of culture, when the very teaching of Jewish values presupposes a distinctive Jewish message and critique of mainstream culture. And it would be a cardinal error both of historical fact and Jewish ethos to enter American Jewish history into the competition lists for the status of ultimate victim.

What then may we conclude? While the Jewish community will occasionally articulate political agendas with respect to the teaching of Jewish history, such agendas must be combated. Although no one may claim complete objectivity, it is our responsibility to strive for objectivity.

Far more desirable are the cognitive and affective goals of teaching the Jewish past—to understand the nature of Jewish experience and to probe its salience and meaning for the contemporary Jew. We return, then, to the original three levels of reading texts—for information, as historical document, and for dialogue with the contemporary reader. Teachers of American Jewish history ought to strive for all three levels—what being Jewish meant and its meaning for contemporary Jews.

Notes

1. Naomi W. Cohen, *A Dual Heritage: The Public Career of Oscar S. Strauss,* Philadelphia: JPSA, 1969, pp. 71–72.

2. Thucydides, *History of the Peloponnesian War,* Baltimore: Penguin Books, pp. 23–25.

3. For two contrasting visions of American Jewry, see Charles Silberman, *A Certain People,* New York: Summit Books, 1985, and Arthur Hertzberg, *The Jews in America,* New York: Simon and Schuster, 1989, esp. pp. 301–388.

4. On immigration, see Irving Howe, *World of Our Fathers,* New York: Simon and Schuster, 1976; on American Jewry and Israel, see Steven M. Cohen and Charles Liebman, *Two Worlds of Judaism,* New Haven: Yale University Press, 1990. On the Soviet Jewry movement, see William W. Orbach, *The American Movement to Aid Soviet Jews,* Amherst: University of Massachusetts Press, 1979.

5. For the religious movements in America, see Jack Wertheimer, *A People Divided,* New York: Basic Books, 1993.

6. Leonard Fein is perhaps the most articulate exponent of Jewish identity as *tikkun olam.* See Fein, *Where Are We?,* New York: Harper and Row, 1988, especially Part II.

7. See Arthur Schlesinger, Jr., *The Disuniting of America,* New York: Norton Books, 1992.

8. See Richard Bernstein, *Dictatorship of Virtue,* New York: Knopf, 1994, for the most penetrating critique of multiculturalism.

Freedom, Conscience, and Authority in
Jewish Tradition

Let me begin with a word of appreciation. I am grateful to join with you at this conference for two reasons. First, on a communal level, the Fellowship of Traditional Orthodox Rabbis (FTOR) can serve as a bridge group between the movements. For that reason alone it deserves to be strengthened. Secondly, while the rabbinate is obviously energized by issues of ideology and pluralism of Jewish life, communal leaders, academics, and intellectuals are similarly wrestling with these issues. In that sense FTOR represents those who wish to take their stance within the parameters of Jewish law but also wish to be open and receptive to the secular currents of modernity. For them, modern Orthodoxy is not a statement of weakness but rather a statement of strength and conviction in the viability of synthesis between tradition and modernity. FTOR can serve as the ideological leadership for these modern Orthodox Jews.

My address this evening will be divided into three major parts. First, I would like to explore the issue of freedom and conscience as stressed in modern Jewish thought. Secondly, ask ourselves how does this affect the contemporary sociological context of American Orthodoxy. And finally, I would like to challenge you to think programmatically in terms of the role of FTOR in the American Jewish community. So if in part one I ask you to be philosophers, I will challenge you to be sociologists in part 2, and in the concluding section to think in terms of Jewish leadership and the formation of the future Jewish community.

Essentially, we are addressing the core issue of the respective and often conflicting claims of tradition and modernity upon the minds and hearts of contemporary Jews. Tradition represents the voice of authority and Jewish teaching. Modernity emphasizes freedom of choice, autonomy of will, and the role of personal conscience in decision-making and action. Can we make room for those conflicting currents? Or, are we compelled to choose between them?

An address presented to the Fellowship of Traditional Orthodox Rabbis (FTOR), Browns Hotel, August 27, 1990.

The issue of freedom and conscience, like much of contemporary Jewish thought, begins with the challenges of Immanuel Kant. Kant criticized Judaism on the grounds that the ethics of Judaism were an ethics of command rather than an ethics of freedom. Kant pointed to the concept of the sacrifice of Isaac in the Book of Genesis in which the personal freedom and conscience of Abraham was irrelevant given the command of the Almighty to sacrifice his beloved son. On these grounds Kant criticized Judaism for the absence of the ethic of freedom. No ethical action could be truly ethical, in Kant's view, if it did not flow from the free and autonomous conscience of the individual rather than on the basis of an external command.

To be sure, many noted that Kant's critique of Judaism was an unfair and biased one. He ignores the dimension of rabbinic thought which emphasizes freedom of the will, or to quote the Talmudic maxim of Rabbi Akiva, "All is in the hands of heaven, except for the fear of heaven."

Yet there are grounds on which one can note the validity of Kant's critique. In medieval Jewish thought, the philosopher Saadiah distinguishes between commandments which we know on the basis of our own reason and commandments which we know only on the basis of their having been revealed at Sinai. Interestingly, however, Saadiah underscores the importance of command in both these categories. Even though there are many things that we would know on the basis of reason alone, our reason for observing these commands is precisely the fact that they were commanded.

Similarly Maimonides notes that the various Noahide laws, which are accessible to human reason, should be observed by all humanity. However, Maimonides sharply underscores that righteous gentiles will attain salvation only on the basis of their observance of these laws because they were commanded to rather than on the basis of their own autonomous freedom and reason.

Perhaps most directly, Kant's understanding of Judaism represents an adaptation of his German-Jewish colleague's philosophy, Moses Mendelssohn. For Mendelssohn Judaism contains no dogmas. All of its ideas are acceptable to reason. What is distinctive about Judaism, however, is its revealed legislation, which we know on the basis of its being revealed rather than on the basis of human reason alone. In essence, Kant's critique of Judaism is that it is a religion which lacks an autonomous ethic. He contrasts his picture of Judaism with his understanding of Christianity in which Jesus represented the autonomous man. To put this into colloquial language, Kant's critique of Jewish observance is that it is based upon fear of heaven and communal peer pressure rather than the basis of internal conviction that the action itself is worthwhile. For example, one who gives charity under the principles of Judaic law does so because the act of charity was commanded rather than on the basis of inner independent will to give of oneself to those who are less fortunate. How many of us have witnessed Jewish observance being grounded on the basis of keeping up with the Jones or as it is more popularly known, the "chumrah" of the month club, rather than on the basis of an internal conviction that such actions are desirable on their own score. Moreover, there is no question that the essence of Orthodox Judaism remains the notion of the laws being commanded. Orthodox Jews do, to be sure, step outside of the law but only in order to justify it, for example, upon the principle of esthetics or upon the principle of morality. They will not step outside of the law in order to override it.

In that sense, Kant's critique that Judaism lacks the sense of internal ethics ought to be taken somewhat more seriously by contemporary Orthodox Jews. If anything, we should emphasize Judaic traditions which underscore that the observance of commandments requires proper intentions—meaning we must be internally convinced of the desirability of these actions. For example, we are taught that one who transforms his prayer into an act of routine has ceased to pray.

Given these challenges, it was of utmost importance that modern Jews respond to Kant's critique. For Hermann Cohen, Kant's critique applies only to Orthodox Judaism. For Reform Jews, the essence of Judaism is precisely that of individual autonomy and freedom of conscience.

In this regard, it is interesting to note that the conflict between Judaism as freedom of conscience and Judaism as revealed morality continues to play itself out in the Reform movement. For instance, mainstream opinion within the Reform rabbinate remains opposed to rabbinic officiation at interfaith marriages. Yet the Reform rabbinate continually explains its inability to sanction or discipline Reform rabbis who do proceed to officiate at interfaith weddings on the grounds of respect for the individual autonomy and conscience of the officiating rabbi. More generally, the Reform movement remains plagued by a conflict of how one can endorse standards of Judaic behavior if individual autonomy remains an ideal. The Reform philosopher, Emil Fackenheim, has put this well in criticizing liberal Jews for forgetting that morality is also revealed and acting as if it is entirely a matter of personal autonomy.

If this was the Reform response to Kant, much Orthodox thought similarly takes its cue from Kant's critique and challenge. For the Old Orthodox, best epitomized by Rabbi Moses Sofer, better known as the Hatam Sofer, the problem lies in how one defines freedom. For Kant, freedom was a Western concept of individual autonomy. For Sofer, the ultimate freedom lay in obedience to the divine will. In this model of freedom, the answer was ask your rabbi—seek out the scholars of the Talmud and bow to their will—"even if they teach you that right is left and left is right." This notion of freedom as observance to divine will is ultimately transformed into the notion of *"Daat Torah"*—or Torah knowledge, which in turn means that there is a Torah view on virtually every subject. In that context how the individual feels about a particular question or theme is secondary to what is the view of Torah sages upon that question or theme. Therefore, freedom becomes consult the great rabbis.

The obvious problem with such a notion of freedom is that the great rabbis often turn out to be wrong. Take three quick examples from the modern period. The rabbis opposed secular education, they opposed emigration to the United States, and they opposed political Zionism. One shudders to think what would have been the result of modern Jewish history had a mass base of Jews accepted the notion of freedom as obedience to rabbinic will regardless of personal freedom and personal conscience.

A second major response to Kant, perhaps one that is better known, was best embodied in the movement of Samson Raphael Hirsch, popularly characterized as the theme of Torah and Humanism. For Hirsch this combination of Torah morality and Western culture represents a quest for neutral grounds on which there is no particular Torah view but rather the individual is free to obey the dictates of personal conscience. This ranges from relatively trivial matters such as personal taste in dress to questions of politics and secular culture. Hirsch aims towards a more liberal approach to the issue of freedom of conscience, abrogating the coercive role of the community to insure individual behavior.

This approach to Kant's critique, "Torah and Derech Eretz" entails, I believe, four major problems. First, there is a rejection of history and historical scholarship as evident by Hirsch's refusal to accept any of the historical writings of Heinrich Graetz. Hirsch's journal refused even to eulogize Graetz upon his passing. Secondly, Hirsch's philosophy results in a rejection of community—an unwillingness to cooperate with non-Orthodox Jews in common endeavors to benefit Jewish peoplehood. The most dramatic was the refusal to work together with Graetz and other non-Orthodox Jews in building an orphanage in Jerusalem for homeless Jewish children. Thirdly, Hirsch rejected Zionism as a step backward rather than one that would advance the Jewish destiny. Finally, Hirsch rejected the notion of synthesis of Torah and secular culture. On the contrary, he criticized Moses Maimonides precisely for the latter's desire to harness the principles of Greek philosophy in order to understand Judaism. For Hirsch secular culture was desirable on its own grounds—not as a vehicle to understand Judaic values and teachings. Norman Lamm has put this well in his most recent book— that Hirsch wanted co-existence of Torah and secular culture rather than a synthesis between them.

A third model of an attempt to synthesize Judaic tradition with modern culture can be found in the writings and teachings of Azriel Hildesheimer. In contrast to Hirsch, Hildesheimer supported work in Palestine. He was willing to work together with non-Orthodox Jews on projects of international Jewish philanthropy. He cooperated with the Bnai Brith and the Alliance Israelite Universelle on common projects despite the opposition of his friend and contemporary Samson Raphael Hirsch. Perhaps most surprisingly he inculcated a respect for scientific scholarship as it applies to the understanding of Judaic text, arguing that such scientific scholarship will elevate Judaism in the eyes of the public. To be sure, he sets limits on the uses of scientific scholarship opposing his contemporary Graetz for the latter's view of a second Isaiah and for interpreting the 53rd Chapter of Isaiah as referring to the people of Israel rather than to a personal messiah. All in all, Hildesheimer, like Hirsch, is seeking to establish neutral grounds on which individual claims and individual knowledge count on their own score rather than simply looking to a higher authority which contains all truth.

Much of this conflict between the modern claim of freedom and the traditional claims of revelation can be played out in terms of attitudes towards secular education. The essence of secular education inculcates the Western democratic values of freedom and questioning. The essence of Jewish education inculcates a greater reliance on dogma, faith, and the teachings of those who know better than we. In that sense these three models of responding to Kant's challenges are best expressed in how these very same authors responded to the challenges of secular education. For Moses Sofer, secular education essentially was of purely utilitarian value. It was permissible if it was necessary to earn a living. Otherwise, it constituted at best wasting precious time or, at worst, heresy and denial of Torah truths.

For Hirsch, secular education was valid in its own right as the creation of God. However, as we noted earlier, it was not valid if used for purposes of studying Torah. Even more importantly, it should never be seen as a source of values. Values and beliefs emanated only from Torah and not from secularism.

Hildesheimer offers perhaps the most liberal interpretation of secular culture, making room for a limited use of scholarship as a vehicle of understanding of Jewish text. Hildesheimer, in turn, acted to sharply limit that freedom to analysis of Talmudic text rather than Scripture itself.

Given these three views on secular education, it is perhaps ironic that Yeshiva University was actually conceptualized structurally along the lines of Hildesheimer. Its founding president Bernard Revel harnessed scientific scholarship to refute false understandings of Jewish laws prevalent among the medieval Karaites. However, if Yeshiva University was conceived structurally along Hildesheimer's lines, ideologically today it appears much closer to that of Samson Raphael Hirsch. Norman Lamm in his most recent book mounts an eloquent plea for greater co-existence between Torah and secular culture. Perhaps most ironically on a practical level, on the ground, the utilitarian instrumentalist view of secular education as legitimate only for purposes of earning a living prevails among Yeshiva's student body.

Perhaps most ignored in discussions of freedom and conscience and Jewish law has been the ideology of the nineteenth-century Galician rabbi Nachman Krochmal. Krochmal represents a far more powerful model than any of the figures discussed until now. He saw his mission as sensitizing contemporary Orthodoxy to the importance of time and historical scholarship. For Krochmal history connoted the central critical challenge to contemporary Jews. In evoking the title of a modern guide to the perplexed, Krochmal understood the need for a new synthesis not between Torah and Greek philosophy but rather between Torah and biblical and historical criticism.

In turn Krochmal seeks to make room for historical scholarship. He notes the existence of two Isaiahs—that the Book of Daniel was probably a Maccabean work and that neither Ecclesiastes nor the Song of Solomon were in fact written by King Solomon. Krochmal argued that these truths were well known to the rabbis of the Talmud. However, in their time these were esoteric in nature. In our time they have since become public knowledge. It is interesting to take one of his proofs for this doctrine. If one takes a look at the Talmudic rendition of biblical authors on the fifteenth page of tractate Baba Batra, the listing is that of Jeremiah, Isaiah, Ezekiel. Krochmal notes that everyone knew that Isaiah preceded Jeremiah. By changing the order the rabbis subtly hinted at the notion of a second Isaiah who lived much later.

What this amounts to is a full-blown battle for academic freedom—for the liberty of what to study and what claims one could make on the basis of personal research and individual findings rather than on the basis of Jewish tradition and teaching. In essence Krochmal's theology is an attempt, or better yet a plea, for the freedom of historical reconstruction while the meaning and theology that one attaches to history ought to be based upon external teaching and tradition.

Common to all of these Orthodox viewpoints, to be sure, lies an emphasis upon command. In that sense Judaism does reject Kant's criticism, for it finds nothing problematic in defining morality as revealed morality. Even within Reform Judaism, Leo Baeck, unlike Hermann Cohen and Moritz Lazarus, rooted ethics in command. For Judaism liberation from Egypt provided a new freedom within Torah. What distinguishes the "old Orthodox" viewpoint is its location of freedom within obedience to the *gedolim*. Modern Orthodox viewpoints, in contrast, share a common quest for neutral grounds on which we may obey the dictates of personal conscience.

Where does all of this leave us? There is no question that a spirit of triumphalism permeates much of contemporary Orthodoxy. Orthodox Jews and Orthodox leaders take much pride, and justified pride, in the success of Orthodox education and the success of the Orthodox Jewish family. However, Orthodoxy today appears to be experiencing a quest for greater certainty—for a removal of individual doubt—for elimination of individual conscience and its imperatives. This reflects itself first in a certitude towards others—a belief that we have the only truth and that all others must by definition be mistaken. Secondly, it reflects itself in a certitude of politics—even a certitude that the Messiah is imminent and that political action must be taken based on the certainty of the Messiah's coming. Thirdly, this new-found triumphalism reflects itself in pride in greater Orthodox affluence, which in turn justifies secular education upon the purely instrumental grounds of enabling Orthodox Jews to secure that affluence. And finally, the quest for certitude reflects itself in a quest for internal "right thinking" in which those who express doubts and those who challenge prevailing ideologies are immediately read out of the camp of the faithful. It is interesting in this regard that we are witnessing a revision, a rewriting of the biography of Hirsch. The current thinking of contemporary Orthodoxy is that Hirsch's making room for secular education was not meant as a model ideal type but rather a concession to the contemporary imperatives and contemporary needs at the time. To give you one personal example, I graduated from the Maimonides School in Boston in which Rabbi Soloveitchik for many years articulated the desirability of a commitment to excellence in both secular and Judaic education. Now that Rabbi Soloveitchik is infirm, many now argue that the ideology underlined at Maimonides School was a concession to liberal Jews in Boston rather than an ideal model of Jewish values and tradition.

The weaknesses of this triumphalism should be self-evident. First, it is open to the intellectual challenge of "Can we be receptive at all to modern scholarship or must our attitude to modern scholarship be one of ignoring its existence at best or denouncing it as heresy at worst?" In this regard, it is no accident that the Art Scroll series has become the most popular Bible commentary among English-reading Orthodox Jews. Emanuel Rackman is perhaps the primary exception among Orthodox scholars in his openness to modern scholarship and his willingness to ask questions of the Bible stimulated by the findings of modern historical research.

Secondly, this triumphalism leaves us with the question of what exactly we do when the claims of modern conscience flatly contradict the demands of Jewish law. This reflects itself in questions of personal status, in the rights of women, for example, in a context of divorce. And a host of other questions in which modern sensibilities flatly contradict Jewish legal teachings. Eliezer Berkovits, in his recent book *Not in Heaven,* has argued for rabbinic autonomy in applying Judaic principles to solving many of these contradictions between modern conscience and Jewish law. Berkovits, however, remains an isolated voice among the practitioners and ideologists of contemporary Orthodoxy.

Finally, the spirit of triumphalism leaves little room for cooperation with non-Orthodox Jews. Irving Greenberg has argued eloquently for a pluralism built upon principle in which Orthodox Jews should maintain their ideological convictions but enter into dialogue with those who differ. Yet pluralism has become a code word for those who deviate from the Orthodox community.

In this light, and with this I would conclude, the role for FTOR becomes crucial. First, FTOR can serve as a forum for diversity of opinion and pluralism within Orthodoxy. Its message must be that some ideological conflict is desirable because it indicates that people care about what are our beliefs and what are our values. In this regard, the identification of FTOR as an Orthodox rabbinical group remains critical, for it amounts to a statement that rejects ideological relativism. Our concept of pluralism does not mean that all views are automatically equal. In this regard, Norman Lamm is correct that if everything becomes kosher then nothing is kosher. Rather what being open to other views means is not that they are equally valid, but rather that we are part of one people, that we have something to say to one another, and that we are willing to fight our ideological battle within the context of the Jewish family—what Irving Greenberg rather eloquently refers to as "a contentious peoplehood."

The identification of FTOR as Orthodox carries another benefit— mainly a statement that our relationship to modernity is by no means as an uncritical one. Rather that we are willing to critically evaluate modern culture and modern values both for what they say to us as Jews and for what they do not say to us as Jews. In that respect the identification of FTOR as Orthodox amounts to a basic statement that modern culture and modern values have much to offer—enhancing Jewish tradition—but also contain trends that we choose to criticize and that we choose to negate.

Finally, within the Orthodox community we require plural visions of what is our relationship between tradition and modernity. Here, to be personal, I recall my own student days at Yeshiva University where, as an undergraduate, I was challenged both by faculty on the right and by faculty on the left. To extend the model of contentious peoplehood, I submit we require a contentious Orthodoxy.

Modern Orthodoxy requires its own definition. It requires its own independence and freedom to communicate its ideas and counterpoints to the prevailing Orthodox Right. The danger to modern Orthodoxy is that it becomes viewed as a weak, watered-down version of Jewish tradition. On a recent Orthodox radio program, a commentator seeking to explain why the translation of the Torah to Greek was viewed as a calamity, utilized the terms "well they modernized it," meaning that it had become a weakened and water-down version of "Torah-true Judaism." The very label of "modern Orthodoxy" has been dropped in favor of the more neutral "centrist" Orthodoxy. This change in label reflects the same fear of modernization. More importantly it attempts to distance those who call for greater receptivity to non-Orthodox currents and are willing to go out to the frontiers between tradition and modernity.

A second challenge relates to the contemporary code word of pluralism itself. It is clear, as noted earlier, that Orthodoxy as a movement must and should reject relativism. Rather, what pluralism means to me is a recognition that different Jews will require different paths to Jewish community and Jewish traditions. And as Jewish leaders we ought to be supportive of those Jews who have different vehicles of reaching out to our fellow Jews. Finally, I submit that pluralism enables us to learn from the different ideologies, values, and teachings of those who differ with us.

In short, modern Orthodoxy remains embattled. It will continue to suffer the reproach of those on the right who regard it as a fake or weak version of traditional Judaism. Its challenge is to perceive its modernity as an asset rather than its liability; to work together with non-Orthodox groups and with Orthodox groups in a common quest to safeguard Jewish continuity; and, most importantly, to act as a lobby within Orthodox Judaism and within existing Orthodox structures to articulate a coherent ideological version of modern Orthodoxy and to prevent the prevailing currents of extremism and isolation from dominating the traditionalist community.

Assassinations: Ancient and Modern

November 4, 1995, constitutes a day of infamy in Jewish history. Yigal Amir, a devoutly religious Jewish nationalist, assassinated the prime minister of Israel because he opposed the Oslo peace process. Subsequently arraigned in court, Amir justified his actions on religious grounds, saying, "I have been studying Talmud all my life; I have all the data."

This was far from the first political assassination in Jewish history. In biblical times, two Davidic monarchs of the kingdom of Judah, as well as two chiefs of staff, were assassinated by fellow Jews. In the northern Jewish kingdom of Israel, moreover, political assassinations occurred regularly. Religious reasons were often invoked to justify the bloodbaths.

The Murder of Gedaliah

The most prominent political assassination in Jewish history, recorded in the Book of Jeremiah, was that of Gedaliah ben Ahikam. The Babylonians, led by Nebuchadnezzar, had quelled a Jewish revolt in Judea in 586 B.C.E., destroying Jerusalem and the Temple of Solomon. In recognition of Jeremiah's opposition to the revolt, the Babylonians liberated the imprisoned prophet and appointed his ally, Gedaliah, as governor in Judea. Gedaliah's family had long been associated with Jeremiah and the Deuteronomic reform[1] that he and King Josiah had championed.

As governor, Gedaliah pursued Jeremiah's vision of accommodating the Jews to Babylonian rule. Jeremiah's letter to the exiles in Babylon articulated what has come to be known as the political theory of the Diaspora: "Build houses . . . plant gardens . . . marry, and have children . . . and seek the peace of the city in which you are in exile, for in her peace will be your peace" (Jeremiah 29: 5–7). The message was clear: Rebellion is futile at best, destructive at worst. Rather, the Jews ought to become loyal and civic-minded citizens.

Reprinted from *Textures* (New York: Hadassah, 1996), with permission of the Jewish Education Department of Hadassah.

In Palestine, Gedaliah urged the remaining Jews to respect Babylonian authority, promising them, "It will be good for you" (Jeremiah 40:9). Indeed, his policies brought significant economic improvement as the Jews "gathered much wine" (Jeremiah 40:12)—a symbol of prosperity.

These policies of accommodation, however, were not universally popular. Some regarded them as too submissive to Babylonia and hoped to ignite a spirit of rebellion among the Jews. Gedaliah's lieutenants warned him of an assassination conspiracy abetted by Baalis, King of the Ammonites, who wished to rebel against Babylonian suzerainty and regarded Gedaliah as an obstacle. Rumor had it that Baalis had conspired with Ishmael ben Nethaniah, a descendant of the royal line of King David, to assassinate Gedaliah. Gedaliah, however, dismissed these rumors as lies. Foolishly, he sought an alliance with Ishmael.

Invited to dine with Gedaliah, Ishmael and ten associates treacherously assassinated Gedaliah, together with his Jewish and Babylonian allies. Before the deed became publicly known, Ishmael also murdered seventy Jewish mourners on a religious pilgrimage. Gedaliah's remaining allies pursued Ishmael, who escaped and returned to the kingdom of the Ammonites.

Following the assassination, Jeremiah counseled continuation of Gedaliah's policies. Others, however, feared Babylonian retribution. They compelled Jeremiah to join them in fleeing to Egypt—which widened the Jewish diaspora and symbolized the final act in the destruction of the First Jewish Commonwealth.

Many hundreds of years later, the Rabbis of the Talmud condemned the assassination unequivocally. First, a righteous man had been murdered, and the Rabbis equated his death with the destruction of the Temple (*Rosh Hashanah:* 14b). Second, Gedaliah's policies were, from a political standpoint, both well-intentioned and functional. Though his response to Babylonia failed to satisfy ardent nationalists, it paralleled the Rabbis' own response to Rome after the Bar Kokhba rebellion in 135 C.E.; they too eschewed revolt in favor of Roman-Jewish accommodation. Finally, the Rabbis believed that Gedaliah's assassination symbolized Jewish disunity and internal warfare—which in their view led to the destruction of the Second Jewish Commonwealth. For these reasons, the Rabbis elected to commemorate the assassination with a fast day immediately following Rosh Hashanah.

Attitudes Toward the Gentile Nations

The assassination of Gedaliah hardly appears to resemble the recent assassination of Prime Minister Yitzhak Rabin. Gedaliah was a victim of a conspiracy involving a foreign nation. By contrast, the attack against Rabin emanated entirely from within the nation of Israel.

Yet there are haunting similarities. In both cases warnings passed unheeded. Both assassins were ardent nationalists who emphasized national interests over the sanctity of human life. And both leaders were murdered in response to their optimism about the motives of non-Jewish nations.

From its beginning, Zionism has contained at least two distinct visions. One wing sees the Jews cooperating with the democracies of the West, regarding Western leaders as potential allies. Another wing focuses on gentile hatred of the Jews, and it sees the Jews standing alone throughout history. Theodor Herzl was optimistic about the Gentile world; he looked to Turkey and the European powers to facilitate the Zionist cause. Leo Pinsker, by contrast, was pessimistic. Despairing of Gentile assistance, he urged the Jews to become self-reliant and engage in "auto-emancipation." Herzl's vision was later echoed by Chaim Weizmann, David Ben-Gurion, and, most recently, Yitzhak Rabin—all of whom cultivated close links between Israel and the Western powers. Those who followed Pinsker's lead and distrusted Gentile powers include Ze'ev Jabotinsky, and to some degree Menahem Begin and Yitzhak Shamir.

Both views have their merits. Ben-Gurion and his heirs have led Israel to its greatest victories *because* they welcomed the assistance of outside powers. On the other hand, Begin had the genius and courage to recognize that the Zionist alliance with Great Britain had run its course by the end of World War II, prompting him to proclaim revolt. Yet even Begin recognized when Herzlian cooperation is beneficial: in 1978, he signed the Camp David accords and paved the way for peace between Israelis and their Arab enemies.

Rabin, as a follower of Herzl, understood the necessity for war but was prepared to undertake risks for peace. Thanks to his efforts, relations between Israel and the United States have never been closer. Full peace has been extended to Jordan, and the peace process between Israel and the Palestinians continues. In retrospect, Rabin's vision was not so different from that of Jeremiah and Gedaliah.

Jewish Law as Defense for Murder

What then are the implications of Rabin's assassination? The tragedy must be understood as occurring on multiple levels. Personally, a great Jewish leader unnecessarily lost his life. Politically, the assassination raises questions concerning the peace process and its future. Nationally, the assassination exposed deep rifts and fissures within the Jewish people. Finally, the assassination constituted a tragedy for Jewish teachings, because the murderer used Jewish law to justify his crime.

In the months preceding the assassination, Orthodox authorities had declared that, according to the Talmud, Jewish law was unequivocally opposed to Rabin and his policies. Some had even stated publicly that Rabin, a traitor to the Jewish people, should be killed. Today, many Jews believe that these extreme statements nurtured a climate in which previously unthinkable actions acquired religious validation.

Amir cited the law of the *rodef*—the pursuer: If one encounters a pursuer with intent to kill, one has the mandate under Jewish law to kill the pursuer so as to prevent further bloodshed. To Yigal Amir, Rabin's policies were the acts of a pursuer, because the peace process endangered the lives of Jews living in Israel, especially in the territories. To halt the peace process, Amir assassinated Rabin.

Over the past two decades, Orthodox Jewish education has failed to balance the particular needs of the Jewish people with universal teachings concerning the sanctity of all human life. When Yigal Amir stated in court, "I have been studying Talmud all my life; I have all the data," he demonstrated the perverse uses to which Jewish teachings can be applied.

Religious Zionism aimed to define one's personal fulfillment as a Jew through the ideology of "Torah and labor," meaning observance of Jewish law coupled with the practical endeavor of building a Jewish homeland. Each religious Zionist must ask: Has the movement abandoned its historic vision of synthesizing Jewish tradition with the claims of a modern democratic state? The answer would seem to be "yes." Indeed, the movement now espouses a narrow nationalism that emphasizes the unity of the land of Israel over the unity of its people.

This redirection within religious Zionism is linked with the recent growth of messianic fervor. The 1967 war in particular nurtured an atmosphere of imminent redemption—that the Messiah would gather all Jews to Israel and rebuild the Temple, ushering in an era of permanent world peace.

Rabbinic Judaism has generally discouraged messianic strivings as certainly hopeless and probably destructive; but, ironically, the most fervent apostles of rabbinic Judaism in our own day are among the strongest advocates of messianism. In their ardor to bring about the era of redemption, some are willing to use any means to achieve their ends, and so approve even the racism and violence of a Meir Kahane. This milieu breeds fanatics such as Amir.[2]

Rebuilding Jewish Peoplehood

Like Jeremiah in the time of Gedaliah, we need to rebuild the common base of Jewish peoplehood. But Jewish unity does not require uniformity of opinion. On the contrary, some measure of ideological controversy is desirable—both to arouse passions and commitments and to challenge the community's stands and values. Yet divisions must be engaged constructively, with the spirit of enhancing the Jewish people and its collective endeavors, rather than as an attempt by each side to delegitimate the other. Democracies need opposition to survive as democracies, but opposition that rejects the very legitimacy of the government cannot be endured.

Rabin's assassination, in this context, undermines the very essence of Jewish peoplehood. The assassination signaled that legitimate disagreement can degenerate into delegitimization. The response must be the rebuilding of peoplehood. All Jews share in the covenant. No one group should follow the path of Gedaliah's assassin in excluding its opponents from the covenant of the Jewish people.

We may disagree on how we read our sacred texts, but as Jews we must engage continually with them. All too often we cite Torah, Talmud, and other teachings in absolute terms, as if there could be no doubt about their applicability to contemporary situations. An honest encounter and dialogue, however, means distancing ourselves from the texts, then asking questions and being prepared to learn anew. In other words, the Jewish people requires an informed and educated Jewish readership.

The lessons of Gedaliah's assassination ring sharply today. The story line is different, but the need for a national soul-searching and a renewed commitment to building peoplehood remains no less pressing.

Notes

1. The reforms involved a revitalization of religious observance and were spurred by the rediscovery of the scroll of Deuteronomy during the reign of King Hezekiah. King Josiah, Hezekiah's grandson, supported the reforms, and the Rabbis believe that because of the piety of his reign he was able to defeat the Assyrians in battle.

2. Amir himself, however, is not a follower of Kahane.

Beshallach: Not Every Enemy Is Amalek

Military conflict permeates this week's Torah reading. The opening verse of *Beshallach* records that the Jews will leave Egypt via a route that will avoid the land of the Philistines—"lest the people grow faint-hearted at the sight of war and return to Egypt"—an apparent reference to the invasions of the sea peoples from the Aegean Sea and their ongoing battle with the Egyptian empire (Exodus 13:17).

Yet despite these efforts to avoid the sight of war, the *parashah* both begins and ends with military encounters between Jews and their enemies. The Egyptian Pharaoh quickly regrets his decision to permit the Jews to leave and determines to re-enslave them by military might. The ensuing battle by the Sea of Reeds leaves the Jews safe on dry land while Pharaoh's entire cavalry is drowned (Exodus 14:28–30).

Within two months the Jews find themselves in another conflict—this time with a desert people known as Amalek. Moses sends Joshua to battle, and the latter prevails, thereby permitting the Jews to continue on their journey—first to Mount Sinai and, subsequently, to the Promised Land. The *parashah* concludes with a promise from God to Moses of a permanent war between God and Amalek (Exodus 17: 13–16).

Diminished Joy

Jewish teaching reacts to these two battles in starkly contrasting fashion. The rabbis questioned why we refrain from reciting the complete *hallel* or thanksgiving prayer during the intermediate and concluding days of Passover. They respond by noting that this *parashah* forms a critical Torah reading for the final day. On these days our joy in the holidays is significantly diminished by the drowning of the Egyptians in the Battle of the Sea. The rabbis go so far as to ascribe to the Almighty the saying, "My creations are drowning and you should be in a mood to sing?"

Similarly, one of the most dramatic moments of the Passover Seder is the spilling of the wine while reciting the plagues that afflicted the

Reprinted from *The Long Island Jewish World,* February 9–15, 1990.

Egyptians—a reminder again that our joy in the Exodus is diminished when we recall the loss of Egyptian life.

In contrast, the Judaic view towards the Amalekites is one of unremitting hostility. The rabbis interpret the wars with Amalek as a neverending struggle with a radical evil from generation unto generation. When King Saul centuries later pitied the Amalekite king, he was punished with the loss of his monarchy. There appears to be no room for feelings of remorse over the shedding of Amalekite blood. How then can we explain the dissonance between the beginning of *Beshallach* and its termination—the war with Egypt vs. the war with Amalek and the contrasting interpretations Jews ascribed to these similar struggles?

One clue lies in the historical context of the motivation for these battles. In the case of the Egyptians, the motive is clear-cut and explicit. The Egyptians have lost their slave labor force and wish to re-enslave Jews. The Jews cannot surrender to such an enemy. On the contrary, the battle must be fought to a victorious conclusion. However, with the removal of the *casus belli,* room for reconciliation exists. In suggesting that our joy in Passover is diminished by the death of the Egyptian soldiers, Jewish tradition subtly encourages us to keep open the doors to reconciliation.

With Amalek, in contrast, no grounds for reconciliation are possible. Amalek attacked without reason. No a priori grounds for conflict existed. Therefore, the war with Amalek is an unending one until Amalek is fully eradicated. Jewish tradition distinctly rejects pacifism, saying that Judaism will wage a perpetual war with the radical evil symbolized by Amalek. The injunction for the Jew is to remember continually that Amalek attacked "all that were feeble in thy rear" (Deuteronomy 25:18), rather than look forward to a future reconciliation with Amalek.

Necessary Burden

In short, Jewish teaching distinguishes between these two conflicts. Both were to be fought to victorious conclusions. The Jews perceived the first conflict as a necessary burden until the grounds for the conflict had been removed. In the case of the latter, Judaism could envision no possibilities for peaceful accommodation.

Like the generation of the Exodus, our generation also underwent two conflicts within a relatively short period. In our time, however, the order was reversed. We fought Amalek in the trauma of World War II and the Nazi Holocaust. No sooner did we emerge from that nightmare than we fought a second and continuing struggle for Israel's independence and security in the face of a hostile Arab world.

Both battles must be fought to a successful conclusion. Yet many today have forgotten the distinction between the war of Egypt and the war of Amalek. Nazism represented a radical evil which had to be destroyed. The Jewish-Arab conflict, in contrast, stemmed primarily from a political foundation of two peoples claiming one piece of land. In the latter context, Jewish victories are tinged with the sadness of spilled blood. More importantly, our moral imperative is to look forward to a day of peace and to keep open the doors that might lead to that reconciliation. Jews who are convinced that no peace with the Arabs is possible would do well to recall the distinction in wars articulated so beautifully by *Parashah Beshallach* and its accompanying interpretations.

Saddam, Haman, and Amalek

For many centuries Purim has been a source of both joy and embarrassment for Jews.

Some have questioned its unabashed frivolity, including an imperative to consume so much liquor "as not to know the difference between Mordecai and Haman," as a notorious exception to traditional Jewish norms of sobriety. Others have worried over the absence of any explicit theological message in the Book of Esther, which goes to great lengths to avoid any mention of God. Still others have challenged the doctrine of violence associated with the holiday.

Martin Luther, for one, accused the Jews of the bloodthirsty and vengeful spirit of the Book of Esther. Although Luther carried this criticism to anti-Semitic extremes, he does reflect the close association of Purim with the biblical doctrine of war against Amalek.

On the Sabbath before Purim, the Torah reading enjoins the Jews to "blot out the memory of Amalek." On Purim itself, we read of the battle of Moses and Joshua with Amalek, and Haman is described in the Book of Esther as a descendant of Agag, King of the Amalekites in the time of King Saul.

The doctrine of Amalek: The theme of Jewish violence against Haman and his supporters, the doctrine of Amalek, has caused Jews the greatest discomfort with the Book of Esther and the holiday with which it is associated. The general reception of Purim continues the tradition of universal sympathy for Jews as victims and the noticeable reluctance to endorse their right to self-defense.

Significantly, the doctrine of Amalek has been widely condemned as racist. But Jewish commentators and sages have always emphasized that Amalek is not a biological concept but a moral one. When confronted with the reality of evil, the doctrine of Amalek enjoins Jews to resist with force. The doctrine of perpetual battle with evil stands in pronounced contrast to the pacifist doctrines of Tolstoy ("resist not evil") and Gandhi, who calmly counseled Jews to practice nonviolent

Reprinted from the *Washington Jewish Week,* February 28, 1991.

resistance to Hitler, à la his own pernicious equation of Nazi genocide with British colonialism.

Judaism teaches that violence is justified under certain circumstances—particularly defense against aggression and war against radical evil. It is instructive to compare, for example, rabbinic attitudes toward the war against Egypt by the Sea of Reeds with the war against Amalek as recorded in the Book of Exodus.

Against Amalek the attitude toward victory is exultant—rejoicing in the eradication of evil. Against Egypt the rabbis counseled moderation because the enemy was considerably different from Amalek. Egypt had waged a war of national interest. It had enslaved the Jews for reasons of state security and questioned the wisdom of settling them free. Not so Amalek, which attacked the rear guard of the Jews in a particularly treacherous manner with no objective except to inflict violence upon "you who are tired and weary" (Deuteronomy 25:18).

Amalek, the rabbis argue, is the eternally irreconcilable enemy who represents a value system that promotes murder and is therefore inherently opposed to Jewish ethics. Moses Maimonides in his *Guide for the Perplexed* explained that war with Amalek was necessary because it had violated universal laws. In other words, Amalek represented a permanent threat to the rule of law and just living.

Herein lies the enduring relevance of Purim. Aggression must be stopped and evil eliminated. Moreover, an attack upon Jews in one corner of the world (the Jews of Persia and the "tired and weary" in the desert) amounts to an attack upon the entire Jewish people.

Waging war against evil: The meaning of Purim is relevant to the question of war in the Persian Gulf today. The issue is not whether Saddam Hussein is a modern Hitler, although his boast that he would transform Tel Aviv into a crematorium suggests that he, at least, does not mind the comparison. The real issue is the moral use of force to stop aggression, to wage war against evil and to defend Western values.

Saddam Hussein has clearly committed naked aggression against Kuwait. He used poison gas to massacre the Kurds and committed atrocities in Kuwait that are unspeakably atrocious. His unprovoked Scud missile attacks against entirely civilian targets in Israel are reminiscent of Amalek's treacherous attacks upon the "tired and weary"

Israelites in the desert. The State of Israel, to be sure, has long recognized the nature of Hussein's threat and did the entire world a favor by eliminating the Iraqi nuclear reactor nine years ago.

President Bush's use of force to halt Hussein deserves the support of all Americans concerned with preserving of Western ethical values. For, as Purim reminds us, war is justified when it serves as a defense against and resistance to acts of evil.

Passover and Modern Jewish Identity

Research has demonstrated repeatedly that Passover is the most frequently observed holiday among American Jews. Approximately 85
percent of American Jews report that they attended a Passover seder
within the past year, compared with 80 percent who reported lighting
Chanukah candles and 61 percent who report fasting on Yom Kippur.

Communal leaders, however, disagree over the meaning of these statistics. Optimists underscore Passover as the centerpiece of the Jewish
calendar, and note that at this time of year Jews congregate with other
Jews and perceive themselves as performing a distinctive Jewish act.
Pessimists question whether attendance at a seder truly signifies engaging in Jewish activity or simply participating in a family meal under an
artificially Jewish rubric.

In all probability, for most Jews the reality of Passover lies somewhere in the middle. For a minority, a seder truly signifies participating
in the recitation of the Passover Haggadah followed by a meal prepared
in accordance with Passover injunctions.

For others, Passover means little more than an opportunity to see
one's relatives at a festive occasion. For most Jews, however, Passover
combines elements of Jewish tradition with the modern consciousness
of America and American society.

In what ways does Passover resonate so strongly with the self-per-
ceptions and identity of American Jews?

First, Jews perceive in Passover a sense of history and historical
memory. Retelling the story of the Exodus communicates the image
that Jews have of their history—slavery and bondage followed by redemption and liberation. Most Jews experience in Passover an opportunity to recall the Jewish past and thereby stress their solidarity with
Jews everywhere as heirs to a common heritage.

In addition to a communal past, Passover signals Jewish hopes and
aspiration for a better future. The Passover theme and mood is upbeat,

Reprinted from the *Jewish Week of New York,* March 22–28, 1991; distributed by the
Jewish Telegraphic Agency, March 1991.

expressing the optimism of Jews that as their forefathers were redeemed from Egypt, so redemption will occur from present-day misfortunes.

The concluding words of the seder, "Next year in Jerusalem," although ideally meant as a literal statement of return to Zion, has come to mean a metaphorical statement of optimism in the human future—a conviction that we will overcome today's crises.

Moreover, the family messages of Passover are indeed powerful ones. Jews of different generations exchange ideas and experiences on what their Jewish connections have meant to them. Even taken at its minimum, the seder creates a common familial bond of Jewish identity, a collective family memory or a "usable past" to sustain future family ties.

At its best, the seder is child-oriented. Jewish tradition unabashedly encourages rituals, such as partaking of parsley or splitting the matzah, for no purpose other than to encourage children's questions and arouse their interest. Freedom creates our capacity to raise families, and the child-oriented rituals of Passover signify Judaism as family at its finest.

Most important, Passover expresses to Jews values and ideas that Jews perceive as distinctively Jewish. First, the endorsement of freedom itself underscores the conviction of Jews that human beings were meant to be free—that tyranny and totalitarianism are inherently anti-Jewish phenomena.

This freedom of the individual is in turn translated into the freedom of the Jews as a people. Passover recalls the birth of the Jewish nation. It resonates today as Jewish pride in the State of Israel and its accomplishments. Yet that pride in national freedom and sovereignty may never be translated into a narrow chauvinism or contempt for others.

On the contrary, one of the most dramatic of Passover rituals is that of the spilling of wine during the seder when we recite the passage from the Haggadah of the ten plagues afflicting the Egyptians. By spilling the wine, we express our sorrow and compassion at the suffering of others even as we celebrate our liberation from bondage.

Finally, Passover resonates so powerfully in modern Jewish consciousness because it approximates the experience and self-definition of contemporary American Jews. The theme of liberation from bondage parallels the perception Jews have of emerging from the dark night of the Holocaust to the new day of modern Israel—two historical events that have shaped the "civil Judaism" of today's Jews and are best expressed by memorials to the martyrs as well as missions of solidarity to Israel.

Although the twin phenomena of Holocaust and Israel are best understood on their own terms as critical historical events shaping the modern Jewish consciousness, they are forever fused in Jewish historical memory. Passover today enhances that memory.

American Jews, in particular, have an additional point of connection between Passover and their own condition as contemporary Jews. Jews have perceived America as the land of opportunity, a country in which Jews have been truly free to mold their own identity. The blessings of freedom are both individual and communal—the freedom of personal fulfillment and the freedom of communal responsibility and commitment to others.

The opening pages of the Haggadah express the dual meaning of freedom. We are enjoined to recline during the seder, for the capacity to recline while eating signals the mark of a free man. Yet we are also enjoined to share our food with others, to extend our hand of hospitality to those less fortunate than we in material, political and spiritual terms.

For this reason, the plight of Soviet Jews for many years dominated our awareness of Passover—namely, that we pray for their personal freedom to leave the Soviet Union and state that our responsibilities as free men and women compel us to work for their freedom as well.

This dual nature of freedom has often been terrifying. With freedom goes moral responsibility and accountability for one's actions. Some have sought the safety and security of tyranny and authoritarian rule in order to "escape from freedom," as Erich Fromm has so eloquently put it.

But the message of Passover that resonates so strongly among American Jews is that our celebration of American freedom not only permits us to lead our individual lives as free citizens, but also compels us to assume the responsibilities of building community, safeguarding freedom and extending the freedom we so cherish to those who are less fortunate and who have not as yet known the "Passover of freedom."

American Jewry Fifty Years
after the Holocaust

It's a matter of perhaps no small irony that we meet here tonight exactly one week before the sixtieth anniversary of Kristallnacht, fifty-three years after the end of World War II and the culmination of the Holocaust. The changes in the Jewish world that have taken place since that time have been monumental in scope—the return of the Jews to sovereignty and statehood, in the homeland of the Jews in Israel, and the maturation and vitality of an American Jewish community.

A Dual Narrative: The "Inner" and the "Outer" Story
The basic story of American Jews consists of a dual narrative. On the one hand, no society in Diaspora Jewish history has been as receptive to Jewish involvement and Jewish participation as has the United States. In that respect, the outer life of Jews as Americans has been an incredible success story. Jews have become the envy of virtually every non-Jewish ethnic and religious grouping in America. At the same time, if the outer lives of Jews as Americans have been a success story, their inner lives as Jews increasingly are called into question. Do Jews understand the meaning of being a Jew, and do they know why leading a Jewish life is significant? Do they have an adequate grasp of the content of Judaic teachings, and can they make a persuasive case to their children and grandchildren why being a Jew is a matter of considerable significance?

In that sense we have a dual narrative. On the one hand, the American Jewish story is a story of inner struggle, of trying to find out what this Jewish enterprise means and why it might have something of significance to say to Jews living at the end of the twentieth century. If you view the position of Jews in American society today to be characterized by the metaphor of a fluid boundary, there are Jews who know perfectly well what being a Jew means, and there are Gentiles who

Reprinted from *Amerikanisches Judentum heute/American Jewry Today* published by Paulinus Verlag GmbH and the American Jewish Committee (Trier, Germany, 1999).

wish to be Jewish. There are also Jews who have no clue as to what being a Jew means and there are also Jews and Gentiles who practice both faiths simultaneously. That fluid boundary itself is testimony to the Jewish success narrative in America. As American Jews have become so much a part of the fabric of American culture, the boundary line between Jews and Gentile has disappeared. Conversely, for a minority to survive in a democratic majority culture, that minority needs a firmer sense, both of what it is, and what it is not. American Jews face that double challenge. On the one hand they have overcome the boundary with American society. On the other hand, they do not know what distinguishes them as Jews. Or, as the British novelist Charles Dickens once put it in a totally different context: "It was the best of times; it was the worst of times."

Some Data

Let me begin with some data and then offer some reflections on American Jewry one generation after the Holocaust. In terms of size, American Jews today are 5.5 million. That is a figure that has been virtually constant since 1950. In 1950 there were 150 million Americans, and 5 million American Jews. Today, in 1999, there are 265 million Americans, but the number of American Jews remains constant at 5.5 million. Clearly, Jews are not a growing element of American society. If anything, we are witnessing a declining percentage of American Jewry within the American population. If Jews were three to three and a half percent in 1950, today they are two percent or perhaps even less. If current trends hold, we will be witnessing a significant drop in the American Jewish population in the next twenty to twenty-five years, owing to the ravages of assimilation. In all likelihood, Jews may number no more than four million by the year 2020. Four million, to be sure, does not mean American Jewry is disappearing. If Jews remain at four million, they will still be the largest Jewish community known to Diaspora Jewish history. Polish Jewry at its height, 1939, was three million. So we are not talking about the vanishing American Jew. Demographic size alone guarantees that there will be some kind of future. Exactly what the content of that future is, that is very much a subject of discussion.

Similarly, in terms of income, American Jews, generally speaking, are earning $10–12 thousand a year more than the average American white family. As a point of reference with America generally, American Jews are doing quite well by economic standards. College education has become completely normative for American Jewry: close to eighty-five to ninety percent of American Jewish high school seniors will continue on into the college years, twice the ratio among the white population generally. Twenty-five to thirty percent will continue on into graduate education, post baccalaureate. That is three times the average among the Caucasian population generally.

Secular and Religious Education

With educational attainments go, of course, economic attainments. The reasons for American Jewish economic success are very closely tied to the primacy and emphasis Jews have placed upon American educational attainments. But there is an enormous gap between the secular aspirations of American Jews, educationally speaking, and their Jewish attainments. American Jews insist upon high level college and university education for their secular degrees.

In terms of religious education, however, they often content themselves with the most elementary forms of learning. To be sure, there are greater opportunities today for an intensive Jewish education in America than at virtually any moment in recent Jewish history, certainly, and perhaps even all of Jewish history. Every American Jewish child has an opportunity for a full day Jewish education in the finest Jewish schools. There is hardly a university of note that does not offer serious academic Jewish studies to its students. The opportunity is there for high quality Judaic studies. The challenge for American Jews is whether they avail themselves of those opportunities.

The Future—Assimilation or Jewish Being and Living?

Again we have a dual narrative. For some American Jews, the story is one of assimilation. For others, perhaps the minority, the real story is Jews in every community in the United States who are far better Jewishly educated and far, far more Jewishly involved than their parents and grandparents ever could have imagined. Are they a majority of American Jews? I tend to think not. My overall picture of American Jewry is a threefold picture, namely a core of the community, twenty to twenty-five percent who are far more Jewishly engaged than their parents' and grandparents' generation ever would have imagined.

At the other end of the spectrum are ten to twenty percent, for whom being Jewish says nothing whatsoever. The real question is what about the middle group, the fifty to fifty-five percent who essentially affirm their Jewishness, who say being Jewish means something to them but are not quite able to specify what the content of their Jewish identity is all about. The Jewish future is in the hands of that fifty to fifty-five percent. The open question is will they fulfill the opportunities available to them for intensive Jewish living or will they pursue the direction of further assimilation and Jewish disinterest. My hope is that the former will prevail. My fear is that the latter scenario will prevail. But that, in fact, is the dual narrative.

Religious Movements—Liberalism or Return to Tradition?

Jewish power in America today is the capacity to make those choices. For one of the few times in Jewish history Jews control their destiny. In large measure the question is what will happen within the non-Orthodox religious movements. Orthodoxy was once considered—as recently as the 1950s—to be moribund, to be a passing phenomenon on the American scene, a development that would never take root on American shores. Orthodox Judaism has not only survived, but also experienced some growth. But the numbers of Orthodox Jews represent only a tiny percentage of the American Jewish population, no more than seven percent. Therefore, the future of the Jewish community is very much a function of what will happen in the non-Orthodox religious movements. With all the differences that exist between them, they comprise about eighty to eighty-five percent of the American Jewish community. What will take place inside those religious movements is very much an open question. One trend is a return to Jewish tradition. The other trend defines these movements as religiously liberal and therefore religiously less committed. Both trends exist at the same time, and the question of which will prevail remains open.

Jews in American Political Culture

In the realm of politics American Jews exercise considerable influence on the American scene. In terms of Jewish numbers, they are a tiny percentage of the American political culture. However, looking at Jewish influence, looking to what extent are Jewish voices heard, Jews represent a significant voice in American political culture. Let me offer a few illustrations. Probably no more than forty percent of the American population cast ballots in non-Presidential elections. Among American Jews, it is close to eighty percent. While Jews are only two percent of the population, they are probably four percent of the voting population. Certainly we need a lot more people voting than currently do. Nevertheless, the willingness of Jews to participate in a democratic political culture is a critical ingredient in the American Jewish success story.

I suggest that there are three major strengths in America's Jewish political culture and one primary weakness. The first is a demographic strength, that Jews live in a small number of critical states in the American political environment. Therefore Jewish votes count disproportionately because Jews are so concentrated in a small number of states, particularly New York, California, Illinois and several others. Therefore, one political strength of the Jews is the vagaries of the American political system that recognizes each state as having critical importance when it comes to counting votes.

Second, Jews are willing to participate in the political instrumentalities of American life. This represents democracy at its finest. Jews are key members of the constituencies of both the Democratic Party and the Republican Party. They become active in political campaigns, and in political fund-raising.

Thirdly, is the power of Jewish ideas, the willingness and the capacity of Jews to write, to speak and to address the major political issues of the day. One need not necessarily agree with everything the Jews happen to say, but it is a matter of no small significance that among the leading writers, among the major organs of the political process, Jewish writers and intellectuals have always been prominent.

The major weakness has been the predictability of Jewish votes. Since 1928, for a full seventy years, there has been one standard rule that has held regardless of who is campaigning or who is running in any particular election. That rule is: The Jews will vote for the more liberal candidate, assuming that candidate is neither anti-Jewish nor, in more recent years, anti-Israel. Jews will incline towards a more liberal candidate, unless they have a specific tangible reason not to do so. The trouble is that from a political perspective, Jewish votes become eminently predictable. Once they become predictable, they are easier to ignore, and to take for granted. Political activists therefore argue that Jewish political strength requires continued Jewish engagement and involvement on both sides of the political spectrum.

American society has come to admire Jews for what they are. To be a Jew is to occupy a coveted position, to be admired, even to be envied. An interesting irony appeared several years ago in an editorial in the *New York Times*. President Clinton, in the fall of 1993, appointed Justice Stephen Breyer to the Supreme Court. What was interesting in the *Times'* editorial is that it criticized Clinton for having opted for the safe choice. Presumably the *Times* wanted a judge who was more daring, someone more outspoken in his opinions. Lost on the editorial writers of the *New York Times* was the irony that a Jew should be the "safe" choice. Jews are so much a part of America that the appointment of a Jew to the highest judicial office in the land is considered a non-controversial appointment. The story of America is that all doors are open to Jews. The question is what will they do when they enter through those doors? How Jewish will they be as they gain prominence within American society?

Concerns of the Present—Challenges for the Future

And that in turn leads us to what concerns American Jews today. In many ways, our historical agendas have been realized. In the first forty years of the twentieth century, American Jews were concerned with bringing Jewish immigrants into American society. That is an agenda that succeeded remarkably. For the next forty years, our primary concerns were protection of Jews against threats, whether it was anti-Semitism during the Holocaust years and after, and after 1948, threats to the stability of the State of Israel. As we approach the end of the twentieth century, I suggest that we are moving towards a somewhat different agenda of four primary concerns.

First, and to some extent foremost, is preserving the agenda of America. As long as America remains an open society and a healthy democracy, the position of the Jews remains stable. One of the real things we have learned about America has been the wisdom of the prophet Jeremiah some twenty-five hundred years ago: "Seek the peace of the country in which you are living, because in the welfare of that city will be the peace of the Jews." A healthy America has been good for Jews. Our job in the future must be to preserve a healthy, stable America.

Secondly, American Jewry has been preserving the close, special relationship between Washington and the State of Israel. The American Washington-Jerusalem relationship has had many ups and downs in the first fifty years of Israel's existence, but a critical ingredient in maintaining a special friendship between America and Israel has been the strength, stability, and outspokenness of the American Jewish community.

Thirdly, the relationship with other Jewish communities. One of the most fascinating developments of our own time has been the emergence of Jewish life in areas that were thought to be lost to the world's Jewish people. It is that story of emerging Jewish communities that represents one of the most exciting phenomena of contemporary Jewish life. What will be their future, what will be our relationship with them, can we preserve a sense of common Jewish peoplehood, even as we discover that there are so many different types of Jews?

And last, and far from least, to what extent will being a Jew make sense in the twenty-first century? Can we make a persuasive case that Jewish identity is sufficiently exciting, sufficiently demanding, sufficiently inspiring, to be worth the sacrifice of Jewish resources and energies? We have often felt, though luckily not often experienced in the last fifty years, that being a Jew is a function of "look at all the people who are out to get the Jews," a sense of Jewish vulnerability. Our challenge for the twenty-first century is can we reconstruct a meaning of being a Jew that has very little to do with pressures from without, but has much more to do with a sense that Jewish heritage and tradition are so inspiring, so compelling, as to warrant a claim on my resources. That is our challenge for the future: Why be Jewish in an open society?

American society will not compel Jews to be Jews. Those days are over. Whether Jewish choices can be made sufficiently exciting and inspiring will determine whether we answer that question affirmatively. That is our challenge of the twenty-first century.

The Meaning of Jewish Memory, Jewish History, and the Holocaust

The critical historical memory that Jews have, and certainly any attempt at opening up the question of German-Jewish relations must address the question of what is Holocaust memory. Jewish tradition obviously is quite explicit on this point—remember the past, do not forget. Being a Jew is always a matter of continuity, of living between past memories and future aspirations, or as the Zionist philosopher Ahad Ha'am put it so eloquently some seventy years ago: "No people can survive, without memories of the past. No people can survive only on the basis of memories."

So the memory of the Holocaust is not negotiable. What the Holocaust means to American Jews, I submit, are four very distinct memories, all of which have a claim on us as we enter the twenty-first century. First, we remember today the lessons of Jewish disunity. The conflicts internally within the Jewish people weakened the capacity of the Jews to pressure Washington. The head of the refugee desk in the State Department in Washington wrote in 1938 that he had advised President Roosevelt not to engage in any rescue activity, not to liberalize immigration quota laws. Why? Because there were so many different Jews, each demanding different things, and if you try to satisfy one group of Jews, you only alienate others. In that respect, the lessons of Jewish disunity are quite powerful. Jews require a greater sense of common Jewish destiny.

Secondly, American Jews have learned the lesson related in the Psalms many years ago: "Do not place excessive trust in princes." Perhaps too much hope was placed on Roosevelt, on a liberal democratic American administration, which was regarded as the best friend of the Jews. The lesson of the Holocaust is of the need for greater Jewish self-reliance, and the need to avoid excessive identification with any one sector of politics.

Related to that is the third lesson, of excessive faith in human nature. We cannot come to grips with the Nazi experience because we assume the basic goodness of human nature. The lesson of the Holocaust is one of not taking for granted human goodness. Men and women by nature are neither preternaturally good nor preternaturally evil. They can go in either direction. Which direction they go is ultimately a matter of free choice. We cannot assume that people will naturally do the right thing, if given certain conditions. We can hope that that is the case, but we cannot assure it.

This explains some of the skepticism concerning the Oslo peace process. Even if you put good things on the table, even if you give people a fair shake, you cannot always be certain that human nature will respond positively. Unfortunately, despite all of the hopes placed by the liberal imagination in human goodness, our experience has been that men and women often do not, necessarily, respond positively to rational proposals.

The fourth lesson is that of the continuity of Jewish life. When Jews look at the past, they do not say history repeats itself. They do not say that the status quo must be permanent. It is the willingness to continue to lead a Jewish life, even given the memory of the Holocaust, which distinguishes the Jews as a people. Jews do not say "what is is what must be." Rather the Jew looks at reality and says "approach reality realistically, do not pretend that it is something it is not, but work to change it, to make it something better".

On my way to this evening's lecture, I took in an evening service at one of the local synagogues, and I said to myself: this is an incredible story of Jewish history. Here we are, fifty years after the Holocaust, sixty years after Kristallnacht, Jews are still gathering for daily afternoon prayers. They are still willing to offer a constructive model of what leading a Jewish life means. They are willing to say after all this time: "let us rebuild, let us look to the future." The meaning of Jewish memory, Jewish history, and the Holocaust to the contemporary Jews is not only a matter of remember the past. That part is non-negotiable. Our challenge to the twenty-first century is to decide where we want to go. No one will decide that for the Jews as a people. Rather the question is what history will the Jews create for themselves.

THE FORMATION OF JEWISH IDENTITY IN AMERICA

Much discussion has occurred in recent years concerning strategies to strengthen Jewish identity in America. Some argue for a more external or civic agenda. Others call for revitalization of personal Jewish meaning and cohesive Jewish community. The essays in this section engage these questions—in particular the nexus between Jewish politics and Jewish identity, e.g., my response to the argument of Prof. Riv-Ellen Prell in the pages of Sh'ma *magazine, and the inadequacy of a Jewish identity constructed in response to external threats to Jews.*

Ideologies of Jewish Identity

Before the onset of modernity, Jews lived in self-contained communities. Their inner and outer lives were regulated almost exclusively by Jewish teaching, and their identity was clear: They were Jews because they followed the laws of Moses. Survival may have been a problem in such a world, but identity posed no difficulties. But today, Jews no longer live in autonomous communities and therefore do not determine their own social policies, practices, and priorities. As Mordecai Kaplan observed more than fifty years ago, modern Jews live in two civilizations. They function both within the Jewish community and as citizens of a larger state, and thus they are heirs to the values and teachings of two traditions.

In a society that welcomes the participation of Jews, Jewish identity becomes a matter of choice. Does Jewish tradition have a role in a world governed by modern values? Why should Jews remain faithful to Jewish tradition if modern culture itself is so powerful and attractive? This controversy has raged in Jewish life ever since the Emancipation.

The philosopher Baruch Spinoza, for one, argued that there was no reason to remain Jewish in a world of enlightenment, and that the teachings of Jewish tradition were an anachronism in the absence of a sovereign Jewish community. Ironically, this view encountered a mirror image among the ultraorthodox. Rabbi Moses Sofer in nineteenth-century Hungary, for instance, agreed that Jewish heritage and modern values were incompatible. Therefore, Sofer decreed, Jews must reject modern culture entirely, except as a vehicle for earning a living. Values and teachings, he insisted, were exclusively the province of Torah.

Most modern Jews, including the Orthodox, reject the recommenda-

Reprinted from Barry Holtz and Steven Bayme, eds., *Why Be Jewish?* (New York, American Jewish Committee, 1993).

tions of both Sofer and Spinoza, and seek a balance between their Jewish heritage and their citizenship in modern culture. All Jews today are "Jews by choice" in the sense of opting for a particular form of Jewish identity. But for many the question "Why be Jewish at all?" is becoming increasingly difficult to answer. We see the result in the alarming erosion of American Jewish life.

Since the release of the 1990 National Jewish Population Study, much communal concern has focused upon Jewish continuity. Indeed, ensuring the future quality of Jewish life has emerged as the critical priority of the 1990s, reflecting the fears and anxieties of Jewish communal leaders as to whether their grandchildren will be Jewish.

However, despite the consensus on the need to assign Jewish identity higher priority on the communal agenda, there is little agreement about what should be done. Some emphasize intensive Jewish education, particularly Jewish day schools. Others note the importance of trips to Israel. Still others advocate increased funds for outreach programs to mixed-marrieds.

These initiatives cannot, in and of themselves, guarantee future continuity, for they fail to address the underlying weaknesses in the community—the paucity of ideological commitment to leading a Jewish life. American Jews lack the language to explain in clear and compelling terms why it is important to lead a Jewish life. This weakness of ideology underlies the problem of assimilation, for those most committed to leading a Jewish life are those least vulnerable to erosion and assimilation.

In other words, we speak of continuity, but for what end? Without some content to Jewish identity, there can be little in the way of meaningful continuity. At best we can aim for a vague nostalgia, at worst an empty tribalism. For Jewishness absent an anchor in ultimate concerns can add little, either to ourselves or to the society around us. Conversely, if we approach the choices we make out of a base of Jewish knowledge, we may then formulate a distinctively modern Jewish identity that appropriately grapples with the twin and often conflicting claims of Judaism and modernity.

Therefore, the appropriate policy response is to formulate a set of ideas explaining to American Jews all the reasons for leading a Jewish life. To be sure, there are many ideological difficulties. Such a formulation may be divisive, for no single set of ideas can appeal to all Jews, and the more vigorously these ideas are propounded, the more likely they are to prove offensive to some. Moreover, some observers will claim, in the spirit of Karl Marx, that ideology does not motivate behavior. It only serves to justify already-existing behavior patterns.

Although these concerns are real, they must not daunt efforts to make Jewish values salient to those unconvinced that Jewish life is worth leading. Absent ideology, we appear interested in continuity for the sheer sake of continuity, expressing itself primarily in pro-Israelism and a liberal universalism that we dress up in Jewish garb. Moreover, it is the ideas of the Jews that have made them distinctive as a people. In a land of free choice, Judaism may compete for the attention of the next generation only in the open marketplace of ideas. Finally, whatever answers the community provides to the question of why be Jewish must be pluralistic in nature, offering at best partial solutions that will speak with varying degrees of persuasiveness to different Jews.

What, then, are the compelling reasons for leading a Jewish life?

1. *The claims of peoplehood.* We owe it to our fellow Jews. Historically, Jews have been one people despite diversity of practice. We identify with the faith and destiny of Jews elsewhere on the globe. Thereby, we affirm our continuing membership in the Jews as a distinctive, historically evolving people.

2. *Personal enrichment.* Judaism has always posited a triangle of individual, family, and community. The health of one component of this triad rests upon the health and vitality of the other two components. Therefore, Judaism has always supported the family, and family-centered Jewish rituals enrich our intergenerational ties. Judaism addresses the personal and existential sides of our lives, suggesting the possibility of finding meaning in life that transcends our work-a-day world. As Abraham Heschel has eloquently written, the Jewish Sabbath connotes a moment of sacred time—a twenty-four-hour retreat from mundane concerns that enables us to strengthen ties with family and friends and that communicates to us the need to address our personal, spiritual, and social needs. Similarly, newly Orthodox adult "returnees" to Judaism

report that they find in Judaism an antidote to the emphasis placed upon material gain and pursuit of pleasure so rampant in the everyday world.

3. *The claims of Jewish law.* The twentieth-century Jewish philosopher Franz Rosenzweig argued for the salience of Jewish law to personal identity as a Jew. At one point, Rosenzweig fully intended to convert to Christianity. However, he felt he could not undertake such an action without first knowing what it was to be a Jew. This led Rosenzweig to a study of Judaism and its meaning for modern men and women. He noted that historically Judaism had been a religion of law. Therefore, any serious discussion of Judaism had been as a religion of law. The challenge to modern Jews was to see whether the law could be internalized—made personally relevant to our concerns as twentieth-century human beings. When asked if he had become observant of the law, Rosenzweig responded, "Not yet."

Rosenzweig's theology has been extremely influential in American Conservative and Reform Judaism. Both those movements approach Jewish law, in varying degrees, as the core of Jewish religion. They disagree, to be sure, on the nature of the law's binding authority and claims upon contemporary Jews. Following Rosenzweig, however, they are asking: What is the salience of Jewish law and how may we internalize it as modern Jews?

Orthodox Jews, in contrast, do not question the authority of the law. For them, being Jewish follows from the fact of historical command at Sinai. However, they share with Rosenzweig and, and for that matter, with Conservative and Reform Judaism the theme that being Jewish is an existential condition—that what happened at Sinai molded the Jews into a distinctive people and community of faith. The essential task of the Jew, then, is to develop something meaningful of that condition.

4. *The claims of history.* The French philosopher Henri Bergson once commented that he saw no merit in remaining a Jew. However, he acknowledged that he was reluctant to convert, for he deemed it ignoble to desert a sinking ship!

Undoubtedly Bergson was in error. Jews are heirs to a rich tradition that merits preserving and transmitting to future generations. Judaism stands at the root of Western civilization, its values and institutions. Jews were the first monotheistic people. For millennia, they have remained the People of the Book, reflecting the primacy placed upon learning and education.

Most importantly, throughout history Jews have been willing to defy and transform prevailing reality rather than submit to it. Paganism was normative in the ancient world, and its plurality of gods seemed far more logical than monotheism. In asserting monotheism, Jews defied existing currents and ultimately shaped the Western religious tradition. In more recent times, contrary to Bergson, Judaism has not disappeared in modern secular culture, and it has refused to accept the reality of the Holocaust as marking an end to Jewish history.

5. *The claims of community.* Synagogues report that they are succeeding to the extent that they have become anchors of a Jewish community that provides a network of institutions serving the needs of the entire Jewish family. Orthodox Jews, for example, frequently cite the presence of kosher establishments in the neighborhood that enable people to socialize with one another, develop personal and communal ties, and ultimately build a stronger Jewish community.

The underpinning of this community are the institutions intermediate between the individual and society—the schools, neighborhood associations, and religious institutions that bridge individual existence and the broad but impersonal universe at large. Repeatedly, sociologists have underscored the importance of such mediating institutions for social welfare. Churches, for example, have often helped families transmit social values. Within the Jewish community, these mediating structures help create cultural norms, stabilize family life, and communicate both the joys of leading a Jewish life and the obligations that go with it. Orthodox communities have been particularly successful in creating strong communal bonds, in effect stating that one should be a Jew because membership in the community both provides benefits and imposes obligations.

Orthodox Jews, to be sure, find it easiest to say, "Be a Jew because that is your religious obligation." However, the non-Orthodox movements also must be empowered to articulate the distinctive commitments and obligations their religious movements entail. Being a Reform Jew should not mean being a weaker Jew. It should mean serious commitment and obligations to the principles of Reform Judaism.

6. *Religion and ethnicity.* Mordecai Kaplan termed Judaism a great civilization, encompassing religious life, culture, peoplehood, family, and personal Jewish associations and connections. In his magisterial work, *Judaism as a Civilization,* Kaplan proposed an overarching "reconstruction" of the synagogue from a house of worship to a Jewish center containing within it all aspects of the Jewish civilization. Kaplan did not claim Jewish chosenness. Rather, he argued, Jews, like other people, have a responsibility to maintain and preserve their distinctive civilization.

One need not be a Reconstructionist Jew to accept Kaplan's analysis. Jews today generally assert their Jewishness out of some kinship with other Jews. Kaplan's challenge is to see that sense of kinship as an entry point to Jewish life, for ultimately to be a Jew means to share in the maintenance and transmittal of the distinctive qualities and values of the Jewish civilization.

7. *Tikkun olam.* Some Jewish thinkers identify the impetus to leading a Jewish life as a quest for social justice. Indeed, for many otherwise unaffiliated Jews, being Jewish means engagement in progressive politics. Leonard Fein and Harold Schulweis are probably the most outspoken advocates of this meta-theory of Jewish existence.

Critics attack this theory on several grounds. First, they challenge the equation of social justice with liberal politics. Conservatives, for example, do not regard themselves as deficient in their social-justice concerns when they place priority upon individual responsibility rather than programs of public assistance. Second, they question whether it is particularly Jewish to engage in the quest for social justice when this is a universalist concern in which Judaism may or may not play a critical role. Certainly, Judaism ought not be wedded to any specific social program or ideology. Finally, they question whether the values of social justice will in fact provide a sustaining basis on which to lead a Jewish life. To date, organizations and publications aimed at Jews who share this vision of social justice have not captured the attention of great numbers of unaffiliated Jews. The experience, for example, of New Jewish Agenda, an organization dedicated primarily to enabling Jews to pursue as Jews their vision of social justice, is instructive.

Nevertheless, it is true that in the modern period the image that many

Jews have of Judaism is that of *tikkun olam*. Based on the Prophetic vision of Jewish experience, this ideology often stimulates Jewish engagement with the contemporary world. To be sure, a serious presentation of the ideology of *tikkun olam* must acknowledge differing conceptions of what social justice is rather than become a mandate for reformist politics. Its starting point ought be the counsel of Jeremiah, "Seek the peace of the city to which I have exiled you, and pray the Lord for it; for in its peace shall lie your own welfare" (Jeremiah 29:7)—initiating a long tradition of Jewish concern for building a good and just society wherever Jews have lived. Its conclusion, appropriately, may then be that being Jewish remains incomplete so long as the world remains in a state of disrepair.

First, we must be clear that we are serious about Jewish continuity. All too often the *tikkun olam* agenda becomes little more than a thin veneer to justify what we wish to do in any case. If we are serious about leading a Jewish life, then our statements concerning the general social agenda must be informed by a concrete knowledge and careful consideration of Jewish teachings and social concerns and not merely dressed up in selective quotations to make them palatable to our contemporary values.

Second, and in the same spirit of candor, we have to be willing to acknowledge conflict between American universalist norms and the needs of Jewish continuity. One example, and by no means the only example, is our perspective on intermarriage. From the vantage point of American universalist norms, intermarriage represents the ideal marriage in the sense of signaling the acceptance and integration of a Jew into American society. From the perspective of Jewish continuity, we ought to be willing to assert Jewish traditional values even if they fly in the face of universalist American norms.

Third, to be serious about *tikkun olam* means asking what will actually improve the quality of the society around us. All too often, advocates of *tikkun olam* automatically equate liberal social policies with improvement of society. One is no less committed to *tikkun olam* if one maintains that conservative social theory is the actual vehicle of improving society. All too often, however, advocates of *tikkun olam* essentially utilize Jewish teachings and the teachings of social liberalism as if the two were interchangeable.

Fourth, we ought to be willing to investigate whether our commitment to leading a Jewish life challenges our American social norms or do we simply utilize our commitment to leading a Jewish life to confirm our basic sense of ourselves as Americans. Arthur Hertzberg, among others, has criticized American Judaism for transforming itself into a religion that gives "no offense." All too often we are unwilling to confront Judaism as the message of a countervailing culture—of performing an act of *havdallah*—of making distinctions between what it is that we believe that is distinctively Jewish and general American norms. In that respect, an ideology of *tikkun olam* is sterile if it only repeats and confirms where we are in any case. On a pragmatic level, let us acknowledge that the ideology of *tikkun olam* has not insured Jewish continuity as evidenced by the recent National Jewish Population Study to date. On an ideological level, let us acknowledge that utilization of Jewish teachings often becomes little more than window dressing rather than an actual vehicle of enhancing Jewish commitment.

Let me offer a concrete illustration of these tensions. Recently a local Jewish community drafted a statement on the Jewish response to the AIDS crisis. The statement sought to buttress our communal response to AIDS with Jewish teachings underscoring reverence for life, the need for medical treatment, and the imperative for compassion for those who are suffering. Few would disagree with this utilization of Jewish teaching. However, the statement then proceeded to underscore AIDS prevention—equally a desirable goal. Here it argued that while Judaism ought to oppose the utilization of drugs, "when the lesson is too hard to learn, the use and availability of clean needles should be encouraged." The statement concluded by invoking the stand of the Jews at Sinai, *"Na'aseh venishma."*

I read such statements and question how serious are we about Jewish continuity. Can we maintain with any degree of honesty that Judaism as a value system would encourage the utilization of clean needles as a vehicle of AIDS prevention? Are we unable to assert distinctive messages—even on the relatively noncontroversial question of drug abuse—because we are so afraid to give the "offense" that Rabbi Hertzberg so rightly criticizes?

Here, however, is the value of the National Jewish Population Study. It pinpoints the underlying weakness in the community as an ideological weakness that we fail to take our Judaism and our Jewishness sufficiently seriously. Our mandate then is to make Judaism and Jewish teaching salient to contemporary men and women. One way of doing so is to ask what is the relevance of Judaism to contemporary social and ethical questions. To take that mandate seriously, however, means an honest confrontation between Jewish values and contemporary concerns.

Finally, let us recognize that *tikkun olam* cannot substitute for leading a serious Jewish life. If our Jewish continuity agenda becomes yet another vehicle for advancing social liberal concerns, then let us recognize that we will be doing little more than confirming what American Jews have been doing in any case since the end of World War II. That posture has brought us precisely to where we are today in terms of current Jewish identification and affiliation.

8. *Zionism and modern Israel.* The re-creation of a sovereign Jewish state as homeland remains the single greatest success story of modern Jewish history. More than any other ideology, Zionism has united Jewish opinion by capturing the minds and hearts of Jews everywhere. To be sure, Jews may disagree about particular aspects of Israel's policy and actions. However, one must acknowledge that Zionism has done much to restore a public focus of contemporary Jewish existence, mobilize Jewish energies to reclaim a Jewish homeland, and enable Jews to assert their historical role as a sovereign and independent people. Lastly, Israel has functioned as a haven for endangered Jewries— including the historic rescue, in our own day, of Soviet and Ethiopian Jews. Indeed, these momentous events ought to remind everyone of the need for a State of Israel and why it came into existence.

Of course, the Jewish emergence from powerlessness did not come without cost. Yet, in many ways, the existence of Israel as a Jewish state provides the ultimate response to the Holocaust, in which the Jew could be but victim. Pride in the accomplishments of Israel today is therefore a central pillar of the meaning of being Jewish.

Common to all of these responses lies an emphasis on the rewards of leading a Jewish life. To the extent that Jewish identity evokes only nostalgia or sadness at the persecution of the Jews, it is unlikely to be sustaining. Leading a Jewish life cannot consist purely of memories of oppression. First, those memories by no means comprise the totality of Jewish history. Moreover, pride in one's identity must contain both memories of the past and aspirations for the future. Identification of the Jew as victim will, in the long run, encourage only further assimilation, for there is little reason why, in a society of free choices, individuals should opt to remain members of an oppressed people. The reasons for being Jewish cited above—peoplehood, family, personal fulfillment, history, religion, social justice, Zionism—all reflect the positive values and joys inherent of Jewish living.

Arthur Hertzberg has put this well: "A community cannot survive on what it remembers; it will persist only because of what it affirms and believes." Jewish continuity is thus indissolubly linked to what Judaism can actually say to modern men and women. A *spiritual* revival—a meaningful ideology of Judaic commitment—is necessary to overcome the weak commitment of many Jews and guarantee the Jewish future.

Thirty-five years ago the sociologist and theologian Will Herberg wrote an important book, *Protestant-Catholic-Jew.* Herberg celebrated the fact that Jews, who were only 2.5 percent of the population, had become one-third of the religious influence in American society. For that celebration of American Judaism, Herberg is justly remembered. What we forget are the last twenty pages of the book in which he argued that the arrival of Judaism in American society had in some respects become meaningless because in becoming so central to American society the message of Judaism had become too bland to have significant meaning.

That precisely is our challenge in mapping out an agenda of Jewish continuity today. If we are to inspire people to lead a Jewish life, we must formulate a rationale that is sufficiently exciting, sufficiently inspiring to make Jewish life worth leading. In so doing, we run the risk of giving offense, of diminishing consensus, of saying things that are truly meaningful. That, however, is a risk worth taking if we are serious in the pursuit of Jewish continuity.

Further Reading

Cohen, Steven M. *Content or Continuity? Alternative Bases for Commitment.* New York: American Jewish Committee, 1991.

Fein, Leonard. *Where Are We?* New York: Harper & Row, 1988.

Gillman, Neil. *Sacred Fragments.* Philadelphia: Jewish Publication Society, 1990.

Greenberg, Irving. *The Jewish Way.* New York: Summit Books, 1988.

Hartman, David. *Conflicting Visions.* New York: Schocken Books, 1990.

Heilman, Samuel. *The Gate Behind the Wall.* New York: Summit Books, 1984.

Hertzberg, Arthur. *The Jews in America.* New York: Simon & Schuster, 1989.

Heschel, Abraham. *The Sabbath.* New York: Farrar, Straus & Giroux, 1975.

Holtz, Barry. *Finding Our Way.* New York: Schocken Books, 1990.

Kaplan, Mordecai. *Judaism as a Civilization.* Philadelphia: Jewish Publication Society, 1981.

Walzer, Michael. *Exodus and Revolution.* New York: Basic Books, 1986.

American Jewry: Renewal or Erosion?

Co-authored with Sholom D. Comay

Periodically, American media attention focuses upon dire tales of woe forecasting the decline, if not the disappearance, of American Jewry. Thus, we are treated occasionally to articles bearing the titles of "Vanishing American Jew" or "U.S. Jewry Slipping."

Conversely, other commentators inform us that we need not fear the allegedly widespread periods of assimilation and intermarriage.

As we approach Rosh Hashanah, it is a good time to sit back and reflect: Where, in fact, are we? Are we to believe the prophets of doom or the pollyannas of renewal? Is the cup half empty or half full?

To be sure, American Jewry does face considerable dangers of communal erosion. Intermarriage rates are unacceptably high—approximately 30 percent—and, absent conversion, intermarrieds and their children participate minimally, at best, in Jewish communal life.

Jews have the smallest numbers of children of any other American ethnic group, suggesting a "grayer" Jewish community with fewer future members.

Perhaps most precarious for communal vitality is the astonishing rate of Judaic illiteracy. The "people of the book" have remained precisely that with respect to secular education, yet content themselves with the lowest of standards for Jewish educational accomplishments.

Too many Jews know abysmally little of the heritage, values, and precepts—to say nothing of the languages—of the Jewish experience.

However, one need not accept a pessimistic outlook as absolute. Considerable resources of vitality and pockets of energy do exist within the Jewish community to counteract these currents. As studies indicate, Jewish renewal is, indeed, a meaningful term if defined as Jews who are far more involved in private and public Jewish life than their parents ever would have anticipated.

Orthodox Judaism, once considered moribund, is enjoying an un-

Reprinted with permission of the Jewish Telegraphic Agency, August 24, 1990.

precedented revival. Moreover, the most dramatic illustrations of Jewish renewal may be found among the *baalei teshuvah,* or returnees to Judaism, in American and Israeli Orthodoxy.

Even far more numerous are Jews in Conservative and Reform synagogues who have become both more communally active and personally observant than their parents' generation.

Jewish women are beginning to take advantage of unprecedented opportunities for involvement in Jewish religious life. To be sure, these individuals—many of whom are active in havurot or small communities of intensive Jewish learning and commitment—do not outweigh, in numbers, those who are disaffiliating. They serve, however, as powerful resources and signals for future Jewish continuity, rather than erosion.

Similarly, Jewish scholarship in America stands at an unprecedented peak. Only one generation ago, the field of Jewish studies was present only at schools under Jewish auspices and at a select handful of elite universities.

Today, virtually every major university proudly showcases a distinguished Jewish studies program among its catalog offerings. Over 1,000 faculty members currently engage in advanced Jewish scholarship and enable college students to enjoy unprecedented opportunities for enriching their Judaic knowledge.

Even greater opportunities prevail for intensive Jewish elementary and secondary education. Every American Jewish community with a population of greater than 5,000 Jews hosts at least one Jewish day school combining secular and Judaic studies.

The number of pupils enrolled in recent years has grown to 120,000—a critical mass from which a reservoir of future leadership may be developed. Interestingly enough, the central complaints about day schools do not pertain to the quality of education offered but, rather, the capacity of middle-class parents to afford such quality education.

Israel, too, functions as a critical ingredient in safeguarding Jewish continuity. Studies have indicated that spending extended time in Israel—as tourists, for instance, or as participants in youth or university programs—serves to enhance Jewish identity, awareness, and communal affiliation.

More obviously, Israel's presence on a daily basis in the American media serves as a powerful stimulus of Jewish awareness for American Jews. Although many may deride this media connection to Israel and Jewish life as superficial at best, it constitutes an entry upon which greater connections and ties may be built.

Finally, American Jewish organizations have much reason for pride in terms of recent developments concerning Soviet Jews. With some few exceptions, Soviet Jews are now free to emigrate, although we still have reason to worry about a potential rise in anti-Semitism within the Soviet Union.

These developments signify an enormous victory for American Jewish organizations and the Soviet Jewry movement, which have long fought for emigration and human rights for Soviet Jews.

The critical theme pervading this mosaic of Jewish renewal is the element of choice. Jews have unprecedented opportunities for intensifying their Jewish knowledge and commitments in America's open society. American freedom, conversely, provides equally the opportunities for Jewish assimilation and even disappearance.

Neither the prophets of doom nor the pundits of renewal can afford to be confident of the accuracy of their diagnoses. Considerable evidence exists on both sides of the question, confirming the old adage that the cup is both half empty and half full.

Whether Jews choose the route of renewal or that of erosion, however, is entirely in the hands of the Jewish community. That freedom of choice is both the blessing and the bane of the American-Jewish experience and the key to the Jewish communal future.

Judaism and American Public Life

Over a century ago, Y. L. Gordon, the poet laureate of the Russian Jewish Enlightenment or Haskalah, advised his readers, "Be a man in the streets and a Jew at home." As Michael Stanislawski has recently argued, what Gordon was actually recommending was the modernization of Jewish culture—the integration of traditional Judaism with universal values of the Enlightenment. In practice, however, his advice was taken to mean strict separation between the private and the public sphere, the confinement of Judaism to the home and synagogue and its absence from the public square.

American Jewry has reversed this maxim. In the public domain American Jews are assertive. In defense of Israel or to protest the scheduling of school exams on Jewish holidays, American Jews feel few inhibitions about asserting their communal interests, even in the face of an unfriendly public. On elite campuses, observant male Jewish students—and lately some female ones as well—can be seen publicly displaying their *kippot,* or head-coverings, as a public demonstration of Jewish distinctiveness. Secular Jewish organizations, once the bastion of "keep your Jewishness private," increasingly employ traditional Jews intent on proclaiming Jewish values within the broader society.

The primary weaknesses of contemporary Jewish life are in the private domain. The same Jews who unabashedly defend Jewish communal interests in the centers of power in Washington find themselves incapable of articulating a language of Jewish content (let alone endogamy) to their children in the privacy of their homes.

Yet efforts to strengthen Jewish life today continue to focus on the public domain and, more specifically, on the place of Judaism in the public square. Opponents of "strict separationism" between church and state argue that the legal status quo in fact weakens Judaism by relegating it to private life. Others call for the public "marketing" of Judaism. Still others urge greater governmental assistance to Jewish institutions, particularly day schools.

Reprinted from David G. Dalin, ed., *American Jews and the Separatist Faith* (Washington, D.C.: The Ethics and Public Policy Center, 1993).

These advocates assume that greater recognition of Judaism in the public square will lead to increased respect for Judaism as a faith, and will thereby enhance Jewish identity. Yet their well-intentioned proposals appear to ignore the real weaknesses of Jewish life. Whether Jews have the right to wear the *kippah* in the U.S. Air Force may be of concern to some, though the *kippah* has no standing in Jewish law. But to assume that such "rights" will foster Jewish tradition among those uncommitted to it is simply wrong. Similarly, advocates of public funding to Jewish institutions downplay or ignore the question whether such funding will mandate diminution of the distinctive content of Judaism taught within these institutions. Finally, the experience of Jewry in Britain, where an established church does exist, indicates that the presence of organized religion in the public square translates into marginal benefits for Jewish culture, e.g., reduced day-school tuitions, but often carries as its price a diminished capacity to assert publicly Jewish values and communal interests.

Allocating a greater role to religion in the public arena may very well enhance the degree of comfort for traditional Jews in American society. It may also raise issues of Jewish consciousness among those who know they are Jewish but have little idea what that means. However, it will have little effect upon the truly critical issues of continuity and quality in Jewish life. The major problems that Jews confront—increased intermarriage, declining Jewish cultural literacy, and sizable communal erosion and disaffiliation—stem not from the weakness of Judaism in the public arena but from the absence of Jewish content in the home and the consequent attenuation of private Jewish identity. Therefore, efforts to enhance Jewish life ought to be aimed at enabling Jews to partake of the joys of Judaism in their private lives, rather than at marginal—and possibly hurtful—initiatives to weaken church-state separation.

To be sure, there is a legitimate role for religion in the public square, but it is one that may be filled by public education rather than legislation. Jews would do well, for example, to advocate the presence of realistic and appropriate Jewish characterizations in the popular media so as to communicate positive images of Jewish private and public life. Until very recently, the only Jews portrayed on television were characters unable to assert any positive values—let alone joys—of leading a Jewish life.

Moreover, Jews possess a rich tradition that may profitably be applied to the great social and ethical issues of the day. All too often this has been done selectively, to validate a preconceived position. These practitioners of proof-texting are likely to elicit ridicule from knowledgeable scholars rather than enhanced respect for Judaism.

Orthodox Jews cite Jewish tradition in an authoritative and absolutist manner. Their message, too, invites societal rejection, for most Americans, and certainly most Jews, simply do not accept the binding authority of tradition.

Rather, what is necessary is honest and constructive engagement with Jewish sources, an encounter that will enable Jews to measure the salience of their tradition in modern times. The engagement itself would stimulate rethinking of what it means to be Jewish, for it would underscore not only the degree of consonance but also the conflicts between Jewish tradition and American values. Jews would be challenged to ponder the meaning of a distinctive Jewish identity and a distinctive American Jewish synthesis.

The overall impact on society would also be positive without furthering the attenuation of church-state boundaries. American society can well benefit from an overall climate in which religious norms are articulated in a persuasive and intelligent fashion. Jewish teaching can contribute to a climate in which Americans take the positive values of all religions more seriously.

An example is the abortion debate. Jewish organizations have, with few exceptions, advocated a pro-choice position and have cited Jewish sources that at times permit and even mandate abortion. Virtually absent from the public pronouncements of Jewish organizations are statements of the moral gravity of abortion in Jewish tradition, its permissibility only in the most extreme of circumstances, the preferability of adoption, and the unequivocal rejection of abortion on demand, of abortion as an alternative form of birth control, and of the claim that "no one can tell me what to do with my body." An honest and open encounter with Jewish tradition could well result in a pro-choice position that communicates the rich array of Judaism's teachings on abortion. This could help to create a climate of opinion in America in which the legal availability of abortion underscores rather than detracts from the relevant moral questions.

A generation ago the sociologist and theologian Will Herberg wrote that Judaism had attained equal status with Protestantism and Catholicism in the panoply of American religions. However, Herberg cautioned that this status did not really mean very much, for all three faiths had become bland. The challenge to American Judaism today is not to overcome the barriers between church and state, barriers that have served Jews well. Rather, all religions should feel free to articulate their distinctive content, to ask what are their meaningful contributions to American life, and thereby to overcome the apparent blandness, and even more the moral relativism, that so many perceive in contemporary religious life.

Between Left and Right: A New Dialogue?

Riv-Ellen Prell's call for a new politics of dialogue and coalition-building appears, at least in design, addressed ideally to someone like myself. Like Prell, albeit much earlier than the 1980s, I became disenchanted with the politics of intolerance so characteristic of the New Left. Like Prell, I am interested in the relationships between political and Jewish identities. Unlike her, I find myself increasingly on the "conservative" rather than "liberal" side of most political and social questions.

Can our dialogue then be productive? Unfortunately, Prell offers us little substantive basis on which to proceed save a return to the "open-mindedness" and "tolerance" she abandoned in the 1960s. Perhaps this is sufficient, for surely these values are in short supply in an increasingly polarized America of the 1990s. But a commitment to dialogue absent consensus of vision—even in broad terms—is likely to prove as frustrating today as it was a generation ago. Civility of discourse clearly is preferable to name-calling, but it is no more likely to proceed unless both sides are prepared to move substantively beyond earlier "truths."

Here, then, are my guidelines for substantive dialogue between Jewish conservatives and liberals:

1. Abandon Moral Absolutism

Prell recognizes that Leftist intolerance alienated moderates. Militant picketing of classrooms and political speakers did, indeed, infringe civil liberties. Moderation of discourse does not exclude the presence of "nonnegotiable" items, but it does require that those items be carefully limited to what is truly nonnegotiable.

Take, for example, the divisive issue of abortion, on which Prell admits she does not know "how to talk to people who oppose abortion." To speak of abortion as legally available yet ethically restricted

Reprinted with permission from *Sh'ma: A Journal of Jewish Responsibility*, 24:460, October 24, 1993.

is to uphold a woman's right to choose but also to state clearly that having an abortion may not be the ethically correct decision. Pro-choice advocates generally welcome statements that support the legal availability of abortion. However, it is becoming increasingly "politically incorrect"—vide the prevention of Gov. Casey from addressing the Democratic National Convention—to articulate qualms concerning the ethical acceptability of abortion as a choice.

2. Abandon Moral Relativism

It is tempting to replace the absolutism of the New Left with an "I'm okay-you're okay" posture in which there are no universals. People and cultures are simply different—not necessarily better or worse. Yet that moral relativism is as destructive of substantive dialogue as is the absolutism Prell correctly repudiates. Pluralism does not mean that all values are equal. It does mean that not all behavior that we protect is behavior that we prefer.

The example of homosexuality is particularly salient here, albeit missing from Prell's essay. Most American Jews defend the civil liberties of homosexuals and do not wish any equivocation on this point. But that is a far cry from accepting homosexuality as morally equivalent to heterosexual marriage—a position over which there is no communal consensus. It is harmful to make homosexuals the pariahs of the Jewish community. Yet outreach to homosexuals cannot and should not mean that we fail to privilege heterosexual marriage as the norm of the Jewish community.

3. Recognize the Intellectual Integrity of Opponents

Those who disagree do not do so because they are selfish, racist, homophobic, sexist, or otherwise narrow-minded. Their convictions flow from a sincere and deeply felt vision of what is good for society. Those who defended American intervention in Vietnam wished to halt the spread of Asian Communism and prevent further atrocities. They may have erred in considering Vietnam a threat to American national interests, but that does not earn them the epithets of "racists" and "imperialists." Similarly, those who uphold the virtues of the two-parent home are not so simple-minded as to think the problems of the ghetto will disappear if only people will marry and stay together. They are concerned that we do ourselves no favors by avoiding questions of "family values" that underscore commitments to marriage and celebration of the two-parent home as the most effective format for the raising of children.

4. Learn from One Another Rather than Speak Past One Another

Liberals tend to emphasize governmental activism, economics, and cultural diversity. Conservatives prefer the rhetoric of values and social responsibility. Both have much to learn from one another. Increased governmental activism can do little unless it is embedded within a culture of self-help and moral responsibility. Prell's call to abandon the politics of victimization is welcome. It must be followed, however, by a politics that perceives individual, family, and society as closely intertwined units necessary to the health of all, and it is the responsibility of each of those units to be strengthening the other two.

5. Find Common Ground Within the Dialogue on Issues of Jewish Identity and Continuity

Remarkably, given Prell's earlier and justly-hailed scholarship, she has little, if anything, to say about Jewish identity as a bridge concern between liberals and conservatives. Yet both are confronted today with the identical dilemma of preserving and transmitting a specific content of Jewishness in a society that has been so open and receptive to Jews that Jewish disappearance is indeed a possibility. Can liberals and conservatives agree, for example, that intermarriage threatens Jewish continuity and, therefore, that it is not racist to encourage Jews to marry other Jews? Can they agree that Jewish texts and teachings ought to be studied for their own sake as the unique heritage of Jewish civilization? Can they agree, following Prell's earlier research, that ritual and community are the best guarantors of Jewish continuity? Prell eloquently searches for allies on the Right but paradoxically ignores the essential dilemma of her generation and the power of Jewish tradition to address that dilemma.

To be sure, major differences here also exist over the relationship between political and Jewish identities. Jewish liberals invoke social justice—*tikkun olam*—as the core meaning of Jewish identity. Traditionalists question whether *tikkun olam* need be translated as liberal rather than conservative social policy. Both sides must grapple with the durability and sustaining power of *tikkun olam* as an ideology to preserve Jewishness—whether social activism suffices to transmit the distinctive content of Jewishness.

6. Beginning the Bridge-Building

Will these guidelines make for effective dialogue between Left and Right? Many conservatives undoubtedly will dismiss Prell's appeal as little more than a corrective to the excessive dogmatism of the New Left. They will note, with considerable accuracy, that beyond changes in style, Prell continues to appear locked in the orthodoxies of the 60s. Her critiques appear limited to questions of tactics rather than substance.

Yet Prell's call for dialogue is too important to go unanswered. The Jewish continuity agenda is too broad and encompassing for any one sector of the community to address effectively on its own. New coalitions will be necessary to enable different Jews to find their particular way to Jewish tradition and community. Failure to heed Prell's call risks creating a Jewish community so narrow as to exclude precisely those Jews anxious to find the nexus between political and religious identities. Conversely, Prell has the potential to reach Jews disenchanted with mainstream Jewish communal politics. Unlike other veterans of the culture wars of the 60s, she is not prepared to "write off" those who disagree with her. For all these reasons, the appropriate response to Prell's call for dialogue is both to engage her substantively and challenge her to explore the relationship between our political and our Jewish identities.

Teaching Kids Jewish Civic Responsibility

Recently my nine-year-old son returned from school with what was to him exciting news: A classmate's father was running for state-wide office. "Of course you'll vote for him, won't you?" he implored. My wife and I exchanged looks. We had often applauded actions of the incumbent office-holder, and consequently questioned the wisdom of replacing him with a well-meaning but inexperienced politician. But how could we explain that to a nine-year-old?

More troubling was a subway excursion to Manhattan with my eleven-year-old daughter. The day was to be a special "father-daughter" day—a movie, trip to the zoo, and dinner, capped by a visit to a toy store. On our way in, several subway panhandlers approached us, begging for a handout. What should we do? Often we had spoken of the need to assist the poor, and their timing was good, since a day devoted to pleasure should, indeed, be coupled with assisting the needy. Yet helping panhandlers in New York subways is a questionable business, since the suspicion remains that the money collected would be wasted, or worse yet, be used to support drug habits.

One evening during the Palestinian *intifada* (uprising) of 1987–88, my family was watching television news reports of Palestinian demonstrators being beaten by Israeli soldiers. "Are they Jewish?" my daughter asked. When I replied that they were, she asked how such a thing was possible—and we launched into a discussion of Jewish attitudes toward violence. Under the circumstances, there was no point in invoking unfair media coverage. Rather we emphasized the need to understand Israel's desire for security and its responsibility to quell disturbances that threaten its citizens' lives, balanced by an understanding of Palestinian rage at continuing occupation. My child invoked the parallel of the Passover Seder, where we rejoice over the Israelite deliver-

From *The Hadassah Magazine Jewish Parenting Book,* edited by Roselyn Bell (pp. 193–200). Copyright 1989 by Hadassah, The Women's Zionist Organization of America, Inc. Reprinted with the permission of The Free Press, a Division of Simon & Schuster, Inc.

ance but agonize over the destruction of the Egyptians. Naturally, we didn't resolve the issue, but we managed to wrestle with some of the questions of Jewish values as to the treatment of Gentiles.

What these incidents have in common is that they all raise issues for parents related to transmitting Jewish civic and social values to young children. As Jews, we are heirs to a rich tradition of social ethics, communal responsibility, and political wisdom. How best to impart this tradition to a younger generation?

Myths to the contrary notwithstanding, Jewish values cannot be clearly identified with any particular political party or tradition. To be sure, Jews in the post-Enlightenment period have tended to support left-of-center political groups, and some have even endorsed radical movements to reshape society. Proponents of these views often have wrapped themselves in the mantle of Jewish teaching, invoking the Jewish value of *tikkun olam* (perfecting the world, setting right what is wrong) as a mandate for reformist politics.

In fact, however, the most traditional segment of Jews has generally been the most conservative politically. Orthodox Jews today frequently support conservative politicians with enthusiasm. Conversely, those Jews furthest to the left on the political spectrum frequently are the most alienated from their Jewish heritage. This anomaly can best be explained by the absence of, rather than the content of, any specific Jewish political ideology or creed.

In reality, Jewish tradition is neither liberal nor conservative, although, to be sure, advocates of liberal or conservative ideologies often try to buttress their positions by appealing to biblical or rabbinic statements of Jewish values. In the last century and a half, Jews have generally supported liberal parties, for these were the forces that extended liberty and equality to the Jews. Conversely, Jews identified parties of the right with forces of oppression and anti-Semitism. Jewish interests and historical memory, rather than any specific Jewish teaching, has thus translated into Jewish votes for liberal candidates.

Jewish teaching does, however, contain certain explicit political values. The prophet Jeremiah enjoined diaspora Jews of his day to "seek the peace of the city to which I have exiled you, and pray to the Lord for it; for in its peace shall lie your own welfare" (Jeremiah 29:7). Jeremiah's advice begins a long tradition of Jewish concern for building a good and just society wherever Jews have lived. This strategy of coexistence with Gentiles assumes that a healthy society will be less likely to mistreat Jews. Moreover, this political strategy often joined hands with a mystical theology of *tikkun olam,* "repairing the world," which held that salvation would come through mystical actions that increased justice and morality in the world.

Thus, while not supporting any particular ideology, Jewish tradition expresses strong approval for Jews acting within the political system. Jewish teaching underscores the importance of voting, but doesn't tell us for whom to vote. To be sure, candidates seen as hostile to Jewish interests—for example, lack of concern for Israel's society—will rightly be rejected by Jews. Similarly, Jews are unlikely to support candidates whose policies may undermine international harmony and justice, such as advocates of unilateral disarmament. The overall message, however, is Jewish responsibility for the health of the society in which we live—a responsibility fulfilled by pursuing both justice generally and defense of Jewish interests specifically.

Since political attitudes and values are initially formed in the home, children need to be shown that Jews care both about specific Jewish concerns and universal concerns. Encouraging children to read and discuss both the daily paper or newsweekly and the local Jewish newspaper can develop this dual concern. Studies show that at election time Jews evidence the greatest concern with Jewish public affairs. Therefore, an election provides useful opportunities for family-based discussions of Jewish political values.

While Jewish tradition is neither liberal nor conservative, universalist nor particularist, it does supply windows of opportunity for transmitting notions of civic responsibility. On the other hand, few Jewish teachings are as explicit as those relating to *tzedaka,* the Hebrew word for charity, which also connotes justice. The Bible repeatedly admonishes us to remember the poor and set aside a tenth of our crops in the third and sixth years of the seven-year cycle to sustain them. By reaching out to the needy, we express the Jewish value of community—that all members are responsible for one another.

Our compassion for the less fortunate is repeatedly drawn into sharp relief by remembering our Egyptian experience of slavery. In ancient times, selling oneself into slavery was the last recourse of a person overwhelmed by debt. Because Jews recall the experience of being enslaved, and more recently of living in great poverty in Eastern Europe, we ought to be especially sensitive to the needs of the abject poor. Rage at homelessness and starvation ought to be the natural Jewish response. As a people that has experienced so much in the way of human suffering, we cannot stand idly by while others suffer.

Moreover, Jewish tradition provides specific guidelines for assisting the needy. The Talmud enjoins us to maintain the dignity of the poor. Therefore, anonymous gifts are the best, in that neither donor nor recipient knows the other's identity. Similarly, the highest form of charity is empowering the poor to help themselves, by providing employment or assistance in securing a job.

Finally, Jewish tradition instructs us how to prioritize our charitable efforts. The poor of our own city take precedence over others. This theme is closely linked to the Jewish value of community. Someone living in our own community has a natural claim upon our resources. Likewise, the theme of "charity begins at home" translates into giving priority to poor Jews over poor gentiles. But the Talmud enjoins us to be generous as well with the non-Jewish poor "for the sake of peace." Thus, by extending our social policy teachings and practices to the American poor generally, we not only accomplish moral good but enhance our presence in American society. As a prosperous element within the United States, we express our Jewish concerns by translating our traditional commitments to the needy to include all the poor among whom we live.

Perhaps no ritual symbolizes our concern for Gentiles better than the spilling of the wine during the Passover Seder. As we recite the Ten Plagues inflicted on the Egyptians, we spill drops of wine to express our sorrow over the shedding of so much blood. This symbolic action portrays our belief that all humanity is created in the image of God, and that the death even of our sworn enemies is no cause for rejoicing. If this is our attitude toward those who enslaved us, how much more positive ought to be our attitude to American society, which has provided Jews with greater freedom and opportunity than any other diaspora society in history.

Hurricane Gilbert recently provided our family with an opportunity to practice prioritizing our *tzedaka*. Our synagogue established a relief fund for hurricane victims through the Joint Distribution Committee. The hurricane coincided with the High Holy season, when recitation of memorial prayers is an occasion for giving charity. On receipt of the synagogue appeal, we brought it to the dinner table for discussion. The children questioned whether such a donation would benefit Jews. We explained that while Jewish charities take precedence, this emergency situation warranted immediate attention. Weighing this issue was a positive exercise in prioritizing charitable efforts and communicating Judaism's universal concerns.

In the area of *tzedaka*, Jewish tradition offers clear guidance as to how much is to be given as well as to whom. Ten percent of one's income is deemed appropriate, less is considered niggardly. Moreover, the rabbis exhorted Jews to give generously until it hurt—holding out the promise of even greater material rewards to those quick to part with their personal assets.

To be sure, modern sensibilities have made it difficult to apply this relatively straightforward rabbinic teaching. For one thing, the contemporary tax system usually commands high percentages of our income—some of which is then redistributed to the poor. Moreover, in a society in which panhandling has become so common, one can legitimately question whether all requests for "spare change" should receive equal response.

Yet even in the face of these doubts, few would question the desirability of transmitting the Jewish value of *tzedaka*. In this area, children are most likely to absorb parental patterns. Seeing parents reaching into their pockets to give immediately impresses children with the positive value of giving. Moreover, *tzedaka* is a Jewish value in which children can readily participate; the simplest way is by just placing coins in a *pushke* on a regular basis. Children should be encouraged to participate in fund-raising drives for charitable purposes, for example, selling Passover candies for projects whose goals they fully understand. Every Purim they can participate in the *mitzva* of seeking out a poor person to give a direct gift of a generous nature. It is especially important that children participate in family discussions of where to give. Finally, as children are entrusted with their own money, from allowances or in payment for odd jobs, they should take responsibility for fulfilling this *mitzva* directly, setting aside specific sums for charitable purposes.

Jews have never extolled poverty as a virtue. Our attitude to accumulation of wealth is positive, so long as it remains a means rather than an end. However, as Jews have become increasingly affluent members of American society, we face greater difficulty in helping our children understand the value of money. As we have more money at our disposal, the potential for conspicuous consumption and ostentatious materialism increases. The Wall Street scandals involving prominent Jewish figures only heightens the image of Jews placing money over everything else. Yet these scandals also provided us with an opportunity for serious discussion of Jewish business ethics in an age of plenty. In my home, we recently fantasized about what we would do if we were wealthy. By the time we had finished with the litany ranging from trips to Disneyland and Israel to F.A.O. Schwarz, the children had gotten the idea that one needs to limit one's acquisitions and give priority to those of enduring value.

Children, of course, require more than words to internalize basic values. They need to witness those values being practiced. In that sense, Judaism as a faith provides a wealth of opportunities to teach by doing rather than by preaching. As a religion based on commands and actions, Judaism prescribes family-centered behaviors and rituals through which basic social values may be transmitted.

We have already noted in this regard giving of *tzedaka* and expressing concern for the suffering of gentiles at the Passover Seder. The list goes on and on. Take, for example, the *mitzva* of welcoming a stranger into our home. Regular extension of hospitality communicates powerfully that our privacy should at times be suspended to provide shelter and sustenance to others.

Jewish educational programs also provide opportunities for children to practice social values. Some years back a Jewish high school at which I taught set aside Friday afternoons for student *gemillut hesed*— visiting the elderly, working with retarded children, or just providing a helping hand to others. More recently, my daughter's fourth-grade Jewish day school class engaged in regular visitations to the residents of a local Jewish senior citizens' facility. This type of social action educational programming could be enhanced by activities that cut across denominational lines. All too often children attending a Jewish school under the auspices of one of the religious movements lack the opportunity to work on social concerns with counterparts in the other movements. Through such social segregation, the religious polarization of their elders gets transmitted, rather than the concern for the entire Jewish community. Yet the Jewish value that "all of Israel is responsible for one another" should be translated into social action transcending denominational lines.

One example of this type of shared responsibility is the widespread practice of taking children to rallies in behalf of Soviet Jewry. Aside from the political benefits of these rallies, one must underscore their educational value as a statement of Jewish unity and solidarity with our brethren behind the Iron Curtain. Rallies that involve Jews across the ideological and political spectrum signal the values both of Jewish pluralism and of the mutual responsibility of all Jews for one another.

Perhaps no ritual contains as many possibilities for transmitting social values as the near-universal rite of passage, bar or bat mitzva. Becoming a bar mitzva connotes responsibility for one's actions; the challenge to families celebrating this new stage is to increase the celebrant's level of responsibility.

To be sure, few will claim that an early adolescent can suddenly become responsible for all his actions. The goal rather is to begin to assume greater personal responsibility. For one thing, children should be included in planning the event: How many guests and whom to invite? More importantly, children must help decide the material level of the celebration. Leonard Fein and Project Mazon have recently proposed a 3 percent surtax on such events, with the proceeds going to feed the homeless. Whether to accept this voluntary surtax is a decision that should be shared among the parents, who are paying for the event, and the child who will soon become a bar mitzva.

Finally, the child celebrant should be encouraged to help decide what to do with the presents received. Jewish tradition mandates tithing the proceeds with 10 percent to charity. The precise percentage should, of course, vary according to the particular family's economic situation. Yet the principle of setting aside part of the proceeds for charity should be upheld, and the child encouraged to determine the amount and nature of the chosen charity. Of course, the new bar mitzva will wish to help decide how to dispense the remainder of the gifts as well. Should money be set aside for college? What about building a home library? Should the new adolescent receive discretionary funds to use as he sees fit? All these decisions may transform an often mechanical ritual into a learning experience in which the child internalizes the imperative of social responsibility—and that, after all, is the meaning of becoming bar mitzva.

Recently my children were discussing a videotape they had seen in school of the 1988 presidential debates. "Who are you voting for, Daddy?" they asked in chorus. Replying that I was not as yet sure, I asked them about their own preferences. "I'm for Bush!" announced my daughter. "Dukakis!" declared my son. Our subsequent discussion by no means brought a political consensus. We did, however, establish that we were a family with multiple political priorities and that, for my children, politics clearly ran a distant second to dessert.

Families with young children tend to be child-centered. Parents justly lavish so much attention upon children's needs that they unwittingly encourage a climate of "me first." Social reality and Jewish tradition both advise us to nurture within our children an awareness of the world around them and their responsibility to it—no small task in the "me generation." Fortunately, our Jewish heritage provides us with numerous resources and opportunities for inculcating civic and social values. Our challenge as parents is to harness Jewish tradition for these purposes and thereby enrich our own family lives.

Anti-Semitism and Jewish Identity

In the aftermath of the Crusades, Jewish leaders faced the challenge of reconstructing Jewish life. They knew that they needed to preserve Jewish memories of destruction, but chose to join them with positive Jewish aspirations and hopes. Thus, they incorporated memories of the Crusader pogroms into a broader context of Jewish joys. The memorial prayer, *yizkor*, recited on holidays, became an affirmation—memories of the past joined with, rather than separated from, the joyous aspects of the Jewish festivals. Pointedly, the Rabbis rejected the "Mourners of Zion," those for whom memory of the destruction commanded all Jewish communal energies.

By contrast, in Jewish life today the specter of anti-Semitism all too often energizes Jewish communal activity and captures communal resources. Fear of anti-Semitism often dwarfs the joys of Jewish living. An audience of Jews will quickly resonate to a speaker who articulates the language of combating anti-Semitism; all too rarely will such an audience resonate to speakers who communicate a language of Jewish values—the struggle to reconcile Jewish tradition with the culture of modernity and the joy of leading a Jewish life in contemporary times.

Two recent books on American Jewry and Judaism document this divergence: *Chutzpah* by Allen Dershowitz, and *The Search for God at Harvard* by Ari Goldman. Dershowitz perceives anti-Semitism around him and urges that Jews respond to it defiantly. Goldman, in contrast, reports little in the way of anti-Semitism either at Harvard or at *The New York Times,* two elite institutions of contemporary America. Instead, his struggle is to integrate traditional Judaism in the world of modernity—to make Jewish rituals and teachings salient to our lives as modern men and women. Rather than seeking examples of continued anti-Semitism, Goldman demonstrates that one can be at the same time both a traditional Jew and an editor at one of the world's finest newspapers.

To be sure, the precariousness of Jewish life in the Diaspora contin-

Reprinted from *The Forum,* Summer/Fall 1991.

ues to be a theme of Jewish history. It is understandable that only one generation after the Holocaust Jews remain on guard against threats to our security. Moreover, there is no question that anti-Semitism can be encountered even in the relative security of North America. The problem, rather, is the concentration of Jewish resources and priorities on combating Jewish enemies—both real and imagined—rather than on confronting the more difficult challenges of defining, maintaining and strengthening Jewish identity in a world which welcomes Jewish integration and even assimilation.

The case of American Jewry is particularly instructive. Never before in history has there been such an assertive and politically influential Diaspora Jewish community. Although Jews do have conflicts with certain sectors of American society, anti-Semitism is found primarily on the fringes of American politics.

Are We Assimilating Too Well?

Jewish success in combating anti-Semitism has, ironically, facilitated not only integration of the Jews in American society but also Jewish assimilation into that society. The recently released 1990 National Jewish Population Study of the Council of Jewish Federations (CJF) documents the success Jews enjoy in American society in terms of our social and economic status relative to the general American population. But it also highlights the essential weakness of American Jewish identity. Intermarriage rates are at an all-time high. Apostates from Judaism outnumber converts to Judaism. Children of mixed marriages without conversion overwhelmingly are being raised outside the Jewish faith— either as Christians or with no religion at all. The report, in short, documents that the primary threats to Jewish existence come not from an unfriendly America but from an internal Jewish condition in which the bases of American Jewish identity do not appear strong enough to endure.

In this context, excessive Jewish concentration on anti-Semitism in America is both misleading and, possibly, hurtful. We Jews seem to invest so much of ourselves and our Jewishness in focusing upon anti-Semitic threats that we often miss the reality that the struggle to create a free and pluralistic America has essentially been successful. More importantly, however, such a preoccupation with external foes may divert us from our real challenges: becoming Jewishly capable of leading meaningful Jewish lives and transmitting the content of Jewish identity to our children.

The findings of the CJF survey, in short, reveal disturbing news about American Jews. The implications suggest that we need to create a fundamentally different agenda and new priorities for the American Jewish community—with far-reaching policy recommendations for Jewish educational initiatives, Israel-American Jewry relations, and the future of the Jewish family. A recent American Jewish Committee study of American Jewish volunteer leaders reported similar conclusions: In the minds of lay leaders, the Jewish agenda ought to focus primarily upon safeguarding Israel, enhancing Jewish education, and addressing the weakness of Jewish identity. Although we fully acknowledge the need to actively oppose Jewish foes both at home and abroad, a continued focus on anti-Semitism as the wellspring of Jewish existence may prevent us from implementing a more far-reaching agenda. It may also serve as a convenient smoke screen, diverting us from confronting our internal selves and the need to define what we mean by being Jewish in pluralist America.

Two Roads to the Future

Growing up as an Orthodox Jew in Boston in the 1950s, adults regularly admonished me that Orthodoxy was doomed to disappear, assimilation and mixed marriage would increase, and the only basis for continued Jewish identification rested in the hands of anti-Semites who regularly reminded us that we were different.

At millennium's end these predictions appear partially misguided yet also partially correct—validation, as it were, of Yogi Berra's alleged dictum, "predictions can be very hazardous—especially about the future." For American Jewry today is experiencing a dual narrative that is likely to persist into the next century—a story of both erosion and renewal. Patterns of assimilation coexist with reports of Jews who are far more intensively involved in Jewish life than their parents or grandparents ever might have imagined. Which trend line prevails will determine the course of future Jewish history.

There can be no minimizing or underestimating the trend line of continued assimilation. Mixed marriage has increased to the point of being nearly as commonplace as marriage within the faith. Moreover, as mixed marriage has become increasingly acceptable within American society, and even among large sectors of the Jewish community, the stimulus to convert to Judaism has decreased, resulting in critical declines in both numbers and proportions of converts to Judaism.

The losses resulting from mixed marriage, to be sure, have not been felt to date, for most mixed marriages result neither in conversion to Judaism nor conversion to Christianity. However, the real impact of mixed marriage will be felt in future generations. Less than a quarter of the children of mixed marriages today are reared exclusively as Jews, raising the prospect of serious erosion from the community in the next generation. Advocates of outreach to mixed marrieds hope to break those trends. Whether they will succeed is doubtful, at best, given that Jews and Judaism comprise a tiny fraction of the dominant American society and culture. Yet even if outreach proves moderately

Reprinted from the *Jewish Week of New York,* December 15, 1999.

successful, the prospect of continued mixed marriage threatens to erode Jewish cultural distinctiveness, creating a most fluid boundary between Jew and Gentile in which mixed marriage becomes normative and marriage within the faith the exception. By this analysis, optimism regarding the Jewish future appears at best foolish and naive.

Yet the American Jewish story is by no means limited to a narrative of erosion. While assimilation has increased, Jews have greater opportunities for intensive Jewish education and study than at probably any time in Jewish history. The day school movement has grown exponentially—to the point that 40 percent of Jewish pupils receiving any form of Jewish education are doing so in the Jewishly intensive environment of the day school.

On college campuses, hardly a university of note exists that does not have an impressive array of Jewish studies courses and faculty. Jewish women are advocating greater involvement in Jewish religious life, confronting rabbinic authority with the challenge of responding to those who want increased access to Jewish heritage rather than diminished involvement. New and dynamic Hillel programs have enhanced the opportunities for creative and vital Jewish campus life. The success of leadership education programs, e.g., the high-level initiatives of Judaic study sponsored by the Wexner Heritage Foundation, promises not only to create more Jewishly knowledgeable Jewish leaders but also to stimulate greater demand for intensive and high quality Jewish education.

Much has been written of "returnees to Judaism" within Orthodoxy, but within each of the religious movements and within synagogues across the country, one can identify Jews who are far more Jewishly engaged than their parents or grandparents. The Manhattan phenomenon of Congregation B'nai Jeshurun attracting over 2,000 worshipers on a Friday night, although particularly eye-catching, signals a trend of non-Orthodox religious involvement that is occurring as well in many other communities within Conservative and Reform synagogues. These forms of Jewish renewal tell a story of American Jewry unleashing some of the most creative energies within the Jewish experience—Jews determined to mold a positive Jewish experience rather than disappear.

What, then, does one make of the dual narrative? What does it portend for the Jewish future?

One crossroad already passed appears to be the eclipse of traditional models of ethnicity. Anti-Semitism, defense of Israel, and the rescue and relief of beleaguered Jews formed the collective agenda of the Jewish people in the latter half of the twentieth century. Although none of these causes has been eclipsed entirely, all appear an inadequate base on which to construct future Jewish life. If anything, the very success of the Jewish community in marginalizing anti-Semitism, safeguarding the American-Israel relationship, and rescuing Soviet Jewry has made traditional slogans sound outmoded for the Jewish community of the twenty-first century.

Similarly, the very success story of American Jewry, making America receptive and hospitable to Jews, raises the specter of greater assimilation. Indeed, it is difficult to posit the continued danger of anti-Semitism when the Jew has become a desirable in-law.

One implication for the future, then, lies in a change of language from a vocabulary of Jewish fears to one of Jewish hopes and aspirations. Jewish leaders will be challenged to make a compelling case for leading a Jewish life privately and commitment to the Jewish people publicly. To be sure, it remains questionable whether a language of religious renewal will provide the necessary passion and stimulus to preserve the collective base of Jewish communal life. Already, critics have pointed to excessive individualism within the current quest for spirituality among those who define religious renewal in personal and existential terms rather than as obligations to Jewish people.

Similarly, the danger of greater divergence between American and Israeli Jews looms powerfully as American Jews increasingly define their identity in personal forms, while for Israelis the collectivity of peoplehood forms the primary base of Jewish cohesion. The challenge for twenty-first-century Jewish leadership lies in maintaining and enhancing both imperatives for Jewish living—personal fulfillment and collective commitment. Commitment to peoplehood and intensive Jewish education must enhance one another to preserve the Jewish enterprise. Conversely, one pillar of Jewish identity absent the other is likely to lead to continued erosion, for Jewish civilization comprises both religion and peoplehood.

Lastly, and perhaps most important, as efforts to enhance Jewishness intensify, they are likely to increase rather than reduce tensions within the Jewish people. The "Who is a Jew" controversy ought by no means be trivialized as the political issue of who is a rabbi. Rather it signals the very real and existential issue of how we define membership in the Jewish people and the cultural issue of how we define the Jewishness of our communal ambiance. Historically, the ability to marry other Jews has always signaled the unity of the Jewish people. Put another way, the idea that all Jews stood together at Sinai, even if we experience or remember it in diverse forms, formed the basis of commonality of peoplehood. Given the patrilineal descent decision and the absence of consensus concerning conversion to Judaism, the capacity of Jews to marry one another has been lessened and the argument that we all stood together at Sinai sharply undermined.

Even more divisive are the cultural issues of how Jewish do we wish to be. Some argue for greater inclusivity—create a Jewish environment in which all may feel at home. Others desire a more intensively Jewish atmosphere. Both goals are desirable but are often in conflict with one another. Should Jewish institutions conduct business on Shabbat or Jewish holidays? Should synagogues extend membership and honors to non-Jews? In the coming decades virtually every Jewish institution will be challenged on how it defines its Jewish ambience and how Jewish it wishes to be. The final results remain unpredictable, except to say that the tensions over these issues are certain to divide institutions, leaving different groups angry and dissatisfied.

For these reasons, denominationalism is likely only to increase in importance in the coming years. To be sure, much switching among the religious movements occurs on individual levels, and the existence of plural religious movements provides diverse avenues of connecting to Jewish heritage. Moreover, the tension between the movements does signal vitality in that it creates passion and commitment among Jews on these very issues of the meaning of Jewish identity. Nevertheless, the prospect of continued denominational struggle does threaten Jewish unity and may suggest that the process of enhancing our lives Jewishly may prove painful on personal, familial, and institutional levels. Policy disputes over outreach to mixed marrieds already are harbingers of future painful divisions within the community.

The new millennium, in short, poses both dangers and opportunities for American Jews. Gone is the conviction prevalent when I was growing up in the 1950s that being a Jew was a matter of nostalgia for a bygone past. American Jewry today is convinced that it does have a future—the question is what kind of future Jewish community will we, in fact, create.

JEWISH FAMILY POLICY

Since 1980 the American Jewish Committee has housed the William Petschek National Jewish Family Center. I have been privileged to serve as its director since 1987. The Family Center was created to sponsor research and gather information about the Jewish family, articulate the salience of Jewish family values, and advocate communal policies to strengthen Jewish family life.

Family issues serve as an excellent laboratory for testing the manifold relationships of Jewish tradition and modern culture. At times, Jewish tradition can serve as a powerful tool to cement family ties. At other times, Jewish teachings concerning family conflict with otherwise attractive American norms. This section explores the relevance of Jewish teachings to family life today and recommends particular strategies for communal policymakers to consider.

Divorce, Jewish Style

Jewish divorce rates clearly are rising. Los Angeles has more than doubled its Jewish divorce rate in the past 20 years. More particularly, divorce generally has been rising among the younger Jews. As this generation ages, its overall divorce rate may approximate the general American pattern.

Finally, divorce is closely related to Jewish involvement. Among affiliated Jewish couples, the chances of divorce are about one in eight. Among the unaffiliated, however, the chances of divorce rise to one in three. Reform Jews divorce more frequently than do Conservative and Orthodox Jews.

Intermarriage is correlated with higher divorce as is higher education and young marriages. In this last respect, Orthodox Jews are indeed an exception, for Orthodox Jews marry at relatively young ages but experience very low rates of divorce.

Although divorce may be a necessary solution to a hopeless irretrievable marriage, it brings with it its own set of difficulties. One issue stems from the complexity—many would say inadequacy—of Jewish religious law, which requires the divorcing male to issue a religious bill of divorce, or *"get."* In the absence of the *get,* divorced women are prohibited from remarrying and the children of such a marriage suffer under the onus of *"mamzerut"* or bastard children prohibited from marrying other Jews. Complications arise when couples divorce who did not know about the *get* and its implications and, less frequently, when the husband refuses to issue the *get* or uses it as a weapon to secure a more favorable settlement.

More familiar are the psychological consequences of divorce. Children especially have been taken "out of the nest," often caught between two parents, and not wishing to alienate either. For children,

Reprinted from the *Washington Jewish Week*, February 1, 1990.

divorce symbolizes the break up of the stability of the home and may cause further difficulties in school and at play where they experience the continued stigmas society generally attaches to divorce.

Perhaps less well known are the economic consequences of divorce. For men, the rise in standard of living in the year following the divorce may be as high as 42 percent. For women, in contrast, particularly those with children, the downturn in economic living standards may be as high as 73 percent. This has given rise to what many have termed the "feminization of poverty"—custodial mothers in divorce situations. Although custodial fathering may become increasingly popular in the future, it remains exceptional—"Kramer vs. Kramer" to the contrary.

Finally, the Jewish community must consider the consequences of divorce for communal continuity and viability. Contrary to current wisdom, divorced families do not drop out of the Jewish community. Rather, they may find that communal programming is targeted to married couples with children, leaving divorced families to participate as if they were a conventional family. Others feel the cost of participation in Jewish communal activities is too burdensome for the single-parent home. Still others require specific services—full-time day care, for example—and turn elsewhere if the Jewish community does not meet those needs.

In the face of these challenges, the Jewish community has both a moral imperative to reach out to the single-parent home and to maximize the opportunities divorce offers for enhancing Jewish identity and communal affiliation. First, clear and accurate information concerning the *get* and its implications must be given to all divorcing couples. Couples who reject the *get* for its sexist bias are free to make their own decisions, but they should do so only knowing the consequences for subsequent remarriages and offspring.

Similarly, Jewish legal authorities must be empowered to resolve the plight of the woman whose husband refuses to grant her a *get*.

Finally, special sensitivity is needed for celebration of Jewish life-cycle events, such as the bar or bat mitzvah. Synagogue-based mediation could reconcile these and other religious issues from the perspective of the children's welfare and best interests—criteria both parents should affirm regardless of their personal differences.

Yet communal obligations transcend ascertaining that Jewish religion not become a weapon in a divorce situation. The community has an opportunity to provide an anchor of enduring values in turbulent times through links to one's past and heritage. For children of divorce, Jewish communal programming constitutes a powerful message of continuity with the past and hopes for one's future. Successful models of outreach exist within each of the religious movements in which particular synagogues have created a sense of community and special care for single-parent homes, including surrogate grandparenting and Big Brother and Sister programs. Contact with Jewish day-care programs, a virtual necessity for single parents, can intensify the Jewish identity of the home. Special family experiences—a parent and child camp, for example—may empower single parents to strengthen their family lives through introduction of Jewish culture and rituals.

Finally, the Jewish community must address the economic barriers to single-parent families' participation in Jewish communal institutions. Those single-parent homes that can afford to pay the full cost of Jewish education, synagogue affiliation, camping, etc., constitute the exceptions rather than the norm among such Jewish families. Simply saying scholarships are available for the needy will not suffice, for many will not know to ask whether assistance is possible. Others will be inhibited from requesting special financial consideration. Rather what is needed is a general communal policy of special economic consideration for the single-parent home.

In short, there can be no minimizing the reality of divorce and its consequences. However, the Jewish community can serve as a resource to divorced families for services parents need and more importantly, for values that provide comfort, nurturing, and a sense of continuity with the past and faith in the future. Such outreach to the single-parent home will not only enable families to cope with marital break-up, it will also create a stronger and more vital Jewish community.

Strengthening the Two-Parent Home

Is the Jewish family today in decline? Do rising numbers of singles, intermarrieds, childless couples and divorcees posit the eclipse of the traditional Jewish values of marriage and parenting?

As American society loudly proclaims the disappearance of the "Ozzie and Harriet" family of the 1950s is the same true for Jewish families?

Consider the following:

Over 95 percent of American Jews marry by age 40. Most expect to have two children—small families, to be sure, and perhaps insufficient for population stability.

Once children reach school age, the likelihood is great that the family will join a synagogue or participate in Jewish communal events.

In terms of employment patterns, no single model of the Jewish family predominates. Jewish women with children under school age are more likely to stay home. Those with school-age children are more likely to return to work.

Part-time employment has been popular as an appropriate balance between family and career concerns, although part-time employment opportunities often are difficult to locate and provide minimal compensation and career benefits.

All this underscores the enduring value of the family for American Jews and its continuing vitality as our single greatest source of sustenance and self-esteem. The family, as one sociologist puts it, is "here to stay." The widely-heralded "alternatives to the family" of the 1960s and 1970s have never successfully taken root precisely because they lack the commitment that is central to successful families.

Jews in particular perceive the family as the best framework for the nurturance of adults, the socialization of children, and the transmittal of Jewish identity from generation to generation. Although no single model of the Jewish family predominates, most Jews continue to aspire to the traditional norms, marriage and parenting.

Reprinted from the *Washington Jewish Week,* February 8, 1990.

Even the much-maligned "Ozzie and Harriet" framework probably accurately describes the majority of Jewish families with pre-school children.

For that matter, the "Ozzie and Harriet" model is alive and well among American families generally. Half of American women with children under school age do stay at home. Of those who do work, the differences between full-time and part-time employment must be drawn carefully.

How then do we strengthen today's Jewish families? One issue clearly relates to balancing work and family responsibilities. Employers need to recognize that employees have family responsibilities and that one is not deficient if one takes those family responsibilities seriously. The workplace, in short, must be made "family-friendly."

What would such a "family-friendly" workplace be like? It would assist workers in securing quality childcare, provide parental leave for parents of newborn infants, and offer flexible work hours through flextime, job-sharing and part-time employment.

Some of these developments are already taking place in the corporate sector. As employers examine the demographic projections of the 1990s, in which quality employees will be at a premium, they're seeking to create an environment that will attract and retain employees who wish to be responsible parents and workers.

The Jewish community has an opportunity to be pacesetting in this regard. As primary employers within the Jewish community, Jewish organizations should reevaluate their personal policies by the criteria of enabling employees to balance work and family responsibilities.

Through the opportunities Jewish organizations provide in terms of childcare, parental leave, and part-time employment, the Jewish community can signal the value it places upon preserving Jewish family life.

Yes, instrumentalities such as daycare and flex-time may assist only those already committed to preserving families. Overriding these instrumentalities are the values that people actually place on their family lives.

In this sense, to strengthen today's families, we require a program of cultural education to combat the ethos of unbridled individualism and the culture of narcissism that inhibit the commitment and sacrifice so crucial to successful marriages and family.

Methods must be developed to help couples grow together and accommodate one another, and thereby lessen divorce incidence. Divorce ought not be viewed as an alternative to marriage but rather as a course of last resort, after all efforts to save the marriage have failed.

Divorce needs to be destigmatized. Often it is a personal tragedy, but a necessary solution to an irreparable marriage.

Programs are needed to train young people in the art of healthy marital communication and family relationships. Premarital counseling, family life programs, and high school and college courses on the family provide excellent opportunities to sensitize the individual to the heavy demands of marriage, to the need for mutual respect and accommodation, and for the commitment to one another and to the relationship that is so necessary for successful marriages.

Moreover, we need to change the image of marriage conveyed in the popular culture and media. In 1983, an American Jewish Committee report on situation comedies on prime-time television pointed to the underlying problem of portraying all marital difficulties as solvable within 22 minutes or less of program time.

We require programing that portrays realistic role models and that suggests that conflicts may be resolved only if the family members are committed to working together to iron out difficulties.

More consultations with media personnel are necessary to encourage development of realistic portraits of marriage and broader dissemination of successful role models for contemporary families.

Private and public sector alike ought to consider developing programs to strengthen marriage by inculcating greater training for marriage and promoting realistic expectations of what marriage entails.

Author Francine Klagsbrun, in her recent book, *Married People,* urges a bias in favor of marriage. If we consider marriage and family as desirable ends in themselves and as vital to the health of society generally, that bias should be strongly encouraged.

Family policy support therefore makes sense only within the context of a broader program of cultural education.

A particular model may be drawn from the experience of the Orthodox Jewish community. Orthodox families generally have three or more children, invest heavily in quality Jewish education, and maintain very low rates of divorce.

These facts should not be attributed to religious prohibitions against birth control and divorce, which are either minimal or non-existent in traditional Judaism. Rather, Orthodox successes testify to the close interrelationship between family and community.

Strong families build strong Jewish communities. Conversely, vital Jewish communities create a public climate conducive to healthy family life.

For example, the rituals of Judaism tend to be family-oriented, and ties to Jewish tradition therefore cement ties between family members. The most vivid illustration is that of the Shabbat dinner—a moment set aside for quality family conversation removed from the day-to-day struggles of the world around us.

Traditional Jewish families who celebrate Jewish holidays and life cycle events together and with their communities are expressing the particular relationship within Judaism between strong families and strong communities.

They are expressing how the public sector—i.e., the Jewish community—can strengthen the private sphere of family life through a combination of both public norms valued by the community and policy and program initiatives that help parents to be parents.

Young Jewish couples today often lack the knowledge and the resources to harness Jewish tradition so as to enrich their family lives. The policy challenge to the community, therefore, becomes one of empowering Jewish parents to introduce Jewish components within their homes.

Finding Common Ground in the Family Policy Debate

For more than a decade now, liberals and conservatives have been angrily shouting the word "family" at one another. Yet so far, this debate has generated more heat than light, more politics than policies, more slogans than solutions.

Consider the current paralysis. Liberals emphasize government-sponsored day care, mandated parental leave and other flexible workplace policies such as job-sharing, flex-time and part-time employment opportunities. Conservatives, on the other hand, emphasize family values—the need to enshrine the value of family in American society and to transmit the importance of family to the next generation.

Liberals dismiss conservative advocates as nostalgic for a mythical family of the 1950s and, more threateningly, as moral absolutists in mandating a particular form of family for all Americans. Conversely, conservatives dismiss liberals as socially permissive and cultural relative in celebrating all lifestyles as morally equivalent, irrespective of family structure and content.

These divisions have led to policy quicksand. President Bush vetoes the Family and Medical Leave Act, which would guarantee unpaid parental leaves, thus confirming the worst fears of liberals. Liberals frequently seem more intent on redefining the family than on strengthening it, thus confirming the worst fears of conservatives. If we want to make genuine progress on family policy in the 1990s, we must discard this tired contest of liberal vs. conservative and replace it with a new public philosophy on how to help the American family. My own recent experience—editing a book on family issues that brought together authors from across the political spectrum—suggests that the time is right for this new intellectual synthesis.

Despite the apparent irreconcilability of the two traditional positions, in truth they share considerable common ground—recognition of societal responsibility to strengthen families, an urgency that measures

Reprinted from the *Chicago Tribune,* March 4, 1991.

be taken immediately because of the deterioration of current family conditions, and the recognition that American society, the wealthiest and most powerful nation in the world, lags behind other democracies in terms of the social supports given to families to enable them to fulfill their functions. Indeed, the very existence of this common ground raised the hopes of pro-family advocates during the 1988 elections.

Therefore, what is needed is a new coalition of ideas—one that will build upon this consensus, absorb the best thinking on family policy from both left and right, and create a bi-partisan family agenda for the 1990s.

What would this new approach look like? First, it would reject equally both cultural relativism and moral absolutism. It would state unequivocally that not all forms of family living are equally desirable. What is permitted need not be what is encouraged. Rather, such a coalition should assert societal preference for the two-parent home even while reaching out to, protecting and lending assistance to those who, for whatever reasons, do not fit that model.

Second, such a coalition would support initiatives to enable parents to balance work and family responsibilities. The time is long past due to make the workplace more family-friendly. Measures such as government-subsidized child care, mandatory parental leave and broader availability of flexible employment options, including part-time opportunities, would empower parents to improve the balance between public and private needs and between their responsibilities as parents and as employees.

Finally, such a coalition would recognize that these policy instrumentalities favored by liberals—day care, parental leave, flex-time—will be effective only if enacted within a broader cultural climate supportive of family. To do that will require a broad program of cultural education celebrating the ideal of the family and communicating realistic role models of family life through the schools and media. Successful families who express the commitment to family relations so necessary for families to function must be showcased. Such a program of cultural education should be careful to portray marriage realistically—both as the preferred family form for most Americans and as the one that requires the most personal sacrifice and commitment in order to succeed. Divorce should not be stigmatized as evil but rather should be represented as the understandable yet tragic final recourse in dissolving an irretrievable marriage. Recognition of the reality of divorce and seeking to accommodate the realities of the single-parent home through policy initiatives to assist those families must not be confused with advocacy of preferred family forms.

To be sure, such a coalition will anger some on both sides of the family policy debate. Conservatives may shudder at the specter of increased governmental activism. Liberals may find discussion of family values and a program of cultural education to be sanctimonious and self-righteous. Feminists may feel that the goals of the women's movement may be undermined by broader employment choices for parents.

Yet while a new synthesis on family issues may ruffle some ideological feathers and dismay some special interests, such an approach is quite consistent with the beliefs of the majority of Americans who do not support either extreme of the current family debate but who do support steps to strengthen the family as a social institution. Accordingly, the time is long past due for breaking out of traditional polarities regarding family and building a new program in which both sides can truly learn from—rather than simply reject—one another's positions.

Conservatives have no monopoly on advocacy of the two-parent home. Nor are liberals alone in seeking support for single mothers. Rather, our problem to date has been our inability to abandon traditional stereotypes associating "family values" with conservatives and "family diversity" with liberals. Taking action to strengthen families as the cornerstone of our future society requires breaking these stereotypes and building a new pro-family coalition.

Promoting the Jewish Family in the Diaspora

Four major currents affect the Jewish family in the United States: delayed marriage, or the "singles phenomenon;" the rising divorce rate, creating a large number of single-parent families; and the massive entry of Jewish women into the workforce, leading to dual-career couples and the effects this entails for the family; and the rise in intermarriage and the challenges it poses for Jewish continuity.

The net effect of these changes raises particular problems for the Jewish community. Jewish affiliation historically has been highest among married couples with children of school age. As people remain single for longer periods, intermarry, choose to be come single parents, or alter their schedules for work and family life, the implications for continuing Jewish affiliation become serious. The policy challenge in this area is to create Jewish communal institutions to meet the needs and interests of these new Jewish sub-groups.

Analyses of the attitudes of Jewish singles point to their desire for marriage, and show that singles have positive feelings about their Jewishness. However, they are alienated from Jewish life because they find that Jewish institutions cater mainly to couples. Some who do not wish to be stigmatized as single avoid special programs for singles. Nevertheless, certain Jewish communities report success with such programs, which range from special synagogue events, to computer dating and old-fashioned matchmaking. The gamut of programs thus seems to attract different types of individuals to different activities. In truth, we know very little about this growing population group of individuals who defer marriage. It is certain that there is a large Jewish population that is alienated from organized Jewish life and may never rejoin the community, even after marriage.

A difficult challenge exists in America: that of intermarried Jews who insist on remaining part of the Jewish community and are proud of being Jews. Even when there is no conversion of the spouse, many of

Reprinted from the Jewish Population Studies series of the Harman Institute for Contemporary Jewry, Hebrew University, Jerusalem, 1992.

the children are raised at least as partial Jews. Many of the intermarried individuals are active in the Jewish community. This is a complicated situation, and a unique challenge for the Jewish community.

Divorce, similarly, poses serious policy challenges. If Jews value marriage as the ideal setting for family life, the institution of marriage must be strengthened. Ways must be found to help couples grow together and accommodate to each other, and divorce should be seen as an action of last resort. While divorce may be a necessary solution to an unhappy marriage that shows no signs of improving, steps should be taken to improve the cultural climate surrounding marriage.

First, we need programs to train young people for marriage and to nurture realistic expectations of what makes marriage work. High school courses on the family, family life programs, and free marital counseling provide opportunities to sensitize the individual to the demands of marriage, the need for mutual respect, accommodation, and commitment to the relationship. Within the Jewish community, steps can be taken in this area through clergy counseling prior to marriage, Jewish school curricula, and informal education. Consultations with media personnel are necessary to encourage the development of more realistic portraits of marriage in the popular media, and dissemination of successful role models for contemporary families.

The Jewish tradition itself can be used as a vehicle for cementing marital ties. The policy question for the Jewish community, and the challenge, is how to find ways of transmitting the Jewish heritage to young couples so as to enable them to strengthen their family lives by drawing on Jewish tradition. Daycare and after-school programs under Jewish auspices can also enhance Jewish identity within the family. Senior citizens might be trained as babysitters and surrogate grandparents, thereby helping to bring single parents and dual-career couples into the organized Jewish community.

Last but not least, the Jewish community must address the vexing question of how the size of the Jewish population can be increased. Within the community, norms and climates of opinion are important regarding children. The Modern Orthodox community, for example, has inculcated a norm of more than two children per family. The issue of increasing family size must involve women, because if it is seen only as something encouraged by Jewish men, it will rightly arouse the hostility of feminists. Discussions of population growth must be coupled with measures to enable parents to balance work and family.

Most difficult is the question of choices concerning abortion. While the Jewish community as a whole favors a pro-choice position on abortion, little thought has been devoted to the question of encouraging adoption rather than counseling abortion. One choice for a woman pregnant with a child she does not want should be access to adoption. Such a pro-adoption policy would be more consonant with Jewish tradition than a policy which encourages abortion without qualification.

A recent study indicated that rather than planning a family of a certain size, couples take decisions about how many children to have one at a time, on the basis of their experience with the previous child. The incentives to childbearing are economic considerations and career development costs. Conversely, couples reported a sense of joy and of self-fulfillment and the importance of Jewish values as primary considerations in deciding to have children.

For the Jewish community, the policy implications are clear: a need to strengthen the positive inducements for having children by widespread education affecting the cultural climate, and by adopting measures to reduce the career costs of having children for professional couples. At the very least, it is the responsibility of a community of scholars to communicate accurate information about the current and future size of the Jewish community, so that individuals may determine their personal choices in full knowledge of Jewish demographic realities.

Changing Perceptions of Divorce

Recently, I chanced upon a colleague and inquired how a mutual acquaintance of ours had been faring in the aftermath of his divorce. "Not too well," replied my colleague. "He really has old-fashioned ideas about divorce." Sometime later another colleague announced to her co-workers that she had just filed for divorce. The dominant response—"Congratulations! It's about time."

These two encounters reflect changing American attitudes toward divorce. Without question, the incidence of divorce has risen greatly over the past generation. Between 1960 and 1982, the number of divorces per 1,000 people increased from 2.2 to 5.0. In absolute terms, the annual number of divorces tripled during those years, rising from 400,000 in 1960 to 1.2 million in 1982. In contrast to earlier social norms that assumed marital success and regarded divorce as exceptional, couples marrying today confront the prospect of putative marital failure. The negative expectations regarding marriage and the sheer numerical incidence of divorce help nurture a cultural climate in which marriage as an institution seems increasingly under attack, its survival in doubt.

Yet, Americans continue to marry and value family life. Virtually 95% of Americans marry at some stage during their lives. Perhaps more tellingly some 80% of divorced men and 70% of divorced women remarry within five years of their divorce, indicating that even those who have known the trauma of marital breakup aspire to rebuild their marriages and family lives.

These twin currents—the increase in divorce incidence and the continuing stability of marital norms—require reasoned policy deliberation and debate. Some argue that public policy can do little to strengthen marriage or alleviate the psychological trauma of divorce. In this view, perhaps best articulated by Lenore Weitzman (1985), public policy should seek to address the negative economic consequences of

Reprinted with permission from the *Journal of Jewish Communal Service* (Kendall Park, NJ, Winter/Spring 1994.)

divorce, thereby enabling custodial parents and children to regain a viable economic footing. Others, particularly Sylvia Hewlett (1991) argue that redressing the economic consequences of divorce is insufficient. Rather, society must attempt to reduce divorce rates and, after divorce has occurred, enhance ties between noncustodial parents and children.

Unquestionably the economic consequences of divorce are severe, particularly for women who have been dependent on their husbands' earning power and find themselves in single-parent households. No-fault divorce, which has eliminated much of the acrimony and hypocrisy surrounding the divorce proceedings by removing the necessity to establish the "sin" of the offending party, has also led to the reduction or elimination of alimony payments as there is no longer a spouse "at fault" who is required to make fiscal amends. Consequently, women generally experience a pronounced decline in living standards within a year of divorce. Male counterparts, in contrast, may find divorce to be economically uplifting.

Policy initiatives can help redress this imbalance, most particularly for children of divorce living in poverty. For example, divorce settlements generally result in a distribution of assets. Assets acquired during marriage (e.g., property, capital, etc.) can be distributed equitably. However, these represent only tangible assets. Often, a spouse acquires career assets such as professional training and education during a marriage, while the other spouse has been supporting the family economically. Consideration of such intangible assets as part of the divorce settlement would both reflect the reality of assets accrued during the marriage and increase the capital available to spouses who lack job training and skills.

Other policy options focus on child support awards, particularly the vigorous enforcement of payments through wage withholding and basing the size of awards upon sharing of incomes, rather than determining a minimal living standard for the custodial spouse. To be sure, these programs presuppose an earned income for noncustodial spouses. Equally significant are transitional measures to enable custodial parents to join or rejoin the work force through continuing education and job training programs. Similarly, health benefits often lapse immediately after the divorce, as a working but noncustodial parent need maintain only personal health benefits, rather than family provisions. Permitting custodial parents the option to continue paying for coverage under the former spouse's health plan would provide transitional insurance pending reentry into the work force.

These measures merit further policy consideration. The trauma of divorce is real, and the victims are often the defenseless. Yet, proponents of these measures err if they maintain that nothing can be done about divorce except helping manage its economic consequences. If Americans continue to value marriage as the ideal setting of family life, and evidence indicates that they do, further strengthening of the marital institution is necessary. Ways must be found to help couples grow together and accommodate to one another, thereby lessening the incidence of divorce. Divorce ought not be understood as one alternative to marriage but rather as a court of last resort after efforts to save the marriage truly have failed. To be sure, divorce itself ought not to be stigmatized. Often, it is a personally tragic but a necessary solution to an unhappy marriage that shows no sign of improving. Yet, society generally should take steps to improve the cultural climate surrounding marriage and to cement marital ties.

First, we require programs that train young people for marriage and that nurture realistic expectations of what makes marriages work. Romantic love and sexual attraction alone may not suffice to sustain a marriage through the inevitable highs and lows most couples experience. Premarital counseling, family life programs, and high school and college courses on the family all provide excellent opportunities to sensitize individuals to the heavy demands of marriage, to the need for mutual respect and accommodation, and for the commitment to one another and to the relationship that is so necessary for successful marriages.

Moreover, we require greater discussion concerning the image of marriage conveyed in the popular culture and media. A 1983 American Jewish Committee report on situation comedies on prime-time television pointed to the underlying problem of portraying all marital difficulties as solvable within 22 minutes or less of program time (Kovsky, 1983). Real conflicts over extended time can be resolved only if the respective family members are committed to one another and are willing to work together to iron out difficulties. Consultations with media personnel are necessary to encourage development of realistic portraits of marriages and broader dissemination of successful role models for contemporary families.

Clearly most marriages do run the risk of divorce. Virtually mythical are the "happy marriages" that can never fall apart. Policy measures, however, ought not to be limited to coping with divorce. The private and public sector alike ought to consider development of programs to strengthen marriage by inculcating greater training for marriage and promoting realistic expectations of what marriages entail. Francine Klagsbrun (1985), in her book *Married People,* urges a bias in favor of marriage, rather than stigmatizing divorce. If we consider marriage and family as desirable ends in themselves and as vital to the health of society generally, that bias should be strongly encouraged.

The Jewish Community

Within the Jewish community patterns of marriage, divorce, and re-marriage are also undergoing significant change. Jews continue to marry at overwhelming rates—90% of American Jews marry at some point in their lives. Marital norms continue to prevail, for most Jews identify marriage as a core component of their aspirations for self and personal fulfillment. This is perhaps best expressed in the phenomenon of remarriage. Despite the experience of marital discord and breakup, approximately three-quarters of Jewish men and women do remarry within five years of the divorce—signaling both the desire to be married and the recognition that the two-parent home remains the most effective context for the raising of children (Friedman, 1993; Heilman, 1984).

Another recent demographic change in the Jewish community has been a delay in the age of marriage. In 1960, approximately 45% of adult Jews had married by age 25. That percentage dropped to 25% in 1970 and according to the 1990 National Jewish Population Survey (NJPS), less than 3% by 1990 (Fishman, 1993; Goldstein, 1992).

Some have argued that delayed marriage in turn leads to greater marital stability and lower divorce rates. Others see the potential danger of delayed fertility and therefore of decreased fertility.

Another impact stems from the relationship between later marriages and communal affiliation. People often defer joining Jewish communal institutions until there are children in the home. Prolonged periods of singlehood and childlessness may create patterns of nonaffiliation that can become much harder to break the greater the number of years that pass by.

As for divorce itself, clearly Jewish divorce rates have been rising. Historically, American Jews enjoyed a Jewish divorce deficit relative to the general population. Steven M. Cohen in 1982 reported that Jews divorced only half as frequently as do Protestants and were "somewhat below" Catholics, despite the proscriptions against divorce that exist in Catholicism and that are nonexistent in Judaism. To be sure, Cohen (1982) noted that the gap in divorce frequency between Jew and Gentile was much smaller in terms of younger couples, indicating that Jewish divorce rates were beginning to approximate overall patterns of American society generally.

By the 1990s that prediction seems to be on the verge of becoming a reality. According to the NJPS, approximately 18% to 19% of adult American Jews previously married have experienced at least one divorce (Goldstein, 1992). The percentage for Americans generally ranges from 15% to 20%, despite the widely publicized and generally misunderstood statistic of a 50% divorce rate for all Americans. The "divorce revolution" may not have permeated the entire Jewish community, but clearly more Jews than ever before are experiencing the reality of divorce, as is true of Americans generally.

Changing Perceptions of Divorce

Given the increase in divorce incidence, how is the phenomenon being viewed by the Jewish community? Jewish tradition itself both opposes divorce and accepts it as a reality at the same time. Thus, the prophet Malachi records that the very "altar weeps" at the dissolution of a marriage, suggesting that divorce is a profound personal tragedy to be avoided if at all possible through reconciliation of the couple involved. Yet, even if Jewish tradition envisions marriage as a universal norm, it recognizes that at times divorce is a necessary solution to a failed marriage. Thus, divorce is permitted on the grounds of a couple's incompatibility—to say nothing of "at fault" grounds for divorce, such as adultery or abuse (Biale, 1984, 1988; Gertel, 1983).

A particularly troublesome issue in Jewish tradition is related to the woman's lack of control of the divorce situation, in particular her inability to "send" a bill of divorce to her ex-spouse. This inability has resulted in personal tragedies, such as the *agunah,* a woman whose husband had disappeared or who was mentally incompetent to divorce his wife on his own. Certainly, the rabbis recognized the vulnerability of women under Jewish divorce law and tried to make provisions for greater protection of women's rights. To this day, however, the phenomenon of men exacting vengeance (or bribery) from ex-spouses by withholding the Jewish bill of divorce (a *get*) continues to occur, even if sporadically (Biale, 1984, 1992; Greenberg, 1981).

The problem of women's rights in divorce stems from limitations within Jewish law. Far more universal in its implications are the questions of Jewish social attitudes and perceptions of divorce as a cultural phenomenon. Higher expectations of marriage, declining commitments to "making it work," and the general social acceptability of divorce in the cultural climate have all increased the possibility of a divorce occurring.

First, we must address the often unrealistic expectations of marriages today. The wedding ceremony in many ways is a metaphor for couples' expectations of marriage—namely, that "it must be perfect." Observers rightly decry the heavy emphasis placed upon the wedding—at most one day in the course of a lifetime—when what really matters is the interior dynamics of married life over a prolonged period. Yet, the treatment of the wedding has become an expression for the treatment of marriage—that anything less than perfection is simply unacceptable.

The real message, of course, is that a marriage requires a lot of work. Both partners must be committed to preserving it—to work on difficulties until they are resolved, rather than surrendering in the face of complications. Realistic portraits of marriages as including shared commitments and shared struggles often fly in the face of a culture that emphasizes unbridled individualism and personal self-fulfillment above all other concerns. The Jewish message of family as teaching social responsibility through relations to other family members is precisely the appropriate image of family life. However, it is a difficult message to sustain in the contemporary culture of narcissism (Linzer, 1984).

Within that broader culture there are, in fact, very few factors that operate to strengthen marital stability, rather than encourage marital dissolution. The "50%" statistic itself encourages the expectation that marriages will fail. Very few understand what the statistic actually means and why it is so misleading. The 50% figure emanates from a 1981 report citing the number of divorces as equal to half the number of marriages for that year. In fact, since then the number of marriages has actually risen per year while the number of divorce has declined (Medved, 1992).

Aside from the fallacy of statistics, popular media portrayals of marriage advance unrealistic and negative perceptions of marriage as an institution. Such films as "War of the Roses" or "Thelma and Louise" signal that marriage is a trap from which to extricate oneself. Such television programs as "Married . . . with Children" mercilessly pillory the nuclear family. To be sure these are by no means the only portraits of family contained in popular culture. The recent film, "A Stranger Among Us," in fact suggests a portrait of Hasidic family life so attractive that a Gentile policewoman finds it compelling and wishes it were hers! The overall media message, however, is best epitomized by "L. A. Law"—the highly rated network series in which divorce is so pervasive among the characters that it appears as a natural aspect of the lifecycle that virtually all of us will experience at one time or another. "L. A. Law's" emphasis upon young upscale lawyers enjoying the good life underscores society's reverence for the pleasure principle and mutes the messages of personal sacrifice, delayed gratification, and mutual commitment that are so necessary to make marriages work. In contrast, the message of divorce seems to be to give individuals a chance to start over.

Finally, one cannot discuss divorce outside of the context of the feminist movement and its relationship to increased divorce incidence. On a pragmatic level, no-fault divorce, although generally progressive, has also made it far easier to initiate divorce proceedings. At bottom, however, the issues are more cultural than legal. Blu Greenberg (1981, pp. 12, 166) for example, in an otherwise powerful defense of Jewish feminism, concedes that feminism "has elements that are destructive from a Jewish perspective," particularly the attack upon the family and notes "that an exceedingly high proportion of women with feminist leanings have been or are now being divorced." Similarly, Sylvia Barack Fishman (1993, p. 32) agrees that "some contemporary divorces may indeed be linked to the greater ambition of women today." Both these authors are interested in strengthening marriage by proving the compatibility of feminism and family. Equal commitment by both partners to the marriage is the key to making marriage work. Significantly, their voices emanate from the world of Modern Orthodoxy in America, which, in some ways, has modeled images of successful families through shared Jewish experiences across generational lines. In effect, Judaism serves the Modern Orthodox well by providing a framework and structure that bind families together through common commitments, values, and memories shared around the "Jewish table." As a result, it is not surprising that Orthodox Jews have the lowest divorce rates (one-quarter the rate of unaffiliated Jews) and that when they do divorce, it is usually for the least negotiable of reasons, e.g., infidelity or abuse (Brodbar-Nemzer, 1984; Friedman, 1985).

In short, contemporary culture has removed the stigma from divorce. Generally speaking, that has been progressive. However, we ought to have replaced the divorce stigma with a cultural bias in favor of marriage. In turn, that would mean promoting realistic images of marriages, with all of their ups and downs. One should not view marriage as static, but rather as subject to change and development. A cultural bias in favor of marriage means emphasizing commitment to marriage as the key to long-term marital stability. And it means facing honestly and realistically the implications of divorce in terms of economic downturn, psychological impact, and lasting effects upon children. Seen in this light, marriage emerges as imperfect and vulnerable, but clearly preferable to all other family forms.

Finally, the implications of divorce upon children are quite serious and must be confronted candidly. Despite shifts of opinion with respect to divorce, research studies continue to demonstrate that two-parent homes are preferable from the vantage points of children's interest and welfare. Children growing up in single-parent homes are far more likely to experience social, behavioral, and educational problems at school and in their adult lives. These realities are painful to be sure, but they must be communicated openly, for they do underscore the continuing importance of the two-parent home and the marital norm (Whitehead, 1993; Wilson, 1993).

Communal Policy

What then ought the community do? Clearly, we cannot remain impervious to divorce. It is a human tragedy with profound consequences. Nor can we pretend that it is a private matter about which the community can do little, if anything. On the contrary, the implications of divorce are so considerable and the capacity of Jewish heritage and community sufficiently weighty that we ought to do whatever possible to strengthen marriage, protect victims of divorce from unnecessary hardship, and harness the resources of Jewish tradition and heritage to renew Jewish identity in married, divorced, and remarried homes.

This agenda means, first, Jewish participation in the broader cultural debate concerning marriage and family in America. The Jewish community ought to communicate its preference for the two-parent heterosexual family form. To be sure, we ought to reach out to and support those who, for whatever reason, do not fit that model. Yet, not all behavior that we protect is behavior that we prefer. Ways must be found to underscore Jewish family values even in the context of generally supporting nontraditional families.

In particular, the Jewish tradition of family is an especially meaningful message in this broader cultural climate. Judaism posits a triad of individual-family-community. The family serves to mediate between individual fulfillment and communal responsibility. It teaches social responsibility through relationships to others. Family, following the Book of Genesis, is the building block for society. Constructing family, in effect, is a prerequisite for the building of nationhood described in Exodus (Bayme, 1990; Steinmetz, 1991). The distinctive message of Judaism—the family as the antidote to unbridled individualism that teaches us to transcend personal gratification—connotes a powerful statement in current debates about the value of family in society generally.

Moreover, we should not underestimate the role that the community can play in strengthening marriage and thereby decreasing the chances of divorce. The first few years within a marriage are the most vulnerable years. Jewish tradition can enhance family ties by providing shared experiences and common bonds. Abraham Joshua Heschel correctly described the Shabbat as "sacred time," a 24-hour retreat from our mundane concerns and an opportunity to share ties with one another. Enabling young Jewish couples to enrich their family lives by injecting Jewish components would enhance simultaneously both family bonds and Jewish continuity.

Finally, after a divorce has occurred, Jewish tradition can still provide a sense of continuity and history, an anchor of stability in an otherwise turbulent world. Divorce, in fact, rather than closing the door to Jewish affiliation, often opens the way to renewed Jewish involvement (Cottle, 1981; Friedman, 1985; Goldman, 1991).

This is not surprising. It is often true that those who have known the trauma of family breakup are the most in need of the sense of community and tradition that Jewish institutions can provide. At a minimum, we should be especially sensitive to removing barriers to communal affiliation for single-parent homes, such as economic cost and cultural fears of divorce. Maximally, we should view tradition and community as resources that in fact will enrich the single-parent home.

This agenda, to be sure, is by no means modest. Family bridges the particularistic concerns Jews have for their own community with the universalist concerns regarding the place of family in American culture. It requires Jews to be active on a wide variety of fronts—cultural, religious, legislative, and communal. Yet here is precisely an opportunity to underscore distinctive Jewish messages that will enhance not only the lives of Jews and the Jewish community but will also strengthen society generally by balancing American values of individualism and individual opportunity with Judaic values of personal sacrifice, shared commitment, and delayed gratification. Few finer examples of the meaning of *tikkun olam* could be provided.

References

Biale, David. (1988). "Classical Teachings and Historic Experience." In *Spotlight in the Family: Public Policy and Private Responsibility.* New York: American Jewish Committee, pg. 28.

Biale, David. (1992). *Eros and the Jews.* New York: Basic Books.

Biale, Rachel. (1984). *Women and Jewish law.* New York: Schocken Books.

Brodbar-Nemzer, J. (1984, Winter). "Divorce and the Jewish Community: The Impact of Jewish Commitment." *Journal of Jewish Communal Service, 61*(2), 152–153.

Bayme, Steven. (1990). "The Jewish Family in American Culture." In David Blankenhorn, Steven Bayme, & Jean Bethke Elshtain (Eds.), *Rebuilding the Nest.* Milwaukee: Family Service of America, pp. 149–150.

Cohen, Steven M. (1982). "The American Jewish Family Today." In *American Jewish Yearbook.*

Cottle, Thomas. (1979). *Divorce and the Jewish Child.* New York: American Jewish Committee.

Fishman, Sylvia Barack. (1993). *A Breath of Life: Feminism in the American Jewish Community.* New York: Free Press.

Friedman, Nathalie. (1985). *The Divorced Parent and the Jewish Community.* New York: American Jewish Committee.

Friedman, Nathalie. (1993). *Remarriage and Stepparenting in the Jewish Community.* New York: American Jewish Committee.

Gertel, Elliot. (1983). *Jewish Views on Divorce.* New York: American Jewish Committee.

Goldman, Ari. (1991). *The Search for God at Harvard.* New York: Times Books.

Greenberg, Blu. (1981). *On Women and Judaism.* Philadelphia: Jewish Publication Society.

Goldstein, Sidney. (1992). "Profiles in American Jewry: Insights from the 1990 National Jewish Population Survey." In *American Jewish Yearbook.*

Heilman, Samuel. (1984). *The Jewish Family Today: An Overview.* New York: Memorial Foundation for Jewish Culture.

Hewlett, Sylvia Ann. (1991). *When the Bough Breaks.* New York: Basic Books.

Klagsbrun, Francine. (1985). *Married People: Staying Together in the Age of Divorce.* New York: Bantam Books.

Kovsky, Harry. (1983). *Family: The Missing Ingredient in TV Family Fare.* New York: American Jewish Committee.

Linzer, Norman. (1984). *The Jewish Family.* New York: Human Sciences Press.

Medved, Michael. (1992). *Hollywood vs. America.* New York: Harper Collins.

Steinmetz, Devorah. (1991). *From Father to Son: Kinship, Conflict, and Continuity in Genesis.* Louisville: Westminster/John Knox Press.

Weitzman, Lenore. (1985). *The Divorce Revolution.* New York: Free Press.

Whitehead, Barbara Dafoe. (1993, April). "Dan Quayle was Right." *Atlantic Monthly,* pp. 24–31.

The Changing Jewish Family in the 1990s: Implications for the Synagogue

It is my pleasure and privilege to share some thoughts with you on the changing Jewish family and the implications of those changes for synagogue programming and policy. Essentially, I pose to you three questions: In what ways is the Jewish family changing today? What is the place of the Jewish family within the culture of family life in America generally today? And finally, what are the implications of these changes for synagogue programming and policy?

The good news is that we know more about the Jewish family today than ever before. Twenty-five years ago Chancellor Louis Finkelstein, of blessed memory, criticized American Jewry for devoting more resources to the study of first-century Judaism in Palestine than to the study of contemporary Jewry in America. Today, it is perhaps a point of some irony, that while there is some doubt as to exactly what we do know about the first-century Judaism in Palestine, all would agree that we know far more than we ever have before about the condition of contemporary Jews in America. Great credit in this regard is due to the Council of Jewish Federations for sponsoring the 1990 National Jewish Population Study, the single most comprehensive and definitive survey of the internal condition of American Jewry. The study suggests a portrait of a Jewish population doing remarkably well by American standards. It is by internal Jewish standards—the question of Jewish identity—that the real weaknesses and challenges to the Jewish future come to the fore.

This duality of a population doing extremely well in America but doing poorly as Jews is best reflected in the data concerning the Jewish family. First, Jews continue to get married at overwhelming rates, albeit at later ages. In 1970 90% of Jewish women had been married by age 35. By 1990 only 50% of Jewish women had been married by age 35, although, to be sure, 89% were married by age 45. Clearly the de-

Reprinted from the *Journal of the North American Association of Synagogue Executives,* 1993.

sire for marriage is very strong as a norm among Jews, and Jews will continue to marry at rates exceeding 90%. The change relates to postponed marriage, in terms of age—a change with great implications for synagogue affiliation and programming.

The immediate implications are far reaching. Delayed marriage, of course, means postponed childbearing, and we have known for a long time that fertility delayed is fertility foregone. In terms of synagogue affiliation particularly, we have also known that membership in synagogues rises in direct proportion to the presence of children within the home. Prolonged patterns of non-affiliation due to late marriage and postponed childbearing may well be more difficult to break when marriage and childbearing actually do take place.

Secondly, Jews are enjoying a degree of marital stability relative to the population as a whole. Eighteen percent of American Jews have gone through a divorce. That amounts to a divorce deficit in terms of the general population, in which divorce is far more pervasive. More to the point, however, is that Jews enjoy a divorce deficit sharply correlated with religious behavior. Of Jews who identify as members of the Jewish faith, the divorce rate is 13.6%. In sharp contrast, however, for secular Jews—those completely removed from any form of religious identification—the divorce rate is 25%, close to the norm for white Americans. This point also has great implications for synagogue membership patterns and programming to which we will return subsequently.

Most of the media attention concerning the population survey has, naturally, focused upon the intermarriage rate of 52%. Some, to be sure, have challenged that figure. All agree, however, that the concern regarding intermarriage is justified in that the 50% figure does represent an all-time high.

Nevertheless, the data must be analyzed more carefully. The 52% figure includes many children of mixed-marrieds, who themselves have married out at a rate of over 90%—thereby inflating the overall intermarriage rate. Children of two Jewish parents, in contrast, continue to express a clear preference for marriage to fellow Jews. Moreover, among those affiliated with a synagogue, the intermarriage rate is significantly less than 50%—Conservative synagogues in Cleveland in

1986 reported that among affiliated members, 31% had known the intermarriage of at least one child. The point to be taken is not that intermarriage is inevitable. Rather, in certain sectors of the population the odds on it occurring are overwhelming. In other sectors of the population—particularly among two-Jewish-parent homes affiliated with a synagogue—the odds on an intermarriage occurring are considerable but are by no means overwhelming.

Similarly, much attention has been focused on children of mixed-marrieds—72% of whom are raised outside of the Jewish faith. So far all the evidence is that intermarriage by the third generation is a disaster in terms of Jewish identity. This has great implications both for the continued need of discouraging interfaith marriage and for targeted and qualified outreach to mixed-married homes. The important point to bear in mind here is not to oppose outreach. On the contrary, outreach is desirable for both human and demographic reasons. However, we must avoid falling into the trap—articulated by many in the community—that outreach forms our answer to the problem of intermarriage. Continued emphasis must be placed upon prevention of intermarriage, and when an intermarriage occurs, upon the need to encourage conversion of the non-Jewish spouse.

Similarly, the data concerning conversion are by no means encouraging. Conversion has declined to 7% of mixed-marriages contracted within the past five years. That means that we used to think that perhaps one in every three mixed-marriages would end up in a conversion to Judaism. However, as intermarriage has become so normative and acceptable in American society, the drive towards conversion has lessened so that mixed-marriages now are likely to result in a conversion to Judaism in only one of fourteen cases. To be sure, these are data from the last five years, meaning that the conversion rate may increase somewhat as these marriages mature and children are introduced into the home. Clearly, however, we are witnessing a sharp drop in the overall conversion rates. The patrilineal descent decision may, possibly, have contributed to this decrease by articulating to Jewish fathers that their wives need not convert to Judaism in order for their children to be considered Jews. This is a major issue within the Reform movement and one which I hope the liberal sectors in the community would consider most seriously.

Moreover, the data concerning converts themselves are complex. The good news is that 99% of the children of converts are raised as Jews. That means that conversion is our success story with respect to intermarriage and forms our primary ray of hope in terms of preserving Jewish identity when intermarriage occurs. Nevertheless, we do have some communal concerns. Fifty percent of the homes of converts to Judaism continue to have Christmas trees. More significantly, they express little identification with the peoplehood aspects of Jewish life—Israel, endangered Jewish communities, and the importance of marriage to other Jews. Important research has been done here in Chicago by Brenda Forster and Joseph Tobachnik, a work entitled *Jews by Choice: A Study of Converts to Reform and Conservative Judaism.* Forster and Tobachnik discovered that converts in the Chicago area would express no opposition to their own children marrying out. This raises the serious specter of one generation of converts in which the conversion has been so superficial as to fail to sustain the Jewishness in the next generation. This obviously has enormous implications for the need to introduce peoplehood concepts, the need to discourage interdating and interfaith marriages in conversionary homes, and the need to affect the process by which individuals choose to convert to Judaism.

The last change in the Jewish family relates to changing patterns of work and family. The common wisdom is that today's Jewish women are upwardly mobile professionals interested in advancing their careers. While there is some truth to that stereotype, the actual data are far more complex. Mothers of preschoolers are more likely to be stay-at-home mothers if they are Jewish. In contrast, Jewish mothers of school age children are more likely to be in the workforce. Moreover, contrary to the image of the high-powered Jewish professional, part-time employment is especially popular among Jewish women. In Rochester, for example, 25% of Jewish mothers with preschool age children were working full-time. Thirty-three percent, however, were working part-time—with the remainder being stay-at-home mothers.

It is also clear that Jewish parents value independence training for their young children. In Pittsburgh, for example, only 50% of Jewish women were in the workforce. However, 83% were sending their children to daycare or early childhood learning institutions. This creates an enormous challenge, to which we shall return, of harnessing this desire for "independence training" to enhance Jewish identity within the home.

Finally, we have a broader question of the status of the Jewish family in contemporary American culture. Jewish fathers are frequently depicted as workaholics and Jewish mothers as over-protective. The media and contemporary literature focus upon the costs of raising children rather than the joys and benefits. Finally, virtually all married couples involving Jews on television today are mixed-marrieds.

These cultural images by no means underscore the positive values of Jewish family life. We are creating a cultural stereotype in which little is valued of today's Jewish family. Within our Jewish institutions—in our publications, our programs, and in the cultural messages we send out—we ought to be depicting realistic images of a changing Jewish family—one in which the joys of leading a Jewish life are effectively communicated.

Let me be more specific concerning the implications of this to the synagogue. First, we ought to be willing to learn some of the positive lessons of contemporary Orthodox Judaism. Orthodox Jewish communities have effectively underscored the importance of communal norms—Blu Greenberg has written effectively on how the norm of three-children homes has penetrated the Orthodox community—in other words, peer pressure can often encourage larger families. Moreover, Orthodox communal structures have become extremely supportive of family life. The idea that there is a place in the Jewish community which encourages parents and children to participate together and which strengthens families by offering Jewish communal services is a powerful motif of today's Orthodox synagogue. One Orthodox rabbi commented recently that his synagogue of 350 families has become a synagogue of 350 volunteer family life coordinators.

On a philosophical level, we must face the challenges posed by these changes in family life and their implications for Jewish communal norms and values. This is a point of great relevance not only to the issue of mixed-marriage but to a host of changes within the Jewish family—changes related to single parenthood, abortion, adoption, and even gay and lesbian homes. While these are matters of great sensitivity, the need is great to find ways in which we can respect personal choices while upholding communal norms and preferred models. To be sure, there is a natural tension between a legitimate desire to reach out to individuals and an equally legitimate desire to maintain communal values. That is a challenge that we must face with respect to virtually all of these changing family constellations—to find ways in which Jewish values are clearly communicated with a recognition that individuals, for whatever reasons, will not necessarily fall into the models Jewish leaders advocate. By contrast, it would be a cardinal mistake to write people off; it would also be a cardinal mistake for Jewish leaders to abandon statements of what we believe in order not to alienate particular individuals.

Thirdly, we require realistic portraits of what makes families work. All too often, we have failed to underscore the struggle involved in marriage and parenting and the need to keep at that struggle in order to obtain marital success. The fact that we have removed the stigma attached to divorce is generally progressive. However, we should be replacing that with a bias towards marriage. Synagogue personnel, in particular, ought to be trained in pre-marital and marital counseling, and their efforts should be infused with a strong bias towards stabilizing the marriage, seeing divorce only as a course of last resort. This position has been most effectively argued recently by Francine Klagsbrun, in her important book *Married People*.

Finally, the data alluded to before regarding daycare and early learning centers essentially create new opportunities for enhancing Jewish life through "gateway institutions"—settings which Jews will use for a variety of reasons, and which will thereby come into contact with organized Jewish communal life. Divorced and single-parent homes here enjoy an unusual opportunity. Research conducted at the American Jewish Committee by Nathalie Friedman has demonstrated repeatedly that synagogues have enormous opportunities to provide stable settings in the aftermath of divorce—to send the message to children of divorce that the world that they know continues even in the aftermath of family breakup. Jewish tradition can serve as a very effective anchor and source of values for a home that has undergone such trauma. Again, Friedman underscores lessons to be absorbed from the Orthodox synagogues, where once the divorce has taken place, the tightly-knit community synagogue can effectively step in with meaningful religious experiences for families, communicating to children in particular that Jewish tradition has a great deal to say to them experientially in terms of stabilizing their lives.

In short, Judaism has historically posited a triad of individual-family-society. If we believe that strong individuals will build strong families and strong families will nurture strong communities, then it is the business of the community to be strengthening families. To be sure, this triad flies in the face of American individualism. American society in many ways is nurtured as an enlightenment society of individual opportunity. That value system has been marvelous in terms of enhancing Jewish opportunities in American society and is reflected in the degree of Jewish success in America. However, our message as Jews is that individualism alone is insufficient. We believe in the interconnectedness between individual rights and family responsibilities. The sociologist Peter Berger defined the Jewish synagogue as a mediating institution—a buffer bringing the individual into society yet serving as a small-scale, more personal institution enabling the individual to cope with the larger more impersonal universe. By the same token, Berger urged that family was similarly such a mediating institution, operating as a half-way house between the individual and the broader society. For Berger, family served to bring individuals out of their "rugged individualism," teaching them responsibilities to others and to the society at large.

This then is our opportunity. We ought to translate the synagogue into an institution that will work hand-in-hand with families, underscoring the values of leading a family life, and seeking out opportunities to enhance the Jewish components of our family lives. Thinking in terms of new ways of formulating synagogue policies and programs can, in the long run, provide us with new opportunities to enrich our communal institutions and thereby to build a stronger Jewish community.

Between Tradition and Modernity: The Contemporary Family and Jewish Values

To some extent the debate between the traditionalist defenders of family and avant-garde innovators breaks down along the lines of a classic liberal-conservative split. In other ways the family has served as a bridge issue between liberal and conservative concerns. Thus Christopher Lasch, long a spokesman for radical societal change, has decried the prevailing "culture of narcissism" and urged a return to traditional family values as a means of transcending the impulses towards pure self-gratification and self-fulfillment.[1]

Sociologists Briggite and Peter Berger have captured the mood of this debate in their book, *The War Over the Family*: "In one vision the bourgeois family is a natural unit of parents and children, united by love, mutual respect, trust and fidelity, based on religiously inspired values and giving a distinct moral quality to this basic unit of social life. In the other vision the bourgeois family is a narrowly constraining cage, turning its members into mere instruments of production, profoundly destructive of the personalities of women and children (and, perhaps, to a lesser degree, of men) and generally cutting off its members from participation in the larger concerns of society."[2]

As a group, Jews have acculturated well in America—perhaps more successfully than most groups and in some ways more completely than in any previous country of concentrated Jewish settlement. Thus, changes in the Jewish family—singles, intermarrieds, voluntarily childless couples, and homosexuals—all reflect growing patterns of modernization among Jews. How well we cope as a community with these changes will be a direct corollary of American Jewry's engagement with modernity and will test our willingness to impose limits to modernization. Particular questions regarding the family pose enormous challenges to the Jewish community and Jewish continuity: The moral value of the family generally, work-family issues, the Jewish birthrate,

Reprinted from *The Jewish Family and Jewish Continuity*, Steven Bayme and Gladys Rosen, eds., (Hoboken, NY: KTAV) 1994.

divorce, and intermarriage, all evoke the issue of the Jews' relationship to modern culture and their willingness to set limits to modernization. The remainder of this essay will examine these issues and suggest some conclusions for further communal policy and programs.

Moral Value of the Family

Like discussions of moral values generally, this area is perhaps the most difficult to clarify. In 1980, the White House Conference on the Family—unable to agree on any definition of the family—changed its name to White House Conference on Families. A coalition that included both the "Right to Life" movement and the National Association of Non-Parents could hardly have agreed on the ideological issue of what constituted a family. Thus the Conference abandoned the effort at values clarification in favor of a values pluralism in which virtually all types of living patterns might be considered a family. Yet the moral problems do not disappear by redefining terminology. By 1992, 24 percent of unmarried American women under age 45 had given birth to a child. For black women, the percentage exceeded 55 percent. With all respect to the values of pluralism, one may hardly claim that children born to teen-age unwed mothers mature in a privileged environment. Absent fathers, inadequate finances, adolescent parents—all create an atmosphere unconducive to nurturing and personal growth.

All Jews at one time or another have encountered the traditional Jewish family ethic: Marriage and childbearing are good in and of themselves; divorce is legitimate but only as a course of last resort; sexual relations are desirable and sanctified by God albeit within the confines of marriage. Genesis captured the spirit of this ethic in its earliest admonitions: "It is not good that man dwell alone. . . . Therefore shall a man take leave of his father and mother and he shall cleave unto his wife and they shall be as one flesh. . . . Be fruitful and multiply and fill the earth . . ."

Yet how binding are these traditional norms today when 95 percent of American Jews do not accept the halachic system? The traditional norm of family essentially offered a locale in which tradition could be transmitted and demonstrated that life was lived in relation to others with serious sacrifices from all parties. The very concept of childbearing itself communicated the value of creative activity and the affirmation of human life. In other words, the family supplied the structure of Jewish life and the socializing agent mediating between the individual and the community.

In the family the Jew learned respect for authority and tradition, obligations to others, and love for those close to us. Finally, the family offered continuity with history and past generations. The very practice of naming a child after deceased relatives served as one reminder of the association of the family with Jewish history. It is, of course, no accident that the historical festivals of the Jews—particularly Passover—are essentially family-centered rituals.[3]

Demographically, Jews continue to want marriage and to have small families. In 1982, 75 percent of Jewish college students indicated their desire for marriage. Only 3 percent had ruled it out. Well over 90 percent of American Jews do marry at some point in their lives.[4]

What has changed has been a delay in the age of marriage. In the 1960s 45 percent of Jews ages 18 through 24 had been married. By 1970 only 25 percent of this age group had been married.[5] This delay in the age of marriage is consistent with patterns for Americans generally who have higher education and upper-middle-class status. Thus, for today, only two thirds of adult Jews are currently married, indicating prolonged periods of singlehood. This does raise certain policy issues in the Jewish community in the sense that Jewish communal affiliation tends to correlate closely with marriage and having children. Prolonged periods of singlehood and voluntary childlessness may create unbreakable patterns of non-affiliation with the Jewish community. Moreover, prolonged periods of singlehood and voluntary childlessness may result in decreased fertility, owing to the increase in sterility after age 30, and heavy investment in high-powered careers, which may not be able to absorb the presence of small children.

Most divisive have been the questions related to homosexuality, Jewish tradition and Jewish communal institutions. Advocates of gay rights uphold principles of equal rights for all and the need to include homosexuals within the Jewish community. Conversely, their opponents seek to circumscribe homosexual behavior, often citing Jewish tradition as justification. Charges and counter-charges of "gay-bashing" and "moral perversity" further polarize the issue and stifle expressions of legitimate disagreement and dissent.

Homosexuals, like members of other minority groups, deserve protection of rights and liberties. There can be no equivocation on this point. But there is a clear difference between toleration of homosexual behavior and its articulation as a communal norm. Jewish ethics clearly uphold heterosexual marriage as the norm for society. That message, unfortunately, often is blurred in the context of debating gay rights.

Homosexual orientation ought rightly be protected. Gay-bashing serves no social purpose and is morally odious. Yet the moral relativism inherent in declaring homosexuality as an "alternative lifestyle" is similarly unacceptable. We must find ways to articulate societal preferences for heterosexual marriage while at the same time upholding the civil rights of individuals. Advocates of gay rights ought rightly be challenged to articulate a message that underscores rather than detracts from social norms of heterosexual marriage. Homosexuality is an orientation that we protect, not one that we prefer. Judaism is by no means homophobic, nor is it morally relativist.

Work and Family

The popular stereotype of Jewish women is that they are highly educated and therefore most likely to wish to pursue full-time careers and occupations. The actual evidence in this regard is, however, quite mixed. Jewish women who have children under school-age are more likely to stay at home. Those who have children over school-age are more likely to be going to work. Part-time employment has been especially popular among Jewish women representing personal satisfaction in being able to maintain both family and career. For example, the Rochester Jewish community reports that 25 percent of married Jewish women with children of school age worked full-time, 33 percent worked part-time and the rest are stay-at-home mothers. In Milwaukee, 46 percent work either full or part-time, while 54 percent has stayed out of the workforce. In Cleveland, 50 percent hold full-time jobs.[6]

These variations indicate that we need greater care in understanding the relationship between family and work. The notion of the stay-at-home mother as being obsolete is a misconception in light of the fact that many American Jewish women with children under school-age do stay at home. Of those who do work the differences between full-time and part-time work must be drawn carefully. In short, no single model exists of Jewish families in terms of the working mother.

By the same token, however, all of our evidence indicates Jewish parents value "independence training" for their children. Here also the stereotype of the overprotective Jewish mother must be carefully revised. In Pittsburgh, where half of Jewish mothers with children under school-age have opted to stay out of the workforce, 83 percent have sent their children to childcare settings either day care or early childhood, indicating the values Jews place upon early socialization experiences for their children.[7]

Birthrates

Historically Jews have never been the most numerous of peoples. Witness Deuteronomy 7:7: "The Lord did not set his love upon you, nor choose you, because you were more in number than any people, for you were the fewest of peoples." In America specifically, Jewish birthrates have lagged behind general norms, but numbers were replenished by a steady supply of immigrants usually in their peak childbearing years. Recently, greater communal concern has focused upon the Jewish birthrate partly because the Holocaust has left us bereft as a people. Moreover, the end of Jewish immigration has effectively meant that future replenishment must come from within our ranks. Finally, communal leaders have feared that population shrinkage might diminish both political clout and cultural vitality. Yet behind the "Jewish birth deficit" lies the more profound set of questions of the impact of modernization on Jewry. The norm within the Jewish community has become, at best, two children per family. That norm derives from broader American concerns—family cost, impact of children upon personal freedom and career, and ecological concerns such as the environment and the possibility of nuclear disaster. Thus Jews have internalized the value system of the Zero Population Growth (ZPG) movement, and have even gone beyond it for themselves to Negative Population Growth (NPG).

Combating this norm—assuming it is desirable to break the two-child pattern—requires asking whether we can set limits to moderniza-tion. Certain lessons here may be gleaned from the Orthodox. Their incomes are certainly no higher, and in many cases are lower, than the non-Orthodox. The Modern Orthodox, at least, harbor similar expecta-tions of career and personal enjoyment as the non-Orthodox. Added to this is the high cost of leading an intensive Jewish life—day school tuition, summer camps, contributions to synagogal and communal in-stitutions. Yet the Orthodox have succeeded in maintaining a norm of three children (and often more) per family. One might argue that the Orthodox simply accept "Be fruitful and multiply" as divine impera-tive. Yet no one denies that the Modern Orthodox regularly utilize con-traceptives and family planning. Far more significant is the question of modernization. Orthodox Jews have recognized the toll modernity ex-acts and have been willing to set limits to it. The non-Orthodox would do well to acknowledge the necessity for setting limits, albeit more broadly than the Orthodox.

Divorce

One of the key differences concerning Jewish families relates to the Jewish divorce deficit. Approximately 18 percent of adult American Jews have been through a divorce, meaning that for the average indi-vidual, the chances of a divorce occurring are about one in six. More interestingly, among the Jews affiliated with synagogal movements—Orthodoxy, Conservatism, and Reform, the chances of marriages end-ing up in divorce are approximately one in eight. Among Jews who are unaffiliated with the Jewish community the chances of divorce rise to one in three. Significantly, among the affiliated Jews, Orthodox Jews divorce the least while Reform Jews divorce the most frequently.[8] To be sure, rates of divorce are higher among young couples than older Jewish couples, indicating that as the younger generation ages the rates of Jewish divorce may rise and will come close to the overall American patterns.

However, the significance of these statistics points to the strong rela-tionship between Jewish commitment and strong marriages. The expe-rience of Jews indicates that the family that prays together stays together. In large measure, this is true on account of the family context which defines Judaism as a faith. The rituals of Judaism tend to be family-oriented, and ties to Jewish tradition cement ties between family members. The most vivid illustration is simply the notion of the Shabbat dinner as a moment out of time set aside for quality family conversation removed from the day-to-day struggles and travails of the world around us. Furthermore, Jews value marital success greatly. They define themselves as successful when they enjoy happy marriages. Conversely, they suffer significant loss of self-esteem when their marriages fail. This identification of marital success and self-esteem relates very strongly to the concept of commitment to making marriage work that is the basic factor in marital stability and success today generally.[9]

To be sure, divorce causes significant dislocations for Jews as it does for all other families. The single Jewish parent is perhaps most vulnerable in terms of family functioning. There are two reasons for this: First the sheer economic downturn that accompanies the single parents and children raises significant barriers to participation in Jewish communal activities. Similarly, the psychological consequences of divorce, in particular the devastating impact upon children enhances the vulnerability of the single-parent home. Research in this area has indicated, however, that ties to Jewish tradition and involvement in communal activities can serve as a stabilizing factor within a single-parent home, reminding children that in a world of turbulence there are enduring values.[10]

Intermarriage

A fifth area of communal concern that highlights the cultural clash with modernity is intermarriage. Theoretically, if we favor full equality in society, it is difficult to oppose intermarriage. Napoleon recognized this early on by asking newly-emancipated French Jewry if they would encourage intermarriage. After all the ultimate entry into civil society would be acceptance in the family circles of the majority culture. Conversely, of course, Jewish leaders have decried intermarriage as a threat to Jewish continuity.

A nineteenth-century dispute among prominent Reform rabbis highlighted communal ambivalence about intermarriage. In Germany, Samuel Holdheim argued that intermarriage constituted the ideal Jewish marriage because it represented a statement of Jewish universalism.

His colleague and counterpart, David Einhorn, no less a universalist, responded that intermarriage was a threat to Jewish survival.

Similar tensions have been expressed within the Reconstructionist movement. In his seminal 1934 work, *Judaism as a Civilization,* Mordecai Kaplan wrote the following:

> Jews must meet all situations that might lead to mixed marriages, not fearfully or grudgingly, but in the sprit of encountering an expected development . . . With a belief in the integrity and values of his own civilization, the Jewish partner to the marriage could . . . make Judaism the civilization of the home.

Twenty-two years later, in *Questions Jews Ask,* Kaplan returned to the same topic, but with a different nuance:

> Since Jews are a minority and Judaism is exposed to tremendous disintegrative forces from the non-Jewish environment, and since Reconstructionism is concerned with the perpetuation of Judaism, it cannot approve of uncontrolled intermarriage with non-Jews. If, however, a non-Jew who desires to marry a Jew, after studying what is involved in being a Jew and what are the principles and practices of Judaism, is willing to undergo formal conversion to Judaism, he should be given every encouragement and should be welcomed into the Jewish community. Only in this way can we compensate for losses through intermarriage, where conversion is not made a condition. It is unreasonable to expect the Jewish religion and culture will be perpetuated in homes resulting from mixed marriages where no such requirement is insisted on.[11]

Two additional factors have intensified communal ambivalence since the days of Holdheim and Einhorn: surge in the numbers intermarrying and shifting reasons for intermarriage. Until the 1960s, intermarriage rates hovered at the historically low levels of 10 percent. By the 1970s, that figure had jumped to 30 percent. Today one out of two marriages contracted by Jews are likely to be intermarriages. One study has estimated offspring of intermarriage in America as 700,000.

Moreover, the reasons behind intermarriage have shifted. Historically, intermarriage connoted ideological rejection of the Jewish community and Jewish tradition. Today, however, intermarriage signifies a matter of meeting a suitable partner who happens to be Gentile rather than any conscious ideological rejection. As a result, the community has begun to advocate outreach programs to draw the intermarrieds into the community rather than lament their defection.

Indeed, perhaps no issue has galvanized the community as much as the intermarriage phenomenon. Some have emphasized outreach and conversion programs. Others have called for an intensive Jewish education as a vehicle to counteract intermarriage. These, however, may be but stopgap measures. The underlying question is one of the degree of our acculturation and accommodation with American modernity. Obviously, we cannot retreat to a spiritual ghetto, nor would such a retreat be desirable Jewishly. In that sense, intermarriage may be a necessary price to pay for living within the modern culture.

Nevertheless, at least acknowledging intermarriage as a price that modernity exacts should stimulate reevaluation of our overall patterns of accommodation to modernity. In particular, outreach to mixed marrieds must be appropriately designed so that the overall message of the Jewish community regarding Jewish marital values, the importance of building a Jewish home, and the importance of finding Jewish mates are clearly communicated. Is that a message that mixed married couples can hear? Some can, some will not. Our task, while respecting the personal choices of individuals, must be to articulate communal norms that are seen as being the preferred model for Jews generally.

To be sure, that distinction is difficult to make and will often get lost. Failure to make the distinction, however, runs the risk of communicating a vision of intermarriage as simply one acceptable option among others. It is at that point that we have abandoned our responsibility as Jewish leaders and have fallen into a trap of moral relativism that anything the Jews happen to do automatically becomes legitimate.

Conclusion

As indicated earlier, questions of family and family values raise further implications for the broader question of the Jewish confrontation with modernity. Some Jews might agree with Benedict Spinoza that given the incompatibility of modernity and traditional Judaism, Jews ought to abandon tradition and assimilate into the universalist culture. Among the right-wing Orthodox, one may detect similar sentiment—that modernity and tradition are incompatible—leading to opposite conclusions. Thus one frequently finds Orthodox spokesmen echoing the views of Moses Schreiber, the Hatam Sofer, that modernity must be unequivocally rejected save for purposes of earning a living.

For most Jews today both these options are equally unacceptable. Jews committed to Judaism will also be unwilling to reject the attractions of modern culture. Their problem is essentially one of Jewish identity—the role of Jewish tradition in the contemporary world. The various questions explored here are all test cases of tradition's confrontation with modernity. In all cases we should be careful to avoid simplistic notions such as a universal retreat from modernity or, conversely, that we may "have it all" without sacrifice of traditional values. Rather the community must, on the one hand, clarify the values and benefits inherent in tradition and acknowledge that some limits to modernity are unavoidable. The process of defining the limits is necessarily a personal one and of course a difficult one. Yet failure to confront the limits of modernity essentially relegates us to a choice most would rather avoid: Spinoza's assimilationism or ultra-Orthodoxy's retreat to the ghetto. Either of these routes would confirm posthumously Arnold Toynbee's canard of a fossil people.

One medium of clarifying communal values lies in communal policies. Does the community acknowledge effective parenting as worthy of its honor? Do personnel policies of Jewish organizations encourage childbearing? Family issues pose a direct challenge to the community to clarify what it represents and believes.

Historically Jews have always perceived individual, family, and community as closely intertwined. Family offered a route both for individual self-fulfillment and for communal vitality and continuity. Moreover, Judaism posited the need for balance between development of self and enhancement of community in direct contrast to the ethos of unbridled individualism on the one hand and the ethos of state supremacy on the other hand. In other words, family both provides opportunities for personal growth through the nurture, companionship, and love of adults and holds the key to future Jewish continuity through the socialization of children in the Jewish heritage. Therefore, if marriage and parenting constitute both personal and communal goods, it is the responsibility of the Jewish community to encourage and foster family formation and stability.

Notes

1. Christopher Lasch, "What's Wrong with the Right," *Tikkun,* Vol. 1, No. 1, pp. 24, 25.

2. Brigitte Berger and Peter Berger, *The War Over the Family,* Garden City: Anchor Books, 1983, p. 107.

3. Irving Greenberg, *The Jewish Way,* New York: Summit Books, 1988, esp. pp. 52–55, and Steven Bayme, "Teaching Kids Jewish Civic Responsibility" in Roselyn Bell, ed., *The Hadassah Magazine Jewish Parenting Book,* New York: Free Press, 1989, p. 196.

4. Rela Geffen Monson, *Jewish Campus Life,* New York: American Jewish Committee, 1984, p. 16, and Sidney Goldstein, "Profile of American Jewry: Insights From the 1990 National Jewish Population Survey," *American Jewish Yearbook,* Vol. 92, 1992, pp. 116–118.

5. Samuel Heilman, *The Jewish Family Today: An Overview,* New York: Memorial Foundation for Jewish Culture, 1984, pp. 9–12.

6. Sylvia Fishman, "The Changing American Jewish Family in the Eighties," *Contemporary Jewry,* 9 (No. 2, Fall, 1988), pp. 15–18.

7. Ibid., p. 14.

8. J. Brodbar-Nemzer, "Divorce and the Jewish Community: The Impact of Jewish Commitment," *Journal of Jewish Communal Service,* 61 (No. 2, Winter, 1984), pp. 152–153 and Goldstein, op. cit. pp. 119–121.

9. J. Brodbar-Nemzer, "Marital Relations and Self-Esteem: How Jewish Families Are Different," *Journal of Marriage and Family,* 48 (No. 1, Feb., 1986), pp. 90–96.

10. Thomas Cottle, *Divorce and the Jewish Child,* New York: American Jewish Committee, 1985, pp. 52–54.

11. See Mordecai Kaplan, *Judaism as a Civilization,* N.Y.: Macmillan, 1934, p. 418; idem, *Questions Jews Ask,* New York: Reconstructionist Press, 1956, p. 225. Interestingly, a contemporary Reconstructionist rabbi and outspoken advocate for rabbinic officiation at interfaith weddings facilely quotes the early Kaplan as justification, ignoring the later (and more realistic) writings on the subject. See Rabbi Emily Korzenik's communication in *Dovetail, A Newsletter by and for Jewish Christian Families,* Vol. 1, #4 (February-March 1993), pp. 2–3.

Can We Speak of Family Values Today?
Jewish Teachings, Continuity and Repairing
the American Family

This paper raises three questions central to the Jewish family, the Jewish community, and the place and function of family in American society generally. More specifically, I ask what should the Jewish community do to strengthen families? What ought the Jewish community do to enhance Jewish continuity and insure the future quality of Jewish life in America? And finally, what are the implications of the Jewish experience for American society? In this latter context, the term *tikkun olam* or 'repair of the world' has been overused as a code-word for liberal politics yet remains central both to the question of Jewish continuity and to the relationship of American Jewry to the general society. In fact, there is probably no better definition of *tikkun olam* today than the repair of family.

Judaism perceives family as closely intertwined with individual self-fulfillment and with building a healthy society. Not only are these units closely interrelated, but the health of each depends upon the health of the other two. More particularly, strong families by no means undermine commitment to community, as some observers have argued,[1] but rather the family is the essential building block and prerequisite for the construction of human society. To be sure, totalitarian societies have sought to break down the family for its loyalties to its members rather than to the state. Precisely for that reason, it has been no secret that totalitarian societies have oppressed both Jews and Judaism.

Genesis in particular serves as a paradigm for Jewish perceptions of family and family ties. Genesis by no means suggests an idyllic portrait of family. On the contrary, it perceives family conflict as normative and urges working towards reconciling relationships within family units. Ultimately that reconciliation serves as the building block for wider social units and the construction of communities.

"Can We Speak of Jewish Family Values Today?" is reprinted with JESNA's permission and originally appeared in JESNA's publication, *Agenda: Jewish Education,* Spring 1997.

Permit me to illustrate this with several passages from Genesis. The opening chapters narrate a twice-told tale of the creation of Adam. The Adam of Genesis, chapter I is majestic. He is enjoined to go out and conquer, to rule over nature and the universe. By contrast, the Adam of Genesis, chapter II is far more limited. He appears as a vulnerable creature, lonely and in need of human comfort. Rabbinic tradition, looking at this dual account of the creation of man, pointed to the male-female unit as co-creator with the Almighty. To attain the status of majestic man, it was first necessary to create the family unit of husband and wife. In rabbinic tradition, marriage signified *shelemut* or 'wholeness.' Through marriage, men and women were given the opportunity to become partners and co-creators with God. The very term for bride, *kallah,* signified wholeness or completion. To undertake the task of building society, the family unit must first be formulated and its ties cemented.[2]

Yet Genesis quickly proceeds to tell a tale of family breakup. Cain destroys the primeval family by murdering his own brother. Cain's reasons appear to lie in placing personal self-fulfillment over familial responsibility. Yet the tale of Cain's development serves as a Biblical paradigm for repentance. Cain regrets his action, suffers punishment, and undergoes rehabilitation. The vehicle for doing so is precisely his understanding of what family means. Cain marries and has a son—one of the great mysteries of Genesis is whom did Cain marry—but the significance of his becoming a father lies in building a city, the earliest recorded form of civilization. It is as if fatherhood and family have taught Cain that social responsibility transcends personal needs for self-fulfillment. By becoming a "family man," Cain becomes a socially responsible citizen.

Perhaps the clearest illustration of this view in Genesis of individual/family/community lies in the tale of Judah and how he emerged from the sale of Joseph to leadership among the sons of Jacob, and by extension leadership of the Jewish people. Our first glimpse of Judah casts him as destroyer of Jacob's family. He is the architect of the sale of Joseph. Like Cain he appears to place personal self-fulfillment over responsibility to others. After the sale of Joseph, Judah leaves the family nest, perhaps a suggestion that he was responsible for the breakup of

Jacob's family. He meets Tamar, who teaches him the lessons of responsibility. The relationship between Judah and Tamar parallels the relationship between Judah and his family. He commits an error, tries to cover it up, and tends to his personal needs rather than fulfilling his responsibilities to those around him. Tamar, however, does not accept this passively. She points out to Judah the importance of our commitments and how we have responsibility for our actions.

With this lesson in tow, Judah is able to take responsibility for the fate of Benjamin, his youngest brother. Judah demonstrates to Joseph that he indeed has changed. He no longer is prepared to cut simply the best deal for himself and ignore his responsibilities and commitments to other members of the family. Judah's concluding speech effectively "overcomes" Joseph, meaning that Judah has demonstrated his claim to leadership of the Jewish people through his taking responsibility for his actions, fulfilling his commitments to family members. Effectively he shows Joseph what Joseph is not—a family man. Joseph's external successes in Egypt are ultimately of secondary importance for the development of the Jews as a people to Judah's successes in restoring the concept of family to Jacob's household. By building these family ties and reconciling Jacob's sons into a family unit, Judah lays the groundwork for transforming the Jews into a people and thereby asserts his claim to political leadership. By placing Genesis before Exodus, Scripture in effect suggests that building family is the prerequisite for the building of nationhood.[3]

These tales of Genesis are didactic in several senses: First, family here serves as a corrective to unbridled individualism, the "me first" syndrome, or, as Woody Allen once put it, "The heart wants what it wants."[4] These personal needs and drives for fulfillment are by no means illegitimate. On the contrary, they are natural and understandable. However, Genesis teaches the limits to unchecked individualism. As the rabbinic sage Hillel once put it, "If I am only for myself, what am I?" Secondly, these stories in Genesis describe the family as a mediating institution between the individual and the broader society. The family is the setting in which individuals learn social responsibility to others. Learning social responsibility inside the family prepares members for good citizenship in society broadly.[5] Thirdly, these stories suggest the importance of family for ensuring the future of the Jews as a people. It is assumed that conflict will take place within the family. If the solution to conflict lies in murder, à la Cain, clearly the Jews and civilization generally are doomed. Rather, the lessons of Judah lie in the willingness to pursue struggle within the family until reconciliation may be attained. Families require commitment and steadfastness in ironing out conflicts and building relationships.

Lastly, Genesis approaches issues of sexuality in unabashedly moral language. Sexual relations are not evaluated on the basis of functionality but as fundamentally moral in nature. Therefore Genesis evokes a language of authority, demands, and judging of behaviors—criteria that are often politically incorrect in contemporary American society. To be sure, Genesis evokes a healthy sexuality. Jacob is perhaps the first romantic lover in classical literature. Nor were the rabbis embarrassed by sex. On the contrary, they encouraged the fulfillment of human desire and never defined sexuality as purely a vehicle of procreation.[6] But in encouraging a healthy sexuality, Genesis, and later rabbinical commentary, insisted on the primacy of moral values and judgments in evaluating appropriate and inappropriate sexual behaviors. Whether those values and judgments remain salient in America today is a question to which we must return.

Given these general principles, are there implications for Jewish communal policy and program to strengthen families? One principle clearly embedded in Jewish tradition is that society must protect the vulnerable and the powerless—or, more precisely, the widow and the orphan. Interestingly, the Biblical record often appears insensitive to the divorcee, who is characterized as a 'hated woman.' A man is prohibited from divorcing his wife only when he has wronged her. Otherwise, his rights of divorce are virtually absolute while hers are extremely limited. To be sure, rabbinic tradition sought to enlarge the rights of women in marriage. Maimonides, for example, argued that women may marry only of their own free will—a principle that deserves repetition given the recent controversy over the betrothal of twelve-year-olds. Yet the inequity between men and women in divorce remains and requires further redress. More particularly, there is a definite need to equalize power relationships between the sexes. Certainly the inequity of the status of *aguna,* or a woman without a bill of divorce, cannot be tolerated.[7]

More positively, Jewish tradition presents Jewish agencies with a wealth of resources that can cement family ties. Abraham Joshua Heschel understood this beautifully in defining the Sabbath as sacred time for families to be families together. Heschel explained the Sabbath as a 24-hour retreat from our worldly experiences providing us an opportunity to sanctify the time around us through personal relationships and family ties. The Sabbath, in effect, provided a structure by which families could be families together across the Jewish table.[8] This insight has been demonstrated as well by sociological studies. Religious commitment does cement marriage—it provides a common set of values and experiences binding families together. Divorce is much lower among religiously observant Jewish couples not because it is prohibited but rather because families celebrating Judaism together are likely to be stronger families.[9] Most importantly, the community has an educational responsibility to broadcast the message that for families to succeed will require enormous work and commitment. The message of American society for Jews has been one of individual opportunity. Never before in Jewish history has there been a diaspora society so receptive to Jewish involvement. However, the language of individual rights and opportunities often fails to articulate the message of family responsibility. The Jewish community must fill this gap by communicating the synergy Jewish tradition underscores between family and personal self-fulfillment. Moreover, it needs to inculcate realistic expectations of marriage and the commitment necessary to making marriages work.

A particular tension that must be confronted honestly is between the language of feminism broadening opportunities for women and the language of family emphasizing marriage and parenting. Blu Greenberg has written of a high percentage of Jewish feminists who are either divorced or single.[10] Sylvia Fishman has echoed these remarks and pointed to feminist ambivalence concerning childbearing.[11] We must confront these issues honestly balancing the legitimate aspirations for personal self-fulfillment with traditional values emphasizing the importance of family.

The concern with family in the Jewish community has been not only a question of meeting the needs and forms of today's families but also ensuring the future quality of Jewish life and the continuity of the Jews as a people. Today, much of the discussion about Jewish continuity has been frankly disappointing in the absence of any efforts to restructure communal priorities and the inability to articulate normative statements about Jewish behaviors for fear of giving offense to large numbers of Jews. In truth, there is no mystery to Jewish continuity. It will come to those who desire it if they are prepared to pay the price—a cultural rather than economic price of leading a Jewish life even if it comes into conflict with otherwise desirable features of American society. In short, there can be no Jewish continuity without normative Judaism. The challenge for today's liberal Jewish movements lies in their capacity to articulate a language of norms, commitments, demands, and expectations of their adherents.[12] A Judaism that does not require personal sacrifice ultimately cannot sustain itself. In this context, the Jewish family stands at the cutting edge of the relationship between Jews and modern culture. Perhaps no finer example of this tension lies in the question of intermarriage, which, on the one hand, validates modern ideals of human equality and romantic love, yet, conversely, threatens the Jewish future.

The question therefore becomes can we speak of Jewish family values today? What are the normative statements we make concerning family and are those relevant to today's Jews? Martha Ackelsberg, for one, recommends expanding the boundaries of what we mean by family to encompass a broad array of living arrangements.[13] Conversely, Rabbi Samuel Dresner urges that we declare war on American culture and assert traditional norms in the face of an inhospitable American climate.[14] Both positions have the virtue of consistency. For Ackelsberg, there are no applicable norms save celebration of diversity. For Dresner, the Jewish community is bankrupt if it is unable to apply the teachings of Jewish tradition to contemporary culture. Yet the virtue of consistency masks the deficiencies in these respective positions. Jewish family values absent traditional norms lack Judaic distinctiveness. Declaring war on American culture has little commonality with the lives Jews actually lead today.

Therefore I suggest a third position that tries to navigate between Ackelsberg and Dresner. That position suggests that we respect personal choice but at the same time articulate communal norms. It suggests that we operate on an *inclusive* basis reaching out to all Jews interested in leading a Jewish life, yet we articulate statements that are ideologically *exclusive,* restoring the primacy of the inmarried two-parent home as the Jewish ideal and preferred model. This position has the virtue of remaining true to Judaic traditions, articulating normative statements, yet, conversely, remaining able to include operationally all interested in leading a Jewish life but who, for whatever reason, do not meet this family script.[15]

Furthermore, this model of respecting personal choice yet articulating communal norms may also be applicable to American society as a whole. First, we teach by example. Jews may feel uncomfortable with the Christian underpinnings of the "Promise Keepers," yet the message of Judaism—of fidelity and commitment—is remarkably congruent. The Jewish idea of family in many ways approximates Christopher Lasch's model of family as "haven in a heartless world."[16] To be sure, that model is one that will articulate judgments and expectations of responsibility. It is not a model that simply celebrates diversity.

Moreover, this model applies to the political debate concerning family today. Liberals are most comfortable articulating a language of economic measures to strengthen families. Conservatives prefer a cultural language of values and commitments. In effect, the Jewish message is that one without the other is insufficient. Society has an interest in building strong families, and economic measures are critical instrumentalities in enabling families to be families. However, those instrumentalities make little sense unless society perceives an equal obligation to preserve the cultural value of family.

In this context, Judaism has a very specific message directed to media images of the family today. Stephanie Coontz and others have warned against nostalgia for the culture of the 1950s. Ozzie and Harriet were by no means typical and, if anything, their program masked a dysfunctional family.[17] Yet the answer to Ozzie and Harriet does not lie in "Married with Children." Unfortunately, the media culture today emphasizes family breakup and dysfunction. "Kindergarten Cop," for example, portrays a world in which all children are divorced, and the one child who lives in a two-parent home suffers from child abuse. "War of the Roses" and "Thelma and Louise" similarly portray marriage as a trap from which escape is absolutely essential. By contrast, "A Stranger Among Us" portrays a Gentile policewoman learning the values of marriage and family from the community of Hasidim she is investigating. Her Jewish partner does not understand her transformation. The other-worldly culture of the Hasidim, in pronounced contrast to her uncaring Irish father, impresses her that self-fulfillment is closely related to commitment to others—a distinct protest against unbridled individualism.[18]

Moreover, in approaching family issues, let us emphasize the priority of the well-being of children. On one level, that does mean discouraging divorce even as we acknowledge the reality of the single-parent home. Jewish tradition suggests a precedent: S.D. Goitein, the foremost historian of medieval Islamic Jewry, noted how medieval Jewish communities discouraged divorce actively yet also practiced it. Islamic Jewry, noted how medieval Jewish courts spared no efforts to prevent divorce by reconciling conflicts. Yet they also recognized that divorce was often a necessary solution to a failed marriage.[19] Our challenge today lies, first, in encouraging a greater bias in favor of marriage, especially in the therapeutic professions and the media culture. Divorce should by no means be regarded as a natural step in the human life cycle. It should be understood rather as a necessary solution when all other avenues have failed.[20]

This is especially true in the context of young children. Our experience indicates that there are no victimless divorces in families with children. Research indicates that children of single-parent homes simply do not fare as well as children of two-parent homes. As Barbara Whitehead has noted, "Family diversity . . . does not strengthen the social fabric. It dramatically weakens and undermines society. . . ."[21]

Once divorce has occurred, the community can and should seek to strengthen the single-parent home. The values of tradition and religion can often serve as buffer and anchor in the turbulent world following divorce. Research on synagogues has demonstrated that the synagogue can often serve as surrogate extended family providing a message of continuity and stability for children of divorce. By extension, the same should be said for other religious institutions.[22]

Furthermore, in a culture that is so open about sexuality, Judaism counsels a message of sexual restraint. The rite of circumcision, symbolizing the covenant of the Jews as a people, also symbolizes the need for sexual restraint. Scripture criticizes ancient paganism for lacking sexual restraint. Rabbinic Judaism defined heroism not as the heroism of the battlefield but as the capacity to master one's passions.

By contrast, American culture has excessively heightened expectations of sexuality. "L.A. Law" portrays a world of lawyers who revel in daily sexual conquest. The message of sexual restraint is by no means irrelevant to today's society. On the contrary, it serves as an appropriate corrective to the overblown expectations of sexuality propagated in the media that, in many ways, are destined to be unfulfilled in any case.

Can we then answer our original question of speaking about family values today? First, this is not a call for the invasion of the bedroom by governmental organs. Family values should by no means become a code-word for a political agenda of oppression—just as *tikkun olam* should not be considered a code-word for liberal social policies. Rather, family values ought distinguish between what is tolerated and what is endorsed—what is permitted and what is encouraged. The state should not be regulating individual conduct—nor should the state intervene in the private relations within families except to prevent abuses. Yet the voices of society and the moral authority of the public square ought be marshalled in a campaign to restore the primacy of family as a value. We should be willing to assert our cultural preferences for traditional norms such as marriage and the two-parent home while at the same time accommodating and reaching out to those who have chosen to lead their lives within alternative settings. We need have no nostalgia for the mythical nuclear family of the 1950s. Conversely, however, we have no need to redefine the family so as to recognize all possible living arrangements as being equally preferable. Recognizing what exists is not the same as stating what ought to be.

The future of family, therefore, affects both the future of the Jews as a community and the future of American society generally. It captures the dilemma of our desire to continue as a people and our difficulty in making normative statements for fear of offending fellow Jews. Conversely, it challenges our desire to contribute to American society yet at the same time expects departure from our liberal orthodoxies. Whether we have the courage to take measures that will both strengthen families and restore a language of family values will test both our seriousness about Jewish continuity and commitment to *tikkun olam*.

Notes

1. See, for example, Stephanie Coontz, *The Way We Never Were*, New York: Basic Books, 1992, pp. 115–121.

2. This discussion of Genesis, chs. I–II, is heavily indebted to the classic essay by Rabbi Joseph B. Soloveitchik, "The Lonely Man of Faith," *Tradition*, vol. 7, (No. 2, Summer, 1965) pp. 5–67.

3. This discussion of the Joseph epic is heavily indebted to Devorah Steinmetz, *From Father to Son: Kinship, Conflict, and Continuity in Genesis*, Louisville: Westminster/John Knox Press, 1991, pp. 112–133, and Aviva Zornberg, *Genesis: The Beginnings of Desire*, Philadelphia: Jewish Publication Society, 1995, pp. 314–361. My analysis has been heavily influenced by both authors, although neither should be read as completely in agreement with each other or with my reading here.

4. Samuel H. Dresner, *Can Families Survive in Pagan America?*, Lafayette: Huntington House Publishers, 1995, ch. 7.

5. On family as a mediating institution, see Brigitte and Peter Berger, *The War Over the Family*, Garden City: Anchor Press/Doubleday, 1983, esp. ch. 8.

6. Michael Kaufman, *Love, Marriage and Family in Jewish Law and Tradition*, North Vale, NJ: Jason Aronson Inc., 1992, p. 216.

7. For historical treatment of Jewish divorce law, see S.D. Goitein, *A Mediterranean Society: The Jewish Communities of the Arab World as Portrayed in the Documents of the Cairo Geniza*, Vol. III: *The Family*, Berkeley: University of California Press, 1978, pp. 264–267. On how rabbinic law enlarged the rights of women in marriage, see Gerald Blidstein, *Honor They Father and Mother: Filial Responsibilities in Jewish Law and Ethics*, New York: Ktav, 1975, pp. 100–105. Blu Greenberg mounts an eloquent plea for further development in the rights of women within a divorce situation. See Greenberg, *On Women and Judaism: A View From Tradition*, Philadelphia: Jewish Publication Society, 1981, pp. 125–145.

8. Abraham Joshua Heschel, *The Sabbath: Its Meaning for Modern Man*, New York: The Noonday Press, 1951, pp. 8–10, 18. See also Irving Greenberg, *The Jewish Way*, New York: Summit Books, 1988, pp. 140–142, 165–175 and Richard Louv, *FatherLove*, New York: Pocket Books, 1993, pp. 223–225.

9. Steven Bayme, "The Jewish Family in American Culture," in David Blankenhorn, Steven Bayme, and Jean Bethke Elshtain, eds., *Rebuilding the Nest: A New Commitment for the American Family*, p. 153, and Jay Brodbar-Nemzer, "Divorce in the Jewish Community: The Impact of Jewish Commitment," *Journal of Jewish Communal Service* 61 (No. 2, Winter 1984), pp. 152–153.

10. Blu Greenberg, pp. 143, 166, and S. Bayme, "Changing Perceptions of Divorce," *Journal of Jewish Communal Service*, 70, (Nos. 2/3, Winter/Spring 1994), p. 124.

11. Sylvia Barack Fishman, *A Breath of Life: Feminism in the American Jewish Community*, New York: The Free Press, 1993, pp. 47–57.

12. Daniel Gordis, *Behaving and Believing, Behaving and Belonging*, New York: The American Jewish Committee, 1995. See also Jack Wertheimer, "Family Values and the Jews" *Commentary*, January 1994, pp. 30–34.

13. Martha Ackelsberg, "Jewish Family Ethics in a Post-halakhic Age," in David Teutsch ed., *Imagining the Jewish Future*, New York: State University of New York Press, 1992, pp. 149–164, and the important critique by Eliot Dorff, ibid., pp. 169–174.

14. Dresner, ch. 2.

15. This centrist position is very similar to that developed by Bernard Reisman, "A Preferred Family Policy for the American Jewish Community," *Journal of Jewish Communal Service*, loc. cit., pp. 113. See also the critique by Lucy Steinitz, "Welcoming New Family Forms: Implications for American Jewish Life," ibid., pp. 115–119.

16. Christopher Lasch, *Haven in a Heartless World*, New York: Basic Books, 1977, esp. ch. 7.

17. See Coontz, op. cit., and David Halberstam, *The Fifties*, New York: Villard Books, pp. 513–520.

18. See Michael Medved, *Hollywood vs. America*, New York: HarperCollins, chs. 7–8, and Bayme, "Changing Perceptions of Divorce," p. 124.

19. Goitein, pp. 260.

20. David Blankenhorn, *Fatherless America*, New York: Basic Books, 1995, pp. 221–225. See also Francine Klagsbrun, *Married People*, New York: Bantam Books, 1985, pp. 87–88, and Steven Bayme, "Marriage and Divorce: Cultural Climate and Policy Directions," *American Family*, Vol. X (No. 7, September 1987), pp. 1–2.

21. Barbara D. Whitehead, "Dan Quayle Was Right," *The Atlantic Monthly*, April, 1993, pp. 77, 80.

22. Thomas Cottle, *Divorce and the Jewish Child*, New York: The American Jewish Committee, 1981, pp. 27ff.; Nathalie Friedman, *The Divorced Parent and the Jewish Community*, New York: The American Jewish Committee, 1985, pp. 52–54.

Can Jewish Families Survive
in Pagan America?

In Woody Allen's film "Bullets Over Broadway," Rob Reiner, portraying a bohemian artist, answers a colleague's query as to whether she ought to enter into an adulterous relationship, by saying, "You gotta do what you gotta do. . . . We artists follow a higher morality."

Although perhaps satirical, Reiner's comment captures much of the ethos of contemporary American hedonism—a world in which sex, violence and infidelity are accepted as normative and even, at times, are glorified.

Samuel Dresner, a Conservative rabbi, perceives these trends as contradictory to Jewish teachings and, more generally, to the family values of most Americans, who continue to desire strong marriages and stable families. Even more depressing to him is that so much of today's cultural products emanate from Jewish artists. Even more distressing is the fact that Woody Allen's incestuous behavior is far better known to American Jews than Abraham Heschel's insight that the Sabbath is sanctified time for families to be families together.

Dresner presents his case in his new book *Can Families Survive in Pagan America?* (Huntington House). His argument is as follows: The increase in single-parent families has bred greater poverty, illiteracy and delinquent behavior. Rather than combat these trends, Hollywood has glorified them. An ethos of moral relativism, reflecting classically pagan themes that celebrate virtually all types of sexual behavior, has replaced Jewish and Christian ethical norms of sexual restraint. Finally, even monotheism itself is threatened by the introduction of witchcraft and goddess cults.

Dresner's thesis is supported by much other recent writing. Michael Medved, in his book *Hollywood vs. America,* has tellingly demonstrated how a plethora of films have pointedly offended the core values of most Americans. Moreover, recent research, as articulated by David Blankenhorn in his book *Fatherless America* and Barbara Whitehead

Reprinted from the *Jewish Exponent* (Philadelphia), January 11, 1996.

in her *Atlantic Monthly* article "Dan Quayle Was Right," has demonstrated that the decline of the nuclear family is by no means a socially neutral development but is closely related to the problems of the American underclass.

Dresner's most striking chapters concern witchcraft and goddess feminism. He takes issue with idyllic portraits of goddess societies, which in reality were far more warlike and bloodthirsty than contemporary admirers imagine.

He is appalled by the rehabilitation of witchcraft, particularly by America's most renowned witch, Starhawk, a middle-aged Jewish woman, who praises witchcraft as "a noble thing . . . to redeem our right as women to be powerful," and condemns Judaic exhortation for sexual restraint as patriarchal tyranny.

Assessing the Indictment

How, then, may we assess Dresner's indictment of American culture? The tensions between Judaism and classical paganism leave little room for compromise. Ancient men and women saw their lives governed by a plurality of forces of nature, over which they exerted no control. Ancient paganism posited a deity standing behind each of these forces of nature.

This type of pluralism possessed the virtue of religious tolerance. If you have your god, I have mine, and there is no reason we cannot tolerate one another.

Absent, however, was the moral order imposed by monotheism. If nature consisted simply of random forces living in tension with one another, one could not assert any universal morality binding on all. In that respect, natural-law theory emanated from monotheistic rather than polytheistic sources.

Monotheism posited a world view where God was the sole creator of nature and imposed a moral order upon it. Humanity was enjoined to follow God's ways, to become co-creators in building society in accordance with God's moral order. To be sure, monotheism ran the risk of fomenting religious intolerance. The Maccabees, for example, compelled conversion to Judaism in areas that they conquered.

Judaism therefore waged cultural war with paganism. The Jewish message sanctified sexuality, protested its excesses, and glorified marriage and children as human ideals. The covenant of circumcision physically symbolized sexual restraint, which marked the Jews as a distinctive people.

To be sure, Jewish tradition was by no means idyllic about marriage and family. The biblical book of Genesis tells the story of families in tension and even breakdown. Yet Genesis concludes with family reconciliation. Its message is that families require a great deal of commitment and hard work in order to succeed.

Beyond Romantic Love

Marriage is far more than romantic love. It requires steadfastness in reconciling tensions and solving the conflicts that are present in virtually all families. Strong families, in turn, build healthy societies. Thus the story of Genesis precedes Exodus, meaning that building families is a prerequisite to transforming the Jews into a people.

These messages go against the grain in an America beset by high rates of divorce, illegitimacy and public displays of sexuality. Whether Dresner is correct in characterizing American culture as "pagan" depends upon how typical the currents are that he derides.

One is tempted, for example, to marginalize goddess worship as an extreme aberration from American religious culture. Conversely, however, Christian groups such as the Promise Keepers, a mass political group urging Christian men to adhere to the values of marital fidelity and fatherhood, may be far more typical of America today than is witchcraft or goddess worship.

Dresner's criticism of American Jewry, while overstated, raises disturbing questions. Do American Jews, in fact, permit our values to be determined by what Jews do rather than what Judaism teaches? Do religious leaders abstain from articulating normative statements for fear of offending individuals? Have we forgotten that religious messages were intended to challenge rather than affirm existing behavior patterns? In this context, Emil Fackenheim's definition of Judaism is especially apt—a permanent protest against idolatry and pagan culture.

What Dresner overstates is that Jews themselves have actually become pagan rather than fearing to protest paganism. The essential weakness in the Jewish family today is intermarriage rather than illegitimacy. Jews intermarry today not because they are "pagan" but because they are insufficiently committed to Judaism.

Although Dresner is undoubtedly correct to be concerned about goddess worship—a truly pagan phenomenon—far more Jews are affected by intermarriage, a theme that receives, at most, passing attention in his book. And the problem of intermarriage reflects much more the success story of Jews becoming desirable in-laws and a loss of Judaic distinctiveness than an ideological commitment to marrying out of the faith.

Intermarriage does threaten the Jewish future, but not in the ways that Dresner suggests. Intermarriage places Jews at risk of losing the content of their Judaism, rather than of substituting it with pagan culture.

Harsh in his Critique

Moreover, Dresner is perhaps overly harsh in dismissing the organized Jewish community as insensitive to Jewish teachings and values. The American Jewish Committee, for example, established in 1980 its William Petschek National Jewish Family Center to identify family as a bridge issue uniting liberals' desire for greater governmental activism with conservatives' emphases upon values and religious teaching.

May we then answer Dresner's query: "Can families survive in pagan America?"

Clearly, Judaism possesses a powerful message of building family and exercising sexual restraint, and serves as a corrective to the excessive individualism that characterizes so much of contemporary America.

America represents the land of individual opportunity. It has worked marvelously for Jews, in that no country in Diaspora Jewish history has so welcomed Jewish involvement. Yet that unbridled individualism—what Christopher Lasch has designated "the culture of narcissism"—has also nurtured a society in which individuals increasingly proclaim their rights and the pursuit of self-gratification without acknowledging their responsibility to others.

The Jewish ideal of family, in contrast, teaches the value of self-fulfillment, reflected in the emphasis upon sexuality and romantic love in marriage coupled with commitment to and responsibility for others. Indeed, family is the setting that nurtures precisely the values of individual sacrifice and commitment to others.

Secondly, the rabbis of the Talmud define heroism not as the heroism of the battlefield but of self-restraint. The rabbis commented, "Who is a hero—one who conquers his passions."

Sexual restraint rather than prowess is to be commended. No, this is not the message of Starhawk, who preaches that "all acts of love and pleasure are rituals of the goddess." But Jewry has an obligation, as Dresner concludes, not simply to embrace modernity but to critique modern culture as well.

Lastly, we must learn to distinguish between respect for personal choice and articulation of communal norms. In a free society, we respect the right of the individual to choose how to lead his or her own personal life. We oppose public institutions entering the bedroom to mandate particular forms of behavior. Yet this respect for individuals must be coupled with strong statements of ideal family forms and models that society values.

Toleration must not be confused with endorsement. What is permitted is not identical to what is encouraged; recognizing what exists is not the same as stating what ought to be. In an American culture of self-fulfillment, there could be few better definitions of the Jewish value of *tikkun olam* than repairing the idea of family.

INTERMARRIAGE, JEWISH CONTINUITY, AND OUTREACH

Perhaps no issue has proven as divisive in Jewish communal life today as how to respond to the growing reality of mixed marriage. Three strategies are currently in play—prevention, conversion, and outreach. In practice, to be sure, it often proves difficult to maintain any one of these particular policy thrusts without doing violence to the other two. More specifically, well-intentioned policies of outreach to mixed marrieds may, in fact, encourage a communal climate of neutrality toward mixed marriage as a phenomenon. Conversely, the desire to encourage Jews to marry Jews, whether by birth or by conversion to Judaism, may in turn inhibit effective outreach efforts to mixed marrieds for whom conversion is not an immediate possibility. The essays in this section reflect all of these tensions and also embody the leadership position the American Jewish Committee has occupied for almost 30 years in seeking to guide the Jewish community on how to respond to what is probably its single most vexing and divisive issue.

Changing Perceptions of Intermarriage

Addressing a 1989 conference of the Union of American Hebrew Congregations (UAHC), Rabbi Alexander Schindler again urged the Reform movement to proselytize among the "unchurched." Schindler's speech was the keynote address to a conference convened to assess the first 10 years of the UAHC's Commission on Reform Jewish Outreach. The conference itself symbolized the centrality of outreach, particularly among intermarried couples, to the future of the Reform movement and the many changes that have taken place in Jewish communal attitudes about outreach over the past decade.

One can hardly argue with the ideological bases of outreach activity designed to secure conversion to Judaism. As Peter Berger (1979) noted over 10 years ago, a Judaism that is self-assured about its own treasures and truths ought be willing to share them with others. Indeed, the very pluralism of American society that Jews have so valued and advocated legitimates a variety of choices of religious identity or of none. Finally, such outreach compels Jews to re-examine their own faith and beliefs and ask which aspects of their tradition speak with salience for contemporary Jews.

Moreover, Rabbi Schindler was correct in identifying Judaism historically as a missionary faith. There was considerable Jewish proselytization in ancient times; some historians have estimated that Jews comprised a full 10% of the population of the Roman Empire. To be sure, Jews suffered heavily from proselytizing, for conversion to Judaism constituted a radical action necessitating the breaking of ties to the Gentile family. Rome itself expelled her Jewish citizens in 19 C.E. for excessive missionary activity (Leon, 1960). Limitations upon Jewish missionary activity were imposed both before and after Rome accepted

Reprinted from *Journal of Jewish Communal Service,* Winter/Spring 1990 (Kendall Park, NJ, 1990).

Christianity as its state religion. These restrictions upon proselytization became so great that conversions to Judaism virtually ceased by the thirteenth century. As a result, modern Jewish thinkers often defended their Judaism precisely in the terms that Jews do not seek others to join their faith. Responding to Johann Caspar Lavater's challenge that he convert to Christianity, Moses Mendelssohn replied that proselytizing was "completely alien to Judaism." Since "the righteous of all faiths can surely be saved," no motive existed for Jewish proselytizing. Schindler, however, stood on firm historical and rabbinic grounds in advocating a return to missionary outreach.

More tellingly, strong pragmatic grounds existed for an outreach movement. By the 1970s large numbers of Jews had opted for inter-marriage with Gentiles. Outreach to the "unchurched" spouses could well result in conversion to Judaism and the formation of a Jewish home. Conversion thus seemed the answer to intermarriage, and per-haps Jews themselves had to adjust their reluctance to seek converts—a reluctance that, in any case, was unique to the modern Jewish experi-ence and had little basis in Jewish tradition.

Against this background, the Reform movement in 1979 identified outreach to intermarried couples as a core component of its future. To be sure, the movement remained ideologically opposed to intermar-riage. There was special condemnation for the apparently growing practice of raising children in two faiths, resulting in the blurring of two distinct religious traditions and the transmission of neither. During the past decade, vigorous efforts, however, have been made to translate Jewish teachings and experiences for intermarried couples, to draw them closer to the Jewish community, and work for the conversion of the non-Jewish spouse. Even when no conversion results, great ener-gies have been expended so as not to lose the Jewish dimension within the home.

Clearly, Rabbi Schindler and the Commission on Outreach have greatly affected Jewish communal perceptions of intermarriage and conversion. Not only has the Reform movement maintained an effec-tive outreach program for the past 10 years, but considerable outreach has also taken place under the auspices of Orthodox, Conservative, and Reconstructionist Judaism. In many cases, this has resulted in the conversion to Judaism of the non-Jewish spouse. Jewish communal leaders today generally recognize the importance of outreach in attempting to grapple with the increase in the incidence of intermarriage.

Map of Intermarriage

What then constitutes the map of intermarriage in America? Until the 1960s American Jews intermarried at rates that were surprisingly low by historical standards. Virtually every society in which Jews had valued integration into the surrounding culture had witnessed a high degree of intermarriage. Thus, in Berlin in the 1920s one of every five Jews was marrying someone not born of the Jewish faith. By 1933 that rate had increased to 44% for all of German Jewry.[1]

In contrast, for reasons that still remain unexplained, intermarriage rates remained lower than 10% until the 1960s in the United States. Thus, Nathan Glazer and Daniel Patrick Moynihan described the Jews as "the most endogamous of peoples" in their 1963 landmark study, *Beyond the Melting Pot.* Yet a sea change in these percentages occurred virtually overnight. In the mid-1960s Marshall Sklare (1964) noted an increase in individual intermarriage rates to 17%, and by the time of the National Jewish Population Study (Massarik & Chenkin, 1973) in the early 1970s, that rate had nearly doubled.

Since 1973 great variations in rates of intermarriage have occurred regionally. New York City, with its large numbers of Jews, which increases the pool of potential marriage mates, and its high percentage of Orthodox Jews, who rarely intermarry, enjoys a low intermarriage rate of 11% (number of mixed marriages subtracting for conversion). Conversely, Denver has one of the highest current intermarriage rates in the country at over 60%. Generally, the western Jewish communities report a higher degree of acculturation, a lower rate of affiliation, and therefore large numbers of intermarrying couples. Los Angeles, for instance, with its half-million Jews, possesses an astonishingly low affiliation rate of 20% and a high rate of intermarriage of 39%.

As noted earlier, the primary vehicle for containing the effects of intermarriage in terms of Jewish identity and continuity has been the conversion of the non-Jewish spouse. Once conversion has occurred, the marriage may no longer be termed an "intermarriage," for the home becomes Jewish (with all of the ambivalence concerning Jewishness that plagues endogamous Jewish marriages). Thus, of 600,000 marriages in America today in which one partner was not born a Jew, approximately one-fifth have resulted in conversion to Judaism; 85% of these marriages are of Gentile women married to Jewish men (Mayer, 1985). There have been surprisingly few conversions to Christianity, a testimony to the improved status of Jews in American society generally. The current norm, however, is for no conversion to occur, leaving the children in a vague no-man's land occupying the interstices between watered-down versions of Judaism and Christianity. The long-term consequences for Jewish continuity may well be devastating. A recent Philadelphia study of three-generational families found that no grandchildren of intermarriage absent conversion continued to identify as Jews (Schmelz & Della Pergola, 1989).

Each year approximately 11,000 to 12,000 Jews-by-Choice enter the Jewish community. The Reform movement converts about 8,000 per year, the Conservative movement about 3,000 to 4,000, and the Orthodox several hundred. The absence of any uniform conversion procedure acceptable to all of the religious movements heralds an impending crisis in the definition of "Who Is a Jew" inasmuch as thousands of individuals are converting to Judaism annually in good faith only to discover that their conversions are by no means universally recognized. The recent controversy in Israel over the "Who Is A Jew" amendment in many ways symbolizes the continuing disagreements in the United States over definitions of Jewish identity.

In point of fact, the Jewish community as a whole has been enriched by new converts. These individuals often strengthen the Jewish identity of the home and stimulate the Jewish members of the family to intensify their ties to Jewish community and tradition. Moreover, the would-be Jew-by-Choice is most likely to convert to Judaism when the Jewish spouse and family members value their Jewishness. In other words, the key factors stimulating conversion to Judaism are the desire to gain acceptance by the Jewish family and build a united family. Once accepting conversion, the new Jews are as likely, if not more likely, than the born Jews to practice specific forms of Jewish rituals and traditions.

Most intermarriages, however, do not result in the conversion of the non-Jewish spouse. Evidence indicates that, as intermarriages become more acceptable socially, conversion to Jewish may be declining. Those who identify conversion as the primary response to intermarriage may have to acknowledge in the very near future that they are fighting an uphill struggle.

Popular Attitudes:
Increasing Acceptance

As the overall map of intermarriage in America has been changing, so have popular attitudes shifted to greater acceptance of intermarriage. Today, 87% of Americans approve of interfaith relationships marriages between Jews and Gentiles; in contrast, 20 years ago only 60% of Americans approved of such marriages. In one sense, Jews should draw comfort from polling data that point to the high level of respect accorded Judaism. Marriage to a Jew connotes a positive statement in the mind of most Americans, Woody Allen's "Annie Hall" to the contrary. The danger, however, that intermarriage may mean dissolution of Jewish communal ties haunts those concerned with future Jewish survival.

Moreover, popular literature and the media have helped legitimize intermarriage as a viable option. A virtual cottage industry of guidebooks for intermarried couples has arisen, each complete with helpful hints for making interfaith marriage work and with stories of successful couples building happy and healthy homes. Such books as *The Intermarriage Handbook* (Petsonk and Remsen, William Morrow Co.), *Raising Your Jewish/Christian Child* (Lee Gruzen, Dodd, Mead and Co.), *But How Will You Raise the Children* (Steven Carr Reuben, Pocket Books), *Happily Intermarried* (a unique interreligious composition of Rabbi Roy A. Rosenberg, Father Peter Meehan, and Rev. John Wade Payne, MacMillan), *Mixed Blessings* (Paul and Rachel Cowan, Doubleday), and *Intermarriage* (Susan Weidman Schneider, The Free Press) all point to the growing market for such marriage guidebooks and to the increased viability and acceptance of intermarriage as a phenomenon. To be sure, these guidebooks vary considerably in approach and content. Yet, the availability of these handbooks on a mass-market basis indicates how intermarriage has evolved from a marginal to a mainstream phenomenon in American society.

Television too has changed greatly in its portrayal of interfaith marriage. In the early 1970s a popular situation comedy, *Bridget Loves Bernie,* drew considerable protest for its portrayal of a successful intermarriage. Today, in contrast, the networks present several attractive role models of a successful intermarriage. In *L.A. Law,* Markowitz and Kelsey are two upwardly mobile, intelligent, and liberal-minded exemplars of intermarriage. Markowitz' Jewishness comes to the fore when he is confronted by his mother-in-law's social anti-Semitism and the couple's inability to agree about how to raise their child.

The program receiving the most attention for its portrait of intermarriage has been the critically acclaimed series, *thirtysomething.* To date, the Steadman couple—Gentile wife and Jewish husband—has reached no decision on how to raise their child, a theme that symbolizes the struggles and even the failures of the "Yuppie" generation. Two years ago the Steadman family first confronted the December dilemma—Chanukah or Christmas, menorah or tree, or perhaps both? In the end, the spirit of reconciliation pervading the holiday season enables the couple to resolve their problem by spontaneously celebrating both holidays.

One year later *thirtysomething* returned to the theme of intermarriage in a far more sophisticated fashion. Approaching the anniversary of his father's death, Michael Steadman begins to question the meaning of his Jewishness and the viability of his intermarriage. Learning that his wife is pregnant with a second child, he wonders about the future religious upbringing of his children. Steadman returns to the synagogue of his youth and discovers that his people are "doing fine" a remarkable statement on television to the effect of the vitality of Jewish life in America. The program concludes with Steadman reciting the Kaddish for his father, suggesting that he continues to struggle in two worlds—a strong and healthy marriage to a Gentile and an internal quest to link himself with Judaism. Significantly, this episode was showcased at a recent national conference of Jewish educators as a model pedagogic tool, indicating the degree to which even Jewish educators have become accepting of intermarriage as a phenomenon.

For these programs, intermarriage has been at most an occasional theme. Generally, it has been peripheral to the primary interests of the characters, surfacing only for particular programs, such as the December dilemma of Christmas or Chanukah. This television season, however, featured one program that highlighted an interfaith relationship as its primary theme—*Chicken Soup,* starring Jackie Mason and Lynn Redgrave. The show was canceled in midseason.

The importance of tradition was central to the program's theme. Its main characters, Jackie and Maddy, were quite proud of their respective Jewish and Catholic heritages. That reverence for tradition may explain the couple's reluctance to pronounce marital vows.

However, both articulated the overriding importance of love and trust in a relationship over allegiances to ethnicity and faith. Religious differences in their view become obsolete when a couple shares common social values. In fact, their common commitment to helping the underprivileged seemed to bind the couple. Conversely, the opposition to intermarriage expressed by Mason's mother sounded like an anachronism roughly equivalent to the boorish anti-Semitism of Maddy's brother, Mike.

Intermarriages, in short, can be happy marriages even if they do present special problems. More tellingly, the taboo against portraying successful intermarriages on prime-time television has fallen, reflecting the growing legitimization of intermarriage by the viewing public.

Parallel to the growing acceptability of intermarriage within the general society has been its growing legitimization within the Jewish community. A Boston survey in the mid-1960s indicated that a quarter of the city's Jewish community would strongly oppose their children's intermarriage, and 44% indicated they would discourage it. By 1985 only 9% of Boston's Jews remained strongly opposed to intermarriage, whereas two-thirds indicated acceptance of intermarriage or neutrality toward it (Israel, 1987; Silberman, 1985).

In the past, Jews who opposed intermarriage usually did so for one of two reasons: religious conviction and a popular stereotype that interfaith marriages would inevitably fail. The 1950s Lakeville studies, for example, indicated strong opposition to intermarriage out of fear of marital discord (Sklare & Greenblum, 1967). Currently, the stronger the degree of ideological religious conviction, the lower the likelihood of intermarriage occurring. Orthodox Jews and graduates of Jewish day schools score especially highly in terms of ideological opposition to intermarriage and a strong desire for endogamous Jewish marriage. These, however, represent at most a tenth of American Jewry.

The strength of the second factor, a lingering stereotype that intermarriages are unlikely to be successful marriages, has been eroded in recent years. To be sure, a recent demographic study finds that intermarriages are still twice as likely to end in divorce as are endogamous marriages (Kosmin et al., 1989). Yet, the reality of successful intermarriages belies this generalization. Role models of happily intermarried couples communicate that tales of "it can't work" are mere vestiges of less tolerant eras. Added to this is the overall American perception that today's marriages are as likely to fail as to succeed. In such a context, success in marriage becomes the luck of the draw, and intermarriages are as likely to succeed or fail as are any other type of marriage.

Communal Attitudes: Outrage and Outreach

Attitudes of Jewish leadership have also changed as intermarriages have become both more widespread and acceptable. Jewish leaders initially responded with shock and dismay to the National Jewish Population Study findings suggesting that one of every three marriages involving Jews was an intermarriage (Massarik & Chenkin, 1973). Articles in Jewish and general periodicals pointed to intermarriage as the glaring weakness of Jewish communal life. Jewish organizations began holding conferences to assess the "intermarriage crisis" and determine whether communal policy might reduce the ever upward rates. There was general agreement that intermarriage threatened Jewish continuity, and each of the religious movements adopted resolutions firmly stating their opposition to the phenomenon. Gradually, this reaction of shock and dismay evolved into a more pragmatic, many would say more constructive, attitude of resistance and containment. In this view, intermarriage remained a threat to the Jewish future, but intermarrying couples remained potential members of the Jewish community, and all efforts should be directed to enlisting their affiliation. In effect, this attitude, best articulated in Rabbi Schindler's 1979 address announcing the formation of the Commission on Outreach, distinguished between respecting the personal choices of individuals to intermarry and opposing the

phenomenon of intermarriage generally as a threat to Jewish continuity.

This policy of "outrage and outreach" theoretically remains the official stance of Jewish leadership: reach out to intermarrieds, encouraged the conversion of the non-Jewish spouse, but articulate clearly the
support for Jewish in-marriage and opposition to interdating and out-
marriage. To be sure, these policies are not always consistent with one
another. Does the existence, for instance, of workshops for intermarried couples under the auspices of Jewish communal organizations in
and of itself signal communal acceptance and even endorsement of intermarriage? By and large, however, communal leadership has successfully defined outreach to intermarrieds as a necessary response to the
difficult problem of Jews living in an open and secular society in which
marriage to non-Jewish mates has become unsurprising. Moreover,
Jews marrying out are no longer communicating their rejection of Jewish heritage by doing so. They are signaling their acceptance of the
open society and the secular courtship process, not their rejection of
Judaism. Religion may well become a critical factor in the subsequent
development of these marriages, and outreach to these intermarried
couples is unquestionably the key to stimulating conversion and formation of Jewish homes, thereby stemming losses and attrition resulting
from intermarriage.

Yet, several signs point to the possibility of a communal redefinition
of intermarriage—as beneficial for Jews, rather than a danger to be
contained. Some sociologists have argued that intermarriage may well
produce a numerical gain for the Jewish community via conversion and
that Jewish identity, in any case, has been so diluted that intermarriage
is by no means aggravating the situation (Bayme, 1987; Hertzberg,
1989; Silberman, 1985). These sociologists intend to counteract the
alarmism and hysteria over the vanishing American Jew. Yet in underscoring that Jewish biological survival for the present seems assured,
the message has been blurred into one that states that intermarriage
may no longer threaten Jewish vitality.

Ideological issues related to intermarriage have also helped change
communal perceptions of the phenomenon. Few communal questions
in recent years have attracted as much attention as the controversial

1983 decision by the Central Conference of American Rabbis on patrilineal descent. The decision in effect affirmed long-standing Reform practice to accept as a Jew the child of either a Jewish father or a Jewish mother, provided that the parents expressed a commitment to Jewish continuity through engaging in specific acts of Jewish affirmation in the child's upbringing. Many have sought to explain the decision as one of principle that is irrelevant to the intermarriage phenomenon generally. Traditional rabbinic law had defined identity via the mother. In an age of gender equality, should not equal weight be given to a Jewish father? Moreover, Reform leaders pointed to the anomaly of children of Jewish fathers raised as Jews, yet not being recognized as such, whereas children of Jewish mothers who had never identified in any substantive or even symbolic way as Jews were automatically recognized as Jews under Jewish law. Traditionalist Reform rabbis, in fact, pointed to their refusal to officiate at marriages in which one partner was born of a Jewish mother but had never affirmed membership in the Jewish community.

Yet, in addition to questions of principle, the patrilineal descent decision must also be considered in the sociological and demographic context of American Reform Judaism. For one thing, the overwhelming majority of Reform rabbis had been practicing patrilineal descent since World War II by their de facto acceptance of children of Jewish fathers and non-Jewish mothers as Jewish. Moreover, Reform rabbis who oppose patrilineality in the name of communal unity had to face the harsh reality that the Orthodox rabbinate was unlikely to accept Reform conversions in any case. Finally, and most importantly, as the numbers of interfaith marriages increased, the numbers of children of Jewish fathers and non-Jewish mothers within Reform temples naturally increased as well.

However, objections to the patrilineal descent decision are considerable. First, its effects upon Jewish unity weigh heavily. For the last 2000 years the Jewish community has acted upon a single principle of matrilineal identity. Any child of a Jewish mother, no matter how involved or uninvolved in Jewish activity, claimed equal status as a Jew under Jewish law. Orthodox and Conservative Jews agree on the continuing validity of this principle. Thus, individuals who are told that they are Jews by Reform rabbis would find their Jewishness rejected, in the absence of formal conversion, by Orthodox and Conservative Judaism alike. To be sure, Orthodox rabbis generally rejected Reform conversions in any case. Yet, the decision for patrilineality, rather than for insistence upon the conversion of children of Jewish fathers, drove a wedge between Conservative and Reform Judaism, the two largest religious movements within contemporary American Judaism. Finally, as Reform Rabbi David Polish (1989) has recently noted, the insistence that the Jewishness of children of either Jewish mothers or Jewish fathers depends upon certain Jewish "affirmations" threatens to divide the Reform movement itself over differing criteria of what such affirmations might be.

Equally serious are the implications for Israel-Diaspora relations. Reform leaders, like their Conservative and even many Orthodox colleagues, oppose proposed changes in the Law of Return that would have the effect of denying Jewish status to those who convert to Judaism under non-Orthodox auspices. They argue that the State of Israel, through legislative action, ought not drive wedges between Israeli and Diaspora Jews by declaring that converts to Judaism in the Diaspora are less than full Jews. This argument, however, collapses in the face of the patrilineal descent decision. The Reform movement itself has driven such a wedge by declaring offspring of Jewish fathers as Jewish. Should Israel now be compelled to amend the Law of Return in a more liberal direction, extending the definition of who is a Jew to children of Jewish fathers, recognized as Jews by the Reform and Reconstructionist movements in America, yet whose Jewishness is denied by more traditionalist sectors of Jewry? Significantly, the Reform movement in Israel itself recognized the implications of the decision for their claims to recognition within Israel and vociferously, yet vainly, opposed the patrilineal descent resolution.

Finally, we must weigh the consequences of the patrilineal descent decision on conversion to Judaism in America. In theory, patrilineality may obstruct rather than encourage conversion. Intermarried couples are now offered the consolation that even without the conversion of the Gentile mother the offspring of such marriages are still Jews. They may well be entitled to ask why convert at all and submit to a rigorous program of Jewish study if the children are already Jews. Although little statistical evidence exists to date to corroborate this claim, historically one motivation to conversion has been to enable children to be raised within the Jewish faith—a motivation possibly undermined by the patrilineal descent decision.

In the final analysis, the patrilineal descent decision, motivated by legitimate concerns for expanding Jewish numbers and the principle of gender equality, may not be taken out of the context of the outreach movement and the intermarriage phenomenon. It affirms the growing reality of intermarriage and says to intermarried couples that their identifying children are still presumed to be Jewish, even without conversion. As laudable as such a statement may appear, not only does it undermine Jewish unity but it also goes beyond a pragmatic accommodation to intermarriage toward ideological legitimization.

What are the alternatives? Recently, several "centrist" Orthodox leaders have been urging the universal conversion of the children of non-Jewish mothers. Legal requirements for the conversion of minors are said to be less austere than those imposed upon adults and might be accepted by all sectors of Jewry without undue hardship. Working toward such a unified conversion procedure would also carry with it the two side benefits of enhancing intermovement relations and encouraging those who truly wish to raise their children as Jews to signal their desires through a meaningful conversion procedure. In the case of adult children of Jewish fathers committed to leading a Jewish life, facilitating reconversion may well be desirable in any case to ensure marriageability with Conservative and Orthodox Jews.

Even more divisive than patrilineality has been the issue of rabbinic officiation at interfaith marriages. Orthodox and Conservative rabbis are universally opposed to officiation and will suffer sanctions should they even attend such weddings. Reconstructionist rabbis have worked out guidelines permitting rabbinic participation in civil ceremonies. No issue has so divided Reform rabbinic leadership than the question of officiation, whether singly or in cooperation with Gentile clergy. About half of Reform rabbis do officiate at mixed marriages under certain conditions, most usually the promise to raise children as Jews. The official stance of the Central Conference of American Rabbis (CCAR), however, opposes officiation, but leaves the final decision to the individual discretion of the particular rabbi. The Joint Placement Committee of UAHC, CCAR, and the Hebrew Union College has sought to support the CCAR position by opposing publicly the decisions of Reform congregations to refuse to employ rabbis who will not officiate at mixed marriages.

Proponents of rabbinic officiation claim it is the natural extension of outreach, opening doors of entry to intermarried couples. Opponents claim that rabbinic officiation accomplishes little except to send normative signals of rabbinical acceptance and even blessing of interfaith marriages.

What little research that exists tends to argue against rabbinic officiation. Studies sponsored by the American Jewish Committee and executed by Egon Mayer (1989) indicate that the rabbinic refusal to officiate causes some bad feeling and resentment, but does not discourage communal involvement. Conversely, little evidence indicates that rabbinic officiation does in fact lead to greater communal involvement, much less conversion. Seen in this light, ideological and theoretical reasons underlying this issue would appear as more weighty and substantive than the pragmatic questions of outreach effectiveness.

To be sure, some rabbis justify officiation as the morally desirable alternative. Thus, Rabbi Roy Rosenberg cites the universalist concern with humanity as grounds for officiation. Common brotherhood with Gentiles should naturally result in marital unions between Jews and Gentiles, and rabbis ought to bless such unions and even co-officiate with Christian clergy. This position ironically echoes Napoleon's erstwhile request—denied by the Paris Sanhedrin—that the French rabbinate encourage one in every three unions to be an interfaith marriage!

Rosenberg's position reflects those who no longer fear interfaith marriages. It is doubtful whether he and like-minded colleagues could subscribe to the official position of the Reform movement, which continues to oppose intermarriage. Yet, rabbis who refuse to officiate generally respect the right of colleagues to do so and will often refer couples to them out of consideration for the couples themselves and their parents. Thus, not only has the number of Reform rabbis willing to officiate increased significantly but also a position supportive of officiation, which once was considered virtually heretical, has become a mainstream, albeit minority, position within the Reform movement. The net effect, of course, becomes further communal legitimation of intermarriage.

Further evidence indicates that Jewish leadership attitudes have become more accepting of intermarriage. A recent study of Reform Jewish leadership indicated that 80% of converts or those married to converts expressed approval of their children marrying out without conversion. More startlingly, 50% of this group indicated they would not mind their children converting to Christianity (Winer et al., 1987)! In other words, as intermarriage becomes more acceptable within Jewish leadership circles, increasingly Jewish leaders no longer perceive it as a stigma. Whether the removal of the stigma attached to intermarriage in fact increases intermarriage is an unprovable supposition, but, over the long term, it certainly helps legitimate intermarriage as an option for American Jews.

Similarly, among the current spate of handbooks to intermarriage are those that extol the virtues of raising children in two faiths. Embracing both faiths may, of course, be understood as an extension of American pluralism and a way to deepen experience and understanding. Thus, oblivious to the theological contradictions between Judaism and Christianity, Lee Gruzen in *Raising Your Jewish/Christian Child* argues that the dual-faith option is the most compelling route for today's intermarried parents. Yet, if Gruzen's book is the work of a solitary journalist, more weighty are the statements of rabbinic leaders who similarly support a two-faith scenario. Thus, Rabbi Steven Reuben in *But How Will You Raise the Children* admits that his earlier opposition to dual-faith child rearing had been misplaced. Far worse, for him, is raising children in no faith at all. Although Rabbi Roy Rosenberg joins with Protestant and Catholic colleagues in *Happily Intermarried* in opposing two faiths for children as theologically inconsistent and confusing to children, he nevertheless concludes that two faiths can happily co-exist within one home. He praises intermarriage as a model human relations phenomenon that will enable Jew and Christian to lovingly accept one another.

In fairness, not all of the recent guides to intermarriage extol the phenomenon generally or endorse the two-faith solution specifically. Paul and Rachel Cowan, for example, clearly prefer conversion to Judaism and criticize the two-faith solution as all but impossible. Similarly, Judy Petsonk and Jim Remsen support a single faith within the home with occasional introduction of cultural and ethnic traditions of the other heritage in the child's upbringing. Susan Weidman Schneider also urges that children receive a unified religious identity, arguing that two faiths can work only if both parents are equally committed to their respective religion.

An Appropriate Communal Response to Intermarriage

Some sociologists recently have claimed that the increase in intermarriage is by no means a watershed event in American Jewish history. Calvin Goldscheider (1986), for example, dismisses intermarriage as an insignificant threat for "the data indicate strong Jewish communal and identification ties for the intermarried." Goldscheider bases his argument on structural factors—friendship ties, neighborhoods, and religious affiliation—rather than on ideological perspectives on intermarriage and Jewish continuity. Recent intermarrieds, in any event, look like most other Jews. He therefore concludes that the fuss over intermarriage, in effect, is unwarranted. Steven M. Cohen (1989), in contrast, acknowledges that, the greater the number of intermarriages, the greater the number of offspring who are less committed to Jewish life. For Cohen, intermarriage poses the danger of decreased involvement in the Jewish community even if windows of opportunity exist for outreach to intermarrieds. In other words, intermarriage poses the specter of serious losses for Jewish life, although the phenomenon is by no means an unmitigated disaster. In pronounced contrast, Israeli demographers Uziel O. Schmelz and Sergio Della Pergola (1989) emphasize the declining rate of conversion and the dilution of Jewish identity over the long term. Thus, whether intermarriage matters sociologically in terms of Jewish survival is currently arguable, although majority opinion tends to see more losses in intermarriage than gains.

Yet, over and above the sociological and demographic effects of intermarriage, the phenomenon matters in how Jews interpret it—the very ideological issues that some of the sociologists dismiss as irrelevant to the Jewish future. For what has occurred has been a shift in the perceptions and attitudes of American Jews toward the increased acceptability of intermarriage. The challenges to Jewish leadership are considerable. First, Jewish leaders must acknowledge intermarriage for what it is—a threat to future Jewish unity, identity, and continuity. Efforts to reinterpret intermarriage as a positive step in terms of human relations and accommodation to American modernity understate the degree of assimilation that intermarriage signifies and lay the groundwork for conflict in terms of future Jewish identity. It must be recognized that opposition to intermarriage in some ways runs counter to Jewish perceptions of American values and civilization as fully consonant with and nurturing of Jewish values. American culture extols the ideals of romantic love and equality for all of humanity. Yet, Jews cannot articulate continued opposition to intermarriage—something Jewish leaders would still prefer to at least pay lip service to—without at the same time acknowledging that Jewish values and American ideals are at times in conflict. Intermarriage proves that America has worked in terms of the acceptance of Jews. The question for leadership now becomes whether Jews can maintain their unique identity in a friendly America.

Second, Jewish leaders must now confront conversion as the antidote and perhaps the sole bright spot on the map of intermarriage in America. This means that Jews must abandon their long-held opposition to proselytization and their ambivalence about the presence of converts in their midst. Programs of outreach to would-be Jews-by-Choice, such as those pioneered by the Reform movement, should receive full communal encouragement. New outreach initiatives are necessary, particularly those that harness the barely tapped potential of the electronic media. Yet, in the absence of a uniform conversion procedure acceptable to each of the religious movements within contemporary Judaism, Jews face the specter of thousands of individuals entering the Jewish people in good faith each year only to find their conversion delegitimized by other sectors of the community.

In the absence of conversion, accurate information must be disseminated about the implications of patrilineal descent and raising children in two faiths. Communal leaders must clearly inform individuals that the identity of patrilineal Jews as Jewish is rejected by Orthodox and Conservative Judaism. Whether the patrilineal descent decision itself discourages conversion and legitimates intermarriage is a painful issue that must be studied honestly. Communal leaders must also inform intermarried couples that no denomination of Judaism has a category of being both Jewish and Christian. Individuals who choose to raise their children in two faiths must recognize the theoretical absurdity they are communicating, to say nothing of the psychological identity problems they are creating for their children.

Finally, the challenge of preserving Jewish unity warrants careful attention to the divisive issues of conversion, patrilineality, and rabbinic officiation at interfaith weddings. Differing standards and procedures operative within the respective movements threaten to drive wedges between Israel and Diaspora Judaism and sow divisions among Jews of different movements and persuasions. At a time of considerable opposition and dangers from without the Jewish community, the Jewish community can ill afford the disunity that the climate surrounding intermarriage breeds from within.

Notes

1. Discussion about intermarriage rates is often blurred by confusion between individual rates and couples rates and between cumulative rates and current rates. Individual rates refer to the percentage of Jews who marry out. Thus, if three of every ten Jews marry out, you have an intermarriage rate of 30%. Couples rates refer to the percentage of marriages involving Jews that are intermarriages. Thus, of the same ten Jews, the seven who married endogamously would form 3.5 marriages, whereas the three who intermarried will form 3 marriages. Thus, the couples rate, in this case, is 45%. Generally, the couples rates will be half again as large as the intermarriage rate. Because these rates are frequently confused, statements about rates of intermarriage often sound artificially high.

Similarly, cumulative rates of intermarriage refer to all marriages. Current rates refer to marriages currently taking place. The current rate, for obvious reasons, tends to be much higher than the cumulative rate. In general, unless noted otherwise, this article uses individual and current rates of intermarriage, rather than couple and cumulative rates.

Further confusion results from statistics and percentages that do not distinguish between intermarriages in which no conversion to Judaism occurs and intermarriage in which the non-Jewish spouse has chosen to join the Jewish people. Technically, intermarriages in which conversion occurs are no longer intermarriages. Moreover, conversion often occurs after marriage, particularly when children are involved. Therefore, the term "intermarriage" should properly be restricted to marriage absent conversions to Judaism.

References

Bayme, Steven (1987). "Crisis in American Jewry." *Contemporary Jewry, 8,* 127.

Berger, Peter. (1979, May). "Converting the Gentiles?" *Commentary,* pp. 35–39.

Cohen, Steven M. (1989, December). *Alternative Families in the Jewish Community: Singles, Single Parents, Childless Couples, and Mixed-marrieds.* New York: American Jewish Committee, p. 8.

Cohen, Steven M. (1989). "The Quality of American Jewish Life: Better or Worse?" In Steven Bayme (Ed.), *Facing the Future: Essays on Contemporary Jewish Life.* New York: KTAV Publishing Company.

Goldscheider, Calvin. (1986). *Jewish Continuity and Change.* Bloomington, IN: University of Indiana Press.

Hertzberg, Arthur. (1989). *The Jews in America: Four Centuries of an Uneasy Encounter.* New York: Simon & Schuster, pp. 362–384.

Israel, Sherry. (1987). *Boston's Jewish Community: The 1983 CJP Demographic Study.* Boston: Combined Jewish Philanthropies, p. 60.

Kosmin, Barry, Lerer, Nava, & Mayer, Egon. (1989). *Intermarriage, Divorce, and Remarriage among American Jews, 1982–87.* Family Research Series #1. New York: North American Jewish Data Bank.

Leon, Harry. (1960). *The Jews of Ancient Rome.* Philadelphia: Jewish Publication Society, pp. 17–19, 33–36, and 250–252.

Massarik, Fred, & Chenkin, Alvin. (1973). "U.S. National Jewish Population Study: A first report." *American Jewish Year Book, 74,* 292.

Mayer, Egon. (1985). *Love and Tradition: Marriage between Jews and Christians.* New York: Plenum Publishing Company.

Mayer, Egon. (1989). *Intermarriage and Rabbinic Officiation.* New York: American Jewish Committee.

Polish, David. (1989). "A Dissent on Patrilineal Descent." In Ronald Kronish, ed., *Toward the Twenty-first Century: Judaism and the Jewish People in Israel and America.* New York: KTAV Publishing Company, 1989.

Schmelz, Uziel O., & Della Pergola, Sergio. (1989). "Basic Trends in American Jewish Demography." In Steven Bayme, ed., *Facing the Future: Essays on Contemporary Jewish Life.* New York: KTAV Publishing Company.

Silberman, Charles. (1985). *A Certain People: American Jews and Their Lives Today.* New York: Summit Books.

Sklare, Marshall. (1965, April). "Intermarriage and the Jewish Future." *Commentary, 37* (4), 46–52.

Sklare, Marshall. (1970, March). "Intermarriage and Jewish Survival." *Commentary, 43* (4), 51–58.

Sklare, Marshall, & Greenblum, Joseph. (1967). *Jewish Identity on the Suburban Frontier.* New York: Basic Books.

Winer, Mark, Seltzer, Sanford, & Schrager, Steven J. (1987). *Leaders of Reform Judaism.* New York: Union of American Hebrew Congregations.

Opportunities for Jewish Renewal

Findings of the Council of Jewish Federations' survey of American Jews raise serious concerns about the future vitality of the Jewish community.

Since 1985 virtually as many Jews have married out as have married other Jews. Only 5 percent of these intermarriages have resulted in the conversion to Judaism of the non-Jewish spouse. Perhaps most ominously, only 28 percent of children in mixed households—except those who have converted to Judaism—are being raised as Jews. Forty-one percent are growing up in a faith other than Judaism, and 31 percent are being raised in no religion.

These statistics are by no means absolute. The percentage of conversions may rise as these marriages endure, children begin to grow up, and the parents begin to think about what will comprise the home's religious identity.

Similarly, the 50 percent rate of intermarried individuals includes children of mixed marriages who are born Jewish, but who are now marrying out at an extremely high rate.

In contrast, children of two Jewish parents in all probability will continue to express a clear preference for marrying other Jews.

Nevertheless, the trend is clear: Intermarriage is increasing, posing serious risks to Jewish continuity. Intermarriage also endangers Jewish unity, for the various Jewish religious movements have contrasting definitions of who is a Jew and lack a uniform conversion procedure acceptable to all.

What can be done?

First, there must be candor. The news regarding intermarriage is by no means comforting, but it must be confronted realistically and honestly. Jewish communal planning will not benefit from utopian predictions of net gains to Jewry via intermarriage, when there is a real question whether we will preserve at all the Jewish identity of the home—especially in the second and third generations.

Reprinted from *The Jerusalem Post* (Jerusalem, Israel, July 2, 1991).

A sobering statistic emerges in Philadelphia: Among the sample studied in its 1984 demographic survey, not a single grandchild of intermarried parents—except those who converted to Judaism—identified as a Jew. This trend will hardly be broken if three quarters of intermarried couples today say that they are not raising their children as Jews.

Moreover, Jews must be clear about their marital preferences. We lack a "language of endogamy" enabling Jewish parents to explain to their children why they should seek Jewish mates. We cannot and should not permit the data documenting the increase in intermarriage to determine Jewish norms and values, which have always articulated an ideology of in-marriage.

By the same token, Jewish teachings mandate a single standard for those born Jewish and those who join the Jewish faith and people. Conversion to Judaism should therefore be treasured as a gain to the Jewish people, and we must overcome any lingering ambivalence or resentment against "new Jews" in our midst. For these reasons, a uniform conversion procedure among the various Jewish religious movements is necessary to avert further tragedies.

We must be realistic, however, and acknowledge that most mixed marriages will not result in conversion to Judaism.

Here, then, is the important role for outreach: Welcome mixed couples, engage them in candid dialogue, and share with them the beauties of the Jewish heritage—in the hope of securing the Jewish identity of their homes.

These individuals, to be sure, cannot, in themselves, guarantee the Jewish future. Safeguarding Jewish continuity will require a serious commitment to the content of Jewish identity—ideological conviction that Jewish heritage and experience merit preservation and transmission to the next generation.

Strengthening the core commitments of American Jews requires more intensive Jewish education, informal Jewish socialization experiences, and extended study trips to Israel.

In an era of limited resources, it will be difficult to set priorities for funding and to target the people who indicate the most promise for leading a Jewish life and providing for a vital and vibrant Jewish future. Yet serious initiatives to strengthen Jewish continuity will require precisely such painful choices and decision-making.

Finally, the population data should be assessed in relation to the qualitative strengths of American Jewish life generally. Sociological or ideological pronouncements of the inevitable demise of American Jewry are misleading. Jews, in fact, are prospering in American society.

Greater opportunities for intensive Jewish renewal exist in virtually all Jewish communities in America, and American Jewish leaders increasingly are being sensitized to the significance of Jewish education and Judaic literacy. Jews feel few, if any, inhibitions about articulating Jewish communal and political interests within American elite institutions and centers of power.

In short, the public quality and structure of Jewish life appear sound; the challenge for the twenty-first century is preserving Jewish identity in the privacy of the Jewish home.

Communal Policy and Jewish Continuity: Future Guidelines and Directions

Formulation of demographic policy can be even more hazardous than interpreting demographic data, for policy requires utilization of communal resources to realize goals that may, in fact, not be attained, or attainable. Nevertheless, we cannot satisfy ourselves with diagnostic statements of what is—as important as those statements are, in terms of clarifying the existing situation. We must move towards prescriptive solutions to current Jewish demographic dilemmas.

More significantly, since the release of the National Jewish Population Survey, there has been a sense of urgency and a compelling need for action among Jewish communal leaders. In particular, much of the debate has focused around intermarriage and the challenges it poses to future Jewish continuity, although, to be sure, much of the data contained within the population studies have implications that range far beyond the question of intermarriage and the Jewish future. In particular, policy advocates concerning intermarriage generally divide between those who advocate strategies of intermarriage prevention and those who advocate strategies of outreach to mixed-married couples.

There is both conflict as well as consonance between these two camps. Advocates of outreach agree that it would be far better for Jews to marry other Jews. Advocates of prevention similarly agree that writing off intermarried couples would be most harmful in terms of the Jewish communal future. Where they disagree is on the questions of *priority* and emphasis and on the larger cultural question of what message to send to the Jewish community.

To some extent this is a conflict between traditionalists and liberals. Traditionalists argue that a strategy of outreach alone would amount to declaring intermarriage to be perfectly normative and acceptable for American Jews. Dropping a language of constraint and endogamy would, in the long run, increase the intermarriage rate even more and

From an address to the Association for Demographic Policy of the Jewish People, Jewish Agency for Israel, Van Leer Institute, Jerusalem, Israel, February 11, 1992.

thereby effectively consign American Jewry to oblivion—given the tiny percentage of Jews in American society. Liberals frequently counter that prevention strategies have been futile, continued emphasis on prevention may make it impossible to reach out to intermarried couples, and therefore the emphasis and focus should underscore outreach. Moreover, to some extent the debate is a function of communal context and institutional base. Those who feel most directly the presence of intermarrieds will naturally incline towards greater outreach. Those who are surrounded by singles or by those committed to building Jewish homes will, most generally, underscore prevention. Conversely, to be sure, many who have worked directly with interfaith couples have, in turn, decided to stress prevention initiatives—a point we shall return to below.

In addressing this debate, we first have to be conscious of the limits of policy. We are dealing in an area of private decision-making, in which public policy has, at most, secondary impact upon decisions of marriage and family. Moreover, those decisions will be influenced by a larger climate of public opinion in American society which Jewish public policy, per se, can affect at most marginally. Finally, we ought acknowledge that policy decision-making is often fueled by a sense of emotional urgency and desire that one's own grandchildren be Jewish—certainly noble sentiments, but not the most rational base on which to formulate decisions for the entire community.

What then can be done? First, there is a need for candor within Jewish leadership bodies. Little will be accomplished by telling people that Jewish continuity is assured when scientific evidence appears to the contrary. More specifically, to date we have no evidence that Jewish identity can be preserved within mixed-married homes in the second and third generation. Telling people that their grandchildren can be Jewish even when mixed-marriage absent conversion signals terminal Jewish identity reflects more wishful thinking than candor and honesty.

In this regard, it must be said that some of the statements emanating from the social science community have been harmful. Some sociologists and social scientists in the mid-1980s argued that intermarriage posed no danger to Jewish continuity.[1] Not only was that view inaccurate, it was also harmful. It gave Jewish leaders a message that was comforting and illusory rather than a message on which concrete action and policy to enhance Jewish continuity could be developed.

More recently, several social scientists have been arguing that the "battle against intermarriage is over—now is the time for a new focus upon outreach."[2] Such statements in and of themselves create a climate that is more conducive to intermarriage as a phenomenon. Telling the Jewish community that resistance to intermarriage is futile only increases the sentiment that intermarriage is now acceptable and normative for American Jews.

Finally, any policy that is formulated must be realistic rather than a statement of wishful thinking. Advocates of outreach inform us that we require realism about intermarriage as a phenomenon. True enough, yet these very same advocates often lack realism when it comes to the successes of outreach. Any outreach policy must confront the serious questions of what realistically can be accomplished through diverting significant communal resources towards outreach programming targeted to mixed-married couples.

In terms of positive steps, a multi-track and nuanced policy is necessary. The American Jewish Committee adopted such a policy statement that would emphasize intermarriage prevention, conversion to Judaism of non-Jewish family members, and continued outreach to mixed-married couples absent conversion.

A strategy of prevention will require diverse elements: It means enriching Jewish life generally to the point that a Jewish community is sufficiently attractive so that few will wish to leave it and others will wish to join. It means providing intensive Jewish experiences to all Jews so that they may perceive the riches and joys of leading a Jewish life and wish to build such a life for themselves and their families. It means raising endogamy to a communal imperative in which we clearly articulate our preferences for marriage within the faith even if they fly in the face of prevailing norms and culture. Barry Shrage, president of the Combined Jewish Philanthropies of Greater Boston, has articulated an action plan for strengthening Jewish life and slowing the growth of mixed-marriage by investing in family education experiences, informal Jewish education, trips to Israel, and Jewish singles programming. To these should be added investments in Jewish day schools of all of the religious movements, in line with Shrage's overall plea that the appropriate policy response to the CJF population study lies in creating a quality Jewish life that people will wish to lead.[3]

But most importantly, an emphasis upon prevention means recognition of where lies the core of the Jewish future. Clearly the future vitality of Diaspora Jewry will rest in the hands of those most committed to leading a Jewish life. That, in turn, will translate into marriage to a Jewish partner and building of a Jewish home. Investment in that core represents our critical hopes for a Jewish communal future that is both creative and vibrant. Investment in mixed-marrieds should not come at the expense of efforts to strengthen the core Jewish population. Pockets of Jewish energies among the mixed-marrieds, to be sure, should be cultivated and enhanced, but, realistically, the large population of mixed-marrieds and their progeny cannot be expected to form the core of the Jewish future.

Conversion means encouraging those factors that will lead to the conversion of the non-Jewish spouse. Here, research has been helpful and can shed new light upon what factors are most likely to bring about the dynamics of conversion and what factors are most likely to inhibit conversion. Policy can build upon previous research and experience in this area, e.g., the theme of addressing the Jewish commitment of the Jewish spouse and the Jewish side of the family, which, if strengthened, holds out great promise for the conversion of the non-Jewish spouse. Similarly, the community should address those factors that seem to send out negative messages regarding conversion in the Jewish community. These include the absence of a uniform conversion procedure acceptable to all the religious movements. More generally, the Jewish community would do well to acknowledge its traditional value and teaching that no distinction can be made between one who is born a Jew and one who has chosen to join the Jewish people. Finally, further research is required to ascertain whether the acceptance of patrilineal descent by liberal sectors of the community has affected the downward trend in conversion rates.

A strategy of outreach means continued dialogue with mixed-married couples. However, to be effective, outreach must be both properly targeted and qualified. We need to identify those target populations where outreach is likely to have an impact and do the most good. Chasing people who express no desire to be chased will only waste valuable communal resources and demean the choices people have made in a free society *not* to lead a Jewish life. Similarly, outreach must be properly qualified by clear statements of Jewish values underscoring communal preferences for marriage with other Jews. Failure to do so, in the name of tolerance and not wanting to alienate people, will succeed only in creating a climate in which it is impossible to discourage interfaith marriage. We should reasonably expect that, in the context of outreach, mixed-marrieds can hear Jewish marital teachings rather than insist that we dress up our tradition so as to make it palatable to them.

Moreover, as Dr. Jack Ukeles has argued, distinctions ought to be drawn between human outreach and communal outreach. Human outreach means encouraging all members of the family to warmly welcome Gentile spouses and family members as human beings all created in the image of God. That is both the right thing to do and the initiative that would hold out the greatest promise for ultimately forming a Jewish home. That is a far cry from heavy investing in communal programs that may or may not have a similar impact.[4]

Moreover, previous experience has already demonstrated that outreach to mixed-marrieds holds out the greatest chance for success when it is targeted to those who have already expressed some commitment to leading a Jewish life. In other words, the appropriate target for outreach initiatives are those who are marginally affiliated with the Jewish community rather than those who have signaled no desire for contact with Jews or Jewish communal institutions.[5]

Finally, outreach to mixed-marrieds works best when placed within the context of broader services and programming for Jews generally, in turn attracting mixed-marrieds as part of a larger service clientele. Experience has already demonstrated this to be the case in terms of early child care programs—namely services which Jews need and which ought to be provided by the community and which mixed-married couples would equally need and thereby establish a point of contact with Jewish communal institutions.[6]

The irony here is that only a few short years ago many of today's eloquent advocates of outreach to mixed-marrieds told us not to worry about the decline in the Jewish birth rate. "Quality, not quantity" was the key to Jewish survival in their view. Suddenly the news of mixed-marriage seems to have altered that ball game. Outreach, we are now told, has become a demographic imperative. However, it will not do to intone "outreach, outreach, outreach" with little idea as to the content of outreach programming, its ideological messages to Jews, or its long-term transforming effects upon the Jewish community.

Peter Medding has put this well in arguing that the challenge of future Jewish continuity depends on an "unambiguous Jewish identity" within the home. For most American Jews, that translates as the absence of Christianity and Christian symbols. The long-term outlook for mixed-married homes in which Christian symbolism is preserved is not sanguine in terms of preserving and transmitting an "unambiguous Jewish identity".[7]

Moreover, the track record regarding mixed-marrieds to this point is clearly not good. A 1984 Philadelphia study uncovered no Jewish grandchildren of mixed-married couples.[8] Egon Mayer, in research for the American Jewish Committee, pointed to intermarriage as a disaster for Jewish identity by the third generation.[9] Most recently, the NJPS itself uncovered that only 28% of mixed-married couples were raising their children as Jews.

Outreach advocates expect to break these patterns. By all means, the community should hope that they succeed. However, our caution here is to recall that we are trying to maintain the rather tenuous ties of a minority increasingly comfortable in the majority culture and unsure of themselves as Jews. Will Jewish identity be retained among this target population? Again, advocates of outreach argue that we don't know but we must try. Those efforts are significant and merit communal support. Yet given skepticism concerning the success of those efforts, it would be a cardinal mistake to invest valuable and limited resources in an "outreach-alone" strategy.

Therefore outreach would do well to limit its goals rather than to expand them. Massive ad campaigns searching for unaffiliated mixed-marrieds have already proven wasteful in terms of communal resources—chasing lots of people who have no desire to be chased. Rather, outreach initiatives should be limited to those who signal a desire to link up with the Jewish community—what Steven M. Cohen has termed the "middles of Jewish life"—those who desire Jewish continuity but have no sense of the content of what that continuity means.[10] Jewish communal policy should seek to supply the content to those middles. Moreover, outreach initiatives must be clear about Jewish communal goals, values, and priorities. Outreach initiatives cannot be supported if they carry the price of making it impossible to discourage interfaith marriage. Finally, I cannot see how the Jewish community should be supporting outreach as a form of marital therapy. Its raison d'être must be clearly underscored as enhancing the Jewish quality and content of the mixed-married home.

Given these concerns regarding outreach, I call for a larger and overarching strategy—one that includes the elements of prevention and conversion as well as outreach. But a final element relates to rehabilitating the role of ideology in Jewish life—attacking the root causes of intermarriage by exploring who we are as Jews and why do we choose to lead a Jewish life.

To be sure, ideology is rarely a popular subject. For one thing, it is divisive among Jews. Social scientists often dismiss it as meaningless and not as motivating behavior. But what makes the community distinctive are the ideals and principles it espouses. Some ideological conflict within the community is healthy, for it shows that at least some people care about what it means to be a Jew. In this regard, no generation of Jewish leaders has failed to resist intermarriage. Raising endogamy to a clearly articulated value of the Jewish community will go a long way towards clarifying what it is we believe in and why we choose to continue as Jews.

An interesting example of these difficulties recently occurred in one of the larger Jewish Federations in North America. A memo went out to a Federation leadership group inviting individuals to participate in an upcoming discussion on whether we may preserve endogamy as a Jewish value while conducting outreach to mixed-married couples. One member, married to a practicing Gentile, refused to attend arguing that a language of endogamy was by definition racist. Federation leadership responded that clearly greater sensitivity would be necessary in the future.

Such sentiments are understandable and perhaps to be expected in the context of dealing with mixed-marrieds. The question here is whether Jewish leadership can permit itself to sacrifice a language of endogamy within the Jewish community as the price of a campaign for outreach to mixed-marrieds. Such a stance, I believe, would be dissonant with Jewish history, would nurture a climate of greater acceptance of intermarriage as a phenomenon, and logically would lead to a higher rate of mixed-marriage. Finally, and most importantly, it would signal a Judaic culture attempting to be all things to all people and therefore bland and meaningless to its adherents.

In this sense, Jewish religious and communal leaders must be empowered to speak a language of norms, expectations, values, and commitments to leading a Jewish life. Absent these, we are at best talking about a Judaism that is bland and empty of content. With a language of values, we are then talking about those who are most ideologically committed to lead a Jewish life, to build Jewish homes, and create a vibrant and vital Jewish future. In theory, all forms of Judaism share the importance of values, norms, expectations, and commitments. The trouble is that our perceptions of ourselves as Jews are so weak that we fear to articulate those expectations lest we drive people away. Here is the role for an ideological strategy. Clearly stating what we are, what we believe in, and why we choose to be Jews may well alienate many who do not share those values. Hopefully, it will also inspire others that leading a Jewish life means something and stands for concrete principles with which people can identify. In this respect, ideology can address not the symptoms of intermarriage but the underlying causes— namely the weakness of commitment to leading a Jewish life. Strengthening the ideological commitments, like strengthening outreach, will never be a panacea. However, a serious effort to ensure Jewish continuity will have to operate on a multiplicity of fronts—preserve those as Jews who are preservable and simultaneously enhance those who hold out the promise of leading creative and vibrant Jewish lives.

Notes

1. See, for example, Charles Silberman, *A Certain People* (New York: Summit Books, 1985), ch. 7, and Calvin Goldscheider, *Jewish Continuity and Change* (Bloomington: Indiana University Press, 1986), ch. 2.

2. Egon Mayer, quoted in *New York Times* article, June 7, 1991.

3. Barry Shrage, *Journal of Jewish Communal Service,* forthcoming.

4. Jack Ukeles, "Does Outreach Justify Investment?—Alternatives to Outreach," in *The Intermarriage Crisis* (New York: The American Jewish Committee, 1991) pp. 17–19.

5. See Steven Bayme, "Outreach to the Unaffiliated: Communal Context and Policy Direction," Memorial Foundation for Jewish Culture, forthcoming.

6. *Ibid.*

7. Peter Medding, "Jewish Identity in Conversionary and Mixed-Marriage," *American Jewish Yearbook* (forthcoming, 1992).

8. Uziel Schmelz and Sergio DellaPergola, "Basic Trends in American Jewish Demography," in Steven Bayme, ed., *Facing the Future* (New York: KTAV, 1989), p. 93.

9. Egon Mayer, *Children of Intermarriage* (New York: The American Jewish Committee, 1983).

10. Steven M. Cohen, *Content or Continuity* (New York: The American Jewish Committee, 1991).

The Intermarriage Crisis

It is my great pleasure and privilege to appear before you this afternoon as you, the professional leadership of the Conservative movement, debate the major issues confronting Jewish continuity and survival in America today. As Jewish leaders, we are constantly challenged to shape and mold the values of the Jewish community and to apply our knowledge of and identification with Jewish tradition to the critical issues affecting Jewish life in the modern context. In that respect, you deserve considerable praise for devoting substantial time at this distinguished convention to intermarriage—a subject which defines our relationship to both tradition and modern culture.

Rabbi Steven Fuchs, a Reform rabbi in Nashville, Tennessee, writes in a recent issue of *Sh'ma* magazine:

> The early thrust of outreach in the Reform movement, as emphasized in speeches by Rabbi Alexander Schindler, was to accept the intermarried while continuing to discourage interfaith marriage. Our movement has been phenomenally successful in accepting the intermarried and integrating them into our congregations. That success, though, does make it more difficult to discourage interfaith marriage.

Rabbi Fuchs's comments reflect a longstanding debate within the Reform movement on appropriate responses by Jewish religious leaders to the phenomenon of intermarriage. Napoleon Bonaparte recognized this as early as 1806 in requesting Jewish leaders then to endorse intermarriage. For French Jewry, however, resistance to intermarriage became the key component of defining Jewish identity. Even those who advocated total fusion with France refused to accede to Napoleon's recommendation that Jewish leadership go on record endorsing unions of Jews and Gentiles.

Published by the William Petschek National Jewish Family Center of the American Jewish Committee; based upon an address delivered to the national convention of the Rabbinical Assembly at the Concord Hotel, Liberty, NY, April 30, 1991. Reprinted with permission of the Rabbinical Assembly.

Forty years later, German Reform Judaism witnessed an internal debate on responses to intermarriage. For Rabbi Samuel Holdheim, intermarriage connoted the ideal marriage, for it recognized the acceptance of the Jew in universal German society. For his colleague Rabbi David Einhorn, every intermarriage signified another nail in the coffin of Jewish identity.

Similar tensions have been expressed within the Reconstructionist movement. . . . In his seminal 1934 work, *Judaism as a Civilization,* Mordecai Kaplan wrote the following:

> Jews must meet all situations that might lead to mixed marriages not fearfully or grudgingly but in the spirit of encountering an expected development. . . . With a belief in the integrity and values of his own civilization, the Jewish partner to the marriage could . . . make Judaism the civilization of the home.

Twenty-two years later, in *Questions Jews Ask,* Kaplan returned to the same topic—but with a different nuance:

> Since Jews are a minority and Judaism is exposed to tremendous disintegrating forces from the non-Jewish environment, and since Reconstructionism is concerned with the perpetration of Judaism, it cannot approve of uncontrolled intermarriage with non-Jews. If, however, a non-Jew who desires to marry a Jew, after studying what is involved in being a Jew and what are the principles and practices of Judaism, is willing to undergo formal conversion to Judaism, he should be given every encouragement and should be welcomed into the Jewish community. Only in this way can we compensate for losses through intermarriage, where conversion to Judaism is not made a condition. It is unreasonable to expect that Jewish religion and culture will be perpetated in homes resulting from mixed marriages where no such requirement is insisted on.

What this debate signifies is that intermarriage stands at the cutting edge of our relationship with modern culture. As a phenomenon, intermarriage has accompanied our desire to be part of the modern world— our refusal to reject a modern culture which welcomes Jewish involvement and participation. Conversely, as Einhorn's and Kaplan's comments indicate, intermarriage connotes a weakening of Jewish heritage and tradition and a threat to future Jewish continuity and identity.

These tensions within Reform and Reconstructionist Judaism are beginning to be felt within the Conservative movement as well. I submit to you that the Conservative movement has clearly defined where it stands on the questions of rabbinic officiation at intermarriages, which it fundamentally rejects, and patrilineal descent, on which it has also taken a clearly negative stance—a subject to which I will return later. Conversely, the Conservative movement has been in the forefront of arguing for a clear and unequivocal acceptance and welcoming of those who choose to join the Jewish faith via marriages to Jews that result in conversion to Judaism.

Where the Conservative movement to date has not clearly defined its stance is on the question of intermarriage and on the policy implications of outreach to intermarried couples absent conversion to Judaism. This is a subject on which the Jewish community itself is divided and on which the Conservative movement could well play a leadership role in striking the appropriate balance between concerns for Jewish tradition, for Jewish continuity, and for the human and demographic imperatives of outreach to mixed-married couples.

My task this afternoon will be to challenge you as friends and colleagues to formulate communal policy positions and program directions for the future.

Let us begin, however, with some background. In the United States, intermarriage rates remained at historically low levels until the 1960s. Until that time intermarriage stood at less than 10 percent—that is, fewer than one out of ten Jews were marrying outside the faith. In the 1960s we witnessed a significant rise to the point that intermarriage appeared to reach a level of one out of three, or 33 percent, by the end of the decade. Recent indications point to a significant rise in intermarriage, possibly well beyond those projected by earlier studies.

The reasons for this increase are quite clear. First, as a small people, we simply have a limited pool. Small Jewish communities report very high rates of intermarriage, while large Jewish communities report significantly lower rates.

Moreover, it is very clear that the courtship process in America today is essentially a secular process. Differences of religion that we believe may harm long-term marital relations simply do not seem significant to young couples today. In this regard, we must recognize that to oppose intermarriage in some ways violates our universal ideals that we are all human beings created in God's image. More to the point, American society values romantic love more highly than it values differences of religious beliefs.

Moreover, in some respects Jews stand alone in their opposition to intermarriage. Recent polls indicate that 87 percent of Americans welcome marriage to a Jew—a remarkable statement of Jewish arrival in America, namely, that the Jew at long last has become a desirable in-law. More seriously, it means that if we are committed to opposing intermarriage, we will require a distinctive Jewish response, one that underscores a distinctive Jewish identity, one that states clearly and explicitly that we as Jews value marriage within the faith in order to ensure the continuity of our mission and culture.

It will be difficult, without question, to articulate such a message. That is because the overriding factor behind the growth in intermarriage is a decline in Jewish commitment, a weakness in Jewish identity, a failure of Jewish education and the Jewish family to bring about the commitment to Jewish continuity that we all so fervently desire. I would add here that all too often Jewish parents do not feel capable of articulating a language of Jewish endogamy to the next generation. They, in turn, look to the Jewish school system to provide that language. And we find, as we have in many sectors of social policy, that school and communal institutions simply cannot replace the home.

So much for the reasons behind the rise in intermarriage. In some ways, more important to us is the communal climate concerning intermarriage, for rabbis are most significant in formulating and articulating attitudes, norms, and values concerning intermarriage.

Essentially we have gone through three stages in our communal responses to intermarriage. When the first news of the growth of intermarriage occurred, communal leaders responded with agony and handwriting. Virtually all Jewish organizations passed resolutions and statements signaling opposition to intermarriage. Conferences were held about what we can do in the face of this tidal wave. That period of *shrei gevalt* soon passed into a more constructive phase often referred to as "resistance and containment" or "outrage and outreach." This phase, best articulated by Rabbi Alexander Schindler in his 1978 call for the formation of an outreach program, continued to underscore communal opposition and resistance to intermarriage, yet called for additional initiatives in which the community would reach out to intermarried couples, form relationships with them, bring them closer to the Jewish community, and ultimately hope and work for the conversions of the non-Jewish spouse.

In more recent years, this second phase has given way to a third perspective—one described by Professor Egon Mayer as "from outrage to outreach"—a perspective that assumes that resistance to intermarriage is futile, the battle cannot be won, and therefore it behooves the Jewish community to accept intermarriage as a reality, to understand that communal opposition will get us nowhere pragmatically, but that serious initiatives can change the nature of the Jewish demographic future. Perhaps most influential in formulating this third attitude has been the pervasiveness of intermarriage in the Jewish community. There is not a family that has not been touched by it. We are all interested in forming relationships with intermarrieds, and we find it difficult to do so when the Jewish community continues to resist intermarriage. The intellectual wherewithal for this third position, perhaps, was symbolized by the reception accorded the publication of Charles Silberman's book, six years ago, *A Certain People*. Whereas others had bewailed the intermarriage crisis, Silberman saw no reason for sadness, for, in his view, intermarriage was not as prevalent as some had predicted and, in the long run, would result in a 40-percent increase in the size of the Jewish community—a set of predictions which, quite clearly, to date has not been realized.

From a perspective of six years later, Silberman's thesis has been largely abandoned if not discredited. His prediction that intermarriage would result in Jewish renewal has proved as ill-founded as his prediction that within a decade the Conservative movement would accept patrilineal descent. For the truth is there is little good news within the intermarriage phenomenon. Intermarrieds participate minimally in Jewish communal affairs. Rather than a growth in conversion to Judaism, a decline in conversion rates has occurred, for as many Jews leave the Jewish community, either via apostasy from Judaism or conversion to Christianity, as Gentiles enter the Jewish community via conversion to Judaism. Most mixed marriages cannot be classified as either Jewish or Christian. Their members live in a vague no-man's-land somewhere between Judaism and Christianity, understanding neither. We are also witnessing a rise in the number of households in which children are raised within two faiths, as if one could communicate the theological absurdity of being both Jewish and Christian. Conversion to Judaism itself is on the decline. Of intermarriages contracted within the last five years, only six percent have resulted in conversions to Judaism. To be sure, that number may increase over the years as children are born and couples begin to worry about the religious identity of the home. However, even assuming an optimistic increase in the rate of conversion within these marriages, we must face the harsh reality that the overwhelming majority of mixed-married homes will never become fully Jewish homes.

Finally, we must be realistic in understanding assimilation as a multigeneration phenomenon. Historians of modern Judaism, in distinct contradiction with sociologists of modern Jewry, underscore how the history of Jewish assimilation has not been a function of a single generation but has been a process that has steadily increased from generation to generation within particular homes. What that means is that even if we are successful in holding on to the Jewish partner in this generation of mixed-married couples, there is a real question what will become of their children, to say nothing of their grandchildren. One sobering statistic emerges from the city of Philadelphia: According to their 1984 demographic study, in the entire city not a single grandchild of a mixed marriage without conversion identified as a Jew. Those who tell us that irrespective of intermarriage we can continue to look to a strong and stable Jewish community because Jews continue to live in Jewish neighborhoods, have Jewish friends, and are concentrated in occupations with large numbers of Jews overlook the reality that assimilation has increased as we go from one generation to the next. Visions of outreach to mixed-married couples will have to wrestle with the overriding historical question of whether we can maintain a Jewish identity within the mixed-married home not for the current generation of the 1990s but for the next generation and the following one.

Despite this rather sobering news about intermarriage, the shift in cultural climate continues. For one thing, there are now books assisting parents to raise children within two faiths. A recent book, *Raising Your Jewish Christian Child,* by a Gentile journalist, contains a preface written by a Conservative rabbi and endorsements from other Jewish communal leaders and social thinkers. The book's thesis communicates the universal American message that, in a land of pluralism, should we not expose children to the riches of both faiths, let them absorb the beauties of our respective religious traditions, and let them decide for themselves what will be their own personal identities. Aside from the obvious theological difficulties Jews will have with such a message, I question the wisdom of communicating to children that two faiths are indeed better than one. Were this book the only example of the current cultural climate that has become supportive of the dual-faith home, my concern would be minimal. Yet even rabbis have written on this issue, endorsing the notion that the home can be both Jewish and Christian. A popular work by Rabbi Steven Reuben, *But How Will You Raise the Children,* and a unique interreligious composition, *Happily Intermarried* by Rabbi Roy Rosenberg, Father Peter Meehan, and Reverend John Payne, both recommend that we should celebrate rather than bemoan interfaith marriages and interfaith households in today's modern universalist society.

Most significantly, lay leaders within the Jewish community are anxious to receive a message of consolation—a statement from the rabbinate that the time has come to view intermarriage in positive rather than negative terms. A recent address by a prominent lay leader before the Jewish Community Centers Association is entitled "Intermarriage—The Challenge and the Opportunity," a clarion call for a fundamental shift in attitude toward intermarriage. Rachel Cowan, otherwise a marvelous example of a righteous convert, writes in a recent issue of *Moment* magazine that, inasmuch as intermarriage is a reality that will not go away, the community must find some mechanism of blessing interfaith unions. To her credit, Cowan admits that such a stance will amount to "effective condoning of intermarriage." However, she concludes, something to this effect must be done for "the need is too great." A member of a support group for children of interfaith unions comments in a more recent issue of the same magazine, "When I hear a rabbi inveigh against intermarriage, I know that's my parents he is assailing." Two columnists in the Boston *Jewish Advocate* recently urged "that Jews must overcome the perception that intermarriage is a threat to Judaism."

This is the climate in which we are currently operating. Jewish leaders concerned with Jewish tradition must function in a world in which Gentile opposition to intermarriage is collapsing, the Jewish community is anxious to hear from us a message of consolation, and those of us wedded to traditional Jewish values find those values increasingly isolated and anachronistic in a world which looks upon intermarriage in such benign terms.

The exceptions, of course, are on the right. Orthodox rabbis seem to have no difficulty counseling resistance to intermarriage. If they are accused of writing off intermarried couples, they are quick to respond, as the executive director of the Rabbinical Council of America recently noted, "The problem . . . in the Orthodox community is, thank God, very low." Whether that will hold for the long run remains to be seen. Current research, to be sure, does indicate significantly lower rates of intermarriage within Orthodox households. Non-Orthodox critics dismiss this as, "We get the Orthodox dropouts." Orthodox leaders respond that they have done the best job at translating the ideological commitments to in-marriage among their constituencies. When charged with writing off the intermarried, they respond that they are preserving Judaism.

On the left, as I noted before, the dominant mood is one of "Let us view intermarriage as an opportunity to be welcomed rather than a danger to be contained." The official policy of the Reform movement remains that articulated by Rabbi Schindler—"Accept intermarrieds but reject intermarriage." However, as Rabbi Fuchs's article demonstrates, it is increasingly difficult to maintain that dual message within Reform congregations.

Therefore, it is to the Conservative movement that I turn with the challenge of ideological clarification. It is the Conservative movement that is best positioned to acknowledge both the human and demographic imperatives of outreach to intermarrieds and the ideological imperatives of encouraging endogamous marriages. In urging you to address these ideological issues, I invoke our shared responsibility as Jewish leaders to provide guidance in terms of the application of traditional Jewish norms and values to the modern context. That has always been the distinctive hallmark of Conservative Judaism as an ideology. For it is the Conservative movement that is wedded to a synthesis of tradition and modernity. Therefore, you have the opportunity to provide ideological clarification to the community—to communicate a message that will uphold traditional values within the modern context of the acceptance of the Jew in American society.

Therefore, I ask, what would such a position comprise?

First, there can be no retreat from candor and truth. We must tell the Jewish community in all honesty that intermarriage does pose significant dangers in terms of future Jewish continuity and identity. Similarly, it poses threats to the future of Jewish unity inasmuch as we have conflicting definitions of who is a Jew within mixed marriages and even conflicting definitions concerning who is a Jew within marriages in which conversion to Judaism has taken place. Attempts to suggest that intermarriage is really not a problem will do little in a positive sense except to offer false consolation to some.

In the same spirit of candor, we must recognize that opposition to intermarriage today makes sense only if grounded in a language of religious values and historical continuity. We can no longer argue that intermarriage doesn't work. We have all seen examples of successful intermarriages. "L.A. Law" and "Thirtysomething" have already informed us that intermarriages are no more problematical than any other form of marriage. Although social scientists report that intermarriage is twice as likely to end in divorce as marriages between Jews, that message is unlikely to be credible in a climate which has so legitimized intermarriage. Therefore, we should be willing to develop a language of endogamy—a curriculum that explains to young people all of the reasons why the Jewish community encourages marriage within the faith, all of the beauties and joys of leading a Jewish life that are best available through marriage to other Jews. It is very difficult for parents to argue against intermarriage. We have not provided the appropriate curriculum materials, the appropriate ideology of in-marriage which can communicate to young people effectively why we prefer marriage within the faith. Such a curriculum will, undoubtedly, offend those who have already intermarried. But that is precisely our dilemma in reaching out to intermarrieds even as we reject intermarriage.

Third, we should continue to underscore the importance of conversion as the goal of communal outreach. In this regard, religious leaders of all the movements should be challenged to secure a uniform conversion procedure acceptable to all the religious movements—in the absence of which we have differing standards of who is a Jew. To date, Conservative Judaism has been most receptive to the idea of a uniform conversion procedure. I encourage you to continue to play a leadership role in this area. To be sure, we do have questions about the long-term effects of conversion. The recent article by Jonathan Sarna in the *Journal of Reform Judaism* poses the danger of "one-generation converts." However, our moral imperative is clear—to welcome Jews by choice, *gerei tzedek,* as assets and resources for the Jewish community. Ongoing, continued work in this area must become a priority for the rabbinate and be made a regular aspect of rabbinical training.

Finally, we must acknowledge that most mixed marriages will not result in conversion to Judaism. Here is the important and positive role for outreach for mixed-married couples. We must maintain lines of communication. We must enable them to raise their children within the Jewish faith. Let us, therefore, discuss openly our concerns with them. Let us share with them our cherished values and beliefs. Let us expose them to the beauties of Jewish peoplehood. Let us dialogue with them on the role of Israel in Jewish life, our concerns for endangered Jewish communities, and our joy and celebration in contemporary Jewish renewal. Let us develop support groups within our synagogues to enable us to maintain such an honest dialogue with intermarrieds rather than signal to them their rejection from the Jewish community.

This form of outreach presupposes that we are clear as to our goals—encourage endogamous marriage, bring about conversion, and develop Jews who will themselves reject intermarriage for their children.

To be sure, this approach is a complex one. It is multitrack in its dimensions. Its nuances will often be misunderstood whether by those who fear legitimation of intermarriage or by those who fear that such an approach will write off the intermarrieds. Yet I submit that this approach is based upon a true pluralism—one in which we can honestly communicate our values, our concerns, our areas of consensus, and our areas of disagreement with intermarried couples. For a true pluralism enables us to assert what we believe in. My own experience with intermarried couples indicates that they will listen to such a message that approaches them with integrity and honesty rather than simply dresses up our tradition in ways that they find palatable.

In 1963 the sociologist Nathan Glazer and the current senator from New York, Daniel Patrick Moynihan, co-authored a book called *Beyond the Melting Pot,* in which they argued that Jews are the most endogamous of peoples and that their very endogamy is the key to their survival. The thrust of my address this afternoon has been to question that analysis. Rather, the key to our communal future rests upon what we mean by a true pluralism. That does not mean that we be all things to all people. It does mean our right to assert our distinctive Jewish heritage and values. My professor of Jewish history at Columbia University many years ago, Chancellor Ismar Schorsch, argued that the distinctive contribution of the Jews historically has been their willingness to fly in the face of reality—to assert monotheism when paganism prevailed, to articulate Jewish renewal in an age of Jewish destruction. Our challenge in America today is to assert our Jewish distinctiveness in the face of a reality that overwhelmingly accepts intermarriage. That is the true challenge that intermarriage poses today. Let us respond to that challenge with policies that assert Judaic values and with programs that ensure Jewish continuity. Such an approach will walk a delicate and fine line between traditional values and modern context—between expression of historical Jewish family values and articulation of the demographic imperatives of outreach. Yet it is precisely those challenges of tradition and modernity that the Conservative movement has always confronted. May you continue to guide those of us who stand committed to living in two distinctive civilizations yet who are equally committed not to sacrifice one for the sake of the other.

Failing to Address Crisis From Within

Co-authored with Alan Silverstein

Some 90 years ago, the Board of Deputies of Anglo-Jews received a report from Limerick, Ireland, of an economic boycott against the local Jewish community. The Board, however, finding it easier to protest the Kishinev pogrom in Russia than confront a threat within its own house, referred the warning to a committee. Ultimately, the Board did protest, but the Chief Secretary for Ireland urged the Board to avoid focusing further attention on the matter. The Board accepted the secretary's letter and congratulated itself on a job well done. By this time, however, Limerick Jewry had begun leaving the town in droves.

Thankfully, this was not the last word on Limerick, but clearly the Board of Deputies was tarnished by its tepid response. Hopefully, the "Report of the North American Commission on Jewish Identity and Continuity" will not represent the final action of Jewish leadership on today's crisis of Jewish continuity. As commissioners, we were privileged to participate in the commission's work. Like the Board of Deputies nine decades ago, the commission, composed of an impressive array of Jewish leaders, failed to address adequately the crisis from within.

To be sure, the commission was limited by a process designed to ensure communal consensus. Moreover, its very existence did herald the need for a new agenda for the community to secure Jewishly-committed grandchildren; thus it identified the internal dangers of erosion and assimilation as the most critical threats to future Jewish existence.

To its credit, the commission avoided the "quick fix" of an isolated summer trip to Israel for all adolescents, noting instead that such dramatic programs can work only when they are encased in a broader rubric of Jewish continuity initiatives—particularly formal Jewish education, which remains the bedrock of Jewish identity. The commis-

Reprinted with permission from the *Jewish Week of New York,* January 6, 1996.

sion did affirm the high cost of Jewish day school education and urged that, in principle, the community should make intensive educational experiences affordable for all Jews. Perhaps most importantly, the commission underscored the need for religious language and experiences—a pronounced shift from the traditional secular focus of Jewish Federations. As Rabbi Arthur Hertzberg has warned: "The need for and the possibility of spiritual revival are clear. If it does not happen, American Jewish history will soon end." In short, there can be no Jewish continuity absent serious commitment to Judaism.

On these many scores we applaud the commission's efforts. Yet what the commission report omits is at least as important as what it includes. First, the commission made no attempt to reorder priorities either on the Jewish communal agenda generally or within the continuity agenda itself. In an era of diminishing resources, if Jewish continuity represents the most critical need, other worthy causes will have to be awarded fewer allocations of dollars and personnel. Moreover, not every type of continuity initiative can claim equal importance. Yet rather than prioritizing among services to adolescents, college students, singles, single parents, immigrant Jews, Jews with disabilities, or intermarried couples, the commission report merely provides a laundry list of potential target populations.

To be sure, priority-setting is divisive. Every program will find its eloquent defenders. Yet the mandates of leadership lie precisely in making difficult choices and the capacity of determining what to affirm and what to reject. In this regard, we urge setting the highest priority in planning for those populations most at risk to intermarry during the next decade: adolescents, collegians, and single adults.

Similarly problematic, the commission avoided normative statements of what values ought to prevail within Jewish communal life. The language of inclusivity, certainly well-intentioned so as to be welcoming to all interested in leading a Jewish life, fails to inspire commitment to desirable behaviors crucial to our Jewish future.

Take, for example, the vexing issue of intermarriage: The commission failed to reaffirm what responsible Jewish leaders have said for millennia—the imperative of Jews choosing Jewish mates and building Jewish families.

Nor could the commission affirm the desirability of certain forms of Jewish education—e.g., day schools, camping—over others despite a body of considerable research establishing precisely that elementary point. We invite other Jewish communal leaders to join in coalition with us in advocating the three routes proven most effective to forge Jewish identity: day schools, post bar/bat mitzvah formal education, and Jewish camping.

Lastly, beyond acknowledging the high cost of day school education, the commission report says little concerning the affordability of Jewish living generally. Intensive Jewish experiences of all types are going to warrant significant claims upon the limited resources of individuals. Therefore, the Jewish choices themselves must be sufficiently compelling to warrant such claims. Secondly, those who have fewer resources will then place legitimate demands upon the community.

In short, there is no mystery to Jewish continuity. We must clearly state our advocacy of in-marriage, our receptivity to sincere conversion, and our opposition to dual-faith parenting. We must allocate sizable dollars and staff resources in programming for populations at risk: teens, collegians and singles. We must persuade Jewish families to send their children to day schools, to Jewish camps, and to post bar/bat mitzvah programs of formal learning. And we must adequately address the affordability of Jewish living for the middle class and the needy. Yet the challenge to American Jewry lies in its willingness to pay the price—in some cases, financial, but more often a cultural price of engaging American culture with distinctively Jewish values and ideals that at times may be quite dissonant with otherwise attractive dimensions of American society. The "Report of the National Commission on Jewish Identity and Continuity" has taken some modest steps in this direction. What is now required is an action plan to bring these general goals into focus.

National Jewish Population Survey: Implications for the Rabbinate

It is my pleasure and privilege to appear before you this morning to discuss current trends within American Jewry and share with you some thoughts on current challenges to Jewish leadership. Those of us who study and interpret the development of American Jewry as a community are indeed privileged to be able to share our thinking with you, the leaders within the Reform movement, who are laboring to preserve Jewish life in the congregations, in the front lines of Jewish communities, and in the trenches of American Jewry.

The good news is that we have definitive information on the nature of American Jews. Our difficulty is that the news is not terribly good. The report points to declining Jewish identity particularly among mixed-marrieds, and particularly among children and grandchildren of mixed-married couples absent conversion to Judaism.

Our community as a whole is disproportionately elderly. Jews are one third times more likely than the overall American population to be over age 65. The median age in our community is 37.3 years, almost four years older than the median age for white Americans. Only 19% of American Jews are under age 15, compared with 23% two decades earlier.

In this regard, we are becoming a community which has few numbers of children. Jewish families have low fertility rates, approximately 1.6 children per couple—by the time the couple has completed its childbearing years. This finding flies in the face of much of our thinking just five years ago, when we naturally assumed that Jewish couples would continue to be able to replace themselves. They would just do so in the later years of childbearing. Our new study indicates that fertility delayed represents fertility foregone.

We also have been surprised by the large number of secular Jews within the community. The survey uncovered 1.1 million Jews who

Reprinted with permission of the Central Conference of American Rabbis, from the *CCAR Yearbook, Volume CII* (New York, 1992).

were *not* members of the Jewish faith—what Rabbi Harold Schulweiss has referred to as the single largest population of Jewish apostates known to history. These are Jews who will not identify themselves as members of the Jewish faith, although they clearly have been born as Jews and are not practicing any other faith. They are Jews who are far less likely to have the benefits of a college education. They are far more at risk of intermarrying. These are Jews who are unlikely to show up at Jewish communal events. They are hidden from our community and have minimal contact with Jewish communal organizations. In contrast, the Jewish community as a whole is quite affluent and well educated. Our median income is some $10,000–$12,000 higher than that of the median American income. Three quarters of our population have had some college—twice the percentage of that of American whites. One quarter has had some graduate education—three times the percentage of the American white population.

Even more surprisingly, one third of Jewish children who are receiving any form of Jewish education at all are enrolled in Jewish day schools—the single most intensive and successful model of Jewish education available. This shift represents a fundamental change in communal attitudes towards day schools within all of the religious movements and foreshadows new sources for leadership in the future.

Moreover, we are a mobile population. Fifty percent of American Jews have changed their residence within the past six years. More significantly, some 700,000 Jewish adults have moved out of state within that time period.

Not surprisingly, the survey has attracted the most attention for its findings concerning Jewish family patterns—marriage, divorce, intermarriage, and conversion. Unquestionably Jews do continue to get married, albeit at later ages. In 1970 some 90% of Jewish women were married by age 35. By 1990 that percentage had declined to 70%. To be sure, close to 90% eventually married, but by age 45 in 1990 rather than 35 in 1970.

Although divorce rates are unquestionably increasing, Jews do enjoy a relative degree of marital stability. Some 18% have been divorced. Most remarry within a few years—what sociologists are fondly referring to as the triumph of hope over experience. More significantly, a divorce deficit may be correlated with Jewish religious behavior. Jews who are practicing a particular form of Judaism have a divorce rate roughly half of secular Jews who are devoid of religious practice or affiliation.

Much attention has been paid to the intermarriage rate of 52%—meaning that approximately one out of every two Jews who has gotten married in the last five years has married someone who was not born a Jew. There has been, to be sure, some questioning of the figure. Yet even if one postulates a lower intermarriage rate, it still approaches the neighborhood of 50%. The real point is who is likely to marry out and who is not. Children of mixed-marrieds themselves have been marrying out at a rate of over 90% in the last five years. In turn, that has inflated the overall intermarriage rate. In contrast, children of two Jewish parents continue to express a clear preference for marriage to other Jews.

Unfortunately, some in the Jewish community have gotten the message of despair from these statistics. They feel it has become useless to attempt to prevent intermarriage. Such despair, however, is unwarranted. We can continue to build upon the preferred model of Jews that they find partners within the faith. This has enormous implications for continued leadership roles, both in discouraging interfaith marriage and in reaching out to mixed-married homes. What we cannot do is accept intermarriage as normative. If intermarriage becomes pervasive among American Jews, then our future is indeed in doubt. For, thus far, 72% of mixed-married couples are raising their children outside of the Jewish faith. It is difficult to see this population as forming the core of the Jewish communal future. Therefore, if the population survey suggests nothing else, it turns to the rabbinate for leadership in formulation of communal attitudes and perceptions of intermarriage.

This has great implications for the very sensitive and important question of rabbinic officiation at interfaith weddings. As many of you know, an American Jewish Committee study on the subject reported few if any differences five years after the wedding between couples who had secured rabbinic officiation and couples who had sought rabbinic officiation but had been refused. At a time when the Jewish community is looking to its leaders for guidance in addressing these very difficult questions, it is my hope that members of the Conference, who have debated this issue on grounds of principle, may revisit it in light of new data and concerns.

Equally significant has been the question of conversion. We used to think that perhaps as many as one in three intermarriages will end up in a conversion to Judaism. Current data indicate that conversion has declined to 7%—meaning that one in 14 intermarriages has resulted in a conversion to Judaism. The good news is that 99% of the children of converts are raised as Jews. To be sure, as Rabbi Joseph Tabachnik and Brenda Forster discovered among Jews by choice in Chicago, we have some concern regarding one-generation converts—those who freely choose Judaism but would not object to their children marrying out or converting to Christianity. Some 50% of converts as a whole continue to maintain Christmas trees in their homes. These concerns, while real, should by no means obliterate the reality that our experience with conversion as a whole has been positive.

Within the Jewish population, the religious movements themselves continue to capture at least the self-identification of American Jews. Reform Judaism itself has become the single largest religious movement with 38% of American Jews self-identifying as Reform. Conservative Judaism is next with 35% reflecting a modest decline from 1970 when Conservative Judaism was the choice of a plurality of Jews. Orthodox Jews today claim 6%—a significant decrease from 11% in 1970. To be sure, 10% of Jews under age 25 do identify with Orthodoxy suggesting some possibilities for future growth. Reconstructionist Jews, as might be expected, represent a mere 1% of the population.

We should not delude ourselves into thinking that these 80% of American Jews who identify religiously are to be found within our synagogues. A mere 30% currently claim synagogue membership—let alone attendance at weekly services. Moreover, even among those who do identify as practicing Jews, 50% of those who claim Reform Judaism have non-Jewish spouses, as do 30% of those who claim Conservative Judaism, and 9% of those who claim to be Orthodox. To be sure, these are all self-definitions rather than concrete statements of reality. An Orthodox synagogue, for example, need not have a nearly 10% intermarriage rate.

These are the findings, how has the community reacted? Some, on the right, have communicated a sense of Orthodox triumphalism—"I told you so"—a conviction that only Orthodoxy would survive while Reform and Conservative Judaism would wither away. Regardless of the merits of this response, Orthodox spokesmen themselves concede that it is hardly a constructive response when 94% of American Jews have already opted to reject Orthodoxy.

Perhaps more surprisingly, some Jewish leaders have openly spoken of the need for revitalization of *aliyah*—presumably on the grounds that Jews living in Israel will undoubtedly continue to lead a Jewish life. For better or for worse, this is equally unrealistic. If American Jews have rejected Orthodoxy in overwhelming numbers, even more overwhelming numbers have rejected *aliyah*. What we should recall, however, is the need to intensify our relationships with Israel. For spending extensive time in Israel at a variety of different age levels has been proven to be one of the most effective guarantors of Jewish continuity.

A third response has been of statements by social scientists and others to the effect that, "The battle against intermarriage is over. The time now is for a new focus upon outreach."

These leaders advocate a "fundamentally different attitude" towards intermarriage, one that will regard intermarriage as inevitable and that efforts to prevent it are futile and even harmful. They suggest that if, instead, we approach intermarriage as an opportunity to enhance Jewish life, then within a generation we can transform entirely the map of the Jewish community in positive and enriched directions.

These advocates, however, are equally mistaken. They will accomplish little through such an undertaking except to succeed in making intermarriage perfectly normative and therefore acceptable for American Jews as a totality. They will thereby undermine those in the community who continue to clearly express their preferences to marry other Jews. Finally, they ignore whatever successes do exist in the realm of intermarriage prevention without setting forth any vision of how Judaism can survive and continue if intermarriage indeed does become routine and dominant for American Jews.

To be fair, the dominant response among Jewish communal leaders is probably best expressed as a sense of confusion and increased anxiety rather than any specific and coherent policy consensus. Lacking a clear vision of what to do, Jewish leaders often find themselves fighting off cries of hysteria coupled with feelings of helplessness and paralysis. It is precisely at this moment that rabbis can exercise leadership in helping to guide our vision of what Jewish life ought to look like and our policy for how to realize that vision.

What then are the implications? First, we ought to be honest in recognizing that much of the optimism of the 1980s concerning intermarriage and conversion was misplaced. We do have serious questions concerning Jewish continuity and therefore issues affecting the continuity and future quality of American Jewish life merit a much higher place on the communal agenda.

By the same token, we ought to be honest in acknowledging that we do have a question concerning who is a Jew in America. If the report suggests nothing else, it is that there are very fluid boundaries of who is in and who is out—people who consider themselves as full Jews, part Jews, and even Jews of two faiths. The size of the Jewish population as a whole depends directly on how broadly one defines the definition of who is a Jew. That size in itself, today, does not reflect a sharp decline in numbers. Contrary to predictions, our numbers remain the same as twenty years ago. Part of the reason for that has been higher immigration. More to the point, however, is that the returns on intermarriage are far from in. Current indications suggest that by the third generation intermarriage leads to terminal Jewish identity forecasting sizable losses within the next 10–20 years.

As a result, we face very significant challenges of policy direction: How may we retain and enrich the core Jewish population, how may we bring in those on the margins, and what do we say to those who are outside of the community and have not opted to join us?

In general, we require a multi-track and nuanced response, one that will continue to encourage Jews to marry other Jews, to make all efforts to reduce the intermarriage rate rather than accept it as inevitable, to work for the conversion of the non-Jewish spouse, and to continue to engage in outreach to mixed-marrieds so as to preserve the Jewish identity of their homes and ultimately work to bring them closer to the Jewish community.

We can best encourage Jews to marry other Jews by enriching the quality of Jewish life generally—by building a community so attractive that few will wish to leave it while others will wish to join. But encouraging in-marriage also means a second step. It means raising the values of in-marriage to a communal imperative. If we are sincere believers in the importance of the Jewish family, we need have no inhibitions about articulating a language of endogamy within the Jewish community. My colleague Rabbi Marc Winer has been especially helpful in developing such a "language of endogamy" for use among American Jews.

Conversion, as I indicated earlier, has clearly been an asset. Reform Judaism deserves enormous credit for revitalizing the concept of conversion for the Jewish community. Most recently, Rabbi Alexander Schindler criticized the tendency in outreach towards adopting a posture of neutrality towards the question of conversion. In line with Rabbi Schindler's admonitions, we ought to be encouraging conversion wherever possible. That will entail removing whatever barriers exist to conversion, including whatever remaining communal ambivalence or even hostility that exists to Jews by choice.

We have a serious and open question in this regard concerning the effect of the patrilineal descent decision. We do not know whether the acceptance of this principle has contributed to the decrease in conversion rates by communicating that your children can be Jewish even if one parent remains a practicing Christian. I do not know the answer to that question. Serious research could advance communal discussion on the question. At a minimum, Reform rabbis and leaders ought to be challenged to clarify what exactly the patrilineal descent decision means. The principle that a child can be Jewish if the child has only one Jewish parent, namely the father, and both parents commit themselves to providing appropriate Jewish experiences for the child has not been understood by the media and the contemporary Jewish public. In those sectors the patrilineal descent decision is understood as a simple statement that a parent of either gender guarantees the Jewishness of the child.

Outreach to mixed-marrieds does remain an imperative for both human and demographic reasons. These are people who are all created in the image of God. They merit our attention and our concern. On a demographic level, failure to reach out to them will virtually guarantee sizable demographic losses in the future.

But this call for outreach requires both appropriate targeting and appropriate qualification. We need to identify those target populations where outreach is likely to have an impact and to do the most good. Chasing people who have expressed no desire to be chased will only waste valuable communal resources and demean the choices that people have made in a free society not to lead a Jewish life. Similarly, outreach must be properly qualified by clear statements of Jewish values underscoring communal preferences for marriage with other Jews. Failure to do so, in the name of tolerance and not wanting to alienate people, will succeed only in creating a climate in which it is impossible to discourage interfaith marriage. Rabbi Stephen Fuchs has appropriately and eloquently cautioned of the need both to target outreach initiatives to appropriate audiences while at the same time clearly articulating what it is we stand for and what it is we believe as Jews desiring to encourage in-marriage with other Jews. In this context of outreach, we can reasonably expect that mixed-married couples can hear Jewish marital teachings rather than insist that we dress up our tradition so as to make it palatable to them.

This leads, however, to some concluding thoughts concerning the need to rehabilitate the role of religious ideology and values for American Jews. We must find ways whereby our people can recapture their religious heritage and treasures. Reform Judaism, in particular, has a unique opportunity in this regard. As a religious movement, it is based upon a serious set of values, commitments, and principles. Reform rabbis must be empowered to articulate that language of norms, expectations, values and commitment. To be sure, religious ideology is by no means popular. On the contrary, it is often divisive among Jews. But this becomes a question of what it is that we stand for—what makes us distinctive as a community. Absent a specific ideology of Judaism, we would essentially form a bland and relatively banal enterprise attempting to be all things to all people and thereby providing significant meaning to few.

In this context, we face the specific challenge of intermarriage. Can we maintain our communal imperative of rejecting intermarriage as a phenomenon, as discouraging intermarriage, even as we reach out to mixed-married Jews and their spouses? No generation of Jewish leaders in this regard has ever failed to resist intermarriage. Our challenge for today is: Can we maintain that message of rejecting intermarriage but welcoming intermarrieds?

Some 35 years ago the sociologist and theologian Will Herberg authored an important book, *Protestant. Catholic. Jew.* Herberg celebrated the fact that Judaism had arrived as one of the three central faiths of American culture. However, he also warned of the dangers that in becoming part of the overall American fabric, Judaism could become virtually bland. That, to me, is the essential challenge emerging out of our most recent population survey. Can we assert Jewish distinctiveness in the face of a reality that proclaims the end to Jewish exceptionalism? That is the challenge confronting all of us. How we respond to it will determine not only the fate of our current generation of mixed-marrieds but it will also be a measure of where we stand as Jewish leaders in the chain of Jewish history.

Outreach to the Unaffiliated

Writing nearly a century ago, Jewish philosopher and theologian Franz Rosenzweig identified the primary requisite of the community as the raising of Jews. "Books are not the order of the day," wrote Rosenzweig. "But what we need more than ever . . . are human beings— Jewish human beings." Much contemporary outreach work is indebted to Rosenzweig's programmatic prescription—renew Jewish life by building upon the *pintele yid* within each Jew to create Jewishly sensitive human beings who can integrate the best of Western culture with the enduring values of Judaism. Judaism, Rosenzweig believed, could provide answers to the ultimate questions of the meaning and purpose of life.

Rosenzweig's concept of Jewish renewal through Jewish learning provides an ideological basis for outreach. Contemporary demographic facts make outreach imperative.

Recent data from the Council of Jewish Federations 1990 National Jewish Population Survey confirm a picture of Jewish life that many have long suspected: Although some Jews are intensifying their Jewish commitments, the major trends within the community are widespread disaffiliation, increasing intermarriage, and ongoing secularization. Jewish renewal is real, for many have enriched their personal and family lives by turning to Judaism. Erosion and assimilation are equally real, for Jews are marrying out in record numbers, and the overwhelming majority of mixed-marrieds fail to raise their children in the Jewish faith, let alone provide a meaningful Jewish identity.

This picture has been obscured in recent years by certain sanguine sociologists who see no erosion and even predict gain to the Jewish community through the conversion of gentile spouses. Equally misleading have been the dire predictions of other observers who see no prospect of a Jewish future in the Diaspora.

In large measure, these contradictory views derive from different expectations for the weakly committed "middles" of Jewish life. Many

Published by the American Jewish Committee, September 1992.

of these "middles" sincerely desire Jewish continuity—usually defined as Jewish grandchildren—but their own lives lack the Jewish content on which continuity depends. They represent the central challenge to outreach: Intensify the Jewish commitments of the weakly committed "middles" by demonstrating to them the beauties and joys of Jewish living.

Analysis and Recommendations

The Target Population

Much communal confusion exists as to appropriate target populations for outreach initiatives. The popular slogan "outreach to the unaffiliated" means little, for it assumes a large population that can be targeted and affected by communal initiatives. Similarly, the term "outreach to mixed-marrieds" presupposes that those who have married out are waiting for and are receptive to contact from the Jewish community.

Actual affiliation rates vary widely by both community size and geography. Small communities often enjoy very high affiliation rates—e.g., Flint, Michigan, has a rate of 87 percent. Conversely, Los Angeles, the second largest Jewish community in the country, has only a 25 percent affiliation rate. Areas of new settlement have low rates—e.g., central Florida, to which many Jews have only recently migrated. Affiliation will also vary by life-cycle stages, reaching its peak when children are just prior to bar-mitzvah age. Thus the widely cited statistic that 50 percent of Jews are unaffiliated with a synagogue actually means that at any one moment in time half the community is unaffiliated. Most will become members at some stage of their life cycle. The numbers that are truly unaffiliated over their lifetimes are much smaller—perhaps 10–15 percent of the community. The challenge then becomes more to work with the large numbers who have demonstrated some minimal commitment or attachment—enrollment in Jewish education, contribution to Jewish philanthropy, subscription to a Jewish newspaper, or synagogue membership—rather than chasing the truly unaffiliated who have shown no desire to be chased.

Again, the implication is focusing on the "middles" of Jewish life, those who express a commitment to continuity but are unable to express the content of that commitment. Jewish identity for them is often instinctual—responses to anti-Semitism or threats to Israel's existence. Often they are parents of young children enrolled in religious schools who themselves rarely appear in the synagogue. Although most identify with the traditional denominational labels of Judaism, the number claiming to be "just Jewish" has been increasing in recent years. Most express comfort at being in the company of other Jews—a somewhat vague feeling of tribalism devoid of ideological commitment. Their reasons for noninvolvement in the Jewish community range from personal circumstances such as just beginning a family, cost of affiliation, and recent geographic mobility ("I don't know anyone in the community") to psychological alienation from the community—negative memories of Hebrew school, marginality associated with intermarriage, and simple ineptitude with matters Jewish.

What the marginally affiliated or underaffiliated Jews have in common is a vague but expressed desire that they and their children remain Jewish. The decline in Jewish religiosity coupled with acceptance by the general society suggests that these are people who may drop out of the community completely. The communal challenge is to enrich these "middles" of Jewish life Jewishly, creating a population that is intensely rather than marginally committed to leading a Jewish life.

Who precisely are these middles? Generally, they observe the major holidays as family events and opportunities to reenact positive childhood memories. Occasionally they support Federation campaigns. They articulate the belief in a watchmaker deity who plays little role in human events. Most important, they are a Jewishly illiterate population, lacking a knowledge and vocabulary of what it means to be Jewish. They express little opposition to intermarriage and therefore are likely to marry out of the faith, as many have already done.

In short, this is a population that is aware of its Jewishness but is unsure what that connotes. They have not experienced the joys of living Jewishly, often perceiving the content of Jewish identity in sorrowful rather than jubilant terms. For some, being Jewish equates with a vague sense that social-justice concerns spring from Jewish roots. Most perceive themselves as Jewishly committed but are not rooted in any particular Jewish institution.

Finally, this target population often express significant grievances with organized Jewish life. Synagogues are regarded as large and distant, unable to serve the inner existential needs of those not firmly rooted in its communities. Serious questions are raised concerning Israel and whether it is practicing Jewish social values in its public policies. Israel's particularism runs against the universalist ethic of many Jews, and Israel's central position on the Jewish communal agenda communicates little but irrelevance to those for whom being Jewish is far more private and personal. Lastly, many report that costs are a barrier to Jewish communal affiliation. The Jews they see involved in Federation and synagogue are often individuals with whom they cannot identify for reasons of social and economic class, and they resent the glitz associated with these public Jewish institutions.

Communal policy initiatives designed to enhance the Jewishness of this target population have many opportunities for success. Communal interventions may tip the scales in favor of Jewish identification and subsequent communal affiliation. Parents with young children are particularly receptive to programs that enhance the overall quality of family life. Recent migrants to new communities are eager to make new friends and establish connections. Singles generally welcome opportunities to meet and socialize with other Jews. Mixed-marrieds are also unsure as to the religious identity of their homes and will join settings that enable them to explore the Jewish dimension and what it may offer their personal and family lives.

To be sure, the process is time-consuming and presents many frustrations to the outreach worker. Individuals who have not been involved in the Jewish community for quite some time may have created a pattern of nonaffiliation that can be very difficult to break. Although outreach may be an imperative for human and demographic reasons, it requires, as we shall see, enormous follow-up efforts with few guarantees of success. Conversely, where successful, outreach holds out the promise of enriching personal lives and strengthening the Jewish community.

What Is Outreach?

Outreach may be defined as initiatives targeted to Jews far removed from the core community and designed to effect behavioral changes bringing the target population closer to the communal core. Often, but not exclusively, outreach initiatives are addressed to the spiritual hunger of individuals for transcendental meaning beyond their daily concerns and their work and family responsibilities. Thus outreach must be differentiated sharply from adult education, which aims simply to make Jews more knowledgeable with no goal of effecting behavioral changes. The ultimate success of outreach is the *baal teshuva,* the adult returnee to Judaism. The term is often used to characterize Orthodox returnees but it should not be used exclusively in that sense. Returnees to Judaism under Conservative or Reform auspices are no less evidence of the success of outreach. As we shall see, community is a critical ingredient in successful outreach, enabling the returnee to join a warm and welcoming community of like-minded Jews, who encourage further behavioral modification through subtly (and sometimes not so subtly) expressed communal norms and standards.

A further distinction should be made with respect to in-reach programs. Leadership-education programs are designed to strengthen communal activists who comprise the community's core. Some of the more notable leadership-education programs—e.g., those under the auspices of CLAL and the Wexner Heritage Foundation—have sought to enhance Jewish leaders by empowering them to make choices informed by Jewish knowledge, share Jewish values and rituals with their families, and create a community of Jewish leaders inspired by visions of Judaism and Jewish life. Outreach itself often has an in-reach component in terms of its transforming effects upon outreach staff and the institutions in which they work. Yet outreach often stumbles over the failures of in-reach, namely, the absence of enough Jews sufficiently secure in their Jewishness to create the type of community so attractive that others will wish to join it. This last issue relates closely to policy issues of concern to outreach initiatives—the importance of role-modeling by Jews in the public arena and whether outreach conflicts with initiatives to enhance the core community in terms of cost and priority. Many will argue that all outreach is a form of in-reach because of its effect upon those already inside the community. The dichotomy is one of form vs. content. Outreach initiatives, with some exceptions, will try to bring Jews into contact with other Jews and strengthen the community structurally. In-reach initiatives tend to be much stronger on content, seeking to address the ideological and ideational weaknesses of the community rather than its numbers or forms.

Programmatically, the critical distinctions in outreach are between Orthodox and non-Orthodox initiatives. First, there is significant difference in what is meant by outreach. Orthodox outreach aims to have Jews "return" to Judaism. Outreach under non-Orthodox auspices, in contrast, often is aimed at Gentiles involved in family relationships with Jews.

Second, Orthodox outreach focuses heavily on the content of Jewish life. Outreach workers, frequently rabbis, are convinced that people will respond to a message of ideological coherence that makes significant and even radical demands for changes in thought and deed. Particularly when articulated by Orthodoxy's right, this "maximal" approach declares a fundamental distinction between Judaism and the broader culture, which is often denigrated as pagan and hedonistic. Modern Orthodox outreach, to be sure, seeks to articulate Judaism's salience in the modern world. Yet it is a point of considerable sensitivity within Orthodoxy that its most notable outreach programs exist under rightist or *haredi* rather than Modern or centrist auspices. The "modern" components of this outreach are formal rather than intellectual—e.g., use of modern technology, including radio spots, and modern country or rock music as vehicles to articulate the message of return.

For example, Rabbi Irving Greenberg, founder and president of CLAL, the National Jewish Center for Learning and Leadership, has long criticized Modern Orthodoxy generally for its failure to articulate a distinctive synthesis between tradition and modernity. Greenberg bemoans the excessive concentration on outreach within Orthodoxy on the extreme right and claims there is no need for such a radical break with contemporary culture. Rather, outreach initiatives should offer multiple models aiming to create more Jewish Jews along an entire spectrum of identity. Moreover, Greenberg argues, the more drastic the change, the less stable it will be. In other words, it is preferable to facilitate individual Jewish growth in which different people will find different avenues and entry points to Jewish tradition. Greenberg therefore articulates a "principled pluralism" in which Jews can learn from one another and respect the validity of alternative expressions of Judaism.

Orthodox outreach workers define themselves as "countercultural" in the sense of offering a criticism of prevailing cultural norms. They target their message to those who express disillusionment with the world around them. Phrases such as "American society is fundamentally sick" reflect their rejection of the excesses of contemporary mores—e.g., the promiscuity accompanying America's sexual revolution. They use popular music to transmit their message that ultimate meaning is to be found in Torah alone. The chorus of one popular outreach lyric goes:

> *Come on home . . .*
> *What you are looking for*
> *Is right there by your door.*

Critics assail this approach on two grounds: First, they quarrel with its content—its abandonment of any distinctive synthesis, once the hallmark of Modern Orthodoxy, between Judaism and Western culture. Others question the neutrality or even ambivalence within *haredi* outreach toward Zionism and the State of Israel. Methodologically, critics claim that the maximalist approach implies an "all or nothing" attitude in which most will opt for nothing. They note that most American Jews do not consider themselves "bad Jews" and will resist a language of outreach that they perceive as a language of reproach. Orthodox outreach professionals concede that more leave than stay but argue that the dropouts are likely to find their way into Conservative or Reform synagogues, thereby benefiting the community as a whole. Thus the "maximalist" program allows for fallback positions even while its exponents criticize those positions as weakened or watered-down and possibly heretical versions of Judaism. Even Yeshiva University failed, in this view, for lowering standards in an abortive attempt at "synthesis" with Western culture.

To be sure, Orthodox outreach workers are quire sophisticated in understanding where their target population is coming from and will not ask that they publicly renounce home or university. Rather the aim is to subtly undermine the potential *baal teshuva*'s background by exposing the excesses of moral relativism, materialism, and spiritual emptiness. Thus the *baalei teshuva* yeshivas in Israel, for example, seek to engage in gradual "people-changing." The capstone of this approach is the marriage of the *baal teshuva* and integration into the *haredi* community of which the yeshiva is representative.

Israeli observers comment that *haredi* outreach activities have generated a backlash. So negative have been the perceptions of *haredi* Orthodoxy within Israel that programs that might otherwise have proven attractive to those seeking to satisfy their spiritual needs never, in fact, reach their target population. In other words, Israeli secularists may never give traditional Judaism a fair hearing because of *haredi* political activities, especially their efforts to strengthen religious legislation in the Jewish state. Indeed, as we shall see, alternative nonharedi programs—e.g., those of Gesher—were initiated, to some extent, as countermeasures to the virtual *haredi* monopoly on outreach activities within Israel.

Orthodox outreach in North America is similarly largely under *haredi* auspices. Significant exceptions have been the Torah outreach programs of Yeshiva University and the Lincoln Square Synagogue in New York City and its recent outgrowth, the National Jewish Outreach Project. The former, university-based outreach, seeks to emphasize Judaism's intellectual depth and its capacity to provide ultimate values. Lincoln Square Synagogue similarly emphasizes the intellectual dimension and the permissibility and even desirability of constant questioning. These programs constitute the distinctive tenor of "Centrist Orthodox" outreach.

Analysis

Several points of commonality emerge from an examination of existing programs. Programs succeed to the extent that they combine social, intellectual, and communal elements. People enjoy the group dynamics and interaction with others; they seek a supportive community that will nurture their growth Jewishly. Yet structural and institutional forms do not suffice. The content of outreach programming and the Judaic knowledge it imparts are equally critical to its success. Here the recurring themes appear to be Judaism's relevance to the personal situation of individuals—including major life crises, human loneliness and alienation, and the limits of modern science and secular values, Israel addresses a part of this personal and existential direction by communicating a sense of homecoming and national pride as well as the group dimension of Jewish family and friends. That may be one factor underlying the success of trips to Israel in outreach initiatives. In Israel various themes of history, meaning, and transcendence are joined with community and social interaction among Jews.

A second point of commonality relates to staff and staff effectiveness. Virtually all program directors underscore the need to meet people where they are—not where the Jewish community expects them to be. Therefore, staff has to be open and nonjudgmental—although clearly committed to Judaism—rather than threatening. Their message and role-modeling ought to signal that the Jewish community cares about the person as an individual.

An important exception is Orthodox outreach, which appears far more confrontational with the target population. However, Orthodox staff must also be intellectually sophisticated, committed to outreach, receptive to doubt, and personally open-minded and tolerant. Generally, Orthodox outreach workers are "people persons," who make themselves available literally at all hours of the day and can tolerate widespread failure. Their strong belief system enables them to withstand the constant frustration of outreach work.

Conversely, Orthodox returnees to Judaism are by no means "home free." Many report continued difficulties with their families, difficulty integrating with the Orthodox community, and continued ambivalence regarding various aspects of Orthodoxy. One key to their success is familial: Secure marriages make for easy acceptance into the community. Perhaps more overriding, however, is their capacity to integrate radical changes in attitude and behavior with their past lives and sense of self. Too radical a clash with other values and lifestyles will lead to dysfunction and cultural dissonance rather than wholesome integration.

This dissonance often extends to the Jewish community generally. Jewish communal life all too often revolves around politics and fundraising. But unaffiliated or marginally affiliated Jews are looking to their private and personal identities, searching for meaning and transcendence. Serious outreach to these people requires translation of the Jewish communal agenda into language they can hear. It also requires greater focus on the spiritual components of Jewish identity. The current public agenda of American Jews, in failing to address the real personal and existential needs of individuals, may not form a sufficient basis on which outreach may be undertaken. The State of Israel, for example, which dominates so much of Jewish communal discussion, may be virtually irrelevant to the private needs and spiritual hunger of those on the margins of the community.

Finally, the concept of pluralism is critical to the success of outreach initiatives. Different individuals require different points of entry and connectedness to Jewish tradition and community. Holidays, family, and foods are entry points; so are Jewish history and Jewish music. Outreach workers' ideological approaches will differ; no one ideology can address the needs of all Jews.

This pluralism distinguishes the non-Orthodox from the Orthodox outreach programs. Orthodox outreach staff describe their programs as maximalist and express enormous conviction that theirs is the appropriate way. They aim to replace the "sickness" of contemporary society with the values of Torah. Orthodox successes in this area are notable and have captured widespread media attention. According to the Council of Jewish Federations' 1990 Population Study, some 12 percent of currently Orthodox Jews were *not* born into Orthodox families. Michael Medved, the author and film critic who is perhaps the best known example of this *teshuvah* phenomenon, has written eloquently of the absence of values in contemporary culture generally. Yet most unaffiliated Jews are by no means disenchanted with Western society. They are far from willing to jettison their Western values for Judaism. Here lies the weakness of the so-called maximalist programs and the need for plural models that can reach people where they are.

The non-Orthodox programs also have a problem with ideology. If Orthodox outreach is too "maximalist" for some, non-Orthodox outreach must ask how it can be as inclusive as possible without dilution of distinctive Jewish identity. For example, can we reach out to mixed-marrieds without abandoning the ideals of the Jewish family and its values of endogamy? Here, outreach staff ought constantly to recall that their initiatives make sense only if they are part of a broader commitment to preserve the vitality of Judaism as a distinctive value system. Continuity for its own sake amounts to little more than tribalism.

For this reason, outreach programs to mixed-married couples have caused some concern within the community. Mindful of the human and demographic imperatives of outreach to mixed-marrieds, synagogues, family-service agencies, and Jewish community centers have begun support groups and special workshops for mixed-marrieds to explore the nature of their marriages and their religious identities. The objective, obviously, is to bring the couples closer to the Jewish heritage, secure the conversion of the non-Jewish spouses, or, when that is not possible, try to maintain the Jewishness of the children.

Advocates of outreach to mixed-marrieds perceive these programs as constructive steps to adopt in the face of an ever-increasing intermarriage rate. The successes here of the Reform movement are particularly noteworthy. Yet critical voices have been heard. First, they ask what messages we are sending to the broader Jewish community. Does outreach, where successful, make it difficult to discourage interfaith dating and marriage? Can Jewish professionals embrace interfaith couples and simultaneously urge teenagers to date only Jews? May rabbis advocate in-marriage when so many congregants are themselves intermarried?

A second question relates to the durability of outreach successes. Can Jewish identity be maintained in a home where one parent is a Gentile? Research thus far indicates that Jewish identity has generally disappeared among the grandchildren of a mixed-married couple. Whether increased outreach activities can change this result is an unanswered question.

Funds for outreach to mixed-marrieds must be diverted from other programs. Allocation committees have to make difficult decisions in identifying which populations hold the greatest promise for the Jewish communal future. Many question whether there is more to be gained by working with mixed-marrieds rather than with those currently active and involved Jewishly.

These questions have no easy answers. Outreach to mixed-marrieds is a new program area and merits some experimentation. The need is obvious, but whether the Jewish community will increase and sustain such programs will be determined only by our answers to these questions and by our experiences.

Research Agenda

To plan for the future, the community should consider various types of research to determine which outreach programs are working and where communal investment should be targeted for maximum results. A research agenda might comprise the following elements:

1. Evaluation research. In most cases, our experience with outreach dates back a decade. Various claims are made for program successes ranging from the modest to the messianic. It is necessary to look at particular programs and track participants over an extended period to determine what proved effective and what failed. This will require some consensus on how to define success.
2. Participant research. Who are today's unaffiliated Jews? How do they differ from affiliated Jews in terms of their images of Judaism? Are they receptive to communal intervention and, if so, under what circumstances and of what sort? Is age a factor in their receptivity?
3. Method research. Who have been the charismatic teachers who have successfully transmitted Jewish identity and why have they been successful? Are there institutional contexts of outreach that have been noticeably successful? If so, why, and under what circumstances?

These questions by no means exhaust the research agenda. But research is necessary if we are to avoid mistakes and channel limited resources effectively.

The Outreach Experience

Lincoln Square Synagogue

The Lincoln Square Synagogue has become internationally renowned for its capacity to attract Manhattan's affluent Jewish professionals. Its founding rabbi, Shlomo Riskin, identified the goal of its outreach programs as raising consciousness among those currently uninterested in being Jewish. Today, nearly a decade after Riskin's *aliya*, the synagogue houses an extensive adult-education program, a weekly beginners' minyan, and twice-yearly "Turn Friday Night into Shabbos" programs. Together these programs have garnered great support from their target population—often in reaction to Manhattan's "yuppie" culture with its emphasis upon career and with its hectic pace. The synagogue corroborates the theme of the movie *Baby Boom* that there is more to life than Manhattan's "rat race." Women professionals in particular are attracted by the centrality of family life, a supportive community, and a sense of connectedness to roots, history, and tradition—all themes that *Baby Boom* finds lacking in Manhattan's professional culture.

National Jewish Outreach Project

The National Jewish Outreach Project has extended the Lincoln Square Synagogue program across the country with the goal of providing every Jew an opportunity to acquire basic Jewish knowledge. It sponsors Hebrew literacy courses, a crash course in basic Judaism, Turn-Friday-Night-into-Shabbos programs, and beginners' minyans. Approximately 30,000 have enrolled in the basic Hebrew course, 8,000 in the basic Judaism course, and 20,000 have participated in the Turn-Friday-Night-into-Shabbos program. Additionally, 65 synagogues conducted beginners' minyans. NJOP organizers concede that approximately one-third of the registrants do not complete the basic Hebrew course. Of the 500 synagogues participating, 40 percent are non-Orthodox. NJOP organizers provide these non-Orthodox synagogues with materials, but they will not place them on their list of referrals where Jews can receive additional information or guidance.

In becoming a national network, NJOP turned to modern electronic media to market its message. Some fifty one-minute radio spots have been aired across the country advertising the basic Hebrew and Judaism courses. A national newsletter has been developed carrying information of beginners' services and Turn-Friday-Night-into-Shabbos programs. The mailing list of the newsletter has been carefully developed from respondents to the twice-yearly ad campaigns.

Again, borrowing from Lincoln Square Synagogue, NJOP identified the teacher as critical to the success of outreach. It works with the local synagogue to create volunteer teachers—a lay outreach worker who is warm, outgoing, and eager to engage in personal follow-up. It is follow-up which is critical to outreach and which distinguishes it from adult education, in which the primary requirement is only that the teacher be knowledgeable and articulate rather than willing to engage in personal follow-up with students.

The Basic Judaism courses consist of five ninety-minute lectures on God, prayer, sexuality, Shabbat, and Jewish observance. The emphasis is on the salience of these concepts to twentieth-century men and women, communicating an understanding of the divine order in creation, prayer as self-expression, and sexual restraint as enhancing relationships, Shabbat as an antidote to the workaday world, and the efficacy of Jewish ritual in creating ethical human beings. The common denominator underlying these themes, as noted earlier, is Judaism as a counterculture to the prevailing norms of modern society. Turn-Friday-Night-into-Shabbos, again an outgrowth of Lincoln Square Synagogue, has grown to over thirty participating synagogues in the past four years. These programs feature an abridged Friday night service followed by a dinner matching observant families with newcomers. There are usually subsequent invitations to the homes of these families, a re-union of participants one month after the event, and follow-up mailings to participants. The involvement of host families from within the synagogue in turn creates a virtual "lay outreach committee," who will build and develop the synagogue's outreach programming.

For all of its successes, NJOP leadership remains convinced that American Jewry is suffering irreparable losses and erosion. It perceives its program as necessary to counteract these trends but admits that it is fighting a losing battle. Ultimately NJOP calls for a change of priorities within the Jewish community so that Jews may be saved for Judaism. Absent the change in communal priorities, NJOP regards all the expressed concern about Jewish continuity as largely lip service.

Lubavitch

Perhaps best known—not only in America but internationally—are the outreach initiatives of Chabad Lubavitch, whose exponents feel most comfortable in the role of missionaries of Judaism. In the 1960s, under the leadership of Shlomo Carlebach and Zalman Schachter, who utilized the teaching of mysticism and Jewish music to reach Jewish souls, Chabad was the first to recruit on college campuses. In turn, this led to the creation of Chabad houses across the country, at times even on campuses with few Jewish students. In more recent years, Chabad efforts have featured an aggressive and visible approach. Their "mitzvah mobiles" operate very publicly, trying to encourage Jews to perform rituals. The addresses of the Rebbe have been carried via radio and cable television. Huge Chabad menorahs may be found at public sites in most cities around Hanukkah. Recently, Chabad has purchased ads in major newspapers proclaiming to Jews the imminent arrival of the messiah.

The strategy appears to be an attempt to capture Jewish attention through highly visible public statements and symbols. To be sure, this approach has drawn considerable criticism. Some claim that religious symbols on public property violate traditional church-state separation. Others criticize Lubavitch intellectually, particularly its difficulty with modern science and evolutionary theory. Gerson Cohen and Arthur Lelyveld each attacked the "cult-like" atmosphere of Lubavitch, although neither could document evidence of snatching or mind-control, nor a turning against one's parents for their lack of Jewish observance. Finally, Lubavitch messianism has drawn considerable political opposition as, at best, a waste of valuable resources and, at worst, as arousing a wave of messianic hysteria that could lead to disappointment should the messiah fail to arrive.

Despite these criticisms, Lubavitch remains intent upon its mission. Its mood, informed by traditional Kabbalism and articulated by the Rebbe, looks upon the world with benevolent optimism. Every Jew is a soul ready to be saved by igniting Jewish sparks of good within it. Despite an enormous dropout rate, Lubavitch remains intent on its aggressive missionary approach.

Havurot

The attractiveness of Orthodoxy has often been its sense of community—closely knit networks of families and individuals who share similar values and experiences. That type of Jewish community is rarely found outside of Orthodoxy. An important exception in recent years has been the growth of *havurot,* surrogate extended families of Jews connecting to one another through the Jewish tradition without a commitment to *halakhah. Havurot* hold out the promise to non-Orthodox Jews of enriching personal and family life through experiencing the intellectual and emotional treasures of the Jewish heritage.

As *havurot* have matured, they have become increasingly family-oriented. Children are nurtured in the Jewish heritage by participation in *havurah* family events and rituals. In essence, the message becomes Judaism fosters family, and the *havurot* strengthen the family by providing a supportive external structure in some ways analogous to contemporary Orthodox communities.

For some, *havurot* form an alternative Jewish community. Its members criticize the spiritual emptiness of suburban synagogues. The countercultural *Jewish Catalog* series has become their guidebook—a do-it-yourself Judaism rather than reliance on rabbinical authority. The significance of *havurot* to outreach is considerable. In celebrating Jewish life, *havurot* provide multiple points of entry or return for many uninvolved with Jewish life. Although their members may not be numerous, *havurot* constitute a dimension of outreach that is working and strengthening Jewish life.

Project Link

The principal outreach initiative of the Conservative movement was a four-year initiative entitled Project Link. Funded by a pilot grant from the Leonard and Phyllis Greenberg Foundation, Project Link was unable to secure permanent funding from either the Conservative movement or from outside sources subsequent to 1989. Nevertheless, it did reach out to over 100 mixed-marrieds in the northern New Jersey area during its four-year existence.

Project Link began as a rather intensive course of twenty-five sessions over a twelve-month period. By its final year, the number of sessions had been reduced to thirteen, a decision regretted by its director, Rabbi Alan Silverstein, as diminishing content without expanding enrollment. Significantly, the project did not utilize the term "outreach" for fear that it connoted too great an acceptance of the lifestyle of the target population, namely, intermarriage, which was Judaically unacceptable. Rather, it employed the term *kiruv,* implying an effort to bring those who had strayed closer to the community rather than transform the community in ideologically unacceptable directions.

The course dealt with Jewish holidays, life-cycle events, theology, and contemporary Jewish identity with particular emphasis on the Holocaust and modern Israel. Where conversion did not appear feasible, Project Link aimed to have couples commit themselves to raise their children as Jews—a goal that, retrospectively, appears to have been realized universally. Following the course, the project focused on bringing these people into synagogues. Apart from these goals, the project provided Conservative rabbis with an opportunity for dialogue with mixed-marrieds. Nevertheless, the project failed to inspire sufficient support among communal leaders to win the resources necessary for its continuation.

According to its director, Project Link did succeed in uncovering a process mixed-marrieds could pursue if already linked to a synagogue. In other words, it provided a critical final step for those who had already indicated some commitment to leading a Jewish life. Where the project failed was with those who were completely unaffiliated and who had simply responded to ads placed in newspapers. For them, Project Link was, at most, a tentative first step on a lengthy journey whose outcome was most uncertain. In this regard, at least according to this single evaluation, more should be done to reach those marginally affiliated with the community rather than expend limited resources pursuing the totally unaffiliated.

Reform Jewish Outreach

The core component of Reform Judaism's outreach program is the "Introduction to Judaism" course held in synagogues in virtually every community in the country. The overall goal of the course is conversion, but that goal is not likely to be attained in most cases. Rather, the hope is to enhance the Jewish identity of the home and preserve the Jewishness of Jewish family members, especially children. Thus outreach to Gentiles functions as in-reach to the Jewish partner.

This program, originally proclaimed by Rabbi Alexander Schindler in a landmark 1978 address, actually took root in the mid-1980s under the aegis of the UAHC-CCAR Joint Commission on Outreach. To be sure, there was some ambivalence regarding a conversionary posture—"converting the unchurched"—rather than an exclusive focus on mixed-marrieds. Others were concerned over diversion of energies and resources from those within the synagogue to those outside it. Those for whom conversion is not the primary stimulus may simply not be ready to make the commitment; for these individuals the courses are doors of entry into Judaism. Program staff note that the courses include many born Jews exploring what it is to be Jewish.

The course curriculum is affective rather than academic. It encourages people to lead a Jewish life by teaching them how to observe Shabbat, holidays, and life-cycle events. Throughout the course, averaging eighteen weeks but with considerable variations among communities, participants keep personal journals of their experiences and Jewish growth.

Much as Orthodox outreach raises questions about its transforming effects upon a community—namely, the tendency toward isolation and rejection of outside culture—so Reform outreach raises philosophical and policy questions. Reform outreach expects to have a transforming effect upon the community as well as upon the target population. Ideally, it will compel the community to examine its own Jewishness and make Judaism attractive in a world of free choices. However, its outcomes remain unknowable. We do not know if this degree of Jewishness can be sustained, what losses will ensue, and whether the cultural impact upon the community will translate as the dilution of Jewish identity. Finally, it is unclear what are the boundaries of outreach. Rabbinic officiation at mixed marriages was once considered unacceptable. Today it is too often a litmus test for the employment of Reform rabbis. Similarly many couples today practice varying forms of religious syncretism and dual-faith scenarios for their households. Guidelines are necessary to determine what within outreach is Judaically acceptable and what is not.

Project Connect

Project Connect of New York's 92nd Street YM-YWHA defines its target population as those who do not belong to a synagogue, who do not give to Federation, and who do not enroll their children in Hebrew schools. Thus it seeks to reach a population completely unaffiliated with Jewish communal life.

The project originated in the mid-1980s with a Shabbat retreat followed by the creation of mini-*havurot* at the Y. These met twice monthly and included holiday workshops, classes, Shabbat dinners, and parallel children's programs. Throughout these meetings some confusion existed as to whether the program was religious or secular, highlighting the difficulty American Jews have in formulating a distinctive Jewish identity that is not particularly religious. Moreover, it was difficult to form a common culture among people of varied backgrounds. As a result, in more recent years the emphasis has been on monthly events rather than on a Shabbat retreat. Today, Project Connect functions as an umbrella for a variety of programs targeted to unaffiliated Jews, including after-school programs for children, workshops for interfaith couples, and Derech Torah, a thirty-week introduction to Judaism involving nine classes of sixteen students each.

Project Connect claims its greatest successes in Derech Torah. Over a four-year period 575 people have enrolled. Retention rates have been quite high; in 1990–91 there were only three dropouts out of 150 enrolled. Instructors present Judaism as holding existential meaning, posing questions of personal existence.

The director of the program, Rabbi David Woznicka, argues that the program's success depends on its excellent faculty, its nondenominational content, and its emphasis upon people meeting other people in a Jewish context. He perceives a spiritual thirst existing in the community which Jewish institutions should try to satisfy. Moreover, by definition, Derech Torah can meet the needs of only a small number of people—larger classes would be far too impersonal.

The curriculum of Derech Torah includes the existence of God, suffering and evil, death and mourning, and the relevance of Jewish teaching to such major contemporary issues as marriage, abortion, and euthanasia. The course also covers Judaism's sacred texts, holidays, dietary laws, and Shabbat, as well as life-cycle events. The experiential component includes two Shabbat dinners during the year, and every holiday is preceded by a special workshop. Some instructors take their students to local synagogues and perform a havdallah service together with them.

The staff dedication just alluded to is critical to the success of the program. Staff are encouraged to act as role models, displaying a passion for Judaism in many ways similar to outreach conducted under right-wing Orthodox auspices. Even though there are non-Jews in the classes, the instructors do not disguise their commitment to Judaism. They perceive themselves as Jewish educators seeking to instill a love for Jewish learning, values, and peoplehood.

Following the program, Derech Torah directs alumni to existing synagogues. Bnai Jeshurun, a prominent Conservative congregation on New York's West Side, today has approximately seventy-five Derech Torah alumni as members.

Jewish Community Centers

Nationwide, Jewish community centers increasingly define themselves as outreach agencies. Professional staff see themselves as a sales force for the Jewish heritage, and, in recent years, significant efforts have been mounted to enhance the Judaic literacy of center staff. The objective is to create a Jewish environment within the center, reflected in associations with other Jews, with Jewish foods and customs, and ultimately with Judaic ideas. Thus the center aims to replace the much-vaunted Jewish neighborhood as a force for Jewish cohesiveness and continuity.

Much of JCC outreach programming focuses on the uses of leisure time and on the services people require during nonleisure hours. Thus the centers, historically, have focused on sports and, more recently, on child care. The assumption is that these are programs that people want and need. If the community can offer these programs in a Jewish context, it will bring Jews into contact with other Jews and ultimately enhance them Jewishly.

For similar reasons, the number of infant day-care centers under JCC auspices has been expanding despite some ambivalence about taking infants out of the home. The operating assumption has been that Jews, at certain stages of their life cycle, will require specific types of services. If these services are provided under Jewish auspices, they provide opportunities for enhancing communal connectedness.

A third type of outreach program under JCC auspices has been the Shalom Newcomers Network. Reacting to studies documenting the increased mobility of Jews and their disaffiliation with the community, JCCs began sharing information as to who is moving into which town and then welcoming them in their new place of residence. Thus the JCC can serve as a place for communal institutional contact in the new environments.

Most recently, JCCs have been experimenting with pilot programs of outreach to mixed-marrieds. These have been informed by a vision of meeting people where they are and ultimately mainstreaming them into synagogues and other communal institutions. Moreover, by providing other services—sports, infant care, etc.—the JCC hopes to attract mixed-marrieds among its broader target population and clientele and thereby provide them with greater Jewish associations.

Memorial Foundation for Jewish Culture

The Memorial Foundation for Jewish Culture has piloted two outreach programs—one in St. Louis, Missouri, and one in Metro-West, New Jersey. Each program—termed "Connections" or "Contact" by its respective sponsor—services 300 unaffiliated or underaffiliated families, to which it provides opportunities to network, celebrate holidays together, and exchange ideas and experiences about parenting and Jewish concerns. A special project coordinator was engaged in each area to locate potential recruits, discover what programming would appeal to them, and present Jewish materials in an open-minded and nonjudgmental fashion.

The experience indicated that parents with young children were the most receptive to this outreach—that parenting, indeed, is a gateway to

Jewish life. Synagogue and Jewish education may or may not lie within these families' futures. Therefore Jewish communal outreach may well tip the scales toward greater identification and affiliation with the community by communicating to the participants that the organized Jewish community cares about them as individuals.

For these reasons, central to the program's philosophy was the idea that no communal or institutional demands or expectations would be placed on participants. The program aimed strictly to demonstrate how Judaism could enrich their personal and family lives, empowering them to introduce Jewish components in their homes. Shabbat dinner, holiday workshops, and family *havurot* were all designed to enable families to place Jewish concerns upon their personal agendas. Organizational agendas, in contrast, were deemed irrelevant. Only at a later point will they, on their own initiative, move on to other Jewish institutions.

In short, the Memorial Foundation programs aim not at communal enhancement but at personal enhancement. Its directors believe that Judaism can and should speak to the human existential condition. All too often, however, Judaism fails to say anything meaningful to these groups, for the language of the Jewish community places communal interests and concerns above personal development.

European Outreach

The Strassbourg-based Yechiva des Etudiants de France prides itself on being the pioneering outreach institution to secularized French Jews. By broadening its activities to serve entire families rather than just full-time students, the institution claims to reach 250 families and over 800 individuals, particularly through sponsorship of lectures and public events.

Given initial successes with families of students, the Yechiva hopes to triple its enrollment in the next five years, in turn having a multiplier effect upon the entire community. Its female students are expected to become teachers in the French Jewish educational system. In this way, the Yechiva hopes to alter a picture of increasing assimilation and defection from the world's fourth largest Jewish community.

To be sure, the Yechiva is intellectually indebted to the Gateshead

Yeshiva in England, to which it turns for spiritual leadership and guidance. As a result, its ambience and ethos are distinctly *haredi,* with all of the concerns raised by *haredi* outreach institutions in both Israel and North America.

In pronounced contrast, the Yakar outreach program in England emphasizes the presence of an open-minded faculty prepared to learn as well as to teach. As a result, Yakar boasts of the diversity of its target population, which includes Reform and Hasidic Jews, Yakar eschews the "people-changing" model of *haredi* outreach, aiming instead to enhance informed decision-making. Its goal is the creation of an educated laity prepared to enter serious dialogue rather than the provision of personal comfort to alienated individuals. For this reason, Yakar has attracted overwhelmingly favorable press comment and currently services 200 people weekly through evening classes and 80–100 individuals in Shabbat study sessions.

Leading Yakar is Rabbi Michael Rosen, a young and dynamic rabbi who, for the past twelve years, has been conducting weekend groups of Shabbat observance and traditional study. Rosen prides himself and his faculty on intellectual openness and absence of missionary zeal. Moreover, he has infused his program with social consciousness, raising questions of Jewish responses to issues like apartheid and poverty. Through encounters with figures such as Archbishop Tutu, Rosen seeks to break the image of traditional Judaism as parochial, broaden the community outlook, and demonstrate the salience of Judaism to the modern world.

Israeli Outreach

Most Israeli outreach takes place within a variety of Israeli yeshivot—almost exclusively under *haredi* auspices—with a clientele consisting of Israeli secularists as well as several hundred visiting American students. Contrary to popular opinion, these yeshivot are not flooded with hippies. Most enter out of curiosity and leave quickly. Those who stay gradually modify their lifestyles to accommodate that of the yeshivot. Wide variation exists among these settings. The Yeshiva of the Diaspora began as a refuge for hippies near the Western Wall. In direct contrast is Yeshivat Hamivtar, whose director, Rabbi

Chaim Brovender, eschews "people-changing" in favor of study. Ohr Someach takes a middle approach. Its original goal was to make everyone religiously observant. Recently it has focused primarily on a campaign against Western culture in an effort to counteract intermarriage.

Aish HaTorah began as an Israeli institution but has, in recent years, invested heavily on the American scene. Its approach is unapologetically "I am all right, you are all wrong." The Discovery Program in the States rails against the bankruptcy of American society. The approach is frankly confrontational, challenging students as to why they know so little and supplying them with appropriate intellectual tools to counteract the evils of secularism. It offers intellectual proofs of God's existence, eliminating doubt and confusion about human purpose. Aish HaTorah takes its name literally, aiming to create firebrands and revolutionaries for the cause of Torah.

Although Aish HaTorah has numerous critics who dismiss its approach, many of their criticisms are unfair. There is no cult of personality, nor are brainwashing techniques utilized. The freedom of the individual to leave at any time is absolute. Gurus are absent, as is physical force. The institution's presence in Jerusalem leaves students with the constant prospect of city life and its relative openness. To be sure, Aish HaTorah is far from a modern institution. The rejection of modernity extends even to great ambivalence about Zionism, which it sees as fortifying the bankrupt secular values of modern Jews.

IsraeLight constitutes a liberal offshoot of Aish HaTorah. Founded in 1986 by David Aarons, IsraeLight offers a three-week co-ed seminar in Jerusalem designed to portray Judaism in positive terms. This program is meant to lead to a regular yeshiva program focusing on study of texts in a single-sex context. Approximately 350 students have gone through the program. Program officials claim the overwhelming majority have taken steps toward greater Jewish communal investment.

Gesher, meaning "bridge," aims to bring together religious and secular Israelis. Over the past two decades, Gesher has sought to create mutual understanding between these two groups by demonstrating what they have in common and shattering their stereotypes of one another.

Gesher was established by Rabbi Daniel Tropper, an American-born rabbi who was concerned that the ultimate threat to Israel lay in the serious divisions and conflicts over religion within Israeli society. Tropper assumed that the religious right in Israel had erred in thinking that further religious legislation would inspire Israelis to become more Jewish. Conversely, he felt all Jews ought to be concerned about the future Jewish identity of Israelis, which was not adequately addressed in existing Israeli curricula.

As a result, Gesher sought to develop encounter groups involving secular and religious Israeli high-school students. The program aimed to nurture common values among them as Jews and to demonstrate for secular Israelis the importance of Jewish identity. Through dialogues and retreats, study days in high schools, films and curricula on Jewish history, Gesher utilized informal education techniques simultaneously to nurture pluralism and understanding and to combat assimilation among Israelis. To date, over 44,000 Israelis have participated in the seminars and 85,000 in the study programs.

Gesher is frankly confrontational about Jewish identity, but it eschews the "people-changing" techniques popular in right-wing yeshivot. Rather, Gesher's premise is that secular Israelis be exposed to the beauties of the Jewish tradition, its claims upon us as modern Jews, and the interdependence of Jews everywhere. For example, Gesher developed a high-quality television program for Hanukkah emphasizing the right to be different as a vehicle for combating assimilation.

Although Gesher is well-known for the excellence of its materials and the open environment it nurtures, Gesher leaders concede that they have had little real impact on Israeli society, which continues to be polarized between religious and secular. Some inroads have been made within the public school system, and Gesher is now developing a curriculum for the system. By and large, however, Gesher sees itself as impacting primarily upon individuals in Israeli society but as accomplishing little change in society generally.

Both right and left within Israel have criticized Gesher vigorously. The *haredi* world opposes the co-ed nature of Gesher activities and the utilization of secular Israeli counselors in the study programs. The left claims that Gesher is a camouflaged missionary movement, one that is not truly pluralist in terms of recognizing Reform and Conservative rabbis. Gesher leaders reject the latter charge, pointing to the participation of non-Orthodox rabbis in Gesher programs. Rather, they see the primary intellectual leadership as emanating from the *hesder* yeshiva world with its more open, intellectual, and religious Zionist outlook. Tropper himself refuses to permit Gesher to be drawn into the controversy surrounding religious pluralism in Israel. He argues that religious pluralism will result naturally from the immigration of more Conservative and Reform Jews to Israel. The critique of Gesher from both right and left, in fact, affirms Tropper's centrist position and enables Gesher to define itself as walking a tightrope between the religious movements and passions within Israel.

Nevertheless, the outreach activities of Gesher clearly do serve as a counterweight to the better-known outreach efforts of the *haredi* yeshivot. By nurturing pluralism and open intellectual questioning, Gesher's message to secular Israelis is clear: Deepening one's attachments to tradition need not result in fanaticism and intolerance.

Bibliography

Aviad, Janet. *Return to Judaism: Religious Renewal in Israel.* Chicago: University of Chicago Press, 1983.

Cohen, Steven M. *Content or Continuity? Alternative Bases for Commitment.* New York: American Jewish Committee, 1991.

Commission on Reform Jewish Outreach of the Union of American Hebrew Congregations and the Central Conference of American Rabbis. *Outreach and the Changing Reform Jewish Community.* New York: UAHC, 1989.

Danziger, Herbert. *Returning to Tradition: The Contemporary Revival of Orthodox Judaism.* New Haven and London: Yale University Press, 1989.

Davidman, Lynn. *Tradition in a Rootless World: Women Turn to Orthodox Judaism.* Berkeley and Los Angeles: University of California Press, 1991.

Goldscheider, Calvin. "The Unaffiliated Jew in America: Sociological Perspectives." *Humanistic Judaism* 18 (Spring 1990): 15–22.

Gordis, David, and Yoav Ben-Horin, eds. *Jewish Identity in America.* Los Angeles: Wilstein Institute of Jewish Policy Studies, 1991.

Heilman, Samuel. *A Tale of Two Cities: A Report to the Committee on the Stabilization of the Jewish Family.* The Memorial Foundation for Jewish Culture, 1990.

Hochbaum, Jerry. "Center and Periphery: Reaching Marginally Jewish Families." *Journal of Jewish Communal Service* 64 (Spring 1988): 234–237.

Kaufman, Debra. *Rachel's Daughters: Newly Orthodox Jewish Women.* New Brunswick and London: Rutgers University Press, 1991.

London, Perry, and Barry Chazan. *Psychology and Jewish Identity Education.* New York: American Jewish Committee, 1990.

New Pockets of Jewish Energy: A Study of Adults Who Found Their Way Back to Judaism. New York: American Jewish Committee, 1982.

Padva, Patricia. *Attitudes Towards Israel and Jewish Identity: A Focus Group Study.* New York: American Jewish Committee, 1991.

Prell, Riv-Ellen. *Prayer and Community: The Havurah in American Judaism.* Detroit: Wayne State University Press, 1989.

"Reaching Out: Ideology, Strategies, Policies, Theologies." *The Melton Journal,* no. 18, Summer 1984.

Ukeles Associates, Inc., "The State of 'Outreach to the Unaffiliated' in the Jewish Community of North America," unpublished paper, 1988.

What Is Reform Jewish Outreach? New York: UAHC, 1991.

Wollman, Yisroel. "A Meeting of the Hearts: Reducing Tensions Between the Religious and the Non-Religious." In Charles Liebman, ed., *Conflict and Accommodation Between Jews in Israel.* Jerusalem: Keter Publishing House, 1990, pp. 193–214.

Woocher, Jonathan. *Jewish Affiliation: An Agenda for Research.* New York: American Jewish Committee, 1990.

"Working With Unaffiliated and Disaffected Jews: Struggling for Spiritual Survival." *The Melton Journal,* no. 19, Summer 1985.

Who Controls the Jewish Continuity Agenda?

It is my great pleasure to be with you this morning and to address issues concerning the Jewish continuity agenda. Many of you have been my teachers, others my friends, and others my students.

My goal this morning is to discuss two major questions: What is the map of the Jewish continuity agenda—who are the players and what are the major issues to be confronted? Secondly, and perhaps more importantly, what are the implications for the Orthodox rabbinate—what roles ought Orthodox rabbis be playing as the community wrestles with ensuring its future continuity.

The Jewish continuity agenda in large measure has been set forth by the 1990 National Jewish Population Study. Great credit ought be given to the Council of Jewish Federations, which supplied us with the single most comprehensive survey and analysis of American Jewry in the twentieth century. The message of the CJF study is a clarion call to alert Jews to the serious problems we face in the years ahead of ensuring that our grandchildren will be Jewish. The Population Study sets forth a picture of a Jewish community that is doing incredibly well by American standards in terms of our professional and educational attainments. We are doing incredibly poorly by Jewish standards of transmitting a meaningful Jewish identity. Moreover, the Population Study points to a Jewish community with incredibly fluid boundaries between Jew and Gentile. We have Jews practicing Judaism. We have Jews practicing Christianity. We have Jews practicing both faiths, and we have Jews practicing no faith at all. That fluidity of boundaries between Jew and Gentile is in some measure part of the Jewish success story in this country, in that it symbolizes the acceptability of being a Jew in American society. However, for a minority such as ours to survive in a democratic culture which welcomes its presence rather than rejects its presence, that minority requires far firmer boundaries between itself and the broader world than do currently exist.

From an address to the National Convention of the Rabbinical Council of America, June 16, 1993.

In this atmosphere of heightened concern regarding the future of American Jewry, Jewish Federations around the country are seeking to find new ways and new funding to allocate greater priority and resources to those programs that hold out the greatest promise of ensuring future Jewish continuity. Federations are seeking to change philanthropic norms among non-Orthodox donors so that they should see Jewish education as a critical focus of philanthropic activity.

In this climate, there are many who claim the mantle of Jewish continuity. Whether it be in Jewish community centers, day schools, Israel programs, or synagogal outreach, all programs have eloquent advocates for arguing that what they do is to maximize Jewish continuity. At the same time, there are a host of programs lining up behind the banner of Jewish continuity to justify their mission as preserving the future health and vitality of the Jewish people.

In this climate, there are a number of skeptical and perhaps unhealthy reactions. Perhaps the most common reaction is one of "give us the funds and we'll produce. After all, continuity is our business." This is a reaction by no means uncommon among rabbis. Nor is it restricted to the Orthodox rabbinate. The second reaction is one of "I'm okay-why don't you change?" This is a reaction that puts the finger of blame and responsibility at the hands of secular Jewish leadership, in a sense mounting an argument that the people who have led us down this road until now have suddenly awakened to the dangers of the Jewish future. This reaction, too, is popular among rabbis, by no means limited to the Orthodox rabbinate, and in many ways destructive of any future communal efforts to enhance continuity. Still a third reaction is one of ingrained skepticism. Those who are deeply steeped in Jewish law and learning question whether a continuity agenda can be realized in any case because the Jewish continuity envisioned simply does not meet up to the standards of the skeptics. This reaction is expressed most vigorously in a recent issue of the *Jewish Observer.* Needless to say, it will add nothing to the continuity debate except to increase polarization within the community and to paint Orthodoxy as the eternal naysayers.

In other words, these responses are at best wrong-headed, at worst counterproductive. We do have a moment of opportunity to change the priorities and values of the Jewish community. This debate is far too important for anyone concerned with Jewish continuity to take a back seat and to throw darts at those engaged in serious efforts at preserving the Jewish future.

In particular, there are five critical questions that must be addressed in this debate. First, who is the target for continuity initiatives? Are we talking about outreach to large numbers of Jews who are out there presumably waiting for our message or would we do far better to work with those whom we already have—the moderately affiliated—and build upon their interest in leading a Jewish life? This is a fundamental policy debate of outreach to the unaffiliated or inreach working with those Jews who have already signaled some desire to lead a Jewish life.

Secondly, if we are serious about adopting new priorities within the community, priorities of Jewish continuity and education, what then will become less important? It is often far more difficult to decide what is to be excluded than what is to be included. It is a far more challenging task, and one that is heavily politically charged, to be able to underscore what is of lower priority to the Jewish community than it is to underscore what is our core priority.

Thirdly, if we are to fund continuity programming, what mechanisms will exist for evaluation, for determining what works and what does not work? Several years ago I did a survey on behalf of the Memorial Foundation for Jewish Culture on outreach programs to unaffiliated Jews. Perhaps my most stunning finding was that when seen through the eyes of outreach program directors, there is not a single program in the Jewish community that is failing. As I mentioned earlier, every one of these programs will have its eloquent advocates and defenders. We need mechanisms to determine what will actually work and what will not. Nor, I would add, should we have any fear of failure. We need to be able to experiment with new programs in the hope that these will reach new and larger numbers of Jews. But if we operate in a climate in which every program by definition guarantees success, then our continuity initiatives will, by definition, amount to little more than self-congratulation and deception.

Fourthly, as we address certain populations—those whose self-image and self-definition do not meet what the Jewish community would like them to be—we will have to find ways to distinguish between respect for personal choice and autonomy and articulation of communal norms and values. This is especially the case, and perhaps most painfully the case, in addressing mixed marrieds and Jewish homosexuals and lesbians.

Finally, as we pursue the Jewish continuity agenda, we require debate over what is our overarching vision of what a Jewish community ought look like? What is the purpose to our continuity? What are we trying to achieve? What vision do we foresee of a Jewish community in the twenty-first century?

These are all questions on which the voice of the Orthodox rabbinate is necessary and must be heard. However, it will be heard only if that voice is articulated in ways that are supportive of rather than dismissive of large parts of the broader Jewish community engaged in serious efforts to enhance the Jewish future and ensure continuity.

This has specific implications in terms of the Orthodox rabbinate. First, let us recognize that Orthodoxy has much to teach in terms of the continuity agenda. Orthodoxy has produced models of successful Jewish families—of families that do Jewish things together, of families that have strengthened themselves as families through intense commitment and sacrifice on behalf of Jewish tradition. In numbers alone, the Orthodox Jewish family has set forth a model of three children per family—the only Jewish subgroup in America to have a norm of actual population increase. Orthodoxy has modeled projects of Jewish learning at all ages—whether it be the success of the Jewish day school, especially on high school levels, which are the most critical in terms of development of values and self-identity, or whether it be programs that are serious about adult Jewish learning and literacy. Orthodoxy has had experience with outreach. It has invested considerable resources in trying to reach out to unaffiliated Jews and bring them back into the Jewish community. The entire *baal teshuva* phenomenon requires careful study to understand what has succeeded within it and, conversely, what have been its failures. On the level of values and cultural ethics, Orthodoxy has demonstrated the critical importance of personal sacrifices and commitment to leading a Jewish life—values that ought well be replicated in non-Orthodox circles. Finally, Orthodoxy offers a very important and corrective voice on some of the most controversial issues of the day. Whether it be questions of intermarriage, abortion, or homosexuality, we need to hear the voice of Orthodox leadership to remind us that not everything that is politically correct is Jewishly acceptable.

In short, Orthodoxy has much to offer. But it will succeed in doing so only if it realizes that its message cannot be the self-righteous message of "We're okay—you're all wrong." Rather it requires Orthodoxy to face up to the critical importance of pluralism within the Jewish community. Jews do require different avenues and different points of connectedness to their traditions. It is in the interest of Orthodoxy that there be strong Conservative and Reform movements. What we need is a literate and a vigorous Jewish community—one that battles over and cares about the interpretation and understanding of Judaic truths rather than one that is simply indifferent to those truths and the texts upon which they are based. The real threat to Orthodoxy in America does not come from religious pluralism. It does come from religious indifference.

In this light, we must recognize that no one institution or one sector of the Jewish community can control the issues of Jewish continuity. This issue is much larger than the resources of any one group among us. Rather, what we do need, and this is what the promise of Federation-driven Jewish continuity plans can accomplish, is an overarching strategy that enables different groups of Jews to strengthen their own programs of continuity, to do it in different ways, but all aimed at the common goal of ensuring the Jewish future. In this context, some measure of dissent within the community is desirable. If nothing else, at least it will demonstrate that people care about these issues. But more to the point, it will enable us to experiment with different models some of which will be effective and some of which will not be effective.

Moreover, it must be understood that Jewish day schools today are a critical and most important setting for the Jewish continuity agenda. Graduates of day schools do score much better on measures of Jewish identification. They are least likely to marry out of the faith. That means, in turn, that in advocating for a continuity agenda, greater resources ought be allocated to Jewish day schools, particularly high schools, which hold out the promise of impacting upon their students' values and Jewish identification.

In short, I don't think there is any denying that a remarkable change is taking place in the community. At Federation meetings around the country lay leaders openly speak of the need for greater Jewish study and greater religious commitment. The president of the Boston Jewish Federation, Barry Shrage, has educated lay leadership—not only in Boston but across the country—of the centrality of religious commitment to the transmittal of Jewish identity. Shrage is not speaking in terms of theology. He is arguing the language of what works—that it is only through our Torah and through commitment to our religious traditions that we stand a chance of ensuring a Jewish future.

At the American Jewish Committee, too, major changes in culture, values, and priorities are beginning to take place. AJC national president Alfred Moses, in an important address to the board, "Jewish Survival in America," argues for greater religious commitment and greater focus upon *mitzvot* to ensure Judaic distinctiveness and continuity. The American Jewish Committee for the last year has been engaged in a public ad campaign of prominent Jews speaking proudly and unabashedly of what being Jewish means to them. Perhaps our most important statement was articulated on our behalf by Senator Joseph Lieberman who, in such a *New York Times* ad some months back, noted how proud he was as a Jew of his religious traditions. To me such a statement is historic. Never before in American history has a politician of national prominence spoken with such pride and such absence of embarrassment about his Jewish identity and Jewish commitment. That ad campaign did not come from Agudath Israel. It came from the American Jewish Committee—long touted as the most secularist and assimilationist of agencies.

To be sure, there is no denying that "Orthodox bashing" still exists. I was at a meeting just last week where a prominent Jewish intellectual said in very explicit terms that he sees himself as having no commonality of values with ultra-Orthodoxy except that somehow they may meet a common end should a Holocaust reoccur. Those stereotypes exist, and they ought properly be combatted. But the challenge to the Orthodox community is to look beyond its narrow self-interest and to see this moment as an enormous opportunity for overall enhancement of the Jewish community at large, an opportunity to strengthen the Jewish identity of our children and grandchildren. That is an opportunity that Orthodoxy cannot afford to ignore. On the contrary, a serious effort in this regard, while by no means guaranteed of success, can only benefit from the support, commitment, and teachings of Orthodox rabbis.

Jewish Organizational Response
to Intermarriage

American Jewry today is debating how to secure its future continuity. Some, proclaiming that the battle against intermarriage is over, call for a fundamentally new, more liberal and inclusive attitude toward mixed marriage and broader outreach to mixed-married couples. Others claim the sole hope for American Jewry lies in a renewed commitment to Jewish religion and tradition.[1] The release of the 1990 National Jewish Population Survey (NJPS), however, signaled the demise of civic Judaism and constituted a clarion call to the Jewish community to address its internal religious and cultural life. Assimilation, it seemed, posed a far greater threat to the security and well-being of Jews than anti-Semitism.

The 1990 NJPS was surprising in several respects. First, intermarriage had risen to the historically high rate of 52 percent. But perhaps more surprising was that conversion, once regarded as the appropriate antidote to mixed marriage, had not increased with the rise in mixed marriages. This finding strongly suggests that as intermarriage became more pervasive in American society, it no longer appeared necessary to modify one's religious affiliation to have a single-faith household. Dual-faith households appeared no more problematic than other family models in an America in which family life was endangered in any case and seemed so welcoming of the prospect of marriage with Jews. Moreover, the decision by the liberal Jewish religious movements to accept patrilineal descent as a criterion for Jewish identification removed one of the major stimuli to conversion to Judaism. In other words, the message of patrilineality was that one need not be a Jew to raise Jewish children.

To be sure, this story of Jewish assimilation coexisted with a narrative of Jewish renewal. High rates of mixed marriage and low rates of

Reprinted with permission of the University Press of New England, from *Jews in America: A Contemporary Reader,* eds., Roberta Farber and Chaim Waxman (Hanover, New Hampshire, 1999).

conversion, synagogue affiliation, and childbearing accompanied smaller, yet by no means insignificant, numbers of Jews who had enriched their lives Jewishly in ways their parents or grandparents could never have imagined. Certainly, American Jews had greater opportunities to lead creative Jewish lives than at any time in American Jewish history. The question was whether they would avail themselves of those opportunities. In short, it was the best of times and the worst of times simultaneously.[2]

More particularly, the debate rages as to how to secure the Jewish future. Several themes are already discernible and must be confronted realistically in any discussion of Jewish continuity. First, the acceptability of mixed marriage must be addressed. No generation of Jewish leaders in history has failed to resist mixed marriage. However, we hear today, for the first time, calls for a "fundamentally new attitude" in which we define mixed marriage no longer as a threat to the Jewish future but as an opportunity for Jewish renewal. In short, one question in the current debate over Jewish continuity is the desirability of a new attitude toward mixed marriage. Others suggest that the new attitude reflects more wishful thinking than sober diagnosis of contemporary Jewish realities.[3]

Second, in terms of numbers, we must confront the reality that some losses are virtually inevitable. These will often be painful, for they may involve the personal families of communal leaders dedicated to the Jewish communal enterprise. Yet a realistic look at the demographics does not suggest the disappearance of the Jews. On the contrary, those committed to leading a Jewish life are doing so in ways that are incredibly vibrant by Jewish historical standards. Smaller numbers will, to be sure, lead to a decline both quantitatively and qualitatively. Fewer Jewish institutions will connote decreased potential for a Jewish cultural elite. Smaller is by no means greater. Yet, that said, the second major demographic conclusion is that the core of the Jewish community, those committed to renewing Jewish life, represents a powerful resource and reservoir of energy. A community declining from 5.5 million to 4 million is clearly a likely if not an inevitable forecast.

Yet 4 million Jews still represent a critical mass capable of sustaining much, albeit by no means all, of the current Jewish communal enterprise. To date, the demographic strength of the Jewish community has been fairly constant since 1950, at 5.5 million American Jews. By comparison with American society generally, Jews have shrunk as a portion of the American population, which has increased from 150 million in 1950 to 265 million today. Despite continued low birthrates, American Jews preserved their numbers by virtue of a temporary baby boom until the mid-1960s and some immigration from abroad through the 1980s. Moreover, the effects of intermarriage, which has risen only in the past twenty years, have not yet been felt numerically by the Jewish community—meaning that although only 20 percent of mixed-marrieds raise their children exclusively as Jews, Jewish partners in mixed marriages continue to self-identify as Jews. Therefore, the numbers have held steady for over two generations. Some losses for the future are likely, given that so few mixed-marrieds are raising their children exclusively within the Jewish faith. Yet if we forecast a Jewish community of 4 million, we would do well to remember that vibrant Jewish societies have been built with far fewer demographic and economic resources.

Third, what is in question is whether the broad middle range of Jews interested in Jewish continuity but lacking the wherewithal to provide it to their children and grandchildren can be empowered by the community to transmit Jewish heritage and identity. If losses are virtually inevitable among the 20 percent at the periphery and Jewish life remains strong among the 20–25 percent at the core, the debate rages concerning the broad middle of 50–55 percent who want Jewish grandchildren but lack the knowledge and capacity to transmit a meaningful sense of identity to their progeny. Jewish continuity initiatives at present appear to be targeted toward these "middles" of Jewish life. The optimists of the 1990s do not believe that Jewish continuity in America is in question. For them, what is in question is the future quality of Jewish life. Pessimists, however, worry that if intermarriage continues unchecked it will have a spiraling effect, whereby rates of intermarriage can approximate 90 percent, further opening the door to assimilation and erosion.[4]

At the core of efforts to enhance Jewish continuity lies the centrality of religion and religious institutions. For American Jews there can simply be no continuity absent commitment to Judaism. Pockets of energy and renewal exist within each of the religious movements, but none is lacking for problems and challenges. Although the Orthodox are generally doing well by standards of Jewish continuity, their actual demographic numbers are smaller today than a generation ago. Whereas in 1970 Orthodox Jews constituted 11 percent of the American Jewish population, today Orthodoxy stands at 6–7 percent. To be sure, among Jews under age twenty-five, 10 percent identify as Orthodox, signaling reservoirs of strength in the future. More to the point, the predictions of the demise of Orthodoxy, so common in the 1950s, appear stale and hollow in the 1990s. Orthodoxy is succeeding in retaining its young and has demonstrated great capacity for the future. Perhaps the most telling symbol of contemporary Orthodoxy was the *siyum hashas* in Madison Square Garden. The idea of Jews setting aside time for the study of Torah on a daily basis represents a powerful symbol for American Jewry. If we are to learn lessons from Orthodox experiences with Jewish continuity, it will require equal dedication on the part of the non-Orthodox movements toward strengthening Jewish education and preserving Jewish family life.

The cultural battles within Orthodoxy are perhaps more disturbing. The past forty years have witnessed the ascendancy of ultra-Orthodox groupings and the eclipse of Modern Orthodoxy as the dream of a creative and vital synthesis between Jewish tradition and modern culture. The power of ultra-Orthodoxy is particularly felt in Jewish education circles. Modern Orthodox educators routinely complain that they are forced to hire *haredi* instructional personnel. Moreover, the one-year program in Israel that has become normative for graduates of Orthodox high schools has had an enormous effect on the culture of Orthodoxy here in the United States. Students returning from the program with renewed commitment to Israel, to Jewish observance, and to the Jewish people often see little value in the ideology of Modern Orthodoxy which calls for a creative engagement with secular culture.

Perhaps the greatest challenge to Orthodoxy lies in the question of Jewish communal relations. As Orthodox Jews become more self-confident about their future and more skeptical of the continuity of the non-Orthodox movements, Orthodox triumphalism becomes expressed in ever more abrasive and contemptuous terms. The gulf between Orthodoxy and non-Orthodoxy widens, both with respect to the capacity for cooperation within American Jewry and with respect to the breach between religious and secular in Israel. Demonstrated Orthodox successes in ensuring Jewish continuity, while justly hailed by all concerned with the Jewish future, run in tandem with continued Orthodox triumphalism and dismissal, if not outright contempt, for non-Orthodox expressions of Judaism.[5]

Conservative Jewry similarly conveys a dual image of strength and weakness. Approximately 47 percent of Jews affiliated with synagogues today are found in Conservative synagogues. Numerically, therefore, it is the largest of the Jewish religious movements. The recent study of Conservative Jews reports continued low rates of mixed marriage for current members of Conservative synagogues. Moreover, approximately 86 percent of current Conservative members believe it is important to marry other Jews. That percentage, however, declines to 32 percent among current Conservative teenagers, what Jack Wertheimer, director of the study, refers to as the "soft core" of Conservative Jewry. At present, it is probably fair to say that most Conservative Jews do not define themselves as halakhically observant. However, they do perceive the Conservative synagogue as a wholly Jewish institution and framework in which they can lead full Jewish lives and raise Jewish families. Whether they will succeed in doing so for the future remains, as per the Wertheimer study, very much an open question.[6]

The picture of the Reform movement is considerably different yet in some respects similar. The Reform movement reports enormous numerical strength. More Jews call themselves Reform than any other denomination. However, many of these are wholly self-defined as Reform Jews, without any significant commitment to a particular Reform synagogue. In other words, part of the reason for the numerical success of Reform Judaism is that many Jews who wish, at most, a minimal connection with Jewish life define themselves as Reform. Thus, where some 38 percent of American Jews call themselves Reform, far fewer are actually members of Reform congregations.

Within Reform temples, considerable tension exists between the imperatives of in-reach to those committed to lead a Jewish life and outreach to mixed-marrieds. The current leadership of the Reform movement is signaling renewed efforts at enhancing Judaic literacy. The president of the Hebrew Union College and his counterpart at the Union of American Hebrew Congregations articulate a language of "Torah, Torah, Torah." Yet philosophically, real tension exists between personal autonomy and commitment to Jewish peoplehood and tradition. In effect, two trends are occurring simultaneously within the Reform movement. A trend of serious Jewish education and effort to define Reform Judaism in a language of norms, values, commitment, and demands is paralleled by a trend toward more inclusive outreach to those with the most minimal attachments to Reform Judaism. Whether the Reform movement can succeed in navigating both trends simultaneously is questionable. Already, Reform rabbis often report that the inclusion of mixed-marrieds within Reform synagogues makes it difficult, if not impossible, for the rabbi to discourage interfaith marriage.[7]

All of this points to some definite policy directions for the future. First, within all of the Jewish religious movements a renewed commitment to serious expressions of Judaism and Jewish identity is needed. Jews who are informed, literate, and knowledgeable about Jewish tradition are most likely to be committed to preservation and enhancement of the Jewish community. Thus, the test for the future should lie not so much in who is a Jew but, rather, are we the possessors of a serious Judaism?

As a minority religion in America, it is essential to declare both what is and what is not a serious Judaism. The boundary in contemporary America between Jew and Gentile is incredibly fluid. Efforts to enhance Jewish continuity cannot be limited to transmittal of what Judaism is, as important as that may be, but must also acknowledge that aspects of American culture that otherwise might be quite positive, such as the triumph of romantic love, may often be dissonant with the imperatives of Jewish continuity, which emphasizes marriage between Jews.[8]

Third, we ought to acknowledge the plurality of Jewish expression in America as resource and asset rather than as a threat and danger. That is where so many of the contemporary religious polemics in Jewish life are hurtful to the cause of Jewish continuity. Different Jews will require different avenues of expression of their Jewishness. The success of Jewish continuity rests very much with the success of all the religious movements to retain their current members and attract new adherents.

Finally, what of the vexing problem of communal responses to mixed marriage itself? A single statistic has dominated discussion on the extremely rich and comprehensive portrait of American Jewry emanating from the NJPS of 1990: 52 percent of American Jews who married between 1985 and 1990 chose unconverted Gentile partners. Though this finding evoked wide and profound concern, it was not at first explored in depth, nor were its implications for communal policy examined carefully. Responses took a polarized form. On the one hand, some argued that "the battle against intermarriage is over," suggesting that a skyrocketing level of intermarriage was inevitable in the open society and that the only appropriate Jewish communal response was outreach to intermarried couples. Others argued that an exclusive focus on outreach based on an assumption of the inevitability of accelerating intermarriage was a serious mistake and that the outreach itself had the effect of validating intermarriage from a Jewish communal perspective. They pointed out that mixed marriage was not randomly distributed among American Jews. While intermarriage had become normative in some sectors of American Jewry, it remained uncommon in others. This suggests that efforts to lower the incidence of intermarriage were not doomed to failure; they should be pursued more energetically and deserved a larger portion of communal resources.[9]

A recent study by Bruce A. Phillips, commissioned by the American Jewish Committee and the Wilstein Institute of Jewish Policy Studies, suggests some directions for communal policy with respect to mixed-marrieds. One interesting, though preliminary, finding in this study indicates that the rate of intermarriage has leveled off and may even be declining. Phillips speculates that this development may be related to the fact that communal leaders, rabbis, and parents have begun to speak more clearly and forcefully about the value of marrying within the faith. Jewish communal efforts to reinforce the norm of endogamy are particularly significant in view of the overwhelming acceptance by non-Jews of the prospect of their children marrying Jews, a finding reported on as early as 1983 in a Gallup survey.[10]

An important section of Professor Phillips's study demonstrates in detail the impact of Jewish education on rates of intermarriage. Among other conclusions, he challenges the widely held assumption that only day school education will lower the rate of intermarriage. All Jewish education during the adolescent years is particularly crucial, whether formal or informal. It is clear from this study that the Jewish community's continued investment in education for its teenagers—apart from the core reason of creating Jewishly literate Jews—will have an impact in reducing the incidence of intermarriage. The adolescent years demand this special focus because it is at that point that questions of dating, marriage, and family become critical. Jewish education during the high school years nurtures Jewish dating patterns, and these are probably the strongest predictors of Jewish intermarriage. Generally, those who date Jews in high school are most likely to do so as adults. Establishing patterns of Jewish dating during adolescence and inculcating norms of endogamy, therefore, appear to be critical in Jewish communal efforts to lower the incidence of intermarriage. Youth groups and overnight Jewish camps are identified as particularly significant in this regard.

One specific example of wise communal policy is the landmark resolution, adopted in 1991 by the Conservative movement's United Synagogue Youth (USY), urging its members to refrain from interdating and barring officers of the movement from doing so. The resolution was criticized by some who saw it as a violation of individual autonomy and as undermining future efforts at outreach to mixed-married couples. But Phillips's study reaffirms the wisdom and appropriateness of the USY resolution.

In its discussion of outreach to mixed-married couples, the study focused on the intermarrieds' openness to outreach efforts. It did not attempt to evaluate the effectiveness of these efforts in bringing about conversion or encouraging Jewish education for the children. By dividing intermarrieds into subgroups based on the religious patterns of the two spouses, Phillips was able to identify those intermarrieds who expressed the most interest in outreach efforts. The painful reality, however, is that the overwhelming majority of mixed-marrieds are not interested. The most promising target of outreach is what Phillips calls the "Judaic mixed marriage" in which Judaism remains the sole faith practiced in the home. Only about 14 percent of mixed marriages currently fit this profile. Those divorced from mixed marriages constitute a second target for outreach initiatives. Therefore, even the most enthusiastic advocate of outreach should acknowledge that the community must deal with difficult questions in assessing outreach efforts and deciding on the allocation of resources to provide them. How much effort should be devoted to pursuing intermarrieds who show little interest in outreach efforts? What are appropriate objectives for outreach efforts, and how should their effectiveness be evaluated? How should the community respond to interest on the part of some intermarrieds in outreach programs that will help them raise their children in two faiths? Are such efforts compatible with Jewish communal interests? What are appropriate Jewish communal responses and policies that will enable the community to deal with the current intermarriage crisis?

Frequently, policy discussion is colored by well-intentioned desires to provide human consolation to those affected. These, to be sure, are noble sentiments but constitute a disastrous base on which to formulate communal policy. Overall, the Jewish community must continue to pursue a multitrack and nuanced approach, consisting of prevention, conversion, and continued outreach to the mixed-married.

There are at least four reasons for pursuing a policy of prevention. First, we do it because we must. Throughout history, no generation of Jewish leaders has ever failed to resist intermarriage. Therefore, no matter how unsuccessful prevention policies may prove to be, it remains our historical mandate to continue to encourage Jewish in-marriage.

Second, were we to abandon prevention policies, the results would be even more disastrous. A climate in which there are no constraints against intermarriage would result in even higher intermarriage rates, since Jews are a mere 2.5 percent of the total U.S. population. It is precisely because we have continued to maintain the Jewish communal preference for in-marriage that intermarriage rates have not risen even further. Italians and Irish already experience out-marriage rates in excess of 60 percent, while Lutherans and Methodists marry outside their respective faiths at rates exceeding 70 percent.

Third, it must be acknowledged that certain forms of prevention *do* work. We know, for example, that intermarriage rates are lower among those who have gone to graduate or professional school. This runs counter to traditional assumptions that intermarriage increases as social and educational attainments increase. But in fact the concentration of Jews is greater in graduate schools than in undergraduate colleges. There is a clear policy implication here: send our children to colleges where a significant proportion of the students are Jewish.[11]

Fourth, there is a real question of who will articulate the message of intermarriage if Jewish organizations do not. Jonathan Sarna has argued that if Jews are serious about resisting intermarriage, they must recognize that they are unique in American society.[12] The difficulty in making this point is illustrated in an article in *Moment* magazine by Rabbi Rachel Cowan, a prominent advocate of outreach to mixed-married couples. A woman approached her at the conclusion of a week-end program and express gratification that her son had been unable to attend. Had he been present, the woman said, he would have heard from Cowan only the message of outreach and nothing at all about the importance of marrying a Jewish partner. Cowan writes that she considered the subject and the woman's thoughts but concluded that, were she to do it over again, she would say exactly the same things.[13]

The second pillar of Jewish communal policy toward intermarriage is conversion to Judaism. This has been our primary response to the reality of intermarriage. The policy imperative appears clear: to overcome remaining barriers that may inhibit conversion. In this regard, there appear to be at least three initiatives that may be undertaken. First, we must underscore the Jewishness of the Jewish partner. When the Jewish side of the family cares about Jewish identity, the likelihood of the non-Jewish partner's converting to Judaism is all the greater.

Second, there is the issue of the communal reception of converts to the Jewish faith and fold. Our tradition here is very clear—make no distinction between those who are born Jews and those who have accepted the Jewish covenant. A policy that is serious about conversion must encourage the Jewish community to adopt a receptive and positive attitude toward converts to Judaism.

Finally, serious discussion is necessary concerning the absence of a uniform conversion procedure acceptable to the various religious movements in North America. In the absence of a uniform procedure, we are creating both personal and communal tragedies when people converting to Judaism in good faith find their conversion invalidated by other sectors of the community. The failure to develop a uniform procedure signals that the traditionally primary response to intermarriage—namely, conversion—can never really succeed. To be sure, there are questions concerning conversion. The 1990 NJPS refers to "self-declared converts"—30 percent of those currently practicing Judaism but not born Jews did not undergo any official conversion ceremony or procedure. It is hard to avoid skepticism about the commitment of such self-declared Jews.

Similarly, we have concerns regarding "one-generation converts." Joseph Tabachnick and Brenda Forster, in a study of converts to Judaism in the Chicago area, underscored the weakness of Jewish identity among converts to Judaism in their failure to oppose the intermarriage or interdating of their own children. Fewer than 50 percent of the Jews by choice in the Chicago area sample placed importance on their children marrying within the Jewish faith. Only 28 percent felt that it was important for their children to limit their dating to other Jews. Tabachnick and Forster rightly conclude that a serious conversion policy must explain to those entering the Jewish fold the importance of marriage to other Jews and the building of Jewish families. Otherwise, conversion only postpones the ultimate dissolution of Jewish identity through the out-marriage of one's children and grandchildren.[14]

The most sensitive and difficult area is that of continued outreach to mixed-married couples. Questions have been raised concerning the effectiveness, appropriateness, and priority level of outreach programming to mixed-married couples. First, there is the question of respective costs and priorities. Is more to be gained by working with those who are outside the community or by attempting to enrich those who are already committed to leading a Jewish life? It is not enough to say that we must do both. In an age of limited resources, serious questions arise as to what is the most effective channeling of the resources available to us.

Second, we must ask whether the community really has the capacity to reach mixed-married couples. Do they wish to be chased by us? Or do we waste valuable communal resources in a vain pursuit of people who have no desire for contact with the Jewish community? Actually, we do not even know if our costly advertising to mixed-marrieds even reaches its intended audience.[15]

Third, we must address the question of tension between outreach efforts and efforts designed to ensure the conversion of the non-Jewish spouse. Rabbi Alexander Schindler, in an important address to the UAHC biennial in November 1991, criticized the tendency of outreach efforts to become neutral toward conversion. Very often, in a well-intentioned desire to build bridges to mixed-marrieds, outreach advocates do not make strong cases for conversion to Judaism. When mixed-married couples tell the community they want involvement but not conversion, a serious question arises as to how effective outreach has been.[16]

Finally, there is the question of the sustaining power of outreach. Absent conversion, can outreach sustain the Jewish identity of the mixed-married family in the second and third generations? Thus far, the evidence is negative. Research conducted by Peter Medding of the Hebrew University points to the importance of an "unambiguous Jewish identity" in preserving the Jewishness of the home. The Jewish identity of a mixed-marriage home is often highly ambiguous, due to the presence of Christian symbols and the observance of Christian holidays. It should come as no surprise, therefore, that, absent conversion to Judaism, mixed-marriages result in "terminal Jewish identity" by the third generation.[17] Medding's research corroborates the earlier findings of Egon Mayer in research undertaken by the American Jewish Committee in 1983.[18]

Given these questions, it still remains necessary to advocate outreach on both human and demographic grounds. On the human level, these are all members of our families, and the Jewish community clearly is not about to turn its back on them. On the demographic level, mixed marriage poses serious dangers of significant demographic losses within a generation.

Therefore, outreach must be carefully targeted to those mixed-marrieds who are interested in leading a Jewish life. Steven Cohen's analysis of the Jewish community differentiates between the 20–25 percent who are core activists, the 15–20 percent who are totally uninterested, and the 50–55 percent who form the "middles" of Jewish life—those who are interested in Jewish continuity in the form of Jewish grandchildren but are unsure how to attain it. Cohen, as well as Jack Ukeles, has argued that outreach efforts ought be targeted to those middles—to those who have already expressed some interest in leading a Jewish life. Our goal ought to be to enlarge the core by shrinking the middle.[19]

To be sure, that route presupposes that some losses become inevitable. Moreover, it is probably only a minority of mixed-married couples that actually fall among the middles. The majority have already signaled, by their decisions to raise their children outside the Jewish faith, that they have little interest in the Jewish community. Here again it becomes a question of how we utilize limited resources to the best effect.

Moreover—and this is of equal sensitivity—outreach must be appropriately designed so that the overall message of the Jewish community regarding Jewish marital values, the importance of building a Jewish home, and the importance of finding Jewish mates is clearly communicated. Our task, while respecting the personal choices of individuals, must be to articulate communal norms that are seen as being the preferred model for Jews generally. To quote Charlotte Holstein, past chair of the AJC's Jewish Communal Affairs Commission: "Certainly, on a personal level, I felt touched by the new research findings and revised policies. However, it was necessary to draw the distinction between what I felt emotionally and what rationally was good for the survival of the Jewish community as a whole. . . . The basic question was at what point do one's personal experience and one's communal responsibility blend or act in concert and when do they conflict or cause tension?"[20]

To be sure, that distinction is difficult to make and will often get lost. Failure to make the distinction, however, runs the risk of communicating a vision of intermarriage as simply one acceptable option among others. It is at that point that we have abandoned our responsibility as

Jewish leaders and have fallen into a trap of moral relativism that anything that Jews happen to do automatically becomes legitimate.

Some initiatives indeed have been launched that address these concerns. The Memorial Foundation for Jewish Culture has started programs in the Metro–West New Jersey and the St. Louis Federations focusing on outreach to "underaffiliated" Jews, including mixed-marrieds, within a broader population of those who are only marginally affiliated.[21] Those programs wisely identify the underaffiliated rather than the mixed-married as the problem. They target outreach to those who have expressed some desire to lead a Jewish life. And by including mixed-marrieds within a broader outreach program they do not blur the crucial message of endogamy.

In conclusion, we face four pressing tasks, and we must confront them with candor and honesty: First, let us acknowledge that this is a disaster in the making. Left unchecked, intermarriage will dilute both the quantity and quality of the Jewish community. Pretending that this is not a problem will succeed only in providing false comfort to some. Second, Jewish leaders must distinguish between their personal needs and those of their families and the good of the community for which they have responsibility. Comforting statements are important, but they are a poor basis for framing communal policy. Third, the community of social scientists must realize that what they say and do creates a cultural climate and communal norms affecting intermarriage. Statements of "pure" social science often get translated as prescriptive advocacy and can prove harmful. The Talmud's advice to sages, "Watch your words," is no less applicable to contemporary social scientists.

Finally, outreach advocates must lower their sights, avoiding messianic claims and focusing on what is doable and realizable rather than holding out false visions to the community. Statements to the effect that outreach will "transform the intermarriage crisis into the greatest opportunity of modern Jewish history"[22] are simply irresponsible. We must acknowledge that the core of the Jewish future is not likely to come from the ranks of the mixed-marrieds. Nevertheless, we should pursue outreach with the objectives of preserving Jewish identity and enabling mixed-married couples to incorporate a sense of Jewishness within their homes.

American Jewry, in short, as it enters the twenty-first century confronts significant challenges, not to its status as Jews in America but rather to its identity as American Jews. All Jewish organizations are continually faced with the challenge of transforming their agendas so as to advance the all-inclusive goal of Jewish continuity. Whether American Jewry and its leadership succeed in realizing that goal remains very much an open question. The currents of renewal coexist with the currents of assimilation. Whether American Jews envision their future as empowered and enriched by Judaic heritage or as overwhelmed and demoralized by the reality of assimilation will, in many ways, determine the course of future Diaspora history.

Notes

1. See the contrasting viewpoints in Alan M. Dershowitz, *The Vanishing American Jew* (Boston: Little, Brown, 1997), esp. pp. 42–44, 320–24; and Elliott Abrams, *Faith or Fear* (New York: The Free Press, 1997), chap. 5.

2. Samuel C. Heilman, *Portrait of American Jews* (Seattle: University of Washington Press, 1995), pp. 5–7.

3. Steven Bayme, in *Approaches to Intermarriage* (New York: American Jewish Committee, 1993), pp. 9–15.

4. Steven M. Cohen, *Content or Continuity?* (New York: American Jewish Committee, 1991), pp. 40–42, 51–52.

5. Steven Bayme, "On Orthodoxy and Non-Orthodoxy," *Jewish Week,* May 2, 1997, p. 26.

6. Jack Wertheimer, ed., *Jewish Identity and Religious Commitment* (New York: Jewish Theological Seminary, 1997), pp. 15–16, 61–62.

7. Stephen Fuchs, "A Reform Jewish Response to the Intermarriage Crisis," in *The Intermarriage Crisis: Jewish Communal Perspectives and Responses* (New York: American Jewish Committee, 1991), pp. 51–53.

8. Jack Wertheimer, Charles Liebman, and Steven M. Cohen, "How to Save American Jews," *Commentary* 101, no. 1 (January 1996), pp. 47–51.

9. Steven Bayme, "Enhancing Jewish Identity: Form and Content," in David M. Gordis and Dorit P. Gary, eds., *American Jewry: Portrait and Prognosis* (West Orange, N.J.: Behrman House, 1997), pp. 394–403.

10. An earlier version of this section appeared previously as the preface, jointly authored with David M. Gordis, to Bruce A. Phillips, *Re-examining Intermarriage* (New York: American Jewish Committee and the Susan and David Wilstein Institute of Jewish Policy Studies, 1997), pp. vii–x. See also Tom W. Smith, *What Do Americans Think about Jews?* (New York: American Jewish Committee, 1991), pp. 16, 56.

11. Steven M. Cohen, *Alternative Families in the Jewish Community* (New York: American Jewish Committee, 1989), pp. 9–10, 30.

12. Jonathan Sarna, "Interreligious Marriage in America," in *Intermarriage Crisis* (New York: American Jewish Committee, 1991), p. 4.

13. Rachel Cowan, in *Moment,* April 1992, p. 14.

14. Brenda Forster and Joseph Tabachnick, *Jews by Choice* (Hoboken, N.J.: KTAV, 1991), pp. 100–102. See also Jonathan Sarna, "Reform Jewish Leaders, Intermarriage, and Conversion," *Journal of Reform Judaism,* Winter 1990, pp. 1–8, which also raises the specter of "one-generation converts."

15. Jacob Ukeles, "Does Outreach Justify Investment? Alternatives to Outreach," in *Intermarriage Crisis,* pp. 17–19.

16. Alexander Schindler, "The Reform Jew: Values, Practices and Visions" (paper presented to the 61st General Assembly of the Union of American Hebrew Congregations, Baltimore, November 2, 1991).

17. Peter Medding, et al., chapter 12 in this volume.

18. Egon Mayer, *Children of Intermarriage* (New York: American Jewish Committee, 1982).

19. Steven M. Cohen, *Content or Continuity: The 1989 National Survey of American Jews* (New York: American Jewish Committee, 1991), pp. 51–52.

20. Charlotte Holstein, "When Commitments Clash: One Leader's Personal Dilemma," in *Intermarriage Crisis,* p. 35.

21. Steven Bayme, *Outreach to the Unaffiliated: Communal Context and Policy Direction* (New York: American Jewish Committee, 1992), p. 15.

22. See, for example, David W. Berlin, "Confronting the Intermarriage Crisis with Realism and Effective Action," in *Intermarriage Crisis,* p. 39.

Outreach Has Its Risks

- A young woman newly employed by a Jewish organization po-
  litely refused a colleague's offer to introduce her to an eligible
  man claiming that she dated only Jewish men. Her colleague responded, "You know, that's being racist."
- A small Jewish community undertaking a program of outreach to
  mixed-marrieds discovered via focus-group research that its potential clientele wished a Christian educator present to teach the
  Christian perspective within the program. When some Jewish
  communal leaders objected to utilizing communal funds in such a
  fashion, a Conservative rabbi successfully supported the request
  on the grounds that both Jewish and Christian educators agreed
  that one faith within the home was preferable to two.
- A group of teenagers, all officers of a Reform synagogue's youth
  group, responded to a question regarding intermarriage that the
  phenomenon is now acceptable so long as the children are raised
  as Jews. Presumably these were the most committed and involved
  young people within the congregation, and all were of dating age.
- At a national convention of Jewish leaders, a participant urged that
  the community develop new rituals enabling mixed-marrieds to preserve both their respective heritages. She suggested adoption of a
  "Chanukamass" for these purposes. The speakers at the session—
  themselves advocating greater outreach to mixed-marrieds—lacked
  the fortitude to "just say no" to this religious sycretism.

These vignettes occurring within the past year are by no means typical, but they do pose grounds for concern. The numbers of mixed-marrieds and their children are vast, and the Jewish community faces the
prospect of serious demographic erosion given the small percentage of
converts to Judaism within such marriages. On a human level, Jewish
parents and grandparents of mixed-marrieds are not likely to reject this
progeny. Therefore, efforts to reach out to mixed-marrieds—enabling

---

Reprinted from the *Jewish Week of New York,* October 21–27, 1994.

them to raise Jewish children, introduce Jewish components within their homes, and keep the door opened to potential conversion of the non-Jewish spouse—deserve careful communal consideration and support.

As the *Jewish Week* correctly editorialized on the report of the Council of Jewish Federations' Task Force on Services to Intermarrieds, outreach to mixed-marrieds does not mean sanctioning intermarriage. Rather, the communal challenge lies both in preventing mixed marriage and in reducing further losses to Jewry among the mixed-marrieds and their families.

Yet the risks in such an approach deserve equal consideration. First, as the CJF task force itself learned, it was not the mixed-marrieds clamoring for Jewish communal outreach but rather their parents and grandparents. If the Jewish community does not adopt a serious effort toward outreach, it cannot be certain of success. Rather we run the risk of chasing large numbers of individuals who have no desire to be chased.

Even more significant, however, are the cultural risks of communal outreach. Some rabbis have already lamented that outreach, where successful, has had a transforming impact upon their synagogues—making it difficult if not impossible to discourage interfaith marriage. In other words, including large numbers of mixed-marrieds in Jewish communal institutions can, albeit with the best of intentions, prevent articulation of Jewish values that encourage intermarriage for fear of offending the mixed-married.

Undoubtedly, outreach to mixed-marrieds merits a place on the communal agenda. Yet to be effective, it must be carefully targeted to those mixed-marrieds actually interested in, or at least open to, leading a Jewish life, and carefully designed so as to preserve rather than negate the preferred model of Jews marrying Jews.

In short, we require a multi-tracked and nuanced approach to intermarriage. The core of the Jewish future lies in encouraging Jews to marry other Jews. When that fails, efforts should be targeted to securing the conversion of the non-Jewish spouse. When conversion is not an immediate possibility, outreach programs can preserve the dialogue with mixed-marrieds and maintain the potential of future conversion. At its best, outreach should strive to include mixed-marrieds within programs targeted to Jews generally.

The Jewish Community Center and the Jewish Continuity Agenda

It is a great honor and privilege to serve as keynote presenter for this conference of the Jewish Center movement. Unfortunately, I do so on one of the darkest days of modern Jewish history. The Jewish people stands at a moment of tragedy and bereavement on multiple levels—personal, communal, national, and a crisis of Jewish values. The peace process that Prime Minister Rabin spearheaded challenges world Jewry to create a unity of the Jewish people around pride in being Jewish and identification with the Jewish collective endeavor. That work of building community which has been the hallmark of the Center movement remains even more important today. Much will have to be done in the days and months ahead to restore the bonds between Jews and to create that sense of common peoplehood that has sustained us over the millennia.

There are two metaphors that currently describe American Jewry. One metaphor is that of the paradox between our inner and our outer lives. Our outer lives as Americans are quite successful. We have the best educated, most affluent, most stable and secure Jewish community known to Diaspora Jewish history. No society has been as receptive to Jewish involvement as has America. The paradox lies in that, with all our external successes, our internal lives as Jews constitutes our weak point. In the privacy of our own homes, we are unable to define for ourselves the meaning of being a Jew, much less transmit it to the next generation.

A second metaphor relates to the fluid boundary between Jew and Gentile in America. To some extent, that is a reflection of the first image of Jews being so successful in American society. Jews today constitute a revered element within the mosaic of American ethnic and

Reprinted with the permission of the Jewish Education Service of North America from *Agenda: Jewish Education,* Spring 1996.
(This article is based on a presentation to the JCC Association/Association of Jewish Center Professionals Biennial Conference on November 5, 1995.)

religious groups. As a result, the boundary separating Jews from Gentiles has become incredibly porous. We have Jews practicing Christianity, Jews practicing no faith, and Jews practicing both faiths. Conversely, we have born Christians practicing Judaism, born Christians involved in intimate relations with Jews, and born Christians practicing a syncrestic mixture of both faiths. That fluidity of boundary is testimony to how successful Jews have been in America—namely, that the Jew has become a desirable in-law. Conversely, however, for a minority to survive with any measure of distinctiveness within a democratic majority culture, that minority requires firmer divisions and boundary lines between itself and the broader society.

Therefore, these two metaphors concerning American Jewry present new challenges to the Jewish Community Center: how to address the personal, existential, and religious needs of Center clientele. More broadly, how can Centers both handle diversity within the Jewish community and among different types of Jews and at the same time set boundaries and limits upon what is Jewishly acceptable?

First, who are the Jews? In terms of size, we remain a community of 5.5 million American Jews. That number has remained flat over the past 45 years. In 1950 we were 5.5 million while the general American population was 150 million. Today there are 260 million Americans but still 5.5 million American Jews.

Our educational and income attainments are considerable. Median American Jewish income is $10–12,000 higher than the median income of white Americans generally. Similarly, American Jews are three times as likely to have attained postgraduate education as the American Caucasian population generally. In terms of mobility, 700,000 Jewish adults have changed their state of residence within the past five years—usually a barometer of greater economic opportunities.

Perhaps the most predictable thing about American Jewry remains their continued political liberalism. Jews will vote for the most liberal candidate in an election, provided that candidate is not perceived as hostile to Israel.

The denominational labels continue to possess salience for American Jews. Almost 80 percent of Jews define themselves as Orthodox,

Conservative, Reform, or Reconstructionist. To be sure, that does not mean that four-fifths of American Jewry are members of synagogues. If anything, all it means is that the synagogue they do not go to is an Orthodox, Conservative, Reform, or Reconstructionist synagogue. More broadly, it suggests that Jews define themselves as members of one of these religious movements yet fail to translate that self-definition into concrete activities and behaviors.

In short, we are talking about an American Jewry that is secure yet feels vulnerable. It has the greatest opportunities for Judaic enrichment, yet only a minority of American Jews participate, let alone maximize, the opportunities available to them.

Over the last five years Jewish continuity has become the buzzword of the Jewish communal agenda. It means a change in rhetoric in which we state that our challenge for the next generation is ensuring the future quality of Jewish life. New coalitions will be necessary across institutional lines and religious movements, for the Jewish continuity agenda is simply too large for any one sector to appeal to all Jews. Different individuals do require plural entry points to Jewish heritage and Jewish connectedness.

Yet much of this agenda has been more rhetoric than reality. The communications barrier has been penetrated so that we do acknowledge the serious problems we have of assimilation, erosion, and continuity. What has actually been accomplished is, however, in reality, far more limited.

Some have suggested a magic bullet approach—a quick trip to Israel which will miraculously transform our youth into committed American Jews. Others articulate a language of broader outreach and inclusivity. More concretely, within the Center movement greater emphasis has been placed upon Jewish education, particularly under the leadership of the executive staff of the Jewish Community Centers Association and its important COMJEE II plan for maximizing Jewish educational effectiveness in Jewish Community Centers. Lastly, within the Reform movement a very important shift is taking place towards emphasis upon Judaic literacy for adult Reform Jews.

What has not happened is at least as important as what has happened. First, there has been no change in communal priorities. The budgets of the Jewish community remain severely limited, and while there has been a general shift in direction towards increased funding towards Jewish continuity, there has been no fundamental shift in communal priorities.

Related to this is that little has been said about the cost of leading a Jewish life. We have known for quite some time that intensive Jewish experiences can be expensive. Yet the social policies of the Jews are not targeted towards enabling middle-class Jews to participate in quality Jewish experiences. The main complaints about Jewish day schools, for example, relate less to the quality of day school instruction and more to the capacity of middle-class parents to afford them.

Lastly, the community has been unwilling to issue normative statements about the meaning of being Jewish for fear of giving offense to key constituencies. Communal reaction to the crisis of intermarriage is a good barometer of the difficulty we have in articulating a language of norms. Serious Jewish continuity will require commitment to Judaism. Of particular importance is whether we can learn to be inclusive operationally in terms of being receptive to any Jew interested in leading a Jewish life while at the same time articulating a language of norms and values that many will perceive as being ideologically exclusive.

In addressing this agenda, there are currently four strategies that are on the communal table. One strategy, often voiced within Orthodox circles, suggests an all-or-nothing approach, declaring the bankruptcy and essential paganism of American culture. The fruits of this strategy lie in the much-heralded *baalei teshuva* phenomenon which has attracted great attention in the media. My sense is that this type of maximal strategy will not work. First, I have my own ideological doubts about the extent to which American culture is "pagan." Conversely, I have no doubt whatsoever that if it is a choice between all or nothing, the overwhelming majority of American Jews have already decided to vote for nothing.

A second type of strategy is known as the *"tikkun olam"* strategy, best articulated by Leonard Fein and others on the Jewish political left. This strategy enjoins the community to become truly committed to social justice, and then masses of otherwise unaffiliated American Jews will join in. I have my doubts about this strategy as well. First, *tikkun olam* has been the agenda for the Jewish community since World War II. It has prevailed precisely at a time when we have become more assimilated. It has, in effect, brought us to where we are today. Moreover, I am by no means convinced that advocates of *tikkun olam* are actually committing energies towards a Jewish continuity agenda when all too often *tikkun olam* becomes a code word for Jewish support for liberal politics.

Between these two poles lie two more centrist strategies. One is the well-known strategy of outreach emphasizing bringing people into institutions and avoiding language that might be threatening or off-putting. The outreach strategy suggests placing minimal demands or expectations upon people so as to avoid giving offense.

By contrast, the in-reach strategy urges that we build a community internally to the point that it is sufficiently vibrant and attractive so that others will join. In-reach suggests that we work with those who express some interest in leading a Jewish life. Its programs are much stronger on content, more willing to challenge belief systems, and place greater emphasis upon Judaic literacy and norms.

Clearly we need both types of strategies. They are not mutually exclusive. But we must pay greater attention to priorities and emphases. In particular, excessive outreach may well damage the core of the Jewish community by broadcasting messages that undermine a language of commitments and obligations. This is particularly the case with the sensitive and vexing issue of mixed-marriage.

What then are the implications for Jewish Community Centers? Clearly the Centers have a unique role in providing a neutral and trans-denominational setting for serious Jewish continuity. However, the Centers cannot afford to be neutral regarding Judaism, for there can be no Jewish continuity without a commitment to serious Judaism. The Centers can and should avoid interdenominational polemic but must maximize the Judaic presence within their programs.

In this light, it is clear that some losses are inevitable. Many will by definition avoid a language that they regard as threatening. However, we are naive if we believe that in any case we can retain all Jews. The pressures of assimilation and the broader culture are so great that we clearly will become a smaller Jewish community. The question is whether a smaller Jewish community can become more intensively involved and identified Jewishly.

There is no mystery to Jewish continuity. Jewish continuity will be attained by those individuals and families who are prepared to commit themselves to it and are willing to pay the price in terms of cultural engagement with Judaism as a civilization. To the extent that American Jews are prepared to say to themselves that the Jewish heritage is sufficiently attractive to warrant commitments of their resources, time, and cultural values, to that extent can Jewish continuity be assured.

In his last trip to America, Prime Minister Rabin consistently called for a new agenda of Israel-Diaspora relations in an era in which Israel will live in peace with her neighbors. That agenda, he claimed, should not be built upon the traditional foundations of politics and fundraising but on shared commitment to the continuity of the Jewish people. Twenty-four hours after his assassination, we are all in mourning. It is far too soon to engage in assessment of what has happened, let alone prognosticate where we are going. Yet his passing means that the nature of our work towards building a stronger Jewish people is all the more important.

The rabbis in the Talmud had it right. In describing the Roman siege of Jerusalem in the year 70, they told the story of the leader of the rabbis who was related by marriage to the leader of the Jewish terrorists. The Talmud claims that the terrorists controlled the city. They burned the stores of food and caused massive starvation. When the leader of the rabbis approached the leader of the terrorists, he asked him how he could support such destructive activity. The latter responded that were he to say anything, the terrorists would kill him as well. The two then conspired to "save a little." The rabbinic party reached an accommodation with Rome by which Judaism and Jewish life could be rebuilt and reconstructed. The terrorists opted for Jewish destruction. We, like the rabbis of old, must continue the work of rebuilding and renewal.

Assessing an Outreach Effort

Several years ago the American Jewish Committee initiated a series of public messages placed on the op-ed pages of the *New York Times* featuring different Jews explaining what being Jewish meant to them in contemporary America.[1] I wish to address the goals, methods, and outcomes of this advertising campaign and then weigh its implications for the agenda of outreach programming to mixed-married couples.

The American Jewish Committee is unique among the so-called Jewish defense organizations in that it sponsors a department working to enhance Jewish identity and continuity. Our underlying hypothesis for over a generation has been that unless there is a critical mass of Jews willing to lead a creative Jewish life, our defense and human relations efforts are at best transitory and at worst meaningless. Although this work has been continuing for over a generation, it assumed a new track and direction in the aftermath of the release of the 1990 National Jewish Population Survey. Rather than limit ourselves to analysis of data and policy recommendations, we determined to engage directly in a broad-ranging program trying to explain to Jews the meaning of being Jewish today. This "Why Be Jewish?" program has had many different components including research, public education, chapter programs, a Judaic Literacy Institute for AJC professional staff and lay leadership, and a college essay contest done in conjunction with Hillel. The ads themselves were not a program. They were meant to be the capstone of a far more expansive and substantive program as well as to be the most effective vehicle of communication to Jews at large.

Our central goal was to change the language of Jewish identity—to move from a language of fear and painful memory to a language of joy and aspiration. We wished to demonstrate the different paths to leading a Jewish life—whether they be through social action, religious commitment, intellectual learning, or identification with Jewish people-

Reprinted with permission of the Jewish Outreach Institute and the Center for Jewish Studies of the Graduate School of the City University of New York from *Making Jewish Outreach Work,* ed., Egon Mayer (New York, 1996).

hood. Our most effective ads sought to communicate in a substantive yet sufficiently light-hearted and engaging way. Authors of messages were chosen either because they were well-known personalities easily identifiable among Jews everywhere or because they had a particular story that would inspire others to explore their own path to leading a Jewish life. In my own view our most important statement was articulated by Senator Joseph Lieberman, who noted how proud he was as a Jew of his religious tradition. For me, such a statement was historic. Never before in American history had a politician of national prominence spoken with such pride and such absence of embarrassment about his Jewish identity and Jewish commitment.

The process in going ahead with such a campaign was fairly straightforward. Authors were identified and invited to submit a particular text. Numerous drafts were developed between the author and AJC staff to determine what would play most effectively within the limited parameters of a 350-word advertisement. Special attention had to be paid to follow-up. A staff member was assigned to field calls and to prepare follow-up material, including those publications on Jewish identity that AJC had prepared and a resource guide for utilizing the Jewish community. The publications included the essays *Why Be Jewish?* by Barry Holtz and myself, as well as a collection of grassroots voices entitled *Twentysomething and Jewish—Personal Reflections on Jewish Identity.* All who responded to a particular ad were immediately placed upon the mailing list for future AJC publications. Ads that were seen as being particularly effective in other contexts were placed in newspapers targeted, for example, to people in their twenties or early thirties, or in college newspapers. Local AJC chapters developed their own ads utilizing local personalities. These messages appeared in local general and Jewish media.

What were our outcomes? Each ad generated over a hundred responses or inquiries. This is by no means an overwhelming number, yet it clearly is comparable with what AJC ads on other subjects such as intergroup relations or questions of national policy have generated in their contexts. For most people with whom we spoke, the ads legitimated being Jewish in America. The basic message was that being Jewish is something that Jews should be proud of and that continues to have salience in the modern American culture. Much as Israel legitimates being Jewish, that it is good to be Jewish in a Jewish state, the AJC ads in a different way communicate the acceptability and desirability of leading a Jewish life in the American context.

Moreover, these ads have had multiple uses. People have told us how much the ads meant personally in terms of furthering their particular Jewish quest. A Jewish day school informed us that teachers utilized the ad as a document for a high school class discussion. Others have reported how the ads served to stimulate discussion within their synagogues and social groups.

To be sure, there has been criticism as well—albeit of limited range and scope. Some have argued that the ads potentially delude the AJC into thinking that it is making a serious dent in the problems of assimilation and Jewish continuity. In effect, the ads may have no impact upon uncommitted Jews generally.

A second criticism has centered around our choice of personalities. In our quest for well-known names, we have often chosen people who may not be all that connected with the Jewish community. In that respect, we have been accused of rewarding those who effectively do the least. Thirdly, some have argued that the ads are a waste of money and resources when only intensive Jewish experiences and education can really do the job in terms of enhancing Jewish identity. Finally, some have questioned whether this is legitimate use of the public square. What is essentially a private conversation becomes conducted in the public arena.

I listen to these criticisms and take them quite seriously. When I weigh them, however, I am convinced, first, that the only way to communicate with Jews generally is via the public media. To insist upon the private nature of this conversation invites speaking only to the converted. Outreach means engagement with Jews who may have differing views. We have to find the right vehicles of conducting that engagement.

Secondly, I believe all these criticisms underestimate the enormous symbolic statement for the American Jewish Committee and more generally for the American Jewish community as to what our priorities are and what is the role of Jewish identity within a Jewish agency. To some extent this ad campaign is an ironic and historic statement. It did not emanate from the ranks of Agudath Israel. Rather it has come from the American Jewish Committee—long touted as the most secularist and most assimilationist of agencies—and has played an enormous role in the internal transformation of agency culture and self-image.

Lastly, I think these ads are succeeding in terms of the culture they are trying to promote within the Jewish community. Our original objective of changing the language of being Jewish from one of fear to one of joy is reflected in a wide array of avenues within the Jewish community. I cannot be so bold as to suggest that the American Jewish Committee has done this single-handedly. Rather, by focusing upon the language of being Jewish, what being Jewish means to us today, providing a statement of why being Jewish is important in the modern era, we are furthering a much larger project within the Jewish community—to inspire Jews to the meaning and salience of leading a Jewish life.

What are the implications of our experience for outreach to mixed-marrieds? One issue concerns the choice of personalities. In the year ahead we hope to have the story of a convert to Judaism. Around Super Bowl time we featured the story of a professional football player who determined to marry a Jewish mate. We have not focused to date upon a mixed-married couple per se. This underlines our broader philosophical view that outreach to mixed-marrieds will do better when we include mixed-marrieds within broader outreach to the Jewish community generally and in effect transform outreach into a form of entry-level Jewish education that is open and available to all who are interested in leading a Jewish life, rather than center upon mixed-marriage per se.

The American Jewish Committee policy to date regarding intermarriage has been a multi-track policy of prevention, conversion, and outreach, meaning that our first track must be that of encouraging Jews to marry other Jews. When that does not occur, our efforts ought to be geared towards conversion of the non-Jewish spouse. When that is not in the cards, the dialogue ought to be kept open so as to keep alive the possibility of raising Jewish children and ultimately of conversion of the non-Jewish spouse. Our ad campaign fully reflects that policy.[2]

These experiences, however, pose a number of challenges to outreach advocates. First, I believe it is a legitimate question as to whether the message of outreach makes it difficult if not impossible to preserve our primary messages of in-marriage and conversion. Secondly, are we targeting our message to those who express an interest in leading a Jewish life, or are we squandering valuable resources on the large numbers of mixed-marrieds who have simply chosen to take a walk? Thirdly, and perhaps with greatest sensitivity, we must ask questions about the content of outreach to mixed-marrieds. Are we in fact enhancing Judaism and the Jewish community, or are we creating a safe place for mixed-marrieds to feel comfortable with their situation of mixed-marriage? Fourthly, a serious question ought to be asked about our priority of resources. Are we utilizing resources in areas where they do the most good, and, if so, what are we giving up in terms of the core Jewish community by focusing upon mixed-marrieds as mixed-marrieds? For example, one Jewish community center recently reported a budget of $100,000 for an outreach program servicing thirteen interfaith couples. Is this the most effective utilization of limited communal resources, given the likelihood that the majority of these couples will not end up establishing wholly Jewish homes? Lastly, outreach advocates ought to be challenged in terms of their long-term vision of what the Jewish community ought look like. Will there be anything distinctively Jewish in a community consisting of half-Jews, Gentiles involved with Jewish mates, people of mixed-ancestry or people practicing two faiths? This to be sure is a painful subject because many of these individuals are people whom we know well and are members of our own families. However, serious questions must be confronted in terms of what are the implications of a long-term Jewish future.

One interesting example of these difficulties occurred last week at the White House. Hillary Clinton's brother married Senator Barbara Boxer's daughter in a White House ceremony with lay Jewish participation. A rabbi had originally been scheduled to perform this mixed-marriage. In the month preceding the wedding, at least one senior Jewish communal executive praised the event as evidence that Judaism in America was flourishing. Yet if we cannot bring ourselves to the realization that intermarriage does indeed threaten future Jewish continuity, if we create a cultural norm in which intermarriage is perceived as beneficial for American Jewry rather than a phenomenon that endangers the Jewish future, all the outreach activities in the world will accomplish little more than salving our consciences and deluding us into thinking that we have solved our problem.

Fortunately, these are by no means the only voices addressing Jewish family and marital values today. A newly published book by Joel Grishaver, *40 Things You Can Do to Save the Jewish People,* urges parents to reward materially their children who choose to date only Jews. That message, although somewhat awkward, remains appropriate. The United Synagogue of Conservative Judaism has published several pamphlets addressed to young people underscoring communal opposition to interdating and encouragement of endogamy. My concern is that outreach advocates, with the best of intentions, may be creating a climate in which it becomes politically incorrect to articulate the message and values of in-marriage.[4]

In short, we need a language of realism in discussing intermarriage today. Intermarriage does pose serious risks and dangers to the Jewish future and to Jewish continuity. The likelihood of population loss is exceedingly great and many of those losses will come directly from the ranks of mixed-marrieds, even if they be within our own families. For those mixed-marrieds who are interested in maintaining the dialogue and preserving their Jewishness, keeping the road open to conversion, outreach has a world of importance. Yet we have to be equally realistic in acknowledging that the core of the Jewish future will not come from the ranks of the mixed-marrieds but from those Jews committed to leading a Jewish life, and most of those will express that commitment in the choice of a Jewish spouse.

In conclusion, I believe we must probe the ideological content of what outreach means today. Are we promoting Jewish family and marital values or do we avoid doing so as not to give offense to those whom we are seeking to address? I believe we must recognize that outreach to mixed-marrieds can never be more than an accommodation to reality. Outreach cannot become a normative statement of what Jews ought to transmit to their children and grandchildren. The content of outreach must challenge Jews Jewishly, not validate whatever Jews do.[5]

Endnotes

1. See the *New York Times,* September 27, 1992, December 6, 1992, March 7, 1993, April 25, 1993, September 12, 1993, November 21, 1993, March 20, 1994, May 4, 1994.

2. See *The Intermarriage Crisis: Jewish Communal Perspectives and Responses,* American Jewish Committee, 1992, pp. 67–69.

3. Egon Mayer forecast such a scenario but failed to address the question of Judaic distinctiveness in a community whose boundary lines are so fluid and blurred. See Mayer, "The Coming Reformation of American Jewish Identity," in *Imagining the Jewish Future: Essays and Responses,* David Teutsch, ed. (Albany: SUNY Press), 1992, p. 181.

4. Jack Wertheimer has argued that Jewish communal leaders have become silent on these issues for fear of offending their constituencies. Although Wertheimer's concerns are real, he overstates the case in ignoring those who, at considerable risk to their personal careers, have been willing to articulate precisely the messages of Jewish family and marital values. See Jack Wertheimer, "Family Values and the Jews," *Commentary,* January, 1994, pp. 30–34, and the resulting correspondence in *Commentary.* April, 1994, pp. 2–11, and May, 1994, pp. 19–20.

5. Paul Ritterband has argued similarly that the long-range response to intermarriage must be to enable Jews to recapture Torah as a "common, compelling culture." Outreach can do little, in his view, unless we address the far more fundamental issue of the decline of Torah. See Ritterband, "Only By Virtue of Its Torah," *Jewish Intermarriage in Its Social Context,* Paul Ritterband, ed. (New York: Center for Jewish Studies, City University of New York and the Jewish Outreach Institute), 1991, pp. 99–108.

INTRACOMMUNAL ISSUES: PLURALISM, ORTHODOXY, AND JEWISH UNITY

Pluralism has often been a defining theme for the American Jewish Committee. For American society, pluralism has served as a guarantor of Jewish security. Indeed, never in Diaspora Jewish history has there been as assertive a Jewish community as American Jewry. Within the Jewish community, however, it has proven far more difficult to nurture a climate of pluralism among diverse Jewish religious groupings. This section analyzes a variety of intra-Jewish communal tensions and attempts to articulate a theory of contemporary Jewish pluralism.

A New Agenda for Tomorrow's Jewish Community?

What does it mean to be a Jew in the modern world; on the one hand, to carry on Jewish tradition and, on the other hand, to be open, receptive to, and influenced by the currents of Western culture?

I. Introduction

A few years ago, Charles Silberman, the noted author and journalist, published his important book, *A Certain People*.[1] Silberman's earlier books had been called *Crisis in Black and White* and *Crisis in the Classroom*. Most observers on hearing about the book automatically assumed it would be about a crisis in American Jewry. That was not at all Silberman's thesis. Silberman suggested a totally different view of Jewish life. He argued, first, that anti-Semitism was by and large unimportant except within the black community. Moreover, he commented that Jewish economic affluence was such that we should think in terms not of Jewish poverty but of Jewish resources. Finally, he described the internal health of the Jewish community as quite positive. Jews were in no danger of disappearing either because of paucity of births or because of a multiplicity of intermarriages. In other words, Silberman's thesis was celebrative of American Jewish life. His argument was that the Jews had really arrived in American society and, therefore, we should begin thinking in terms not of Jewish weakness but rather of Jewish power.

Since publication of Silberman's book there has been a great deal of discussion of these issues—some under the auspices of the American Jewish Committee and certainly a great deal under other auspices.[2] There has been no question that Silberman hit upon a number of proper themes. Certainly, when one speaks of Jewish renewal, a great many

Reprinted with permission from the *Journal of Jewish Communal Service* (Kendall Park, NJ, Summer 1989).

positive developments have occurred that signify that Jewish culture and Jewish life in this country really do rest upon strong foundations: the renaissance of Jewish scholarship, for instance—over 300 universities offer majors in Judaica; or Jewish cultural production—witness the plethora of books on Jewish subjects published each year specifically by not only Jewish publishing houses, but by Harper and Row, Random House and others; also the development among younger Jewish families of informal networks, so-called *havurot,* of individuals and families trying to lead a more intensive Jewish life by grouping together around Jewish concerns; and in the field of Jewish education, the enormous development of Jewish day schools in major cities around the country, offering intensive forms of Jewish education under all denominational auspices, Orthodox, Conservative and Reform. These developments would not have been predicted years ago. They do signify real signs of Jewish renewal.

Yet, if Silberman is correct in positing that renewal is taking place, serious questions are raised about the depth of that renewal. How involved are Jews in their community? What are the real imperatives of Jewish life? What are the values that Jews live by? What are the ideologies of Judaism that Jews can speak about intelligently? In that sense some observers argued that Silberman was correct in positing a Jewish renewal that was "a mile wide" in scope but which was only an "inch deep." I would suggest taking it a step further and carrying the discussion onto a new stage. While the debate continues about the accuracy of Silberman's thesis, a number of new issues have come onto the Jewish agenda within the past three years that are not all touched upon in Silberman's book or in the considerable literature that has sprouted around it.

Three major issues have programmatic implications for the Jewish community: first the question of unity and disunity between Orthodox and non-Orthodox Jews; second, the growing cultural alienation from Israel as the focal point of Jewish identification by American Jews; and third, the vision of Jewish leadership as we approach the end of the twentieth century. We will discuss these three issues in detail, including the connecting links among them, and then suggest some of the possible directions to explore in the future.

II. Jewish Unity and Pluralism

Jewish unity has been a theme much discussed within the past three years. One view is that there is a primary polarization of Orthodox and non-Orthodox Jews, both here and in Israel; polarization that has taken place both on the level of rhetoric, of stereotyping, of delegitimatizing one group at the expense of another, and on another level, over concrete issues of Jewish identity. The question of "Who is a Jew" comes sharply to the fore in America in certain issues of personal status, in matters of divorce, remarriage, and patrilineal descent. Debates have taken place over whether these issues can be resolved, and whether, in broader, cultural terms, a Jewish community can be created in which all within it have real mutual respect and feeling of kinship. The prevailing stereotype among the Orthodox is that the non-Orthodox are less committed Jews, less involved, and weaker in their Jewish identity. Conversely, among the non-Orthodox, the prevalent stereotype is that the Orthodox are rigid, uncompromising, unbending and, perhaps most importantly of all, lacking in concern for the unity and welfare of Jews everywhere.

To discuss this complex question, we must begin with what we mean by Jewish unity. It has never meant that we are one Jewish people, slogans to the contrary. It has never meant a Judaism that has been or is monolithic. It has never meant a community in which agreement is the rule of thumb. If anything, the old saw, "where there are two Jews, you have three opinions," is a far stronger theme in Jewish history than the theme of "we are one." This former theme is by no means a recent one in Jewish history. As early as Talmudic times, the rabbis were fond of saying there are seventy different interpretations of Jewish tradition. One ought not delegitimatize another Jew because he happens to hold a different interpretation of what is correct and what is true. We have to recognize, then, that historically we have never been a unified, monolithic Jewish people.

Rather, pluralism has actually been the norm in Jewish history. There have always been different Jews expressing different concepts of what it means to be a Jew. In that sense our response to the contemporary debates and contemporary polarization is to raise the question: What degree of religious pluralism do we want to encourage in

America and what degree of religious pluralism do we want to encourage in Israel?

A successful pluralism has to have three major features. First, it encourages the view that each expression of Judaism—Orthodox, Conservative, Reform, and Reconstructionist—contains both strengths and weaknesses, that no one movement has the complete answer, but rather that each of the movements has made major contributions to Jewish life and, as a result, members of each denomination ought to see those in other denominations as allies, as friends in building Jewish life rather than as destroyers of it. In other words, pluralism encourages a certain degree of modesty, a recognition that one cannot have the final truth because one happens to belong to a particular branch of Judaism.

To examine the implications of this criterion of pluralism for each of the denominations, let me begin with Orthodoxy. The Orthodox have compiled a commendable record in the education of their young. Jewish day schools are now the envy of the non-Orthodox community and have been emulated by Conservative and Reform leadership. The Orthodox family is extremely cohesive. Orthodox Jews enjoy a high birth rate and a low divorce rate, perhaps proving the proverb, the family that prays together stays together. When one enters into an Orthodox community, one is immediately struck by the intensity of commitment to Jewish life. Jewish values, issues and concerns permeate the day-to-day life of the Orthodox Jew. There is a strong commitment to, and a strong feeling of identification with, the Jewish people. And, finally, some Orthodox groups have compiled a commendable record in outreach to unaffiliated Jews. Large numbers of adult Jews have rediscovered their Judaism in their adult lives and have joined up with Orthodox communities. Some parts of the Orthodox community are well-known for their hospitality, their willingness to accept people who want to join their ranks.

To be sure, Orthodoxy is by no means monolithic, and observers have frequently underestimated the degree of pluralism in contemporary Orthodox life. Hasidim, for example, are perhaps best known for their tightly woven communities and their utilitarian relationship to the outside culture. In recent years, however, the Modern Orthodox have succeeded in building their own subcommunities while maintaining closer and more positive ties to secular culture than their more right-wing counterparts. Modern Orthodox institutions have succeeded to the extent they have provided their members with strong communities fulfilling a wide range of social, cultural, and educational needs.

On the other hand, the Orthodox are plagued by a number of ideological problems. They have failed to confront the challenges of modern scholarship, in particular, modern Biblical criticism. Only recently have they begun even to debate the impact on Orthodox tradition and law of feminism and the drive for women's equality, involving some very grave matters, particularly the rights of women within marriage and divorce.

The Conservative movement, similarly, combines both points of strength and points of weakness. Traditionally, the Conservative movement has fostered the academic study of the Jewish past, and to this day the Jewish Theological Seminary is probably the fountainhead of Jewish scholarship in this country. The problem with the Conservative movement, or as some have called it, its dilemma, is the wide gap between observance by its religious leadership and by its laity. Sociologists have commented that if Conservative Judaism is truly devoted to living by Jewish law, then it essentially failed to transmit that message to the hundreds of thousands of Jews who are members of its synagogues.

The Reconstructionists have only recently begun to emerge as a movement. For many years, Mordecai Kaplan hoped that Reconstructionism would serve to bridge the various religious movements. Only recently has it emerged as a fourth religious current. It is unclear what Reconstructionism's ideology currently is. It strikes many observers as eclectic. On the other hand, it is also a point of entry for many Jews who otherwise would remain unaffiliated.

Reform Judaism has traditionally prided itself on its emphasis on social action and on the ethical dimension of Jewish values. In more recent years, Reform has witnessed a greater return to tradition and to Jewish ritual. The debate between Zionism and anti-Zionism has disappeared from the Reform camp as Reform spokesmen and laity have become overwhelmingly supportive of the State of Israel, and indeed the State of Israel has become what some have called the "civil" religion of American Jews. That is a theme I will return to later. Yet, the dominant perception remains, even among Reform Jews themselves, that Reform Jews are somehow less committed, less involved than their Orthodox counterparts. As many Reform Jews have stated to me personally, they feel Reform is the last way station before one opts for secularism or even out of Judaism entirely.

I think the point to realize regarding all four of these movements is that all four represent reformulations of Judaism in the light of modernity. All four represent attempts to couch Judaism in distinctively modern terms yet retain a dimension of Jewish tradition and values. The dilemma of the modern Jew is precisely this question of what is the proper synthesis between tradition and modernity. All four of these movements are grappling with these questions. What modernity has done is to shatter the unity of our faith and confront us with the dilemma of being a Jew in the modern world. In terms of the specific issue of Jewish unity, if we do not have a unity of faith, do we still retain a unity of people?

Recent events in Israel and the Diaspora may further challenge this unity of peoplehood. Proposed amendments of the Law of Return threaten Jewish unity by driving wedges, via legislation, between born Jews and those who have chosen to convert to Judaism under non-Orthodox auspices. Conversely, the absence of a uniform conversion procedure raises the specter of large numbers of individuals choosing, in good faith, to join the Jewish people, yet being rejected by other portions of the community.

Secondly, I think pluralism has to recognize some pragmatic realities, and one is that different Jews require different avenues or points of entry into Jewish life; what works for one set of Jews is not necessarily going to work for another set of Jews. At a time when we speak so much of Jewish alienation or disaffiliation, or of young Jews dropping out of the community, or of people being attracted to forces outside of the community, one has to recognize each of the movements as offering different points of entry for those who want to buy into the Jewish community and to find a Jewish identification that will speak meaningfully to them in terms of their particular and communal situation. Sadly, we don't do that. Each of the movements has been so vigorous in propounding its own ideology that it has also communicated the message that it is *the* entry point for Jews who are alienated.

This leads to the third point that if each of the movements is vigorous in propounding its own system, each must also recognize the intellectual integrity of the other movements. Each movement ought to acknowledge the spiritual authenticity and religious expression of the competing movements. Each must also recognize that when we call for pluralism we cannot call for ideological compromise. One can call for ways of working together, of refraining from delegitimizing one another in terms of public rhetoric, but at the same time one has to recognize that a religious movement would not be faithful to its ideological principles if it could not defend and articulate those ideological principles with rigor and with intellectual integrity. To be sure, the Orthodox, by their own ideology, do not recognize the legitimacy of non-Orthodox formulations of Jewish teaching. Nevertheless, Centrist Orthodox spokesmen, notably Norman Lamm of Yeshiva University, have argued that the non-Orthodox movements must be recognized as "valid groupings," i.e., strong movements that represent large numbers of Jews, and their spokesmen be accorded a measure of "spiritual dignity."[3]

It is in that context that the question of Jewish religious polarization has occupied a great deal of the Jewish communal agenda in recent years. There are those who would argue that the degree of cooperation and unity far overshadows disunity. On the other side of the spectrum there are those who argue that disunity is actually an asset in Jewish life. It permits each movement to proclaim its own autonomy, to develop its own creativity, and what's more, and in perhaps a somewhat more cynical fashion, that some ideological controversy is desirable because it shows that people at least care about these issues.

I would suggest that the problems of disunity are quite real, both in Israel and in America, and they are directly related to the theme of the collapse of Modern Orthodoxy. Modern Orthodoxy as a movement was developed and nurtured as a bridge between Judaism and Western culture. It was seen as ushering in a new era, one in which Jews could firmly identity within their tradition, yet be open, receptive and influenced by the currents of modernization. Within the last twenty years, certainly 1967 may be a very good benchmark, developments within the Orthodox world have witnessed a sharp turn to the right. Yeshiva University, once considered a flagship of Modern Orthodoxy, today has as its primary intellectual influences individuals who delegitimize the culture of modernity and the effort at synthesis. The same is true of the rabbinical leadership in Israel. In other words, the weakness of modern Orthodoxy has undermined the bridge between Orthodox and non-Orthodox Jews and has contributed to polarization of rhetoric and relationships between one movement and others.

I would say in assessing the issue of Jewish unity and polarization that it is important to distinguish between attitudes of Jewish leadership and attitudes of the rank and file. Survey after survey of attitudes of rank-and-file American Jews, and to some extent those of Israeli Jews as well, indicate that the rank-and-file Jews are not that concerned with these issues. The recent furor over who is a Jew in Israel revealed why so many Israelis failed to comprehend why an issue that affected so few individuals could become such a core and vital question for American Jewish leadership. They are far more concerned with such basic questions as do Jews live in my neighborhood, or, are members of other religious movements part of my society, than they are with the ideological issue of who is a Jew and what is our attitude toward other members of other Jewish movements. Where the issue is crucial is on the leadership level. We have, in other words, an interesting conflict over what is important in Jewish life. Are the ideological factors with which the leadership is concerned more important than the structural factors which concerns the rank and file, such as: who are my friends, with whom do I work, who are my business associates and who are my social acquaintances. If one were to go back to Silberman, he would argue that social factors are more important, and as a result, polarization is probably not that crucial an issue. On the other hand, I would argue that what makes Jewish life interesting are the ideas Jews profess. In that respect the ideological voices today point to increasing polarization. The policy response must be to encourage and nurture a pluralistic Jewish community.

III. American Jewry and Israel

A similar set of issues confronts my second major theme, that of the growing cultural alienation of American Jews from the modern State of Israel. We have gone through a number of phases in attitudes of American Jews towards the reality of the State of Israel. For many, Israel long served as a transcendental imperative for American Jews. It was the answer in terms of Jewish identity. Israel was the noble dream being created by a group of young, vigorous, intelligent Jews who wanted to create a Jewish state and a Jewish homeland that would essentially be a beacon unto the Gentile world. Perhaps 1967 was the capstone of this period in which Israel has served as a cohesive force for American Jewish identity.

What did it mean to be an American Jew? It meant to be inspired by the State of Israel. Certainly the triumph of Zionism, a dream which some 80 or 85 years ago was regarded as utopian nonsense, represented one of the most significant revolutions and success stories in the entire history of the Jewish people. The victory of Israel in the Six-Day War against all odds and against a horde of surrounding enemies served to inspire the American Jew with a sense that to be a Jew was not necessarily to be a victim of persecution. To be a Jew meant to be a proud standard-bearer of the Jewish tradition in its current incarnation and in its current phase of Jewish sovereignty. In the aftermath of 1967, Jewish life, certainly in America, was infused with a far greater degree of Israeli content than ever before. Jewish educational programs on all levels—children, adolescents and adults—became infused with the theme of Israeli society as the basic center or area of concentrating one's Jewish identity. It could manifest itself in trips to Israel, seminars for college students and for adolescents, and special one-day programs of Israeli content in Jewish schools. It represented itself around the dinner table; one rarely had a Jewish discussion in which the State of Israel did not play a major role.

It is this definition of Israel as the centerpiece of American Jewish identity with Israel themes providing so much of the programming for American Jews that has begun to undergo a serious reevaluation. Especially since 1982, Jews have begun questioning to what extent their identity is a reflection of the inspiration and models coming out of Israel. Certainly, the Lebanon war in the summer of 1982 created all sorts of analogies with the American experience in Vietnam. Occupation of the territories, something that had been going on since 1967, became much more of a front-page issue in the aftermath of 1982, and began to give rise to the analogy which rings so harshly in our ears today, of comparing Israel with South Africa. On the religious phase the entire question of "Who is a Jew" perpetrated by the Lubavitcher Rebbe in Crown Heights, and his *haredi* supporters in the Knesset, raised the specter of Khomeinism for modern Israel. And, finally, the election in the Knesset of perhaps the one Jew who has been delegitimated by nearly all American Jews, Meir Kahane, symbolized to American Jews the dilemma of identifying with an Israel that contains within its midst, on a leadership level, someone who is so alien to American culture, to American values, and American traditions.

To be sure, all of these analogies are severely flawed. Lebanon was not Vietnam, territories are not South Africa, and Meir Kahane is effectively counterbalanced by Israel's democratic structure. Yet the implications became very powerful for many American Jews. Namely, are we witnessing an Israel that continues to serve as a beacon and an inspiration, or are we witnessing an Israel with which we have an increasing amount of discomfort and difficulty identifying?

The recent controversy over proposed amendments to the Law of Return reflect the growing ambivalence American Jews have about their relationship with Israel. By mounting such a concerted and well-publicized lobbying effort, American Jews were signaling the necessity for continued engagement with an Israeli state albeit with misgivings concerning the state's internal ethos and values. At stake in the minds and hearts of the Jewish leaders who were protesting the proposed amendments were long-range considerations about the future of Israel in terms of its values and public policy that might attentuate ties between Israel and American Jewry.

Several qualifications are in order. First is the exception of the Orthodox in America themselves. They see what is going on in Israel and they, by and large, continue to like what is going on. They certainly have discomfort about many of these issues, particularly in terms of the occupation, but by and large the general shift to the right in Israeli society that has been a fact of Jewish life since 1967 and certainly since the election of the Likud in 1977 has been paralleled by what I spoke of earlier as the Orthodox shift to the right. In that respect the Orthodox look at Israel and like what they see.

Secondly, and I think this is the critical point in terms of the policy discussion, the questions of Jewish support and identification with Israel are primarily a subject of discussion on the metapolitical level rather than the political level. In terms of the political level, as we all know, when our friends are under siege, we tend to rally around the flag. And in that respect we continue to argue that Jewish support for Israel remains strong, and with all of the agonizing over the current conditions in Israel, we never want to see that translated as political weakness or as a crack in the wall of American Jewish support for Israel. It is rather on the metapolitical level that the questions of Israel as the beacon of American Jewish identity must be further discussed and further analyzed. In other words, even as American Jews continue to support Israel's security requirements, they question the degree of their cultural, religious, and spiritual identification with current Israeli realities.

Certainly, one of the things that we are currently beginning to talk about is what do we mean by a real partnership between American Jews and Israel? What do we mean by a new era in the relationship between American Jews and Israel? Does it move beyond Israel as the centerpiece or the beacon of Jewish identity? Are we talking at the same time, a la Charles Silberman, of a Jewish renewal in this country? Does not this mean that we are talking in terms of bi-centralism? Others would argue Israel remains the center, but Diaspora Jews, particularly American Jews, can no longer be regarded as the periphery, but rather must be seen as partners with differing agendas yet with common interests. It is in that respect that some of the exchange programs that have been developed over the last few years represent attempts at developing metapolitical connections and dialogues between Israelis and American Jews. When one group takes the other for granted or one assumes that the other has nothing to say in terms of substantive recommendations and suggestions, then we know we do not really have a partnership. It is the nurturing of that partnership that will allow us to continue to go down a certain road in Jewish history, continuing to build ties between us, yet at the same time realizing that ultimately if we are to work out our Jewish identity, we must have a strong Jewish identity here and a strong Jewish identity in Israel.

I offer one anecdote to illustrate the tensions in the "partnership." I returned recently from the AJC Academicians Seminar in Israel. In our final evaluation session one of the American academics, one of the most thoughtful in the group, said "I'm afraid that one of the things that I consistently get the message from here in Israel is that if I'm going to work out my Jewish identity, it's got to be on my own terms. I wish my Israeli friends good luck, but ultimately their situation is not my situation." It's a problem. The minute we communicate that message, then we're talking no longer of a partnership between our communities, but we're talking of what I call the increasing cultural alienation of American Jews from Israel. In other words, classic Zionism posited a disappearance of the Diaspora. Herzl argued that those Jews who wanted to be Jewish would move to Israel and the rest of the Jewish world would be free to disappear, or enter into Gentile society. For some, he argued, even conversion was desirable. That classic Zionist theory has clearly run its course. The Diaspora, if you will, is here to stay in terms of a vibrant, coherent American Jewish entity, and probably it is true for other segments of the Diaspora as well. The challenge then is overcoming cultural alienation and developing a true partnership.

IV. Jewish Leadership

This leads me to my third theme, namely, who would carry out such a partnership? And that raises the questions of what is Jewish leadership, where is it going, and what do we want to see in terms of American Jewish leadership of tomorrow? In this area we have also gone through three stages. As an immigrant community we tended to choose our leaders from the periphery of Jewish life, namely from those who had succeeded in the Gentile world, had minimal Jewish connections, but were nationally known, recognizable names for everyone in American society. A classic example, of course, is Justice Louis Brandeis. Brandeis was a leader from the periphery, one who discovered Jewish life very late in his career, yet for the Jews he was a major asset because he was a Jew who had succeeded in the American legal profession and had risen to the heights of the Supreme Court. That leadership from the periphery, I understand, is historically characteristic of almost all minority groups, especially immigrant groups who are unsure of themselves in the new society and want to establish that they are loyal, productive citizens of the new community in which they have entered.

The second major phase, certainly the one that characterized the war-time years, was leadership by great rabbis who had become ambassadors to the Gentile world. Stephen Wise, Abba Hillel Silver, and others effectively utilized their pulpits to promulgate Jewish values, concerns and interests onto American society.

Jewish leadership in the third generation became a much more Federation-oriented leadership rather than a rabbinically-oriented leadership and, as a result, much less ideologically concerned and much more concerned with creating consensus in Jewish life. That Federation model of leadership, by and large, is prevalent today. Jonathan Woocher has argued that Federation leaders of today articulate the "civil Judaism" of American Jews, namely, a common denominator of values which all Jews can agree to, such a Jewish peoplehood, support for Israel, identification with America.[4] It is that civil religion of American Jews that Woocher suggests shapes most of the attitudes of today's Federation leaders. It is a form of Judaism which does not express itself in any ideological or ideational values that will cause conflict or dissention within the community. One of Woocher's examples is that today's Jewish leaders are far more interested in the civil questions of Judaism than in the religious questions of Judaism. They are far more interested in the questions of anti-Semitism, of Israel, of Jews and the elections, than they are in the ideals, values and history of the Jewish people. This raises the question of what kind of leader then are we looking for? We have gone through a number of different models, yet we have no consensus either on the lay level or on the professional level as to what kind of leadership the community needs.

I think there are a number of issues that have to be discussed in this area. First what are the values of Jewish leaders? What do they believe in? Where is their current mind-set? Are their attitudes and values "in sync" with the rank-and-file Jews? Are the leaders leading the community or are they reflecting ideologies and values that are totally dissonant with what the Jewish communal agenda is all about? One obvious question is whether the agenda of Jewish communal organizations are "in sync" with the leadership attitudes prevalent in those organizations? In that respect a study of Jewish leadership attitudes is almost a prerequisite to any attempt to grapple with the issue of what are the ideological values of the leaders.

Secondly, on a philosophical level what kind of leader do we want? Do we want strong ideologians? Do we want consensus politicians? Do we want leaders that will move their constituencies towards other values and other goals? Jewish tradition and general thought provide a wealth of models of what we mean by a leader. Within our agencies, within our community, we have very little discussion of what leadership actually means.

Thirdly, on both lay and professional levels what training programs ought to come into being? Or, if they exist, how should they be enhanced to create a leadership that will bring us into the twenty-first century? On the professional level this applies to rabbinical schools and to schools for Jewish communal service. The newly founded Wexner Foundation has been actively trying to develop programs to create the professional leadership of tomorrow by enhancing the various settings and institutions where these leaders are trained. The same thing applies on the lay level. What programs exist to train our leaders for tomorrow and in what ways do we want to see those programs enhanced?

Finally, what do leaders need to know in order to be leaders? This is an area where we are far behind the corporate world in continuing education for people in leadership positions on both staff and lay levels. We have no consensus as to what leaders need to know about their Jewish heritage. What do they need to know about civil issues? What do they need to know in terms of organizational and management skills? We all have a sense that we need leadership, yet we have no clear vision of what we are looking for within that leadership.

No one can doubt that the American Jewish community confronts enormous challenges and opportunities as it approaches the close of the twentieth century. Whether it will foster Jewish renewal or will experience increased erosion will, in large measure, be a function of its communal leadership. Over many years a considerable infrastructure of communal institutions has been created to address the critical issues and public affairs of the Jewish community. The continued vitality of these institutions will, in large measure, turn upon the quality and caliber of the leadership they recruit and retain.

In that context, we must examine the following policy questions:

1. Does the Jewish community require its leadership to articulate a new agenda?
2. What do Jewish leaders need to know in order to lead?
3. Given the changing demographics of work and family, will we be able to draw upon the best talents in the Jewish community for leadership positions?
4. Given the diversity within the Jewish community, can we create a leadership that is itself pluralistic and accepts and advocates the desirability of pluralism?
5. What are appropriate models of lay-staff relationships?

V. Conclusion

In conclusion, let me note that I would suggest as a common theme, running through each of these three areas of Jewish unity, alienation from Israel, and Jewish leadership, is what we mean by a modern Jewish identity. What does it mean to be a Jew in the modern world; on the one hand, to carry on Jewish tradition and, on the other hand, to be open, receptive to, and influenced by the currents of Western culture? At the root of the Jewish unity issue I suggested that the real problem was the collapse of Modern Orthodoxy. As long as there was a movement trying to build bridges between traditional Judaism and Western culture, the Modern Orthodox served as a central focal point not allowing either the right-wing Orthodox or the non-Orthodox to go their separate ways. With the collapse of Modern Orthodoxy we have witnessed polarization. The same phenomenon applies in terms of cultural alienation from Israel. For a long time Jews saw their modern identity as embodied by Israel as a shining beacon, as an inspirational example. In the absence of that transcendental imperative, where Israel can no longer serve as that given form of inspiration, the challenge becomes, what is meant by being a Jew in the modern world? The same applies to leadership. If we had role models of Jews who worked in both civilizations, of Jews who embodied both characteristics of what it means to be a modern Jew, then we could talk more coherently about what it means to be a Jewish leader.

I began with Silberman, so permit me to conclude with him. I do think his thesis has to be seriously revised in terms of many of its premises. It emphasizes far too much the forms of Jewish life and too little the content of the community. But its major contribution to American Jewish thinking is very clear. Silberman is urging us to move away from the survivalist agenda that has dominated so much of our thinking for the past twenty years. Issues of anti-Semitism, assimilation, and intermarriage are all very important issues, and obviously we have to continue paying attention to them. But Jewish life in America does rest upon strong foundations. Therefore, if the survivalist agenda is no longer the most important or the most central agenda for American Jews, what exactly should we be looking at?

One can agree or disagree with some of the issues that are outlined in this article, but I think the common challenge they raise is if our survival is not in doubt, then let us address the question of what kind of Jewish community we want. If we need not worry about our disappearance, and we don't have that many enemies from without that are going to overpower us, then let's ask another question of what kind of Jews we want to be in a modern era. It is to this set of metaphysical questions that Silberman provides a very strong impetus to move beyond the survival issues to questions of the quality of Jewish life.

Notes

An earlier version of this paper was presented at the Board of Governors Institute, American Jewish Committee, February 1, 1988.

1. Charles Silberman, *A Certain People: American Jews and Their Lives Today,* Summit Books, 1985.

2. For example, Silberman addressed the American Jewish Committee, National Executive Council, Miami Beach, Florida, November 1985. See also the following reviews of Silberman, *A Certain People:* Steven Bayme, "Crisis in American Jewry" in *Contemporary Jewry,* Volume 8 (1987), pp. 125–128; Nathan Glazer, "A Dream Fulfilled," *The New York Times Book Review,* September 1, 1985, pp. 1 & 17; Samuel Heilman, "Jews in the Land of Promise," *The New Leader,* October 7, 1985, pp. 16–19; Arthur Hertzberg, *The New York Review of Books,* November 21, 1985, pp. 18, 20–22.

3. See, for example, the exchange between Norman Lamm and Aaron Twerski in *The Jewish Observer,* Summer 1988, pages 13–26.

4. See Jonathan Woocher, *Social Survival,* Indiana University Press, chapter 3. In other words, even as American Jews continue to support Israel's security requirements, they question the degree of their cultural, religious, and spiritual identification with current Israeli realities.

"We're Okay, You're All Wrong"

Current concern with Jewish continuity has sparked renewed interest in American Orthodoxy. Great respect exists for the movement's successes in preserving and transmitting Jewish heritage. Not only have predictions of Orthodoxy's demise been misguided, but the Orthodox have been particularly successful in maintaining the Jewishness of the next generation.

That respect for Orthodoxy is coupled with considerable resentment at the apparent triumphalism and self-righteousness of Orthodox Jews. Many claim, often falsely, that the Orthodox do not recognize the Jewishness of non-Orthodox Jews. Others claim, with greater accuracy, that members of their family who have tried to convert to Judaism in good faith find that their conversion is rejected by Orthodox leaders.

Both currents of thought are important. The respect for Orthodoxy and its successes in the realm of Jewish continuity suggests the power of tradition in the modern world. That message, however, will not be heard if the Orthodox are perceived as adversaries of the rest of the community.

For example, the Orthodox have an excellent record in terms of close attachments to the State of Israel. Specifically, 50 percent of Orthodox Jews have been to Israel more than once, and 22 percent have been there once. In contrast, only 42 percent of Conservative Jews and 29 percent of Reform Jews have ever been to Israel. In other words, proportionately more Orthodox Jews have been to Israel more than once than Conservative or Reform Jews have been there at all. For Orthodox young people in particular, the year after high school has become a study year within an Israeli educational institution.

Similar comments should be made concerning the low rates of intermarriage within Orthodox Jewry. According to the national Jewish population survey of 1990, intermarriage rates among the Orthodox stand at less than 10 percent—what they were for American Jewry generally in the 1950s. More to the point, however, is the low rate of inter-

Reprinted from *The Jewish Sentinel,* (New York, December 23–29, 1994).

marriage among day-school graduates. For instance, a recent survey of Ramaz graduates, who are by no means exclusively Orthodox, indicated an in-marriage rate of 97 percent. The experience of a day school such as Ramaz, which is open and welcoming to non-Orthodox Jews yet preserves the message of Jewish in-marriage, makes an excellent statement on intermarriage prevention.

But if this suggests respect for Orthodoxy, what are the grounds for resentment? First, Orthodox attitudes concerning Jewish continuity initiatives border on the cynical. The *Jewish Observer* dismisses the Jewish continuity agenda as inadequate to secure the Jewish future.

The community deserves better than this type of skepticism. Serious efforts to strengthen Jews as Jews are only to the good and merit the broad support of all concerned with Jewish continuity. For example, Jewish community centers in recent years have been engaging Jewish education specialists to teach within their institutions. Such programs enable a broader cross section of Jews to partake of the joys of a Jewish experience. When the Orthodox react to these initiatives with such comments as "We are okay—why don't you change?" they gain only resentment for Orthodoxy as a whole.

Perhaps even more problematical has been Orthodox self-righteousness toward the non-Orthodox community. This attitude of "We're all right—you're all wrong" raises the issue of the critical importance of pluralism within the Jewish community. Jews do require different avenues and different points of connectedness to their tradition, and it is in Orthodoxy's interest that there be strong Conservative and Reform movements. What we need is a literate and vigorous Jewish community—one that battles over and cares about the interpretation of Judaic truths rather than one that is simply indifferent to those truths and the texts upon which they are based. The real threat to Orthodoxy in America does not come from religious pluralism—it comes from religious indifference.

Moreover, the agenda of Jewish continuity is much larger than the resources of any one group among us. No single institution or set of institutions within the community can secure continuity for all. Rather, we need different groups of Jews working together to secure the goals of preserving the Jewish people.

To be sure, one must acknowledge the reality of Orthodox bashing. We witnessed some of this in the aftermath of the Hebron massacre. Recently I heard a prominent Jewish intellectual state that he shares no commonality of values with the ultra-Orthodox community except that somehow they may meet a common end should a Holocaust recur. Those stereotypes exist; they ought to be properly combatted.

But behind the stereotypes lies a series of issues on which Orthodox Jewry and the rest of American Jewry seriously disagree. These relate to the peace process in Israel, governmental aid for Jewish education, and intermarriage.

At present, the Orthodox appear to be the only group in American Jewry with a clear majority opposing Israel's agreement with the PLO. According to the latest AJCommittee survey, 54 percent of American Orthodox Jews oppose Israel's accord with Yasir Arafat. That more than two-thirds support the agreement with Jordan should not be surprising. On the contrary, on such a vital issue, some disagreement within the community is healthy.

The same ought be said concerning governmental aid to parochial education. In advocating governmental assistance, the Orthodox underestimate the degree of governmental regulation that it will bring. I assume teachers in Jewish schools will not be shy about open advocacy for Judaic positions. Whether that is possible given governmental regulations and assistance is questionable.

Conversely, the Orthodox overstate the degree of governmental support for their institutions. Were legislation enabling the funneling of governmental funds to religious schools to be passed, the funds would most likely be targeted to parents whose incomes fall below middle-class levels—thus, in effect, excluding the Jewish day-school system from receiving significant amounts of funds.

It is a mistake to think that government can come to the rescue of Jewish education. The affordability of Jewish day schools is an issue within the community, but it is most likely an issue we will have to solve ourselves. Again, reasonable people may disagree on this subject without succumbing to polarization and extremism.

Lastly, in the area of intermarriage, the Orthodox generally oppose programs of outreach to mixed-married couples as justifying intermarriage. Moreover, the Orthodox are unclear in their approach to conversion, which for the rest of the Jewish community is the primary response to the reality of intermarriage.

The most recent report of the Council of Jewish Federations Task Force on Services to Intermarrieds reflected this communal difference. No Orthodox representative or leader participated in any formal official capacity in the task force. When the report was released, Agudath Israel dismissed it as "pathetic."

Orthodox and non-Orthodox Jews alike ought to agree that the children of Jewish mothers in mixed-marriages be preserved as Jews. We all have a stake in the future of conversion. Although concerns about the effects of outreach are real—at the recent General Assembly of the Council of Jewish Federations, one college senior interpreted a session on outreach to mixed-marrieds as indicative of the Jewish community's acceptance of intermarriage—legitimate ways of involving mixed-marrieds must be found without undermining the primary message of in-marriage.

What then are the grounds for engagement between Orthodoxy and the Jewish community? First, there is the importance of Jewish learning. At the CJF assembly, Jewish leaders set aside time for the study of Jewish texts. Though we may differ in how we interpret those texts, we should reclaim them as the heritage of Jews everywhere.

Second, Orthodoxy should engage the community with respect to the appropriate targets for outreach initiatives. Are we talking about outreach to large numbers of Jews who are waiting out there for our message, or would we do far better to work with those whom we already have—the moderately affiliated—and build on their expressed interest in leading a Jewish life?

Third, we must answer the question of communal priorities. If continuity is to become the major priority in the community, we must determine carefully what are not priority items for the community.

The voice of Orthodoxy needs to be heard on all these questions. However, that voice will be heard only if it supports rather than dismisses large parts of the broader Jewish community engaged in serious efforts to enhance the Jewish collective enterprise.

Understanding Orthodox Dissent

As my daughter departed last month for a year of study in an Israeli yeshiva, Orthodox friends and neighbors questioned whether I would remain supportive of a peace process that seemed to endanger so many Jews living in Israel. Significantly, these callers and well-wishers never suggested reconsidering my daughter's study plans. Rather, they questioned the peace process itself, noting the spate of protests, anti-government demonstrations and ads in the media by Orthodox Jews against current Israeli policies.

Underlying these calls lie some real tensions within American Jewry, and within its religious movements, concerning its relationship to Israel generally and the peace process specifically. Unquestionably, Orthodox Jewry today forms the sole sector within American Jewry in which an absolute majority opposes the peace process. Orthodox rabbis have been among the most vocal opponents—some going so far as to issue halachic bans against the return of territories. Yet the story is far more complicated than simply pitting the Orthodox vs. the rest of the community.

First, not all Orthodox Jews oppose the peace process. A strong minority of 31 percent, according to the most recent American Jewish Committee survey, support the process. Sixty-four percent oppose the current handling of negotiations, and the rest are undecided. By contrast, approximately three-fourths of Conservative and Reform Jews support the peace process. Orthodox opposition and dissent are real, but a significant minority of Orthodox Jews do favor the peace process.

It is facile and simplistic to suggest that Orthodox theology or *halakha,* or, more crudely, hatred of Arabs, mandates opposition to peace.

Rather, the reasons for Orthodox opposition to the peace process are located elsewhere. Two years ago, in September 1993, a clear majority of Orthodox Jews supported the Oslo accords. Since then, a decline in support has occurred across a spectrum of American Jewry, and the sharpest declines have occurred within Orthodoxy.

Reprinted from the *Jewish Week of New York,* October 6, 1995.

Why this opposition? First, according to the AJCommittee survey, Orthodox Jews have the greatest knowledge of and attachment to Israel. Two-thirds of Orthodox Jews follow news about Israel very closely, compared to 28 percent of Conservative and 15 percent of Reform Jews. These differentials result in wide gaps of knowledge concerning elementary facts of Israeli politics. For example, 72 percent of Orthodox Jews understood correctly that Shimon Peres and Benjamin Netanyahu were members of different political parties, while only 45 percent of Conservative and 33 percent of Reform Jews were so informed.

Increased knowledge concerning Israel also means greater awareness of some of the real weaknesses in the peace process—particularly the rise in incidents of terrorism and the PLO's failure to repudiate its covenant calling for Israel's destruction.

Secondly, Orthodox Jews have visited Israel far more frequently than most American Jews. More than 75 percent of Orthodox Jews have visited Israel at least once and 57 percent have done so at least twice. By contrast, only 41 percent of Conservative and 31 percent of Reform Jews have been to Israel at all. In other words, the average Orthodox Jew has undertaken multiple visits to Israel. My daughter's experience of spending a post-high school year at an Israeli yeshiva has become virtually normative among today's day school graduates.

Lastly, Orthodox Jews report close personal attachments to Israel. Eighty-three percent report that they have close friends or family members living in Israel, compared to 45 percent of Conservative and 29 percent of Reform Jews. Enjoying regular contact with loved ones and fearing for their safety and security is reflected in diminished support for the current negotiations.

In short, Orthodox Jews are by no means "enemies of peace," as some have recently suggested. They are considerably more knowledgeable about Israeli politics, have undertaken multiple visits there, and have close family and friends residing in Israel. Frequently, it is their own children and grandchildren who have undertaken *aliya*. They oppose not the negotiations per se—recall that a majority of Orthodox Jews supported the peace process in September 1993, and a majority today favor some territorial compromise on the West Bank—but worry whether this peace process will further endanger the lives and security of Israelis.

Significantly, while sharing these concerns, a strong Orthodox minority supports the peace process and has been led courageously by rabbinic groups such as Shvil Ha-Zahav, or Golden Mean. This group has called upon American Jews to support the peace process while asking the Israeli government to pay closer heed to the security needs of Israelis residing on the West Bank.

Several Orthodox lay leaders have vigorously defended government policy as the appropriate road to peace. They recall that Rabbi Joseph B. Soloveitchik, of blessed memory, the most renowned talmudic scholar of twentieth-century American Orthodoxy, urged that the question of the territories be considered strictly on the basis of political, diplomatic and security considerations rather than considerations of *halakha* or "Holy Land."

This minority opinion within American Orthodoxy must be heard, if for no other reason than to avoid stereotyping Orthodox Jewry as "enemies of the peace process."

I believe that this peace process, though flawed, is preferable to no peace process at all. Yet as this process and debate continues, let us avoid "Orthodox-bashing." Those few protesters who have sought to delegitimize the government of Israel and its elected officials clearly have transgressed the boundaries of acceptable dissent and civility of discourse. They merit the public repudiation of all Jews regardless of political orientation and perspective.

But let us understand American Orthodoxy for what it is—a community divided over the peace process, as is Israeli society itself, a community deeply attached to Israel and knowledgeable about its situations, and passionately committed to Jewish continuity and the future of the Jewish people. Rather than demonize the Orthodox, let the debate continue in a spirit of respectful disagreement and civil dialogue.

As the rabbis of the Talmud commented many years ago, "An argument for the sake of heaven is destined to prove its worth."

Rebuilding Jewish Peoplehood

The aftermath of the Rabin assassination sent tremors throughout the Jewish world. In an attempt to underscore common ties of blood, kinship, and fate—if not of faith and ideology—the American Jewish Committee invited over thirty intellectual and communal leaders to reflect on the implications of the assassination for the future of Jewish peoplehood.[1]

Some derided these efforts as unrealistic—instead urging the AJC to acknowledge the reality of two distinct Jewish peoples. Others felt that Jewish unity was at most a meaningless slogan. An Israeli delegation pointedly informed us that the real challenge is for Orthodoxy to clean its house and only then to discuss rejoining the Jewish people. Prominent columnists in both Israel and the United States proudly proclaimed their disinterest in unity, challenging their readers instead to choose sides. One writer went so far as to advocate seriously the repartition of Israel into a humanistic Israel and a theocratic Judah.[2]

In short, the aftermath of the assassination witnessed more finger-pointing than shared grief. Thus, the Israeli and American Jewish left rejected any responsibility for inflaming the climate between Jews in the weeks and months prior to the assassination. A spokesman for Americans for Peace Now unequivocally denied that the left bore any responsibility for violent rhetoric.[3] Seemingly forgotten had been the no less polarizing rhetoric of the left during the Lebanon War: "Arik Sharon is a murderer!" At one AJC public meeting in the late 1980s, a prominent member of the Knesset and subsequently a cabinet minister castigated Lubavitch as the "Nazis of our time." Many of these tensions erupted into full public focus at the *Nightline* "town hall" meeting shortly after the assassination, at which a prominent Labor politician violated democratic norms of minority rights by proclaiming of his opponents that "we will crush them."

Since that time, the climate among Jews has only polarized further

Published by the American Jewish Committee in *Diverse Paths: Seeking the Core of American Judaism* (1998).

with no shortage of villains on both sides. Particularly galling have been statements by Israel's chief rabbis referring to Reform Jews as "terrorists" who should be "vomited" out of the Jewish state. Perhaps the saddest part of the unfortunate statement of the once-prestigious but now inconsequential Union of Orthodox Rabbis that Reform and Conservative Judaism were simply "not Judaism at all" was that privately many Orthodox Jews and their rabbis may well have agreed with it. Indeed, only the violently anti-Reform and anti-Conservative animus may explain the refusal to accept any form of validation for the non-Orthodox religious streams. Thus, for example, the professional head of the Union of Orthodox Jewish Congregations of America (OU), a centrist Orthodox organization, found it necessary to disassociate himself from the widely acclaimed "Turn Friday Night into Shabbos" program because it amounted to encouraging Jews to attend a Friday night service in a Reform temple.[4]

The backlash against Orthodoxy, and in some respects even against Israel itself, has, of course, widened the breach. For some, the advocacy of religious pluralism in Israel became a code word for Orthodox bashing. Others, notably Rabbis Eric Yoffe and Ismar Schorsch, called for dismantling the Chief Rabbinate and for redirecting American Jewish philanthropic funds away from Orthodox institutions. Rabbi Sheldon Zimmerman, president of the Hebrew Union College, warned that Knesset members could expect only hostility from Reform congregations should legislation be passed preserving the Orthodox monopoly on conversion. His colleague, Rabbi Simeon Maslin, in a presidential address to the Central Conference of American Rabbis, offered his own rejection of pluralism: "Let me make it clear that when I say we, as in 'we are the authentic Jews,' I refer to the two great non-Orthodox synagogue movements of America, Reform and Conservative. My we includes both Beit Shammai and Beit Hillel, but it does not include those who act and think today as the Sadducees acted and thought twenty centuries ago." Although perhaps couched with greater eloquence, Rabbi Maslin's statement was no less exclusionary than that of the Union of Orthodox Rabbis. In fact, if not in spirit, his statement excluded both Reconstructionist and Orthodox Judaism. Lastly, some go so far as to advocate a new Jewish unity of all committed to pluralism against the antipluralists. Needless to say, such a scenario would both fracture what little is left of Jewish unity and deprive the entire Jewish people of genuine Orthodox contributions to strengthening Jewish life.

The root causes of this polarization lie both in the rise of a triumphalist Orthodoxy and in the increased radicalization of the liberal movements. Orthodox triumphalism expresses itself in the well-known attitude of dismissal of the non-Orthodox movements. In the 1950s, Orthodoxy perceived itself as on the defensive—having to refute the standard wisdom predicting its imminent demise. By contrast, in the 1990s Orthodoxy radiates an almost smug self-confidence about its future based upon its growing numbers and the commitment of its adherents. Aggravating this cultural attitude of "we will survive—you will disappear" has been the political extremism of Meir Kahane and its offshoots in the Baruch Goldstein and Yigal Amir affairs. The ugly racism and cult of violence of Kahane all too often permeated religious Zionist circles. In his last years Kahane remained a respected speaker at Orthodox synagogues and educational institutions long after he had been ostracized by the organized Jewish community in America and by the Knesset in Israel.

More moderate than Kahane, but in some ways no less problematic, has been the growth of messianic activism both in Lubavitch and among settlers on the West Bank and their American supporters. All too often the dangerous roles messianic movements have played throughout Jewish history have been ignored in favor of millenarian sentiment of an imminent end to history as we know it and the ushering in of a final redemption. Predominant opinion within Rabbinic Judaism generally discouraged messianic frenzy as futile at best and dangerous at worst. Ironically, in recent years, some of the foremost apostles of Rabbinic Judaism have become the purveyors of precisely that messianic frenzy. Some deride these activities as a waste of energy and resources. Others question whether messianism inflames relationships among Jews, spilling over into extremist politics and even violence.

The effects upon Jewish unity and peoplehood have been considerable. Confronted with the image of Orthodoxy as obscurantist, politically reactionary, and triumphalist toward non-Orthodox Jews, liberal

Jews react with disdain and even disgust. The Orthodox, of course, respond by reminding their critics of the threats of assimilation and claim that non-Orthodox hostility is really only a reflection of resentment at Orthodox successes in transmitting Jewish identity and preventing mixed marriages.

The collapse of the Synagogue Council of America and Orthodoxy's reaction to its demise is a case in point. Where Orthodoxy had been among the creators of the Synagogue Council in the 1950s, and Orthodox leaders had been among its most senior officers, by the 1990s the Synagogue Council was at best tolerated within Orthodox circles. With its demise, a senior official of the leading Orthodox congregational body commented, "I always felt dirtied by it" and proceeded to pronounce a blessing rejoicing in its collapse.[5]

For non-Orthodox Jews, Orthodox triumphalism and intransigence have fractured Jewish unity. The most common formulation of the problem is that "it's the Orthodox vs. the rest of the community." Modern Orthodox Jews, anxious to build bridges between different portions of the community, are dismissed as inconsequential or as "exception Orthodox." As one woman put it recently to an Orthodox speaker, "I don't mean you, but the other Orthodox are fanatics!"

Less heralded but no less significant as a root cause of the communal fissure has been the radicalization of the liberal movements. Acceptance of patrilineal descent and same-sex marriages within the Reform and Reconstructionist movements has broadened the breach not only with Orthodoxy but also with Conservative Judaism. Within Israel, even many of the strongest proponents of liberal Judaism acknowledge that the adoption of these measures has undermined the credibility of Reform Judaism in the eyes of many secular Israelis. One indication of this radicalization in the United States has been shifting perceptions of Reform rabbis who officiate at mixed marriages. Where, in the 1970s, less than 10 percent of Reform rabbis officiated at mixed marriages, and these were widely considered to be marginal to the Reform movement, by the 1990s the percentage has increased to almost 40 percent, and the prevailing attitude among rabbis who refuse to perform mixed marriages is that "I do not perform them, but I respect the right of my colleagues to do so."

In short, the tensions expressed in the past year over who is a Jew, conversion to Judaism, and the legitimacy of the non-Orthodox movements in Israel only reflect a much larger battle within the Jewish people on how we relate to one another and how we preserve any semblance of common peoplehood.

The Ne'eman Commission recognized the urgency of this situation and developed recommendations to avert a split in our common fabric of peoplehood. Its final proposals called for a joint conversion institute including faculty drawn from the three major religious streams. Graduates of this institute would then undergo a conversion process administered by representatives of the Chief Rabbinate.

This recommendation fulfilled two major objectives within the conversion debate: provide recognition and legitimacy for the non-Orthodox streams and ensure a uniform conversion procedure acceptable to the entire Jewish people. Like most compromises, it failed to satisfy any group completely. However, it did offer the Reform and Conservative movements a "place at the table" without asking Orthodox rabbis for compromise on Jewish law itself.

No sooner was the report released, however, than it became apparent that the Chief Rabbinate was unlikely to approve it. Consequently, Avram Burg engineered an alternate solution, known as the "technical solution." This proposal maintained the existing requirement that all Israeli Jews carry identity cards indicating their nationality as Jewish. The new aspect of this proposal is to follow the identification as Jewish with a date. For those born as Jews, the date would be that of birth. For those converted to Judaism, the date would be that of the conversion. The effect of this proposal would be to signal to any religious authority that for purposes of citizenship the individual is recognized as a Jew but not necessarily for purposes of religious practice. The Burg proposal gained the support of the Reform and Conservative movements in Israel as well as that of the Sephardi Chief Rabbinate. Converts to Judaism would be recognized as Jews by the State of Israel although not necessarily by the Chief Rabbinate. To be sure, the next battle would most likely occur over the rights of non-Orthodox converts to marry within Israel.

Reaction in the American Jewish community has been decidedly mixed. Some reacted with rage to the prospect of an identity card differentiating categories of Jews. Others maintained that the Burg proposal was premature, effectively giving the Chief Rabbinate cause to reject the Ne'eman Commission report prior even to its consideration. Still others were disappointed that a true compromise had been shelved in favor of a very limited and technical solution that only postpones the battle to another day.

Yet the Burg proposal also garnered significant support. The leadership of ARZA, the Reform movement's Zionist wing, followed the lead of Rabbi Uri Regev, a key figure in Israel, in support of Burg's recommendation. Doing so, it was felt, would avert a crisis in Israel-Diaspora relations, establish the principle that no decision could be made without consultation with North American Jewry, and identify Reform and Conservative spokesmen as the statesmen in this dispute, to the obvious detriment of the Chief Rabbinate. Conversely, in this view, the Ne'eman proposals were doomed in any case.

Within the Conservative rabbinate, there was widespread disappointment that the Burg proposals effectively preempted the Ne'eman Commission report. Some Conservative rabbis were never entirely happy with being on record in favor of Reform conversion in any case. As Conservative rabbis committed to Jewish law, they felt they were duty-bound to reject nonhalakhic conversion. However, they maintained that the State of Israel, as representative of the entire Jewish people, should *not* be delegitimating non-Orthodox conversion. The Burg solution, in this view, recognizes all conversions for purposes of Jewish identification in Israel although not for purposes of religious functions such as marriage and burial. This solution, whereby rabbis of different streams may or may not accept one another's conversions, operates de facto in the United States as well. Lastly, there was some concern, as well as division, within the Conservative rabbinate that the Burg solution signals a separation between synagogue and state by dividing religious functions from citizenship functions.

Orthodox leadership is also by no means monolithic. The coalition of Am Echad effectively lobbied the Chief Rabbinate against Ne'eman. The Modern Orthodox rabbinate wished to see the Ne'eman Commission proceed but were effectively undercut by the Am Echad coalition.

Therefore, what can be done? The following represents some modest proposals for rebuilding Jewish peoplehood in an age of polarization:

1. *Strengthen Modern Orthodoxy.* Once considered the wave of the future and a bridge to the non-Orthodox movements, no sector is as beleaguered today as are the Modern Orthodox. As the influence of *roshei yeshiva*—one of whom went so far as to equate the Modern Orthodox of today with Amalek[6]—has increased, moderate voices within Orthodoxy have receded. Yet Modern Orthodox day schools continue to be widely admired models of Jewish education. The conferences in 1997 and 1998 on feminism and Modern Orthodoxy were historic both in the number of participants and in signaling a shift of authority in the community from the voices of ultra-Orthodoxy. These currents merit the support and encouragement of the entire Jewish people.

2. *Cool the rhetoric.* Extreme statements on all sides only polarize the climate further. Statements equating the State of Israel with third world regimes that deny freedom of religious practice and expression defame the Jewish state. Statements contemptuous of the non-Orthodox movements and their followers divide Jew from Jew. Similarly, it does no good to engage in panic hysteria. Public advertisement to the effect that "the last time we were so divided we lost ten tribes" only escalate communal angst. If anything, disunity has been the norm of Jewish history. Periods of actual unity, unfortunately, have been all too often exceptional.

3. *Recognize the reality of the "who is a Jew" problem rather than reduce it to the triviality of "who is a rabbi."* Conservative rabbis by no means automatically accept Reform conversions. Some Reform rabbis acknowledge that there are those within Reform Judaism who perform pro-forma conversions. The acceptance of patrilineal descent by Reform and Reconstructionist Judaism fractured a historical consensus over Jewish identification. Currently, in America, there are at least 50–55,000 self-proclaimed converts to Judaism who have converted without the benefit of any rabbi at all. In short, the questions of personal status cannot be simplified to "Who is a rabbi?" Heated rhetoric of who recognizes whom will not solve the very real problem within the Jewish people of who is a Jew. Conflicting criteria of Jewish status

signal a very real problem of marriage eligibility between Jews. Power politics is no road to conflict resolution. However, the complexity and scope of these problems are far greater than simplistic suggestions of Orthodox intransigence might imply.

4. *Recognize that the common problem facing Jews lies far more in assimilation and religious indifference than in religious pluralism.* On the contrary, the availability of diverse models of religious expression acts as a corrective to assimilation. However, this entails a definition of what constitute a true pluralism in pronounced contrast to religious relativism. I suggest that a true pluralism contains four specific components:

(a) No group possesses a monopoly on religious truth. We all need to learn from one another, or, in the words of the Talmud, "who is a sage, one who learns from all humanity."

(b) Different Jews will require different avenues to connect with Judaic heritage. No single formulation of Jewish expression will work for all Jews. Rather, we need multiple entry points and pathways to Jewish identification.

(c) Pluralism should not be invoked to validate whatever Jews do. Religious relativism, indeed, mandates an "I'm-okay-you're-okay" attitude in which religious truth and conviction lose all meaning. As Dr. Norman Lamm has put it eloquently, "If everything is kosher, then nothing is kosher."[7] Rather, pluralism does mean the freedom to criticize one another but in an atmosphere of respect and cooperation rather than of delegitimation.

d) Pluralism connotes a clarion call to combat religious indifference. Its essential message means increased religiosity rather than freedom from religion. One of the greatest ironies of the current controversy over pluralism has been the common cause that advocates of religious pluralism have made with atheists and agnostics in their struggle against the Chief Rabbinate. Short-term political gains may be realized through such alliances. But defining pluralism as opposition to the Chief Rabbinate or as complete separation of synagogue from state will hardly guarantee the future Jewishness of the Jewish state.

5. Lastly, the fiftieth anniversary of Israel provides occasion for celebration of that which unites all Jews. No event in modern Jewish his-

tory has been so dramatically positive as the return of the Jews to homeland and sovereignty. Israel represents the success story of modern Jewish history. Disagreements over particular manifestations of Israeli policy or resentment of the status of religion within Israel should never overshadow our definition of Israel as a Jewish state for the entire Jewish people and as a connecting theme binding Jews together.

Yossi Beilin, former deputy foreign minister in Israel, was widely criticized for speeches urging American Jews to focus on Jewish identity needs in America rather than upon domestic Israeli needs. Most of his critics claimed that his rhetoric had harmed the UJA campaign and, indirectly, endangered U.S. foreign aid to Israel. The potential harm, indeed, was serious. Underlying Beilin's remarks, however, lay a cogent analysis of the problem of Israel-Diaspora relations. For fifty years the unity of the Jewish people had been constructed on external threats to Jews. But reliance upon potential foes to bind us together constitutes an insufficient basis on which to construct future Jewish unity. Rather, our challenge lies in rebuilding our common Jewishness on the joys of leading a Jewish life and on celebration of the opportunity to build a Jewish state, on ties of common heritage and culture, and on the mutual interdependence among Jews—wherever they reside.

Notes

1. *Rebuilding Jewish Peoplehood: A Symposium in the Wake of the Rabin Assassination* (New York: American Jewish Committee, 1996).

2. Zeev Chafets, *Jerusalem Report,* Nov. 28, 1996, p. 22, Dec. 12, 1996, p. 22, and Dec. 26, 1996, p. 29.

3. Gary Rubin, "Rabin's Assassination Was Not Isolated Act," *Long Island Jewish World,* Nov. 17, 1995.

4. Steven Bayme, "On Orthodoxy and Non-Orthodoxy," *Jewish Week,* May 2, 1997, p. 26.

5. National Conference, UOJCA, November 1994.

6. *The Forward,* May 2, 1997, pp. 1–2.

7. Norman Lamm, "Unity and Integrity," in *Materials from the Critical Issues Conference: Will There Be One Jewish People by the Year 2000?* (Princeton, N.J.: CLAL: National Jewish Center for Learning and Leadership, 1996), p. 56.

Digging their Heels into Pluralism

The assassination of Prime Minister Rabin exposed a deep fissure within the Jewish body politic. The breach between religious and secular, hawk and dove, and even Tel Aviv and Jerusalem long predated the murder. Moreover, the breach has only widened in the past year.

The facts on the ground alone give sufficient cause for concern. Private Noam Friedman, although clearly more deranged than his predecessors, symbolized the continued willingness of some Orthodox Jews to break the law, deny the legitimacy of the Government of the State of Israel, and violate fundamental Jewish moral values concerning the sanctity of human life. The case of Friedman, like those of Yigal Amir and Baruch Goldstein, suggests that the most important victories of Meir Kahane have occurred posthumously, and that the survival of Kahanism posits a serious threat to the moral fabric of Israel and the Jewish people.

Orthodoxy, in short, confronts the identical problems of climate and atmosphere that preceded the Rabin assassination. Orthodox leaders may be somewhat more restrained in their pronouncements, but the Orthodox failure to marginalize Kahane and his ugly racism, as the rest of the Jewish community had successfully done, continues to undermine Judaic teachings that all human beings are created in the image of God. Moreover, Kahanism threatens Orthodoxy's standing in the general Jewish community and besmirches well-intentioned Orthodox efforts to preserve Jewish continuity.

Yet the problems of climate are by no means the monopoly of the Right. Extremist rhetoric was in no shortage, either before the assassination or since, among responsible spokespersons on the Left. Consider the following examples culled from a variety of communal forums and deliberations over the past twelve months:

- An Israeli intellectual, writing in the *New York Times,* characterized the victory of the Likud in the Israeli elections as the triumph of "Israel's dark side."

Reprinted from *The Jewish Sentinel,* (New York, April 4–10, 1997).

- A leading Israeli educator, visiting the United States a year after the assassination, maintained that anyone wearing a *kipa* has no right to eulogize Rabin.
- A non-Orthodox American Jewish scholar serving on a joint commission of Israelis and American Jews recommended that the group study a Jewish text together. An equally prominent secular Israeli academic rejected the proposal claiming that Jewish texts belong to the *haredim,* a group with which he wishes no relationship.
- An American Jewish leader urged that the struggle for religious pluralism in Israel be cast as a struggle for religious freedom, suggesting that a Jewishly democratic Israel may now be equated with illiberal dictatorships.
- An Israeli columnist of American origin advocated yet a new partition of Israel—between a theocratic state governed by *halakhah* and a secular democracy. Lest his words be taken as hyperbole or a reductio ad absurdum, the idea quickly found serious supporters in the mainstream Israeli press.

To be sure, these incidents are by no means typical. Moreover, all should be understood as emanating from a context of a chief rabbinate which exercises power coercively. Yet if we have learned anything at all over the course the past year, it ought to have been the necessity to avoid incendiary rhetoric that only escalates tensions and divisiveness rather than builds bridges between Jews.

What, then, should be done? First, Orthodoxy requires serious internal soul-searching of what it teaches, how it teaches, and who is doing the teaching. Orthodox leaders promised such a reappraisal in the immediate aftermath of the assassination. The need remains all the more urgent today, yet clearly it has not taken place. Israel leaders and institutions rightly should be challenged to follow through on the promised reappraisal, disseminate widely its findings, and implement its recommendations.

Beyond reappraisal of internal education, Orthodoxy should also be challenged on the grounds of pluralism—its dreaded "P" word. Pluralism should never mean that all groups of Jews possess equal legitimacy. No Orthodox Jew can accept so broad a prescription. Nor, for that matter, ought any committed Conservative or Reform Jew subscribe to such a definition. Rather, what pluralism does mean is that different Jews require different avenues for Jewish expression, and all concerned with the Jewish future ought to encourage the viability of those expressions even if he or she would disagree with them.

Orthodoxy, in short, ought to acknowledge that the primary threats to future Jewish continuity emanate from religious indifference rather than religious pluralism. Acceptance of this formulation of pluralism enables Orthodox leaders to cooperate with non-Orthodox colleagues in a common quest to strengthen the Jewish people. It also recognizes the reality that Orthodoxy is not a solution for all or even most Jews. Pluralism does not require Orthodox assent to whatever the non-Orthodox movements are doing. On the contrary, healthy disagreement is a sign of a mature and vital community. Moreover, the constructive criticism traded between each of the movements can act as a corrective to excesses. Lastly, passionate disagreement suggests only the depth of our commitment and concern. What pluralism does require is couching criticism in a spirit of love for the Jewish people rather than one of scorn and contempt. Unfortunately, all too often, Orthodoxy finds it easier to engage in condescension if not outright dismissal rather than to confer a modicum of personal and spiritual dignity upon non-Orthodox religious leaders.

If Orthodoxy requires greater respect for pluralism, the non-Orthodox sectors need to define both the limits of pluralism and its meaning. First, pluralism must not be equated with relativism. If all forms of Jewish expression are said to possess equal validity, then we have so deconstructed Jewish tradition to mean virtually anything one wishes. Torah remains more than an extended midrash. Its claim to be taken seriously is its possession of timeless truths.

Secondly, the liberal religious movements ought to acknowledge their error in mounting their campaign for greater religious pluralism as one of rights and civil liberties—the right to marriages, conversions, etc.—rather than the existential questions of broadening religious expression and Jewish identification. Relatively silent are liberal voices calling for an Israel that clearly and authentically articulates the continued salience of Jewish heritage and tradition. A true religious pluralism, in short, would act as a corrective both to the excesses of Israel's religious establishment and to widespread religious indifference and assimilation. In particular, the willingness of liberal religious voices to ally with post-Zionists who would redefine Israel as a secular democracy with no special status for Judaism and the Jewish people is especially troubling. The failure of religious liberals to rebuke the rhetoric of post-Zionism mirrors the failure of Orthodox leaders to rebuke religious extremism.

A case in point is the recent controversy over conversion to Judaism. Efforts are underway to strengthen the Orthodox monopoly over conversion within Israel. The non-Orthodox movements understandably combat this effort, often in a language of civil rights and liberties. Absent, however, are efforts to build a stronger Jewish people through development of a uniform conversion procedure acceptable to and inclusive of the major religious movements. Such an initiative, endorsed by the heads of the major American rabbinical seminaries, nearly came to fruition during the tenure of former Prime Minister Yitzhak Shamir.

Differences over personal status—i.e., who is a Jew—are real and, unless remedied, herald a split within the Jewish people. A constructive albeit partial approach to healing the breach may be found through developing common conversion procedures. Those unwilling to compromise at all for the sake of peoplehood retreat to a sanctimonious language of civil rights, assuming that the breach has already occurred and is probably irreparable in any case. By contrast, a truly *religious* pluralism would seek to underscore the importance of the non-Orthodox religious movements to preserving Jewish identity and, at the same time, strengthen Jewish peoplehood. Sadly, one year after the assassination, that model of religious pluralism has not prevailed. We prefer to score our victories at the expense of one another rather than mount a common quest on behalf of the Jewish people.

Panic on Pluralism Is Premature

In the intermediate aftermath of the Israeli elections, many American Jewish spokespeople reacted with expressions of deep concern concerning the future of religious pluralism within Israel.

More specifically, the fact that coalition agreements with religious parties promise to strengthen the power of the chief rabbinate has dismayed Reform and Conservative religious leaders in the United States.

Particular attention has been focused on recognition of non-Orthodox converts to Judaism within Israel and the right of non-Orthodox religious leaders to officiate at life-cycle events.

These pessimistic forecasts, although grounded in realism, are not yet warranted.

First, the increased votes for religious parties were by no means necessarily votes against religious pluralism. Of the religious parties, the ultra-Orthodox United Torah of Judaism (formerly Agudath Israel and Degel Ha-Torah) experienced no gain in seats. The increases occurred within the National Religious Party (Modern Orthodox) and Shas (Sephardi Orthodox). The NRP did not campaign for greater religious legislation so much as against a vision of Israel as a secular democratic rather than a Jewish state.

Similarly, 60 percent of Shas voters were non-Orthodox Israelis, but traditionalists of Sephardic background, who supported Shas for its commitment to Jewish heritage and tradition.

The implication of this voting pattern is significant. Supporters of the religious parties do not necessarily desire enforcing an Orthodox monopoly, restricting the expressions of Conservative and Reform Judaism, and increasing religious prohibitions in accordance with a strict interpretation of Jewish law. It does mean, however, that many Israelis are very concerned about the future quality of Israel's Jewish and spiritual life. These represent a potential constituency for religious pluralism.

Efforts to strengthen the non-Orthodox movements within Israel

Reprinted from the *Jewish Week of New York,* October 18, 1996.

therefore may well find a resonant ear among all Israelis concerned with the Jewishness of Israel society and its links to Jewish tradition and heritage.

Moreover, for American Jews, future Jewish continuity is tightly bound up with the future of the Conservative and Reform religious movements in the United States. To the extent that these movements succeed in retaining and increasing the number of their adherents, we will have Jewish continuity. To the extent that they fail and lose members, Jewish continuity is endangered. American Jews will pay close attention to whatever statements are made by the Israel government concerning the future place and legitimacy of the non-Orthodox movements. Statements contemptuous of Reform and Conservative Judaism will be viewed as counterproductive at best and may create serious rifts between Israeli and American Jewry.

The real significance of the "Who is a Jew?" question is not so much its impact upon non-Orthodox converts to Judaism as its dismissal of the principle of religious pluralism, which most American Jews regard as indispensable to Jewish continuity.

To the extent that the Israelis are committed to assisting in preserving Jewish continuity in the Diaspora, statements and actions by Israeli officials ought affirm rather than disparage the non-Orthodox religious movements.

Further, the election accentuated, as did the Rabin assassination, the religious-secular divide within Israeli society as a potential fissure within the Jewish people. The divide was echoed here in the United States between Orthodox and non-Orthodox Jewry.

This divide carries with it serious threats for our future as a common Jewish people albeit with diverse ideologies. Plurality of opinion, even vigorously debated, is by no means a debit. On the contrary, it indicates that at least we care passionately about our future as a people.

However, when diversity of opinion degenerates into delegitimization of one group by another or its demonization, we face a serious danger to our future as Jews.

The recent Israeli election calls into focus greater need for dialogue across ideological and spiritual divides over the question of what is our commonality as Jews. We can debate the differences, but we should also focus on the unifying faces of Judaism. Moreover, the self-interest of Orthodoxy lies in encouraging pluralism and an atmosphere of mutual tolerance.

To do otherwise will undermine future Jewish continuity and mutual understanding among Jews.

Lastly, the election brought into focus the continued need to rethink the meaning of a Jewish state. Many Israelis and American Jews reject the concept of theocracy. Yet probably as many will reject the definition of Israel as a secular democratic state that happens to have a majority of Jews. Therefore, American Jews and Israelis in the months and years ahead must ask what does a Jewish state mean if it is not a theocracy.

In this respect, the non-Orthodox religious movements may well have erred in articulating the message to Israel society as primarily a message of civil liberties—the right to perform marriages, conversions, etc.—rather than the existential questions of broadening religious expression and identifying Jews within a Jewish state in a noncoercive fashion. Significantly, the terms of the coalition agreement do allow for legislation permitting civil marriages in the case of individuals who cannot be married under Jewish law.

Similar vehicles must be found to define the Jewish state and simultaneously make room for individuals who would suffer under a state governed in all respects in accordance with Jewish law.

American Jews recognize that the American model of church-state separation cannot be transplanted to contemporary Israeli society.

The United States, after all, was not founded as a Christian country. Israel was established as a Jewish state.

Questions of the relationship of religion to state, the role of tradition in society, and the role of religion as moral conscience of the state and its policies do provide, however, unique opportunities for testing the viability of Judaic heritage in a modern democratic context. If we opt neither for a theocracy nor a secular democracy, we ought work toward a middle ground in which the Jewishness of Israeli society remains inviolable while affirming the civil rights and liberties of individual citizens, Jew or Gentile, within the Jewish state.

Patrilineal Descent Revisited

A prominent United States government official recently explained to a visiting American Jewish Committee (AJC) delegation that the only reason he was not a practicing Jew today was the refusal of his Conservative rabbi to confer the bar mitzvah rite of passage upon him inasmuch as his father had been Jewish but his mother was Gentile. At virtually the same point in time, Rabbi Yitz Greenberg, a prominent Modern Orthodox rabbi well-known for advocating religious pluralism, also addressing an AJC forum, condemned as "a first-class disaster" the Reform movement's decision to accept patrilineal descent as a criterion for defining who is a Jew.

Similarly, in 1998, at the board meetings of the Memorial Foundation for Jewish Culture, Rabbi Aharon Lichtenstein, a leading Orthodox scholar, commented that he well understood why the Reform movement had accepted patrilineality as meeting the needs of its constituency. However, as a Talmudic scholar and as a Jew committed to the binding power of Jewish law, he noted he could never accept such a definition. Rabbi Alexander Schindler, immediate past president of the Union of American Hebrew Congregations (UAHC), responded that the decision was taken only after ascertaining that sufficient scholarly basis within Jewish tradition warranted it.

Both views exist, yet both cannot be correct. The facts on the ground are self-evident. In 1983 the Reform movement accepted patrilineal descent as evidence for presumption of Jewish status within Reform Judaism. Reconstructionist Judaism had done so as early as 1968, yet, given the small number of Reconstructionist Jews, that decision had caused few ripple effects within the Jewish community. By contrast, the 1983 decision of the Central Conference of American Rabbis (CCAR) underscored major debates taking place within the Reform movement, within the broader Jewish community, and between Israel and the Diaspora.

Background

To be sure, as early as 1909 the CCAR had affirmed patrilineality. More recently, in 1961, it had reaffirmed that decision through its *Rabbi's Manual.*[1] For all intents and purposes virtually every Reform rabbi in the United States had been acknowledging patrilineal descent since the Second World War. What changed in 1983, however, was the public nature of the decision and the surrounding communal debate. Until 1983 matrilineality had been upheld in principle, and patrilineality was at most tolerated. From 1983 onward the matrilineal principle no longer was operative exclusively, leading to the irony that in at least · some cases, persons considered as Jewish under Jewish law were *not* entitled to Jewish status under the Reform definition of who was a Jew.

By 1990 the National Jewish Population Study (NJPS) reported approximately 150,000 patrilineally defined Jews. Those numbers have doubtless increased since then, owing to continued high rates of mixed marriage. Moreover, in the intervening decade many mixed couples have been raising children. In short, a critical mass of individuals exist whose status in the Jewish community is disputed—acceptable as Jews in some sectors yet unacceptable in others. These differences cross ideological and geographical divides. Even within the Reform movement no unanimity exists. In England, for example, Reform Judaism rejects patrilineal descent while Liberal Judaism practices it.

Therefore, the issue has grown in importance in recent years and promises to become even more significant in the future. For that reason it is appropriate to revisit the issue to ask precisely what has been accomplished, what have been the ripple effects, and what are the implications for the future.

The Crux of the Debate

The issues and considerations in the debate may be quickly summarized. The decision in effect affirmed long-standing Reform practice to accept as a Jew the child of either a Jewish father or a Jewish mother, provided that the parents expressed commitment to Jewish continuity through engaging in specific acts of Jewish affirmation in the child's upbringing. Many have sought to explain the decision as one of principle that is irrelevant to the intermarriage phenomenon generally. Traditional rabbinic law had defined identity via the mother. In an age of gender equality, should not equal weight be given to a Jewish father?

Moreover, Reform leaders pointed to the anomaly of children of Jewish fathers raised as Jews yet not being recognized as such, whereas children of Jewish mothers who had never identified in any substantive or even symbolic way as Jews were automatically recognized as Jews under Jewish law. Traditionalist Reform rabbis, in fact, pointed to their refusal to officiate at marriages in which one partner was born of a Jewish mother but had never affirmed membership in the Jewish community.

Yet in addition to questions of principle, the patrilineal descent decision must also be considered in the sociological and demographic context of American Reform Judaism. For one thing, the overwhelming majority of Reform rabbis had been practicing patrilineal descent since World War II by their de facto acceptance of children of Jewish fathers and non-Jewish mothers as Jewish. Moreover, Reform rabbis who opposed patrilineality in the name of communal unity had to face the harsh reality that the Orthodox rabbinate was unlikely to accept Reform conversions in any case. Finally, and most important, as the number of interfaith marriages increased, the numbers of children of Jewish fathers and non-Jewish mothers within Reform temples naturally increased as well.

However, objections to the patrilineal descent decision are considerable. First, its effects on Jewish unity weigh heavily. For the last two thousand years the Jewish community has acted upon a single principle of matrilineal identity. Any child of a Jewish mother, no matter how involved or uninvolved in Jewish activity, claimed equal status as a Jew under Jewish law. Orthodox and Conservative Jews agree on the continuing validity of this principle. Thus, individuals who are told by Reform rabbis that they are Jews would find their Jewishness rejected, in the absence of formal conversion, by Orthodox and Conservative Judaism alike.

To be sure, Orthodox rabbis generally rejected Reform conversions in any case. Yet the decision for patrilineality, rather than for insistence upon the conversion of children of Jewish fathers, drove a wedge between Conservative and Reform Judaism, the two largest religious movements within contemporary American Judaism. Finally, as Reform Rabbi David Polish noted, the insistence that the Jewishness of children of either Jewish mothers or Jewish fathers depends upon certain Jewish "affirmations" itself threatens to divide the Reform movement over differing criteria of what such affirmations might be.[2]

Equally serious are the implications for Israel-Diaspora relations. Reform leaders, like their Conservative and even many Orthodox colleagues, oppose proposed changes in the Law of Return that would have the effect of denying Jewish status to those who convert to Judaism under non-Orthodox auspices. They argue that the State of Israel, through legislative action, ought not drive wedges between Israeli and Diaspora Jews by declaring that converts to Judaism in the Diaspora are less than full Jews. This argument, however, collapses in the face of the patrilineal descent decision.

The Reform movement itself has driven such a wedge by declaring offspring of Jewish fathers as Jewish. Should Israel now be compelled to amend the Law of Return in a more liberal direction, extending the definition of who is a Jew to children of Jewish fathers, recognized as Jews by the Reform and Reconstructionist movements in America, yet whose Jewishness is denied by more traditionalist sectors of Jewry? Significantly, the Reform movement in Israel itself recognized the implications of the decision for its claims to recognition within Israel and vociferously, yet vainly, opposed the patrilineal descent resolution.

Finally, we must weigh the consequences of the patrilineal descent decision on conversion to Judaism in the United States. In theory patrilineality may obstruct rather than encourage conversion. Intermarried couples are now offered the message that even absent the conversion of the Gentile mother the offspring of such marriages are still Jews. They may well be entitled to ask why the non-Jewish partner should convert at all. Why submit to a rigorous program of Jewish study if the children are already Jews?

Historically one motivation to conversion has been to enable children to be raised within the Jewish faith, a motivation undermined by the patrilineal descent decision. Estimates today are that there are between three thousand and four thousand converts annually—a pathetically small number in the vast sea of mixed marriage. Reform leaders once hailed conversion as a historical response to mixed marriage. Yet no sooner did Reform accept patrilineality publicly than the numbers of converts to Judaism began to decrease remarkably.

In the final analysis the patrilineal descent decision, motivated by legitimate concerns for expanding Jewish numbers and by the principle of gender equality, may not be taken out of the context of the outreach movement and the intermarriage phenomenon. Patrilineal descent affirms the growing reality of intermarriage and says to intermarried couples that any of their children who identify with Judaism are still presumed to be Jewish, even without conversion. As laudable as such a statement may appear, not only does it undermine Jewish unity, but it also goes beyond a pragmatic accommodation of intermarriage and toward ideological legitimization.

Implications

One implication clearly has been the communal dissensus and divisiveness concerning the issue. A 1997 AJC survey discovered that American Jews agreed by 50 percent to 37 percent, that the decision had divided "the Jewish people worldwide, especially between Israel and the Diaspora."[3] Perhaps even more significantly, a 1991 survey of Reform rabbis indicated that one-third opposed the patrilineal descent decision, an additional 7 percent were unsure, and over half agreed that the decision "is one of the most divisive acts in contemporary Jewish life."[4]

A second implication relates to the degree of confusion and misunderstanding concerning the decision. First, the boundary line between Jew and Gentile in America is quite fluid—a significant challenge to a minority group's efforts to maintain its distinctiveness. Patrilineality blurs that boundary even more, because in the public eye it has been interpreted nearly universally as meaning that one is a Jew if one simply has one Jewish parent of either gender. In fact, as noted, the patrilineal decision is more restrictive—in some cases even more restrictive than the definition provided under Jewish law.

Moreover, the NJPS reports that approximately one-third of the children of mixed marriages are being raised at least partially outside the Jewish faith. Patrilineality as a criterion excludes these individuals as

Gentiles rather than Jews, for the patrilineal descent decision required the exclusive raising of these children as Jews in order to qualify as Jewish. However, in the public perception, the category of patrilineal Jew encompasses anyone whose father is Jewish and whose mother is not, even if the person was raised partly in another faith.

Reform efforts to draw boundaries on this issue—for example, the decision to deny Jewish education to anyone raised partly in another faith—have not become mandatory for Reform congregations, in turn further blurring the lines and definitions of who is a Jew. For example, even Jewish communal leaders have been known to use the phrase "half Jew," a category unknown to all of Jewish heritage and to all the contemporary Jewish religious movements as well as being at odds with the terms of the patrilineal descent decision. Given this fluidity, one social scientist goes so far as to counsel simple acceptance of all models of Jewish identification irrespective of historical or communal norms.[5] Another sociologist calmly predicts that in the twenty-first century "the mixture of people who comprise synagogue-affiliated families will include ever-greater numbers of intermarried, non-Jews, half-Jews, and patrilineal Jews"—the specter of which should frighten all Jewish leaders, including the most ardent advocates of patrilineality.[6]

The Blurring of the Boundary

In theory, patrilineality has both broadened and narrowed the definition of who is a Jew. Thus, its defenders frequently note how patrilineality may be more stringent in its definition than Orthodox definitions.[7] One advocate, Rabbi Bernard Zlotowitz, even invokes, out of context, the mantle of Rabbi Joseph B. Soloveitchik, dean of American Orthodoxy, as validation for Reform practice.[8]

In reality, however, the trend toward broadening the definition and blurring the boundaries has prevailed in the implementation of the patrilineal descent decision. At a minimum the decision itself has not been understood by the Jewish public and the media, where it is generally interpreted as accepting anyone as a Jew who has one Jewish parent, rather than the far more limited notion of Jewish status resulting from both parents committing themselves to the exclusive raising of the child as a Jew. The latter criterion would in all probability sharply reduce the actual number of individuals claiming Jewish status under patrilineality. In turn, the Reform movement would then find itself in the most difficult position of explaining to large numbers of people why they cannot be accepted as Jews despite the best of intentions.

Other questions flow from the blurring of the boundaries. Should, for example, community day schools, theoretically open to all Jews, accept patrilineal Jews as students even though their status as Jews is not accepted by either the Orthodox or Conservative movements? Claims for inclusion de facto contradict the principle of educating children in an environment presumed to consist of only Jewish students. Moreover, the definitional problem of who is a Jew is compounded by contrasting standards of conversion between the religious movements as well as the presence of a critical mass (50,000 to 55,000) of self-declared converts—individuals born as Gentiles who now claim to be Jewish but without having undergone any type of conversion process.

Finally, it should be noted that the blurring of the boundaries between Jew and Gentile is far more critical for American Jewry today than at any other moment in Jewish history. Shaye Cohen offers impressive evidence that biblical Judaism acknowledged patrilineal descent and that both Josephus and Philo were unacquainted with the principle of matrilineality. Only the Mishnah introduced matrilineality as the exclusive operating principle.[9]

Nevertheless, Cohen underscores how rabbinic law strengthened the boundaries between Jew and Gentile and concludes that boundaries are even more necessary today because the contrast of Jew and Gentile ("us and them") has virtually disappeared as existential reality for American Jewry.[10] Matrilineality in effect ensured common kinship of Jewishness. At a time when common faith has virtually disappeared among Jews, surrendering common kinship marked a break with eighteen hundred years of Jewish history and severed one of the few remaining ties universal to all Jews.[11]

Nor has this split in common peoplehood been limited to Orthodoxy versus Reform, a conclusion frequently drawn in media coverage. For example, liberal and secular Israelis have often seized this issue as illustrative of the harmful effects of an Orthodox monopoly in matters of personal status. However, the actual split by patrilineality has also divided Conservative and Reform Jewry and has driven a wedge between Israeli and Diaspora criteria for Jewishness. Significantly, advocates of patrilineality predicted that Conservative Jewry would soon follow the lead of Reform.[12] To be sure, over two-thirds of Conservative synagogue members express personal acceptance of patrilineality in the case of their own families.[13] Conservative leadership, however, has rejected by increasingly larger margins any departure from the matrilineal principle as constituting rejection of *halakhah,* departure from historical Judaism, and a splitting of the Jewish people. In effect, Conservative Judaism has opted for upholding the criteria of Judaism as law, history, and peoplehood over the potential benefits of patrilineality to individual Jews and their families. In fact, Rabbi Robert Gordis, a leading figure within Conservative Judaism, challenged Reform to abandon patrilineality on account of its divisiveness within the Jewish people.[14] The Conservative position upholds the need for boundaries. Its solution for children of Jewish fathers and non-Jewish mothers lies in the conversion of such children, a solution in fact far more acceptable to the concerns of halakhists.[15]

Surprisingly, a considerable proportion of Reform rabbis agree. For example, 25 percent of Reform rabbis reported that they themselves would oppose the marriage of their sons to a patrilineally Jewish woman.[16] Jacob Petuchowski, long considered an intellectual dean of the Reform movement, opposed the decision as surrendering a universal standard of Jewish status. Whatever our theological disagreements, Petuchowski noted, Jewish distinctiveness lay in our capacity to recognize one another as Jews. A 1997 joint Simchat Torah celebration of Orthodox, Conservative, and Reform synagogues in New York City illustrated Petuchowski's fears. One of the Jewish communal leaders present praised the event as a statement that we all stood together at Sinai regardless of our differences theologically. Within the assembled crowd others commented that this statement, no matter how well intentioned, simply did not ring true once Reform had accepted patrilineal descent, creating a category of Jews whom some sectors felt did stand at Sinai and others felt simply did not.

Reform leaders acknowledge these costs but do not believe they warrant retreat from the patrilineal principle. UAHC president Rabbi

Eric Yoffie, for example, respects the right of Orthodox Jews to reject patrilineal descent but opposes their invoking the coercive power of the Jewish state to endorse that definition.[17] By that logic Israel should reject *any* definition of Jewish status as disenfranchising some who claim to be Jews (for example, Jews for Jesus, Black Hebrews, and so on). Any definition will prove exclusionary to some, and codifying a definition under Israeli law essentially does mean utilizing the coercive power of the state to mandate it. It should be noted that no sentiment exists within any sector of Israeli society (including Israeli Reform Jews) for the patrilineal principle. In this respect the patrilineal descent decision has created yet another wedge between Israel and the Diaspora.

Perhaps the most damaging of the effects of patrilineality has been its impact on the image of Reform Judaism within the Jewish people. Significantly, the Denver Colorado Joint Conversion Institute collapsed in the immediate aftermath of the patrilineal descent decision. Although Reform leaders at the time blamed the collapse of the Denver plan on ultra-Orthodox intransigence, few were willing to question how the decision had in effect undermined those in the Modern Orthodox rabbinate counseling greater cooperation with Reform, especially on issues of personal status. Even as liberal a thinker as Rabbi David Hartmann, who embraces Reform as part of the struggle to preserve the Jewish people and praises it for its emphasis on social ethics, condemned patrilineality as breaking the ties of Reform Judaism to Jewish peoplehood and community.[18]

The larger issue of Reform's self-image and communal perception relates also to the question of the limits of freedom and the need for discipline.[19] Is Reform Judaism so elastic as to permit in the name of inclusivity virtually anything that Jews are doing? By accepting patrilineal descent, is Reform in essence sanctioning mixed marriage even as its leaders claim continued opposition to mixed marriage as a phenomenon?

Conclusion

These questions have no easy answers. But the facts on the ground do speak eloquently. Patrilineal descent benefits individuals at the expense of issues of peoplehood and unity. In accepting patrilineal descent, Reform leadership argued for gender equality, inclusivity, and the fact that Orthodoxy would never accept them no matter what they did. The decision clearly resonated with overwhelming numbers of Reform Jews and even large numbers of Conservative Jews.

Aspects of it need to be articulated more clearly and studied more carefully for their impact and effects: the sustaining power of the patrilineal definition (for example, whether patrilineal Jews identify as Jews as adults), the impact on conversion, and so on. Even absent formal study, it may be hypothesized that, given patrilineality, those who are converting to Judaism under Reform auspices are in fact quite sincere in their conversion. In other words, patrilineality permits those who do not desire conversion to retain Gentile status while raising children as Jews. In that sense a side effect of patrilineality may well be to underscore the sincerity of those who actually do convert to Judaism. Moreover, it should be noted that the Orthodox rabbinate may rightly be challenged for its failure to provide even a modicum of support for the Conservative movement's rejection of patrilineality, let alone for Reform rabbis who similarly oppose the decision.

Clearly, however, the decision does signal placing the personal interests of individuals over the collective welfare of the Jewish people. That individuals pursue their own self-interest is understandable. For Jewish leadership to pursue personal rather than collective agendas and aspirations will result in short-term gains and satisfactions but long-term failures.

Notes

1. Charles Silberman, *A Certain People* (New York: Summit Books, 1985), 322; Meryl Hyman, *Who Is a Jew? Conversations, Not Conclusions* (Woodstock: Jewish Lights, 1998), 226.

2. David Polish, "A Dissent on Patrilineal Descent," in *Toward the Twenty-first Century: Judaism and the Jewish People in Israel and America,* ed. Ronald Konish (New York: KTAV, 1989), 230–32.

3. *1997 Annual Survey of American Jewish Opinion* (New York: American Jewish Committee, 1997), 45.

4. Samuel Heilman, *Jewish Unity and Diversity: A Survey of American Rabbis and Rabbinical Students* (New York: American Jewish Committee, 1991), 50.

5. Martha Ackelsberg, "Jewish Family Ethics in a Post-Halakhic Age," in *Imagin-*

ing the Jewish Future, ed. David Teutsch (Albany: State University of New York Press, 1992), 152–53.

6. Egon Mayer, "The Coming Reformation in American Jewish Identity," in Teutsch, ed., *Imagining,* 181.

7. Bernard Zlotowitz, "Patrilineal Descent," in *The Jewish Condition,* ed. Aron Hirt-Manheimer (New York: UAHC Press, 1995), 259, 265.

8. Ibid., 266.

9. Shaye Cohen, *The Beginnings of Jewishness* (Berkeley: University of California Press, 1999), 266–83.

10. *Ibid.,* 343–47.

11. Hyman, *Who Is a Jew?* 73–78.

12. Silberman, *A Certain People,* 323.

13. Egon Mayer, "From an External to an Internal Agenda," in *The Americanization of the Jews,* eds. Robert Selzer and Norman Cohen (New York: New York University Press, 1995), 424; see also Jack Wertheimer, *Conservative Synagogues and Their Members* (New York: Jewish Theological Seminary, 1996), 10.

14. Jack Wertheimer, *A People Divided: Judaism and Contemporary America* (New York: Basic Books, 1993), 158.

15. Hyman, *Who Is a Jew?* 101–3. See also Jack Simcha Cohen, "Pluralism: Halakhic Obstacles and Solutions," in *Conflict or Cooperation: Papers on Jewish Unity* (New York: American Jewish Committee and CLAL, 1989), 66–67.

16. Heilman, *Jewish Unity,* 51.

17. Hyman, *Who Is a Jew?* 178.

18. Ibid., 63–64.

19. Polish, "A Dissent," 233.

From Coalitions to Partnerships to Mergers

American Jewry has built a network of Jewish communal organizations that not only exceeds by far anything comparable in Jewish history but has also aroused the envy of virtually every non-Jewish group eager to learn whether the secrets of Jewish success in America are replicable. Precisely at a time when forebodings about the Jewish future are legitimate for reasons of assimilation and mixed marriage, the communal structure appears so vibrant that prophecies of imminent doom sound exaggerated.

Yet fewer numbers of Jews will mean weaker and smaller Jewish organizations. Conversely, greater commitment to Judaism translates into more intensive involvement in Jewish communal life. Therefore, despite external perceptions of Jewish organizational and communal vitality, virtually every Jewish organization is reexamining its agenda and asking whether it is well-positioned to meet the new challenges of the twenty-first century. Given the reality of assimilation, some shakedown in Jewish organizational life is likely, and those agencies that demonstrate their capacity to reposition themselves and develop new strengths and expertise will be those most likely to survive such a shakedown.

In this context of looming assimilation and organizational repositioning, new partnerships and even mergers between agencies have already become evident. To be sure, Jewish organizations have often formed coalitions, in particular in the political arena, so as to speak with a stronger voice. These coalitions, however, have often proved little more than loose alliances, fashioned to meet immediate external threats with little impact upon internal communal culture. In recent years, however, new partnerships have developed—between Federations and synagogues, between philanthropists, and between the Israeli Government and Diaspora Jewish organizations—for the specific purposes of addressing current challenges of continuity and assimilation.

Reprinted with permission of the Jewish Life Network from *Contact,* 2:3, Spring 2000.

In at least one case a full-blown merger occurred, creating the newly-formed United Jewish Communities from the relatively disparate Council of Jewish Federations, United Jewish Appeal, and United Israel Appeal.

Several factors have driven these developments. First, limited economic resources suggest elimination of unnecessary overhead and duplication so as to free funds for the programmatic work that underlies organizational purpose. More profoundly, the emergence of partnerships reflects the need to bridge traditional divides in addressing current communal needs. Thus the New York Federation, among others, has increasingly sought to fund creative programming within synagogues, thereby breaking the informal separation between civil and religious sectors.

Most importantly, partnerships reflect the desire of leading philanthropists to dedicate resources to specific needs and launch new initiatives to address them. In so doing, they effectively create "facts on the ground" that existing institutions may well imitate at a future point. Thus philanthropists can lead by action and example rather than await full communal consensus.

Much here can and should be applauded. That leading philanthropists are pooling resources to secure the Jewish future in itself helps alter philanthropic norms and signals to the community that there is no greater priority than combating assimilation. New projects, in turn, may be funded on an experimental basis before the community more generally is prepared to devote resources to them.

The most significant drawback to this development lies in the as yet unanswered question as to whether it may inhibit communal debate by imposing an artificial conformity of opinion in the name of chasing the availability of philanthropic funding. One need not be crudely Marxist to note how concentrations of ever larger amounts of resources in smaller numbers of hands can limit the freedom to dissent for fear of losing one's next potential grant or donor. The Hebrew phrase, *lo hameah, lo-hadeah* ("money talks"), resonates even more strongly in the new world of partnerships. One would do well to recall that one reason American Jewry built so many organizations was precisely to allow the diversity of expression and plurality of opinion that have allowed for both traditionalist and liberal agendas to flourish. One may legitimately ask whether distinctive, minority, and politically incorrect opinions will continue to be heard or whether one will run the risk of finding oneself marginalized for daring to challenge philanthropic wisdom.

These questions have no immediate answers. For the present, new partnerships hold out the possibility of formulating new communal priorities, providing resources to address them, and effecting fundamental communal change. Clearly, new alliances are necessary in critical areas, e.g., advocacy for Jewish education. Moreover, it is precisely on the agenda of Jewish continuity where the "culture of consensus" long favored by the community may be failing our current needs. Precisely because the internal questions of Jewish identity are themselves so divisive, it may not be helpful, and indeed it may prove counterproductive, to avoid divisiveness by lending communal support to whatever programs may interest Jews (and, in some case, non-Jews as well) regardless of their long-term impact upon Judaic cultural and religious distinctiveness. In this sense, philanthropic partnerships wish to act quickly, to realize a "big idea." Yet such "big ideas" usually generate counter-voices, and they need to be heard.

Partnerships, to be sure, have not mandated ideological conformity. Some have tried to be inclusive of dissenting opinion. Yet even as we advocate new coalitions and applaud new partnership initiatives, let us be mindful that the old adage "two Jews, three opinions" no less lauded the diversity of Jewish communal expression than it bemoaned the absence of Jewish unity.

ISRAEL-DIASPORA RELATIONS

The Dorothy and Julius Koppelman Institute on American Jewish-Israeli Relations was established originally in 1982 to strengthen ties between the world's two largest Jewish communities. In becoming associate director of the institute under the leadership of Founding Director Bert Gold in 1991 and subsequently succeeding Bert as director in 1992, I began to focus on areas of tension and conflict in Israel-diaspora relations. Of particular interest to me have been questions of religious pluralism, post-Zionism, and the threats to continued unity of Jewish peoplehood expressed in the atmospherics surrounding the assassination of Prime Minister Yitzhak Rabin. In turn, the hopes raised by the Oslo Process for permanent peace between Israel and surrounding Arab states, to be sure, have since proved unfounded, but these hopes only reflected ongoing American Jewish support for and identification with Israel as a Jewish state.

Israel-Diaspora Relations:
The Case of American Orthodoxy: A True Partnership?

Let me begin this paper with some personal reminiscences. Growing up in the 1950s as an American Orthodox Jew, I regarded Israel as a distant place. Only the wealthiest Jews could afford to visit. Rarely, if ever, did one hear talk of individuals settling there. Moreover, the Jews who were there were said to be secularists—distant from any form of religious behavior or ideology. Finally, those who were truly Orthodox in America generally shunned Israel. To be sure, there were pockets of religious Zionism, but its members were perceived as somehow less than fully authentic in their commitment to Orthodox Judaism.

Since that time major changes have taken place. For today's Orthodox Jew, Israel is anything but distant. On the contrary, Orthodox Jews visit Israel regularly and most do, in fact, at least contemplate permanent settlement there. More importantly, for contemporary Orthodox Jews the personal connections with Israelis are in many ways far stronger than those between non-Orthodox American Jews and secular Israelis. Finally, it is those American Orthodox Jews who distance themselves from Israel who are now regarded as less than authentic in their commitment to Orthodox Judaism.

How did these changes come about? First, the perception of Orthodoxy in America today is that of a growing rather than of a decreasing group. And Israel is a major source of the renewal and strenthening of Orthodoxy in America. In other words, American Orthodox Jews are the primary American Jewish group for whom Israel actually constitutes a spiritual, cultural, and ideological center.

Second, identification with Israel is a critical component in the self-

Reprinted from *Religious Pluralism and Modern Israel: Implications for Israel-Diaspora Relations,* by David Ellenson and Steven Bayme, published by the American Jewish Committee, 1992.

identification of American Orthodox Jews. For them, Israel retains its utopian image. The theme of Israel as redemptive in Jewish history— "the beginning of the growth of our redemption"—permeates the consciousness of Orthodox Jews.

Third, a subtle but detectable shift has taken place in the perception of the ultra-Orthodox or *haredim*. Perhaps in theory the leadership of the *haredi* community remains anti-Zionist. Rarely does that express itself in terms of day-to-day interrelationships among American Orthodox Jews. In other words, the *haredi* Jew living in Borough Park is not regarded as less committed to Israel than the Modern Orthodox Jew living in Riverdale. On the contrary, the Lubavitch movement within Hasidism is now primarily identified through its messianic thrust— namely, that the Messiah is about to arrive and all Jews will quickly move to Israel. Although occasional anger does flare up between Orthodox communities over questions such as reciting the prayer on behalf of the State of Israel, for most American Orthodox Jews these are rather subtle points of ideology. Most will agree on Israel's centrality in Jewish life and the need for American Jewish support—even if doctrinal differences remain about the sanctity of the Jewish state and its precise religious significance.

In contrast, where distancing has taken place is between Orthodox Jews in America and the rest of the American Jewish community. There the presence of intermarriage and the widespread perception that non-Orthodox Jews are less engaged religiously and are facing assimilation has underscored the need to "circle up the wagons"—to nurture greater separatism for the Orthodox community. It is precisely in this context of greater separatism from non-Orthodox Jews that American Orthodox Jews look to Israel for greater engagement and sustenance.

There are at least four forms of this "greater engagement." In the areas of Jewish education, fund-raising, *aliyah,* and politics, American Orthodox Jews are far more directly involved in Israeli culture and public affairs than are other American Jews. This paper will analyze the forms of that involvement and its impact upon the respective communities, and will seek to explain it and its implications for overall Israel-Diaspora relations.

Let's begin, however, with a demographic profile of American Orthodoxy. In 1881 only twelve of the 200 leading congregations in America were Orthodox. A hundred years later, according to the National Jewish Population Survey, American Orthodoxy retained the allegiance of only six percent of the total Jewish population—proportionately the same as in 1881. Today we speak of 350,000 American Jews who profess Orthodoxy. To be sure, this number may underestimate the *haredim,* who are notoriously unwilling to participate in surveys such as that of the NJPS. The six percent figure does represent a decline from 11 percent in the 1970 NJPS. However, in the 1990 survey, 10 percent of Jews under age 25 identified as Orthodox, suggesting that the decline is by no means permanent and that, on the contrary, Orthodoxy may be experiencing some growth among the younger generation. Perhaps more importantly, of Jews active and affiliated in the community, perhaps close to 20 percent are Orthodox, ensuring the Orthodox a greater degree of visibility and accounting for the perception of growth and strength. In other words, the decline in Orthodox numbers parallels a rise in the visibility of those committed to Orthodox norms and a growth in their role and prominence within the broader Jewish community.

In terms of Israel-Diaspora relations, American Orthodox Jews consistently outscore the non-Orthodox on knowledge of Hebrew, *aliyah,* repeat visits to Israel, and the claim of having close friends and relatives in Israel. When one compares Orthodox Jews to affiliated Jews in these areas, the general ratio is at least 2:1. For example, Orthodox rabbis are twice as likely to consider *aliyah* as non-Orthodox rabbis.[1] Although some may regard this as a reflection of the treatment of non-Orthodox rabbis in Israel, it also parallels a general Orthodox perception that they like what they see in Israel and identify with it. It is this identification that is in sharp contrast with the perceptions noted above of the 1950s. For example, a recent study of alumni of the Ramaz day school in New York City indicated that 95 percent of alumni had visited Israel at least once and 66 percent had done so at least four times.[2]

Similarly, albeit on a more personal level, while serving in 1977 on a search committee for a dean for one of the colleges associated with Yeshiva University, I questioned one Orthodox candidate concerning the state of Jewish education in America. He responded that he assumed that all Orthodox Jews would rejoice in the election of Menachem Begin as prime minister in Israel, for that would undoubtedly be a major boost for Jewish education in North America! This, at a moment when non-Orthodox Jews were so fearful that Begin would upset the delicate relationship between America and Israel generally. Again, the Orthodox like what they see—even if in sharp dissonance with the general views of American Jewry.

Jewish Education

It is in the area of Jewish education that one can identify the intensity of the Orthodox relationship with Israel. For American Orthodox Jews, twelve years of day school education is now considered normative. It is considered a most radical step to send one's child to a public high school or a private one under non-Jewish auspices. But even more telling is the increased trend among centrist Orthodox youths toward spending the year after high school graduation in an Israeli yeshiva. This latter trend has become normative for both boys and girls, again suggesting a pronounced change in the nature of Orthodox education and its relationship with Israel.

Moreover, the results and impact of this post-high school year appear to be considerable. Those who return to the States to pursue their college education report increased attachment and allegiance to Israel. This is reflected in their *aliyah* consciousness. The same survey of Ramaz alumni indicated that 11 percent of alumni currently reside in Israel, of whom 80 percent (nine percent of the total) report that they have made *aliyah*.[3] More specifically, for the Flatbush Yeshiva class of 1967, fifteen out of 125 graduates have gone on *aliyah*—again, 11 percent of the total. For the Maimonides Day School in Boston, the 1967 graduating class reported that five of nineteen alumni now reside in Israel.[4] Needless to say, these percentages are far higher than those for any other form of Jewish education in America.

Aside from *aliyah,* the impact of the year in Israel can be felt in higher education here in the States. For the first time, Columbia University students, graduates of a year in a variety of Israeli yeshivot, have engaged a *rosh yeshiva* to conduct regular Talmud lessons while attending courses at Columbia. At Yeshiva University the change is even more marked. In the 1960s Talmud study at night was virtually unknown. The *beit midrash* was empty after dinner. By the 1980s on virtually any weeknight one could encounter a full *beit midrash*. Observers attributed the change almost entirely to the numbers of students who had spent a year studying at an Israeli yeshiva.

The impact can also be felt in terms of increased religious observance. Graduates of Israeli yeshivot increasingly have accepted women's head coverings as a necessary aspect of marriage. When one realizes that this aspect of Jewish law was virtually neglected by their parents' generation, and given the ubiquity of the women's head covering within the Israeli Orthodox community, one must conclude that the year spent in Israel acts for many to intensify the degree of religious observance.

Similarly, those who attend Israeli yeshivot often return with a pronounced sympathy for the political right in Israel. There is, to be sure, an exception among alumni of the Yeshivat Gush Etzion, where the dovish influences of Rabbis Amital and Lichtenstein are felt. Many of these spearheaded support in America for the Meimad Party during the 1988 elections. These, however, are the exceptions. Support for Gush Emunim among the American Orthodox far exceeds support for Oz V'shalom.

Although these changes are often applauded by Modern Orthodox American Jewish leaders, they have not come without cost. More specifically, the "modern" dimension of American Orthodoxy has suffered. If nothing else, in terms of secular education, those who return from a year at an Israeli yeshiva frequently compress their college education into three years or less. In terms of modern Jewish scholarship, it is fascinating to note that the single most popular Bible commentary utilized among American Modern Orthodox Jews today is that of the Art Scroll series—a commentary authored under *haredi* auspices, which ignores modern scholarship or dismisses it as irrelevant at best and heresy at worst. Twenty-five years ago Charles Liebman predicted an explosion within the American Orthodox community over the question of biblical commentary and scholarship. To date, no explosion has occurred. What has happened, however, is the growth of English-language commentaries presenting the words of the Bible in the most simplistic and uncritical senses.[5]

Moreover, Orthodox parents report some unease if not ambivalence about the year in Israel. They fear the added pressure of the *roshei yeshiva* on their children to spend a second year in Israel, during which negative estimates of college and secular education will be nurtured. Others report that those who intend to concentrate in the sciences are not seriously affected by the year in Israel. Rabbinic authorities have already made their peace with the need to study the natural sciences so as to advance professionally. What is in question is the necessity for humanistic studies—for a liberal arts education in America is by no means a sure path to professional success, and the conflict between humanistic scholarship and traditional Jewish learning rages far more intensely today than historical divisions between scientists and Talmudists. It is this instrumentalist vision of secular education—as important primarily for purposes of earning a living—that symbolizes the weakness within Modern Orthodoxy today. The irony here, of course, is that what distinguished Modern Orthodoxy was its unwavering commitment to the importance of secular education as a value in itself. Perceiving secular education as primarily instrumental in purpose signified an unwitting, but by no means illusory, victory of the *haredi* world, which always considered secular education as permissible only for purposes of earning a living.

This vision of the *roshei yeshiva* permitting secular education only in this utilitarian sense of earning a living neatly complements the turn toward professionalism in American higher education generally. Thus, for example, at Yeshiva University in the 1970s and 1980s, virtually entire humanities departments disappeared or shrank to part-time status, while courses in accounting and information science proliferated. Today's undergraduates tend to concentrate entirely in preprofessional areas; rarely in their undergraduate studies are they exposed to the classics of Western intellectual history, literature, political theory, much less compelled to assess their importance for Jewish thought and culture.

This last point has produced a further irony. As American *roshei yeshiva* have observed the products of Israeli yeshivot, they, in turn, have grown closer to religious Zionism. Thus the opposition to religious Zionism within the American Orthodox world has faded, for it is modern Israel that ensures the primacy of the value system of those who initially opposed religious Zionism as too secular and too "liberated" from rabbinic authority.

Nor is this impact limited to yeshiva students alone. Rather, the seriousness of Torah study has spilled over into women's education as well. Israeli institutions targeted for serious Torah study for American Jewish women have left a similar mark upon their constituents.

What all this amounts to, in a most striking fashion, is the reemergence of rabbinic authority. At a time when American Jews generally look to their rabbis primarily for symbolic leadership and guidance on life-cycle events, American Orthodox Jews have returned to the notion of rabbinic authority. In other words, while few rabbis can actually mandate for their constituents, Orthodox rabbis have the greatest capacity for influencing the day-to-day lives of congregants. To be sure, most Orthodox Jews, like American Jews generally, will end up making their own decisions. What is unique to Orthodoxy, however, is the perception that rabbis can influence personal decision-making—on questions of career, family, and culture as well as fairly narrow areas of Jewish law.

To be sure, American Orthodox Jews do express some unease at the preponderance of yeshivot in Israel under *haredi* auspices. They are not comfortable with those who refuse to sing the Israeli national anthem or celebrate Israeli Independence Day. The *haredi* critique that Zionism tried to normalize the Jews—make them a nation like all other nations—causes great discomfort. Nevertheless, even among those who have come under *haredi* influence, one sees greater identification and involvement with Israel. For instance, among New York City *baalei teshuva,* 36 percent have visited Israel more than once—three times the percentage of the non-Orthodox.[6] More to the point, the ideological criticism of Israel as a Zionist state is lost among the Jews in the street—whether they be *haredi* or Modern Orthodox. Israel's centrality in Jewish life is the most critical theme pervading the self-consciousness of Orthodox Jews. *Haredi* leaders themselves acknowledge that as their fund-raising base has broadened to include so many non-*haredi* donors, the ideological critique of Zionism ought best be muted.

All this is not to say that Orthodox Jews have received intensive education about modern Israel. On the contrary, concrete knowledge of modern Israeli life is remarkably weak within Orthodox educational institutions. Rather, what is at stake is the perception of Israel as the critical presence in Jewish life and the necessity to experience Israel as realization of Jewish dreams and aspirations. Israel may not have entered the formal curriculum of Orthodox educational institutions in America, but feeling for it and identification with it permeates the Orthodox school.

Fund-raising

Recent research has documented that a prime factor involved in philanthropy is the satisfaction the donor derives from giving directly to causes he holds dear. In the case of the centrist Orthodox, this principle is especially relevant. The centrist Orthodox give twice as much to yeshivot as they do to the UJA. Among the traditional Orthodox, the percentage exceeds a 7:1 ratio.[7]

Again, the direct involvement of the Orthodox with contemporary Israeli culture should be obvious. American Orthodox Jews in essence have signed on to what Israeli yeshivot represent. They like what they see, and therefore are prepared to fund these institutions quite generously. Moreover, they are well aware that other Jews will take responsibility for other types of institutions in Israel. Therefore they perceive part of their very purpose and mission in the area of Israel-Diaspora relations to be the funding of Torah institutions. Needless to add, Israeli institutions sensitive to the implications of American fund-raising, in effect, must be concerned with the impact of their actions upon Orthodox public opinion abroad. In some respects, this was evident during the "Who is a Jew?" crisis when the heads of the Israeli yeshivot maintained, correctly, that they themselves had little stake in the issue, which had been foisted upon them by external intervention from Lubavitch headquarters in New York City.

Aliyah

Before 1948 American Jewish emigration to Israel could be classified as secular Zionist rather than religious Zionist. Two-thirds of the *olim* settled on kibbutzim. Only one percent cited religious reasons as their most important motivation.

These figures changed somewhat during the 1950s. During that decade 34 percent of *olim* were Orthodox, 24 percent were Conservative, and seven percent were Reform. The remainder reported no affiliation. Significantly, these figures represented virtually the inverse of the American Jewish demographic profile generally. Similarly, *olim* during this decade had twice the number of children as American Jews generally and reported the most intensive forms of Jewish education.

However, most significant has been the shift in *aliyah* ratios since the 1950s. By the 1980s two-thirds of American *olim* were Orthodox.[8]

Chaim Waxman suggests that the key factors behind this shift lie in the social structure of Orthodox Judaism. The Israeli Orthodox community provides a mediating structure between the individual and society, easing the immigrant's absorption.[9]

Waxman underestimates, however, the role of ideological factors within American Orthodoxy. *Aliyah* for the Orthodox suggests *hagshama*—fulfillment of one's life as a Jew. Moreover, for American Orthodoxy Israel today has become a haven for leading an Orthodox way of life. Orthodox parents, while often ambivalent about the prospect of the *aliyah* of their children, nevertheless will be ideologically supportive, thereby forming an important psychological asset. Of course, the personal and professional sacrifices involved in American *aliyah* are no less real for Orthodox Jews than for anyone else. Significantly, however, it is the Orthodox who are the most willing to pay the price. Cases have even been reported of Orthodox physicians engaged in commuter marriages between America and Israel—pursuing career opportunities at home while spouses and children live in Israel.

Perhaps most controversial in this regard has been the presence of American Orthodox Jews among the settlers in the administered territories. Waxman sees their influence primarily as a democratizing element. They continue the tradition of American Jewish liberalism. Their decision to settle in places such as the West Bank reflects pragmatic rather than ideological considerations. Waxman notes that less than 15 percent of American settlers reject democratic values—to be sure, a far higher percentage than one would expect among American Jews generally. In other words, Waxman seeks to refute the stereotype of the West Bank settlers as Jewish ayatollahs. On the contrary, they are clean-shaven and well-educated professionals. According to him, the "large majority of American settlers are among the most rational and moderating forces" on the West Bank.[10] His conclusions, while useful to a point, require further analysis. Only 30 percent of the Americans would extend equal rights to Arabs. As noted above, 15 percent reject the value system of democracy. Waxman notes how most opposed the Jewish "underground," yet it was American Jews who spearheaded fund-raising initiatives on behalf of the underground activists. One questions how they could defend full-blown terrorists. These American Jews usually responded with the justification of personal friendship— namely, that they identified precisely with those Americans on the West Bank, including those close to underground circles.

In this regard, there is a larger question of whether the settlers through their activities nurtured a climate of opinion on the West Bank in which recourse to terrorism became a legitimate option. In other words, by saying territorial compromise is impossible, did the settlers influence the atmospherics on the West Bank in which the previously unthinkable could become possible? In this sense, the ultimate role of Americans on the West Bank remains insufficiently explained. Clearly, their high status and education give them influence. Whether that influence is expressed in the moderating direction that Waxman suggests is questionable. Some of the most notable personalities among the American settlers—e.g., Ira Rapoport and Shifra Blass—have utilized their American-style educations to mount eloquent and articulate defenses of Gush Emunim ideology.

Political Involvement

This last point suggests the most visible area of engagement between American Orthodoxy and Israel. American Orthodox Jews have few inhibitions about direct political activism—including the widespread support for West Bank settlements and orchestrated appeals for underground activists.

One example of this lack of inhibition is reflected in Orthodox responses to what has come to be known as the Pollard Affair. Over 80 percent of Orthodox Jews had heard of the Pollard Affair in 1991—compared to 56 percent of Conservative Jews and 52 percent of Reform Jews. More tellingly, 70 percent of these Orthodox Jews felt that the Pollard sentence was too harsh, and 65 percent felt that American Jewish organizations should campaign for sentence reduction. In contrast, only 22 percent of American Jews generally favored campaigning for a reduction of Pollard's sentence.[11]

Here is a particular example of Orthodox willingness to engage in direct political activism. While many Israelis criticized American Jews for ambivalence regarding Pollard and an unwillingness to raise the Pollard issue for fear of accusations of dual loyalty, that ambivalence seems relatively absent from Orthodox political thinking.

Similarly, it should be noted that while Orthodox political activism on the left is far less evident, it is by no means restrained. The Meimad Party in Israel engaged in considerable fund-raising among Modern Orthodox American Jews—prompting one observer to comment that they "raised more dollars in Riverdale than votes in Israel!"

More generally, among American Orthodox Jews support for Gush Emunim is quite strong. In the fall of 1991, over 40 percent of American Orthodox Jews felt that the Gush currently had too little power. Fifty-seven percent felt that they had either the right amount of power or not enough.[12]

The most visible demonstration of Orthodox political activism occurred during the "Who is a Jew?" controversy in 1988. To be sure, this activism did not take place without protest. The Rabbinical Council of America dissented from legislation designed to amend the "Who is a Jew?" clause in the Law of Return. That dissent, however, was not shared by the Union of Orthodox Jewish Congregations of America—the leading lay arm of American Orthodoxy. Most Orthodox Jews did feel that *haredi* Orthodoxy had overplayed its hand on the issue. Within Israel itself, as noted earlier, there was considerable resentment that Lubavitch in America was forcing the issue.

For most American Orthodox Jews, the agitation brought home the degree of Orthodox alienation from the non-Orthodox. "Orthodox bashing" became quite visible at American Jewish public forums—the CJF General Assembly in New Orleans in November 1988 witnessed explicit hostility expressed at a wide variety of sessions.

However, it is precisely in this context of Orthodox alienation from non-Orthodox Jews in America that the ties and allegiances to Israel become stronger. American Orthodox Jews look at Israel and no longer see a society distant from Torah values. Rather, they see a wholly Jewish society in which the Orthodox presence is quite visible and pervasive.

How, then, may we account for these widespread examples of direct American Orthodox engagement with Israel in contrast to the sense of distance so pervasive in the 1950s? In part, we can ascribe such engagement to the power of ideology to motivate behavior. Orthodox Jews, perhaps, represent the most direct refutation of the Marxist analysis of ideology as entirely a matter of superstructure. Precisely because Orthodox Jews believe in Israel as the fulfillment of Jewish aspirations, they are determined to make Israel as Jewish a society as they can.

Social factors, to be sure, are also significant. Orthodox Jews have, perhaps, the greatest number of personal ties with Israel. They hear from these friends and family constant requests for assistance— whether economic, political, or religious. Because these ties are sufficiently strong, American Orthodox Jews are quick to respond.

Allied to this is the degree of cultural polarization within Israel itself. Orthodox Jews do feel alienated from the Israeli Left—from figures such as Amos Oz or A. B. Yehoshua, who claim little connection with Diaspora Jewry and its historical Jewish experience. Orthodox personalities on the Israeli Left—e.g., Avram Burg or David Hartman—have little following among American Orthodox Jews. Rather, this alienation from the Left is reflected in a counterimage of enhanced relations and strong support for the Israeli right. The Orthodox look at Likud figures and note "their yarmulkes fit on their heads." It is this degree of cultural alienation from the Left coupled with the attractiveness of the cultural and political Right that enables American Orthodox Jews to strongly support those with whom they identify.

Specific changes within Israel itself produced a portrait of Jewish life with which Orthodox Jews could easily empathize. While many secular Israelis lamented the erosion of the Zionist dream (often accompanied by emigration out of the country),[13] Orthodoxy celebrated its youth and settler movements in Israel as the new Zionism. Political rhetoric and cultural symbols invoking Jewish history, the Holocaust, and the sanctity of the entire Land of Israel resonated strongly with Orthodox conceptions of divine mandates and messianic promises.

But perhaps most important to this engagement is the surefootedness of American Orthodox Jews regarding their own Jewishness. They have no feeling of inferiority vis-a-vis the Israelis. As a result, standing secure in their own Jewish identity, they are prepared to engage directly, even to the point of on-site intervention with Israeli political and religious culture.

What then may we conclude from this analysis? First, it is a paradox that the group that is most conscious of being in exile is the least in danger of disappearing in the Diaspora. It is precisely because of the strength of Jewish identity among American Orthodox Jews, their keen perception of living in exile, that they are so tightly intertwined with Israeli society.

Moreover, although there are many facets of this form of direct engagement which non-Orthodox American Jews would object to, the model of direct engagement ought to be taken more seriously. In no other form of Israel-Diaspora relations do we have such an equal partnership as between American Orthodox Jews and their Israeli counterparts. The Orthodox have said they will support those aspects of Israeli society with which they identify. One implication for non-Orthodox Jews is that they might well consider the benefits of supporting directly those aspects of Israeli society that best represent their values and norms.

Yet the long-term implications of direct Orthodox engagement with Israel must be weighed in the overall context of Israel-Diaspora relations. Israel clearly is both a central factor in the Orthodox resurgence in America and a symbol of that resurgence—namely, Israel has not only nurtured American Orthodox Jews, but the willingness of American Orthodox Jews to demonstrate their support for Israel is symbolic of Orthodox assertiveness generally. That assertiveness is often dismissed as self-righteous triumphalism. Yet its message must be carefully considered. To some extent it is an expression of the weakness of secular Jewish identity—of the failures of non-Orthodox Jews to develop models of intensive Jewish living that are sustaining and can be transmitted to the next generation. The Orthodox message when perceived in the political context of the Israeli Knesset appears illiberal and undemocratic. But when weighed reflectively that message challenges us to think what is the content of Jewish identity today—what does it mean to lead a Jewish life. Rather than dismiss Orthodox engagement as fundamentalist lunacy or combat it as a basic threat to Israeli democracy, non-Orthodox Jews both in Israel and America should be asking not only why the Orthodox are as influential as they are but also what has, thus far, prevented non-Orthodox models of Jewish identity and religious expression from capturing the minds, hearts, and commitments of large numbers of our people? Are we, in other words, locked into a permanent siege between those who are Orthodox and those who are not? Or, alternatively, could we draw from the resources of one another in a more broadly based effort to engage Jews Jewishly?

Conclusion

In conclusion, several models of Israel-Diaspora relations are currently in existence. For most American Jews, Israel-Diaspora relations connotes political support for or dissent from Israeli public-policy positions—with some seeking to combine support and dissent. For select leadership groups—e.g., the exchange programs sponsored by the American Jewish Committee's Institute on American Jewish-Israeli Relations or the Moriah Conference of the North American Jewish and Israel Forums—Israel-Diaspora relations means personal ties and dialogues on a one-on-one people-to-people basis. American Orthodoxy, however, suggests a third model for direct hands-on engagement and advocacy on behalf of like-minded groups in Israel.

This latter model, to be sure, causes controversy both in Israel and in America. Yet its effectiveness cannot be negated. American Orthodoxy is clearly strengthened by the Israel connection. Conversely, Israeli Orthodox institutions and causes benefit from the direct engagement of American Orthodox Jews. Non-Orthodox Jews, until recently, have chosen the "high road" of broad overall support without delving too deeply into the specifics of Israeli society. Whether the "Who is a Jew?" issue marks a watershed in terms of significant non-Orthodox direct engagement or is merely a passing footnote in the history of Israel-Diaspora relations is a question yet to be answered.

In short, American Orthodox Jews, perhaps somewhat ironically, have been successful in realizing the vision of a true partnership in Israel-Diaspora relations. The Orthodox, like the Zionists of old, place serious demands upon constituents. In theory all expressions of Jewish identity, to be taken seriously, must articulate a language of norms, expectations, and commitments. That the Orthodox have succeeded in doing so, however, enhances their degree of self-confidence in relations with modern Israel.

At the root of this "partnership" lies the reality that the Orthodox depend far less upon Israel than do the other movements for the rhythms and pulses of Jewish activity. Sources of energy in American Orthodoxy flow from within the community and then are, of course, sustained by Israel-related activity. It is precisely when signals do *not* come primarily from Jerusalem that the Diaspora community can perceive itself as a vigorous and thriving community nurtured and sustained by a partnership with Israel rather than dominated by it.

Therefore it is a point of considerable irony that American Orthodoxy, widely perceived as most reactionary on political questions concerning Israel, has actually realized the vision of partnership in Israel-Diaspora relations. To be sure, if Israel-Diaspora relations is merely a code word for dissent from Likud politics, the Orthodox model will be found wanting. If Israel-Diaspora relations connotes the type of meaningful partnership advocated by observers such as Leonard Fein, otherwise vigorously outspoken in condemnation of American Orthodoxy, then it must be acknowledged that the Orthodox have succeeded most admirably. In many ways, they suggest parallel models for relations between Israel and non-Orthodox Diaspora communities and institutions.

Notes

1. Samuel Heilman, *Jewish Unity and Diversity: A Survey of American Rabbis and Rabbinical Students* (New York: American Jewish Committee, 1991), p. 62.

2. Nathalie Friedman, "The Graduates of Ramaz: Fifty Years of Jewish Day School Education," in Jeffrey S. Gurock, ed., *Ramaz: School, Community, Scholarship, and Orthodoxy* (New York: KTAV, 1989), pp. 106–108.

3. Ibid., p. 98.

4. Personal communications, 1967 graduates.

5. Charles Liebman, "Orthodoxy in American Jewish Life," in Marshall Sklare, ed., *The Jewish Community in America* (New York: Behrman House, 1974), p. 139. See also Lawrence Kaplan, "The Ambiguous Modern Orthodox Jew," in Reuben Bulka, ed., *Dimensions of Orthodox Judaism* (New York: KTAV, 1983), pp. 246–247, and Steven Bayme, "Art Scroll and Scholarship," *Tradition* 20 (Winter 1982): 371–373.

6. M. Herbert Danzger, *Returning to Tradition* (New Haven: Yale University Press, 1989), p. 34; see also Janet Aviad, *Return to Judaism* (Chicago: University of Chicago press, 1983), pp. 63–70.

7. Samuel C. Heilman and Steven M. Cohen, *Cosmopolitans and Parochials: Modern Orthodox Jews in America* (Chicago: University of Chicago Press, 1989), p. 134.

8. Chaim Waxman, "The Impact of Aliyah on the American Jewish Community," in Steven Bayme, ed., *Facing the Future: Essays on Contemporary Jewish Life* (New York: KTAV, 1989), pp. 194–195, and Waxman, *American Aliyah* (Detroit: Wayne State University Press, 1989), pp. 80–84, 98–100.

9. Ibid., pp. 129–136.

10. Ibid., pp. 150–168.

11. Steven M. Cohen, *After the Gulf War: American Jews' Attitudes Toward Israel* (New York: American Jewish Committee, 1992), pp. 48–49, and personal communication.

12. Ibid., and personal communication.

13. See, for example, the following works by Israeli intellectuals and political leaders: Amnon Rubinstein, *The Zionist Dream Revisited: From Herzl to Gush Emunim and Back* (New York: Schocken Books, 1984); Amos Oz, *In the Land of Israel* (San Diego, New York, and London: Harcourt Brace Jovanovich, 1983); Arie Lova Eliav, *New Heart, New Spirit: Biblical Humanism for Modern Israel* (Philadelphia: Jewish Publication Society, 1988). Significantly, all three books postdate the Likud ascendancy and, specifically, the Lebanon War, and suggest that Israel in the 1980s had abandoned its original mission and fallen into the hands of the Orthodox. The well-known term *haredizatia* similarly connotes this shift in political culture.

Changing Patterns in Israel-Diaspora Relations

The widespread assumption in both Israel and the Diaspora is that the September 13 "day of the handshake" has changed everything. In the months that have passed, there have been numerous attempts to redefine the relationship between Israel and Diaspora Jewry. The Reform movement's Al Vorspan calls for renewed emphasis upon the universalist agenda of Reform Judaism, now that the political security and military defense of Israel appear to be less pressing. On the Orthodox side, Irving Greenberg advocates redefining Israel as a learning center for Diaspora Jewry. And within Israel, Deputy Foreign Minister Yossi Beilin urges that American Jews redirect their fund-raising away from assistance to Israel—which, he underscores, is a prosperous country undertaking a peace initiative out of strength rather than weakness—and use the money instead for the perpetuation of American Jewish identity. Indeed, Prime Minister Rabin, at the most recent General Assembly of the Council of Jewish Federations, exhorted North American Jewry to couple Jewish education with Israel experiences as the focal point of a Jewish continuity agenda undertaken jointly by Israel and the Diaspora.

What all these attempts at redefinition have in common is the assumption of a decreased need for political involvement on the part of American Jews, and the acceptance of an enhanced position for Jewish continuity on the Jewish communal agenda as the critical element in Israel-Diaspora relations. To evaluate these efforts by American Jewish and Israeli leaders to reorient the basis of their relationship, it is necessary to look at three major changes taking place in the Jewish world.

One change is demographic. For the past 2,600 years, the majority of world Jewry has lived in the Diaspora. Within the next ten to fifteen years—if present trends are not reversed—Israel will surpass the United States as the world's largest Jewish community, and, at some point within the next generation, Israel will contain within its borders a majority of world Jewry.

Published by the American Jewish Committee, October 1994.

This is a historic change in the map of world Jewry, underscoring that Israel is the center of Jewish peoplehood and international Jewish existence. The suggestion of a bicentric model, in which the Israeli and American communities are somehow of equivalent weight—a common assumption in the early 1980s—is undermined by the demographic transformation currently under way. If bicentralism possesses any merit as a model, it relates to questions of intellectual culture rather than demographics.

This does not mean, however, that the Diaspora is about to disappear. American Jewry is undoubtedly experiencing significant losses that will reduce its ranks to around four million within a generation. That community of four million, however, will still be the largest Diaspora Jewish community known to history. Intermarriage, a symbol as well as a cause of many weaknesses within the American Jewish community, need not necessarily continue its steady increase. Those Jews most likely to intermarry are doing so now, and some of them will leave the community. But one must not underestimate the degree of Jewish conviction among those who do not intermarry. Many may well make the choice to lead a deeply Jewish life, as symbolized by their choice of a Jewish mate. A possible indication of such a trend may be the finding of the 1991 New York City Jewish population survey that no significant increase in mixed-religion marriage occurred over the past decade. I am not suggesting that intermarriage rates among American Jews have plateaued. What I am suggesting is that the deterministic view of history, predicting that intermarriage and assimilation will inexorably increase—a view commonly favored by many Israelis—is not necessarily accurate. Like other understandings of history that are based on the assumption that future human behavior can be extrapolated from present tendencies, this scenario leaves no room for the choices and freedoms that make social trends so difficult to predict.

A second area of transformation is political. Israel is now pursuing a peace process with the PLO and with its Arab neighbors. Only a short time ago most American Jews believed such a thing impossible, given the internal nature of the PLO and the radical tendencies of Palestinian politics. Today, while many American Jews may have fears and anxieties about these developments, they are relieved, at least, about one side effect of Israel's forthcoming negotiating posture: It is much easier than before to make a political case for Israel. This makes the current Israeli government extremely popular with American Jews, who are, therefore, quite likely to follow its lead. The most recent survey of American Jewish opinion about the peace process suggests that as few as five percent of American Jews are opposed to its continuation—in striking contrast with the divided nature of Israeli public opinion.

These political changes are significant. Only a short time ago there was concern that American Jewish support for Israeli policies was eroding and that, by extension, the American government's support for those policies would also weaken. The political challenges of the 1990s, significant though they may be, certainly will not have to be addressed in the context of potential erosion of American Jewish political support for Israel.

The third area of change is the cultural transformation in Israel-Diaspora relations. Our language divide continues to grow: fewer and fewer American Jews feel comfortable, much less fluent, in the Hebrew language—a trend that may be detected even among American Jewish day school graduates. Conversely, Israelis, whether or not they themselves are fluent in English, point to the Hebraic illiteracy of American Jews as a barometer of the cultural divide between us.

We are also growing further apart in our attitudes toward intermarriage. American Jews are increasingly accepting intermarriage, especially as they experience it in their own families. Israelis, in contrast, who rarely experience intermarriage within their immediate families, view it as a primary symbol of North American Jewry's weakness and ultimate lack of staying power. These different perceptions also influence attitudes toward an outgrowth of intermarriage, the question of patrilineal descent. The American Reform movement decided in 1983 to define as Jews children of a Jewish father and non-Jewish mother when both parents commit themselves to raise children within the Jewish faith. That position—which has both defenders and detractors among American Jews—is opposed virtually unanimously by Israelis, who see it as a threat to the unity of the Jewish people.

Another example of the cultural divide concerns religious pluralism. For the great majority of American Jews, plurality of religious expression is an axiomatic aspect of contemporary Jewish identity. Israelis, however, who implicitly recognize Orthodoxy as the legitimate form of Judaism even if they themselves do not practice it, have little interest in religious pluralism for its own sake. At most, they may see recognition of non-Orthodox forms as a human-rights issue, or a step toward a more liberal Israeli society. Indeed, Israeli indifference to the concept of religious pluralism is often cited by American Jews as an important reason for their personal unhappiness and disappointment with Israel.

Given these demographic, political, and cultural transformations, what is the future of Israel-Diaspora relations?

One possibility is the conclusion that the divide is so great that we should agree to part company. Although there are few who would go so far as to advocate a renewed Israeli Canaanism—a literary movement of the 1950s that sought to redefine Israel as totally unconnected with Diaspora Jewish history and experience—similar sentiments are occasionally found in the dismissal of the Diaspora's significance by some Israeli leaders, or the expressed conviction of some American Jews that the problems of Jewish identity in the Diaspora require solutions to which Israel is by no means central.

In pronounced contrast to those who suggest a parting of the ways, others still advocate the status quo agenda of Israel-Diaspora relations: political support, fundraising, and the promotion of *aliya*. Although, as I will show, this set of priorities still retains its old relevance, it fails to reflect the revolutionary changes of the last decade.

There is a third school of thought that is developing a new agenda for Israel and the Diaspora in the hope of refocusing energies upon the new problems of Jewish continuity in the Diaspora. For many Israelis, even talk of such a new agenda is threatening, since it presupposes a continued existence for Diaspora Jewry. This is, the Israelis feel, a violation of classic Zionist doctrine, and a possible encouragement of *yerida*.

What are we to make of this three-way debate?

To begin, I am baffled by the notion that the traditional Israel-Diaspora agenda is obsolete. If nothing else, the inevitable ups and downs of the peace process will require ongoing American Jewish political support for Israel on questions such as Jerusalem, the settlements, continued economic aid, Palestinian statehood, and refugees. In addition, quite aside from the evolution of the peace process, Israel, over the long term, will have to meet the threats of Islamic fundamentalism and nuclear proliferation—threats that endanger not only Israel but Western culture and civilization as a whole. Events since the famous handshake ought to caution American Jews that the euphoria surrounding that event underestimated the real risks to Israelis brought on by the reduced responsibilities of Israeli security forces in the area. We cannot forget that the only Palestinian state known to history materialized in Lebanon a little over a decade ago. The prospect of a Lebanon-type experience in Gaza or the West Bank should be most sobering to those who look forward to a new era of Arab-Jewish coexistence. It is quite possible that the Israeli government may choose a cautious line on the peace process, and American Jewry will need to step up its political support for Israel—perhaps even in defiance of the American administration.

Similarly, American Jewish fund-raising for Israel is by no means obsolete. The $300 million raised by American Jews via the United Jewish Appeal stands as a strong statement of American Jewish involvement with, and support for, Israel and a perpetual reminder to the American government that American Jews still strongly back American political and military assistance for the Jewish state. Perhaps we should consider the suggestion made by Professor Avi Ravitzky of the Hebrew University that American Jewish fund-raising for Israel should be redirected to aiding Jewish education within Israel—to strengthen the Jewishness of Israelis and to enrich educational opportunities for American Jews. Were we, however, to reduce our fundraising for Israel, we would not only weaken ourselves as a people, but also communicate the wrong message to American society and its political leaders.

We must surely acknowledge that *aliya* is not a realistic option for most American Jews. Yet Israelis need not feel any embarrassment for speaking about it. Indeed, American Jewry may well witness a larger proportion of its most committed members undertaking *aliya* in the years ahead. This is already happening among the children of American Orthodox Jews.

While all of these traditional issues remain important, we must also explore the implications of the Israel-Diaspora bond for Jewish continuity. So far, this new agenda has not gotten beyond the stage of rhetoric. We need to determine exactly what, in practical terms, a joint dedication to enhancing Jewish continuity means for Israeli and Diaspora Jews.

There are at least five Jewish identity problems which the two communities can work in common to solve:

1. All Jews—Israeli and Diaspora—struggle with the question of what it means to be a Jew in an open society. This is the fundamental dilemma created by the clash of Judaism and modern culture. What relationship do we—Israeli and Diaspora Jews—have to Jewish tradition in a world that speaks of personal autonomy, freedom of choice, and cultural diversity? Does Jewish tradition speak to us in sufficiently powerful terms that the choices we make will be Jewish choices? For Israelis, the question is national identity—how does Judaism remain salient in a Jewish state? For Diaspora Jews, the problem is personal and communal—what defines us as contemporary Jews?

2. We must begin to define Jewishness within a context of Jewish power and influence rather than Jewish weakness. Despite the existence of a Jewish state and prosperous Diaspora communities, we still prefer to see ourselves as victims endangered by external threats. Our challenge is to assert a Jewishness that is not rooted in the perception of terrible things happening to Jews, but rather in a vision of Jewish life sufficiently inspiring and compelling that we should want to lead it with passion and verve.

3. What is the role of religious practice and belief in our continuity? Diaspora Jews have understood for a long time that Jewish religion is crucial in providing a Jewish identity that lasts over generations. We used to think that Israelis don't need religion because they have a Jewish state. Yet the report issued recently by the Guttman Institute in Israel suggests that Israelis are far more traditionalist than commonly believed. Both Israeli and Diaspora Jews, then, face the task of maintaining and enhancing the religious content of Jewish identity.

4. All Jews share in a common sense of international Jewish peoplehood: what happens to Jews in one corner of the world will affect Jews

everywhere. Diaspora Jews tend to feel this especially when they come in contact with other communities, as recently occurred when the American Jewish Committee hosted an international conference of young Jewish leaders. Over the course of the three-day conference, the common theme was the sense of Jewish bonding across boundaries. More generally, we share a common challenge of assisting endangered Jewish communities.

5. All Jews share in common an interest in defining the Jewish qualities of a Jewish state. Most Israeli and Diaspora Jews would agree that a Jewish state must be liberal and democratic, but that it must also assert a special role for Judaism and the Jewish people. Attempting to define the precise parameters of that privileged role while at the same time preserving liberal democratic values is a challenge we all face.

Despite all these points of commonality, there remain significant obstacles to developing a new joint agenda based on Jewish continuity. Many Israelis simply do not perceive continuity as their issue—in their eyes, it is a problem for Diaspora Jewry only. The only relevance they see for Israel is the ominous fact that less Jewish identification in the Diaspora means less Jewish support for Israel.

Also, too much confidence is being placed in the Israel experience as the centerpiece of the Jewish continuity agenda. Indeed, I suspect that we tend to focus upon Israel precisely because the other burning issues on the Jewish continuity agenda are too divisive for American Jewry to confront—the ravages of intermarriage and religious polarization. We have to recognize that Israel can never serve as a quick fix for Diaspora Jewish continuity. The focus on Israel as a panacea may delude us into thinking that we have solved the problem of Jewish continuity.

Furthermore, in the process of developing a common agenda of Jewish continuity in Israel-Diaspora relations, we must come to grips with the question of whether American Jewry will in fact sustain the same degree of passion for an agenda built around continuity that it has heretofore had for an agenda built on politics. While it is true that the National Jewish Population Survey raised the consciousness of American Jews as to their real dangers, it is hard to know whether that concern can be transferred from the realm of rhetoric to the world of action—let alone action sustained over many years.

We must also acknowledge that Israeli and Diaspora Jews face very different challenges in securing Jewish continuity. Diaspora Jews will have to work hard to secure Jewish continuity for their grandchildren. Such continuity comes only at a price—the price we pay for the commitment entailed in leading a Jewish life. Discussions of Diaspora continuity are often so frustrating precisely because of our unwillingness to consider the price we are prepared to pay. In Israel, however, a Jewish society, the sacrifice necessary to lead a Jewish life is considerably less.

Despite these obstacles, we must continue the work. Clearly, a parting of the ways between Israel and the Diaspora is not acceptable, but unless we pursue a joint agenda we risk just such a cleavage. The forces that seek to dissolve the ties between Israel and the Diaspora are quite strong. They must be combatted.

Israeli president Ezer Weizman expressed the need eloquently when laying the groundwork for his recent international conference on Israel-Diaspora relations. In a letter to AJC executive director David Harris, President Weizman wrote: "I share your view that Israel and the American Jewish community, the two largest Jewish communities, as well as other communities in the world, are inextricably linked and must remain so, for the well-being of Jews in Israel and throughout the world and for the fulfillment of the Zionist ideal. . . . We must make every effort to strengthen the oneness and togetherness of the Jewish people."

Rebuilding Jewish Peoplehood:
A Symposium in the Wake
of the Rabin Assassination

The Jewish people have suffered an enormous loss. Questions persist not only regarding how this happened, but where do we go from here in healing the serious rifts and breaches that have so sorely torn the Jewish world.

To be sure, there are those who argue that this is not the time for repairing divisions. Tom Friedman, in a *New York Times* column, urged that in the aftermath of the assassination we choose up sides between those who favor peace and its opponents. Similarly, Leon Wieseltier in a *New Republic* article commented that this is "no time for healing." The American Jewish Committee has expressed a pronouncedly different view. In an ad printed in the *New York Times* entitled "Beyond Grief," AJC urged that we reassert the unity of the Jewish people, acknowledging significant diversity within our ranks but at the same time underscoring that what unites us as a people is far more important than what divides us.

The tragedy itself must be understood on multiple levels. First, it was a personal tragedy. The prime minister, of blessed memory, had spared no efforts to break the cycle of warfare between Israel and her neighbors. His vision of peace in the Middle East was far from realized. He deserves enormous credit for initiating a process that at least held out the hope for an alternative reality in the Middle East of the twenty-first century. His assassination signals, not the end of the process he initiated, but rather that he, like Moses of old, would be able only to glimpse the Promised Land and not enter it.

On a political level, the assassination underscored the significant opposition to the peace process within Israel itself. No overwhelming consensus exists in support of Prime Minister Rabin's policies. Certainly no linkage ought be drawn between legitimate disagreement

Published by the American Jewish Committee, January 1996.

about the peace process and the assassination itself. But some elements within Israeli society do maintain that the peace process failed to account for their security needs and sensibilities. Politically, therefore, the assassination signals the need to create a broader consensus in support of governmental policies.

On a national level, the assassination exposed deep fissures within the Jewish people and body politic. It signaled the conflicting visions of what is a Jew and what is a Jewish state. Since the assassination, "Orthodox-bashing" has prevailed in a wide variety of circles. Israel and the Jewish people are divided not only along political lines but also along far more existential lines—questions such as what it means to be a Jew today, and what is the definition of a Jewish society.

Lastly, the assassination signaled a tragedy of Judaism and Jewish teaching. That the assassin invoked Jewish heritage to justify murder constitutes a grave desecration of Torah. Nor can the assassin be dismissed as a lunatic—or a loner like Lee Harvey Oswald. Rather, he came from circles which stand at the very center of classical Jewish education.

What are the implications and where do we go from here? First, there is a need for accountability—to determine what went wrong, and how. For one thing, the political debate had become excessively polarized. The tendency to demonize one's opponents prevailed. Words like "traitor," "Judenrat," "Judeo-Nazi," and "murderer" became part of the lexicon. To be sure, this vocabulary was by no means the monopoly of the religious right. However, actual events—e.g., the Hebron massacre in 1994—had broken taboos and made the unthinkable possible. The effect of these murders internationally was to cede the moral high ground on which Israel had positioned itself. We must acknowledge, painful as it is, that we do have our own terrorists. They are not simply an aberration, but must be confronted and dealt with forthrightly. No society can exist unless it is prepared to defend itself against those who would take the law into their own hands.

Second, we have to look at Jewish education and the messages it transmits. Jewish education stands at the center of efforts to preserve Jewish continuity. There can be no Jewish continuity absent serious commitment to Judaism as faith and teaching. However, for Jewish education to fulfill that imperative, it must incorporate and emphasize Judaism's humanistic dimension—that all human beings are created in the image of God. Effective Jewish education requires a constant balance between particular Jewish needs and universal imperatives. The mantle of Torah cannot be permitted to justify hatred. Yet when Yigal Amir intoned, "I have been studying Talmud all my life; I have all the data," he uncovered a dark undertone within Jewish educational circles that speaks in terms of absolutist certainty, and prevents serious dialogue between groups. Prominent Talmudic scholars issued harmful statements castigating supporters of the peace process as sinners. Rather than encourage absolutism, Jewish education needs to recognize the serious differences among Jews, among different Jewish texts, and within a common sense of Jewish peoplehood. As Dr. Norman Lamm emphasized to the students of Yeshiva University:

> Beware of ever lightly cloaking political views, no matter how much you believe in them, in the mantle of *halakhah*. . . . And keep far away from excessive self-confidence that leads to arrogant self-righteousness that, in turn, persuades us that our ideals are greater and better than those of the other fellow; that we are sincere and he is not; that we are unquestionably right and he is indubitably wrong; that we are therefore entitled to force our views on him—by "eliminating" him if need be, in order to have our "truth" prevail.

Third, religious Zionism must undergo its own self-appraisal and reckoning. All too often religious Zionists have placed the unity of land over the unity of the Jewish people. Messianism has, in recent years, prevailed within many religious Zionist circles, ignoring some of the lessons of Jewish history in which messianic imperatives had provided some of the most dangerous currents in the annals of our people. Predominant opinion within rabbinic Judaism has always discouraged messianism as futile and potentially destructive. The irony of recent years was that some of the most fervent apostles of rabbinic Judaism ignored the dangers of "forcing the end" and hastening the imminent arrival of the redeemer. And the ugly racism and cult of violence articulated by Meir Kahane all too often permeated religious Zionist circles.

Kahane in his last years continued to be received within synagogues and Jewish schools even after he had been ostracized for his racism by the organized American Jewish community and the Israeli Knesset.

The Left, too, must face its own accountability. All too often, the Left downplayed the security concerns of West Bank residents. In truth, it had often been the Labor Party that built settlements and encouraged people to move to them. Perhaps most significantly, the Left had little empathy for the religious and historical claims of the settlers. Even if one takes the settlement in Hebron, which is perhaps the least justifiable of settlements, the fact remains that Hebron was the sole place where Jews maintained continuous settlement from biblical times into the twentieth century, and the only reason there were no Jews there after 1929 was that they had been massacred by Arabs. In that sense, the initiative to settle in Hebron, as misguided politically as it may have been, reflected an authentic concern with preserving historical Jewish attachments to one of the most storied cities of Jewish history.

Nor has the Left lacked for extreme language and incivility. Some of its spokespersons claim innocence on the ground that no one on the Left has fired a shot. The response to that is twofold: First, the lessons of the assassination prove that we can never take for granted the sanctity of life. Second, and perhaps more important, we ought to acknowledge that extremist language must be marginalized no matter from where it emanates. When politicans use phrases like, "We will crush them," they are guilty of violating basic democratic norms that acknowledge the right of dissent and the imperatives of preserving minority rights. Let us recall that it was a prominent dovish philosopher, Yeshayahu Leibowitz, who coined the term "Judeo-Nazi." Similarly, at an AJC meeting some years ago, an Israeli politician condemned Lubavitch as "the Nazis of our time."

Beyond facing up to what went wrong, we also must revisit what we mean by common Jewish peoplehood and collective Jewish experience. The reality of a Jewish state challenges the Jewish people to fulfill the responsibilities of sovereignty while acting in an ethical and moral fashion. Powerlessness, to be sure, always has the virtue of the moral high ground. Yet, in many ways, it only signals the classic image of sympathy for the Jew as victim. Zionism posited a much more difficult challenge—what the Zionist philosopher Ahad Ha'am referred to as the unity of ethics and politics—namely, fulfilling the responsibilities of power and sovereignty while preserving Jewish ethics. Israel as a Jewish state constitutes a statement that Jewish history continues, that its most exciting chapters are taking place at this very moment. Jewish peoplehood in this age means that every Jew has a share in that ongoing history, and responsibility to be part of that collective endeavor. Yet we cannot content ourselves with statements of unity. We must acknowledge divisions between us over politics, religion, and even our very definition of who is a Jew. These divisions are by no means necessarily harmful. On the contrary, some ideological controversy is healthy, for it means that at least we care passionately about these issues and values. Unity should not mean uniformity of opinion. On the contrary, for democracy to survive, a government must have an opposition. In terms of our religious disputes and controversies, an ethos of pluralism does not mean we must agree with one another. Rather, as Irving Greenberg has argued, a "contentious pluralism" means the freedom to engage passionately over these issues, debate with one another their merits and demerits, all in a collective endeavor to enhance the Jewish people.

Controversy, in short, is by no means the enemy of the Jews. On the contrary, we have far more to fear from religious indifference than from religious pluralism. But our challenge is to work out these disagreements and divisions in the spirit of shared excitement about the Jewish enterprise, loyalty to the Jewish people and Jewish state, and love for all Jews. Let all Jews recognize that we are all together in this business of preserving and enhancing the Jewish people. For all that we may vigorously disagree over means, our overarching ends and purposes remain the welfare of the Jews as a people and the nurturing of justice for humanity generally.

We must reclaim the Judaic heritage as the treasure of the entire Jewish people. The assassination was not a sign of the normality of the Jews as a people, that, like all other states, they have their fanatics. Rather, the assassination signaled a violation of the Jewish covenant and Judaic teaching. There can be no Judaism without ethics. That humanistic thrust within Judaism, unfortunately, was lost in the circles that fomented hatred within the Jewish people.

The Right today articulates a language of Jewish unity. The Left is speaking a language of democracy and majority rule. Both sides must work toward bridging that gap. There is no contradiction between unity of the Jews as a people and democracy as a political value. From its very beginnings, Zionism contained deep divisions over vision and self-definition. Some maintained that the Zionist endeavor was creating a state for Jews. Others claimed that the endeavor was meaningful only if it resulted in a Jewish state informed and guided by Jewish heritage and teaching. Some Zionists were optimistic about the Gentile world and looked to fulfill Zionist aims through friendly Gentile assistance. Others were pessimistic and claimed that Zionism required self-reliance and self-emancipation. Perhaps the finest moments in Zionist history occurred when these contrasting visions were shared—when those who had known the reality of war were prepared to make peace. Our task today is to nurture and further develop these competing visions of Zionism and peoplehood—to take the best of each, to synthesize tradition and modern culture, and at the same time to critique and engage both value systems—to incorporate those aspects that speak to us and to criticize those aspects that may be foreign to us.

For the Jewish world needs both currents. It needs a vibrant Orthodoxy to sustain Jewish continuity. Yet, for the very same reason, Orthodoxy requires vibrant Conservative and Reform movements to preserve Jews as Jews. Orthodoxy cannot sustain the entire Jewish people alone. By the same token, Israel requires the energies of the entire Jewish world. It too needs Orthodoxy to nurture Jewish tradition and articulate its voice within a Jewish state. Greater religious pluralism within Israel would help counter prevailing religious indifference. Similarly, Israel benefits from a creative and healthy Diaspora. And Israel benefits from the resources of secular Jews who remind us of our obligations to humanity at large and to the protection of minorities.

Thus no single sector of Jews possesses all the answers to today's Jewish agenda. A true pluralism requires not a surrender of principle but rather a recognition that different Jews working together for similar purposes can accomplish much more than a house divided.

The assassination did not create our divisions. They have been with us from time immemorial. Yet the lessons of Jewish disunity have also been with us. The Talmud attributes the collapse of the Second Jewish Commonwealth to internal Jewish disunity. Our job 2,000 years later and fifty years after the Holocaust is to sustain and rebuild that unity and peoplehood even as we acknowledge our serious differences and disagreements.

Israel: Jewish or Post-Zionist?

Co-authored with Alan Silverstein

The forthcoming elections in Israel rightly focus on the current peace process. Prominent Labor spokesmen have warned Conservative and Reform leadership that the question of validating non-Orthodox conversions to Judaism will recede into insignificance—especially if the needs of coalition politics dictate advancing the monopoly of the chief rabbinate on laws of personal status.

What is absent from this assessment is any real understanding of a larger context: the face of Jewish religion in the Jewish state and the centrality of both a noncoercive Judaism and religious pluralism to any vision of a Jewishly vibrant and creative Israel.

Current Israeli political realities suggest that only Orthodox and secular Israeli votes count. Implicit in this assessment is that once Israel achieves peace with her neighbors, she then will be free to choose between two extreme options: a theocracy or a totally secular democracy. No middle ground is seriously discussed, one which would maintain a special relationship between Judaism and state in a noncoercive fashion.

In the meantime, state powers are invoked to enforce the religious edicts of an Orthodox monopoly. This status quo is resented not only by Conservative and Reform Israeli minorities and their Diaspora supporters, but also by growing numbers of nonreligious Israelis.

In fact, some Israel intellectuals are proclaiming a "post-Zionist" Israel. In this view, Israel's future best lies in normalizing relations with her Middle Eastern neighbors as well as in the full integration of non-Jewish citizens into a nonsectarian Israeli state. Post-Zionists regard both Judaism and links to Diaspora Jews as impediments to these objectives. Post-Zionism would sever Israel's link to Judaic heritage and culture. At its worst, post-Zionism easily spills over into an anti-Judaism rejecting any common covenant of the Jewish people.

Reprinted from the *Jewish Week of New York,* April 19, 1996.

The answer to the threat posed by post-Zionism must lie in an Israel that clearly and authentically articulates the continued salience of Jewish heritage and tradition. Here is where the battle for a noncoercive and religiously pluralistic Israel becomes crucial to Jewish survival, for such a religious pluralism acts both as a corrective to the excesses of Israel's religious establishment and as a counter to widespread indifference and to assimilation.

How is this the case? First, greater religious pluralism would rescue the image of Jewish religion from negative stereotyping. In the aftermath of the Rabin assassination, a secular backlash was targeted at religious people per se—irrespective of their political or social views. Jewish tradition was wrongly equated with religious extremism. As a countermeasure, religious pluralism would underscore Judaism's openness to listen to different viewpoints while upholding Judaic heritage as the common treasure of all Jews.

Second, greater religious pluralism would counter the widespread ignorance within Israeli society concerning Jewish tradition and thereby promote Jewish identity. The Shenhar Commission recently decried the abysmal illiteracy with regard to Jewish teachings apparent among the students of Israeli public schools. The report recommended broadening the teaching of Judaism, utilizing pluralistic perspectives such as those of Conservative Judaism's TALI schools.

Similarly, the Municipality of Jerusalem has joined recently with the American Jewish Committee's Institute on American Jewish-Israeli Relations to sponsor an exchange program of Jerusalem high school principals to study how Judaism is transmitted in the pluralistic context of American Judaism and to implement follow-up programming within Israeli public high schools. These efforts stem from a growing recognition that Jewish continuity also is a problem for Israeli society, particularly in a post-peace Israel which will be ever more open to outside influences. Broader Jewish education remains the best vehicle of ensuring that continuity.

As strategies for achieving a proper place for Judaism in the Israel of the future, mainstream Orthodox, Conservative and Reform movements best would be served by avoiding the temptation of politicizing their religious agendas in order to secure tangible benefits. Instead of seeking power through political alliances, religious leaders of all the movements should concentrate upon articulating this important middle ground as an alternative to the status quo's coerciveness and to the ardent secularism of the post-Zionists.

What should supporters of this centrist position advocate?

They should challenge the existing religious establishment, recognizing that Israelis, like American Jews, require pluralistic avenues to express their connection to Judaism. All too often Israeli visitors to other countries report that they never fully acknowledge the importance of leading a Jewish life until they had traveled to Diaspora communities and experienced an array of Jewish religious options. Moreover, the status quo only aggravates resentments toward Orthodoxy and Judaism in general. In sum, under the current arrangements the state of Judaism in Israel suffers.

They must advocate for the preservation of a Jewish society as well as a democratic state. The civil liberties of non-Jews and nonpracticing Jews must be protected, but the public culture of Israel must remain fully Jewish. This means that the power of the state ought not be invoked to coerce religious behaviors; but it also means that the Jewish character of the state—in public symbols, education and fundamental ethos—must be non-negotiable.

The answer to post-Zionism lies not in theocracy but in securing a democratic but fully Jewish Israel.

In laws of personal status, the question of marriageability among Jews historically has been essential to the maintenance of Jewish unity and peoplehood. When we can marry one another, we preserve common peoplehood. When we have been unable to marry among ourselves, we have become fragmented and weakened as a people. Therefore, we acknowledge the real divisions within the Jewish people over issues of personal status, but we call for efforts to forge consensus conversion procedures and laws that maximize marriageability among all Jews.

In Israel, as in America, threats to continued Jewish identity emanate primarily from religious indifference, not from religious pluralism. Jewish religionists on the Right ought to be challenged on the grounds that continued opposition to pluralism only plays into the hands of ardent secularists and assimilationists. Jewish religionists on the Left ought similarly to be challenged to counter the post-Zionism of their allies among secular parties, to maintain greater rather than lesser Judaism within the Jewish state.

The American model of religious pluralism is not necessarily the model most appropriate to a Jewish state. Similarly, a model of complete separation of Judaism from state is inappropriate for contemporary Israel. What Israel needs is a model of pluralism and mutual tolerance and interaction that preserves democratic freedoms but also increases commitments to Judaic heritage and tradition. The particular details of that model will need to be worked out. Yet Israel's place in Jewish history and centrality to Jewish peoplehood would be enhanced by marshaling the energies of all Jews committed to Jewish continuity, albeit with different ideologies over how to secure it.

Just as Israel's physical survival will be determined by its relationships with Arab neighbors, its spiritual survival will depend upon retaining a strong nexus of Judaism and a state in a noncoercive and pluralistic manner.

Continue the Ne'eman Formula

Like most compromises, the recently released report of the Ne'eman Commission in Israel calling for a joint conversion institute failed to satisfy completely any of the participating groups—Orthodox, Conservative and Reform. The proposal provided legitimacy and recognition for the non-Orthodox streams and ensured a uniform conversion procedure acceptable to the entire Jewish people. But no sooner was the report released than it became apparent that the chief rabbinate was unlikely to approve it.

Consequently, Avraham Burg engineered an alternate solution. This "technical" proposal requires that identity cards of Israeli Jews follow the identification as Jewish with a date. For those born as Jews, the date would be that of birth. For those converted to Judaism, the date would be that of the conversion. The effect of this proposal would be to signal to any religious authority that for purposes of citizenship, the individual is recognized as a Jew but not necessarily for purposes of religious practice.

The Burg proposal has the support of the Reform and Conservative movements in Israel, as well as that of the Sephardi chief rabbinate. Acceptance of the plan will probably prevent the controversial conversion bill from passing in the Knesset. Converts to Judaism will be recognized as Jews by the State of Israel, although not necessarily by the chief rabbinate. To be sure, the next battle will most likely occur over the rights of non-Orthodox converts to marry within Israel.

Reaction in the American Jewish community has been decidedly mixed. Some react with rage to the prospect of an identity card containing different categories of Jews. Others maintain that the Burg proposal was premature, effectively giving the chief rabbinate cause to reject the Ne'eman Commission prior even to its consideration and debate. Still others are disappointed that a true compromise had been shelved in favor of a very limited and technical solution that only delays the battle to another day.

Reprinted from the *Jewish Week of New York*, February 13, 1998.

Yet the Burg proposal has also garnered significant support. The leadership of ARZA, the Reform movement's Zionist wing, supported Burg's recommendation. To do so, it was felt, would avert a crisis in Israel-Diaspora relations, establish the principle that no decision had been made without consultation with North American Jewry, and identify Reform and Conservative spokesmen as the statesmen in this dispute. Conversely, in this view, the Ne'eman proposals were doomed in any case.

In short, the ink has barely dried on the proposals and already the parties to the controversy are preparing for the next round. Mutual recriminations dominate the public discourse. Relatively silent have been the voices advocating internal soul-searching, personal accountability and bridge building. Excluding Finance Minister Yaakov Ne'eman himself, absent has been any long-range vision that would preserve Jewish unity in the face of differing standards of conversion.

Nevertheless, even as the current controversy bounces back into the halls of the chief rabbinate, and perhaps the Knesset and the High Court, several lessons ought be noted for American Jewry, its relations with Israel and for relations between the differing Jewish religious movements.

The Ne'eman Commission itself provided a dignified forum for discussion of intra-Jewish affairs. Representatives of all the movements sat together in a collegial atmosphere willing to learn from one another. The civility of discourse that characterized commission discussions ought serve as a model for the conduct and resolution of problems within the Jewish people.

Through its deliberations the commission realized two goals often perceived as mutually contradictory: recognition and legitimacy for the non-Orthodox movements and preservation of the integrity of the halakhic process. Orthodox Jews cannot be expected to compromise on *halakha,* or Jewish law. Conversely, the non-Orthodox movements cannot be expected to acquiesce in a status quo that denies their legitimacy.

The Ne'eman Commission offered a solution accomplishing each objective without doing violence to the other.

Sadly, Modern Orthodox groupings failed to mount an offensive in support of the Ne'eman Commission, even among those rabbis who privately supported the proposal. The Am Echad (One People) coalition consisted of individuals associated with the National Council of Young Israel, once the flagship of Modern Orthodoxy, as well as individuals associated with Agudath Israel, the voice of the rigorously Orthodox, in a joint campaign against the Ne'eman Commission. More generally, the decline of Modern Orthodoxy and the ascendancy of ultra-Orthodox voices have resulted in greater isolation of the Orthodox from the non-Orthodox and augurs a wider split within the Jewish people, and not only over issues of personal status.

The Conservative and Reform movements were much too hasty in advancing the alternate Burg solution, which as noted will not solve the problem and instead introduces a historic shift in distinguishing between convert and Jew.

Some proponents of the Burg solution may have as their real agenda the complete separation between state and synagogue expressed by the distinction between civic Jewish identity and religious Jewish identity. Significantly, the Burg solution emanated originally from Dedi Zucker, a longtime leader within the Meretz Party. Thus, one of the ironies of this debate is that leaders of all the religious movements find themselves in alliance on this issue with proponents of Israel's most outspokenly secularist ideology.

At this point the continued unity of the Jewish people remains in great danger. Differing definitions of who is a Jew jeopardize our capacity to marry one another. A climate of mutual recriminations and incivility threatens to unravel the common fabric that binds Jews together. Only proposals like those of the Ne'eman Commission may offer both a long-term solution to the problems of personal status and provide a viable model for working relationships between Jews.

Continued communal support for both the substance of the Ne'eman Commission proposals and for its procedural model remains warranted. At present, American Jews may feel somewhat marginal to the debate and certainly possess little leverage over the chief rabbinate. Yet over the long term, issues of Jewish peoplehood transcend geographical boundaries and may be resolved only through the ongoing willingness of Jews to work together despite ideological and cultural divisions.

Roundtable on Yossi Beilin's
The Death of the American Uncle

Yossi Beilin's *Death of the Uncle from America* is doubly significant. First, an individual with ministerial responsibility in Israeli politics has focused on Jewish continuity in the Diaspora, which signals a new and welcome attitude in Israel's relationship with world Jewry. Second, Beilin's ideas, which call for fundamental shifts in language, approach, and self-perception from emphasizing Jewish vulnerabilities and anxieties to stressing Jewish potential and aspirations, are stimulating and provocative in themselves.

Beilin claims that Jews today no longer see themselves as victims. Jewish unity and identity were sustained over the past 50 years through memories of the Holocaust and perceptions of external enemies, but the eclipse of this "vulnerability model" signals that traditional modes of thinking will not sustain Jewish life in the twenty-first century. Thus, fundamental change in language and leadership will be necessary. Beilin's ideas are both positive and pro-active. He correctly warns that the traditional agenda of countering anti-Semitism, safeguarding Israel, and rescuing Soviet Jewry has been largely realized, and that new leadership and alternate paradigms will be necessary to address the challenges of the Jewish communal future. Conversely, communal leadership may be too reluctant to change their status quo models sufficiently to meet those challenges.

Beilin's proposals merit serious and careful consideration. Clearly he has helped set the agenda for world Jewry in the twenty-first century. However, if Beilin's diagnosis is sound, his solutions are more questionable. The eclipse of the vulnerability model does create the need for change in the communal agenda and self-image, but whether the passions of the Jewish people can be mobilized for an agenda committed to Jewish continuity, as opposed to rescuing Jews physically, remains undecided.

Consider, for example, the most headline-grabbing of Beilin's pro-

Reprinted from *Israel Studies*, 5:1, Spring 2000.

posals—an end to American Jewish economic assistance for Israel. Understandably, Beilin wishes to declare both Israel's independence and her capacity to tend to her own social welfare needs. The UJA provides annually less than one-half of one percent of the Israeli budget. Rather than continue to foster the image of Israeli dependency, UJA funds, in Beilin's view, would be better targeted toward programs of Jewish continuity in the Diaspora.

These proposals are well-intentioned. They are, in fact, even occurring as Federation funds shift gradually toward domestic American Jewish needs. Yet Beilin does not probe thoroughly whether United States foreign aid to Israel might be imperiled by an end to American Jewish fundraising. Beilin assumes that American aid is not dependent upon poverty wants within Israel, but that it is tied to other criteria. Yet foreign aid remains a difficult question in America during the best of times. The $3 billion targeted to Israel is validated by continued American Jewish fundraising as a statement of Jewish inter-dependence and passion for Israel. The peace process Beilin anticipates, in turn, will prove even more costly for the American taxpayer. Public calls for an end to American Jewish donations to Israel may well become self-defeating in terms of overall U.S. foreign aid to the Middle East. That U.S. aid persists within the current climate testifies only to the continued importance of American Jewish fundraising for Israel. Should the peace process require even greater American economic assistance, doubtless Beilin's ministerial colleagues will be appearing at American Jewish podiums urging increased efforts to secure U.S. aid.

Even more problematic, however, are Beilin's prescriptions for ensuring Jewish continuity. Too quickly he dismisses calls for *aliyah* and for increasing Jewish fertility as unrealistic at best and regressive at worst. Quixotic as such calls may appear, *aliyah* does ensure the Jewishness of the grandchildren of *olim*. Efforts to stimulate non-Orthodox *aliyah*, although largely unsuccessful, do contribute toward a solution, however infinitesimal, for Jewish continuity. Similarly, the fact that Jews have reached negative population growth in the Diaspora provides no cause for rejoicing. Indeed, one of the most positive Jewish self-images emanating out of Israel is that it is the sole society in the world in which Jews have broken the norm of only two children per family—a sign of the very self-confidence and pride in future aspirations that Beilin wishes to inculcate in the Jewish world generally.

In place of *aliyah* and increasing the birthrate, Beilin proposes three additional solutions to the problem of Jewish continuity. Refreshingly, he urges that securing Jewish continuity in the Diaspora become an Israeli responsibility for the twenty-first century. Trips to Israel, use of the Internet, and secular conversion to the Jewish people, if implemented properly, he maintains, will result in an *increased* Jewish population size for the future.

Clearly Beilin deserves credit as one of the godfathers of the Birthright Program guaranteeing every Jewish teenager the right to a tenday expense-paid visit to the Jewish homeland. His leadership resulted in an historic commitment on the part of Israel to preserve Diaspora Jewish life. The partnership with leading philanthropists and Federations in turn signals a profound shift in communal priorities and philanthropic norms.

All this, of course, is welcome news. Yet excessive trust is being placed in a "magic bullet" approach. Ten days is simply too short a time span to effect real change among those initially uncommitted to the Jewish collective enterprise. No incentives are being given to encourage longer visits. Beilin insists that no obligations be imposed upon participants, raising the specter of creating a marvelous moment in time but one with few lasting effects.

Nor does Beilin weigh alternatives to the Birthright Program. Current estimates place the cost of the program at $60 million annually. If the goal of 50,000 participants per year is to eventually be reached, the cost of the program will skyrocket. Might these funds be utilized for more effective purposes—e.g., Jewish summer camps or intensive Jewish education? One of the very few trenchant conclusions of the 1994 North American Commission on Jewish Identity and Continuity was to avoid magic bullet approaches that seek to substitute transformative experiences for the formative and basic building blocks of Jewish education. The expectations placed upon the historically significant Birthright Program run the risk of committing precisely that error.

Less controversial, although by no means less visionary, are Beilin's proposals for harnessing the vast potential of cable television and the Internet to create a global Jewish village of mass communications. Correctly, Beilin urges us to think creatively about utilizing new technologies for purposes of securing Jewish continuity.

What he fails to give adequate attention to are the limits of these technologies. Jewish continuity is best secured by making the rhythms of leading a Jewish life a daily affair—Jewish schooling on a daily basis, living in an intensive Jewish community, or, for that matter, living daily in the Jewish homeland. It is difficult to imagine the virtual community of cyber-space commanding that degree of allegiance. Cable television itself provides viewers with much greater options, but the overwhelming majority of its programs amount to little more than casual incidents in the daily life of the average viewer.

Most explosive is Beilin's call for a new type of conversion—secular rather than religious and conversion to the Jewish people rather than to Judaism. He queries why an agnostic like himself may be considered a Jew by birth yet an atheist cannot, in good conscience, undergo conversion. This argument may satisfy many secular Israelis and their American Jewish sympathizers—especially parents of mixed marrieds who wish to declare their grandchildren as Jews. The negative consequences of this proposal, however, far outweigh potential benefits.

Sociologically, Beilin misreads Diaspora Jewish identity. In America, Jews form a tiny minority, and, lacking distinctive Jewish ties, identity becomes blended with the broader American and universalist culture. Beilin's call for secular conversion is simply too minimalist a standard of transformation to expect long-term and sustained Jewish commitment. He appropriates the dictum of Ruth, "Your people, my people" yet omits the latter and no less significant declaration, "Your God, my God."

Additionally, Beilin does not weigh the consequences of secular conversion for the unity of the Jewish people. Diverse conversion standards among the religious movements have already created real division over who is a Jew. An additional category of "secular convert" will only further polarize divisions and, of course, further undermine marriage eligibility between Jews—the historical barometer of Jewish unity and peoplehood. The phrase "we all stood at Sinai" can mean little without common standards for who is a Jew. David Hartman, for one, urges Reform Judaism to serve as a corrective to the belief that "peoplehood is the necessary and sufficient condition of Jewish identity."[1] Beilin's advocacy of secular conversion will, in effect, undermine the efforts of Reform Judaism—the most liberal of the religious movements—to secure interfaith families into the Jewish fold through sincere and serious conversion to Judaism, and will further divide the Jewish people by creating diverse categories of individual Jews. Reform rabbis, in turn, will be compelled to invalidate secular conversions. Lastly, as Jack Wertheimer warns, no religion can afford to create a standard for conversion so low as commitment not to practice another faith. Proposals such as Beilin's "promise to convert the Jews into something they have never been—a people bereft of religious convictions and religious boundaries."[2] Steven M. Cohen, whom Beilin cites approvingly, has published research questioning the sustaining commitment of converts even to Conservative Judaism.[3] Further dilution of standards for conversion will only exacerbate this problem.

Surprisingly, Beilin stops short of advocating acceptance of patrilineal descent—a logical outcome of his call for greater inclusivity. He fails to ask whether the price of this inclusivity connotes dilution of Jewish identity and cultural distinctiveness. He draws a false dichotomy as religion being exclusive and peoplehood being inclusive. But no group interested in its cultural survival may persist without boundaries connoting both what it is and what it is not. Such boundaries, by definition, prove, in some measure, exclusionary, despite efforts to be as inclusive as possible.

Beilin's call for change within Israeli society, by contrast, is far more constructive. He acknowledges weaknesses within Israeli education and advocates, especially within secular schools, much greater appreciation of Jewish heritage, including the Talmud, and awareness of Diaspora existence. He concedes that the Israeli street has become de facto Canaanite—unconcerned with Diaspora Jewry and the Jewish people. He articulates a refreshing change of perspective and candor about Israeli society, although he perhaps overstates the capacity of the ultra-Orthodox to create a Jewish ghetto in Israel. Indeed, the very globalization and communications revolution Beilin celebrates signals inroads of modernization even within *haredi* [ultra-Orthodox] society.

Clearly, however, Beilin is correct to advocate an end to the coercive Orthodox monopoly in matters of personal status and the religious status quo, and he rightly calls for the possibility of civil marriages and burial for individuals unable to secure these services under traditional Jewish law.

To effect these changes, Beilin wants greater democracy and representiveness in Jewish life. He urges creation of a world Jewish parliament in which the entire Jewish people can address common Jewish matters. He notes that current structures have not promoted a true dialogue between partners. Whether Beilin's "Beit Yisrael" will provide such a setting remains an open question. It is probable that individuals of wealth—what Beilin calls the "plutocrats"—will, in any event, continue to dominate Jewish communal discussion, even given the possibility of communal elections. Historical experience demonstrates that few Jews participate in such elections, and most cannot recognize the names of particular candidates.

In short, Yossi Beilin has provided a treasure trove of ideas for shaping the Jewish world in the twenty-first century. To be sure, there are no short-cuts to securing Jewish continuity. However, Beilin's call for fundamental change within Jewish life cannot and should not be ignored. On the contrary, he deserves enormous credit for helping to chart a new agenda for the Jewish future. Let the discussion begin but by no means conclude with his proposals.

Notes

1. David Hartman, *A Heart of Many Rooms* (Woodstock, VT, 1999), 200.

2. Jack Wertheimer, "Let's Not Undermine Religious Conversion," *Sh'ma,* October 1999, 5.

3. Steven M. Cohen, "The Conversion Illusion," in Jack Wertheimer (ed), *Jewish Identity and Religious Commitment: The North American Study of Conservative Synagogues and Their Members* (New York, 1997) 29–35.

BOOK REVIEWS

Frequently, book reviews have provided a forum to articulate my thinking and beliefs. Editors occasionally tease me that I write opinion pieces masquerading as book reviews. In truth, reading books constantly challenges my thinking and compels me to revisit even strongly held convictions. Reviewing books provide opportunities to share ideas with a broader audience as well as to underscore the importance of continuing Judaic literacy. The reviews in this section reflect an array of interests—Jewish history, the contemporary Jewish community, and the ongoing dialogue between tradition and modernity.

Crisis in American Jewry:
A Certain People:
American Jews and Their Lives Today

by Charles E. Silberman

Charles Silberman's long-awaited work on American Jewry synthe-sizes the most recent sociological research and demographic studies into a coherent and thoughtful analysis of the state of American Jewry. The book's dustjacket identifies Silberman as the well-known author of *Crisis in Black and White* and *Crisis in the Classroom.* Would we now be treated to a "Crisis in American Jewry?"

Silberman answers the question in resoundingly negative terms. Nei-ther external foes nor internal erosion threaten American Jewish conti-nuity. On the contrary, Silberman celebrates the major changes in American society that have opened virtually all portals to Jews. For-merly closed or restricted aspects of the power structure now willingly accept Jews into their highest echelons. Since World War II anti-Semi-tism has been in general retreat. Even the much-publicized AWACs de-bate five years ago is today largely forgotten. Only among young and well-educated blacks does Silberman perceive significant signs of anti-Semitism.

Nor, in Silberman's view, ought Jews agonize over low fertility and high intermarriage rates. Jews remain overwhelmingly committed to marriage and a norm of two children—small, but enough to replace themselves, and Jewish families were never large in any case. Although intermarriage has risen to 25 percent, this rate is far lower than the usual estimates paraded for U.S. audiences. Moreover, in light of the increasing tendency of intermarrieds to raise their children as Jews, in-termarriage may result in a net gain for the Jewish community. Finally,

Reprinted with permission from *Contemporary Jewry,* Vol. 8, 1986.

the open U.S. society has given Jews the freedom to choose to lead a Jewish life. When the mountain of tradition no longer hangs over them, as in the midrashic rendition of God compelling the Jews to accept the Torah, those who freely choose to lead a Jewish life do so with vigor and intensity.

Yet, if the news is so good, why has the book received a fairly harsh press? No doubt many Jews have a natural paranoia about their future. One generation after the Holocaust, we have witnessed the enormous capacities of anti-Semitism. The phenomenom has existed, at least in latent form, in every society in which Jews have sought to preserve a corporate identity as Jews. Only the factors that trigger anti-Semitism and transform it into a real danger for Jews have varied. In that light, it is at least questionable whether the United States is really different from other societies in which Jews have prospered.

In terms of the United States, however, every survey taken since World War II has reported a decline in anti-Semitic attitudes. Even during difficult times, e.g., the Lebanon War, public support for Israel and regard for Jews remained high. American Jews suffer no important disabilities. Jews have at times been considered for the vice-presidency of the country. Critical phenomena—McCarthyism, the George Wallace presidential campaign, the oil boycott—were noticeably free of anti-Semitic content, although at another place and time such currents usually were accompanied by widespread agitation against Jews. To be sure, anti-Semitism among blacks did flare during the controversy over Andrew Young's resignation and more recently during Jesse Jackson's presidential bid. Clearly, Jews may not relax their guard, but by historical standards their situation in the United States is most enviable.

Still, Silberman's opinion rings hollow with respect to the internal condition of Jewry. First, Silberman celebrates Jewish affluence and general professional success. Estimates of Jewish poverty, however, remain around 10 percent. One of four Jewish wage earners do not attend college and in all likelihood enter blue-collar occupations. Inner-city Jews, frequently residing in high-crime neighborhoods without close family, pass unnoticed in Silberman's book. Irving Shapiro of DuPont no more typifies the American Jew than does an elderly shut-in in New York's Lower East Side.

Nor does Silberman manage to persuade that the news is good on fertility and intermarriage. He argues that Jews are delaying childbearing into their thirties but still expect two or more children. Yet Silberman fails to account for the increase in infertility among women over age thirty. Nor does he question whether long-term involvement in careers may inhibit childbearing even if biological capacity and desire exist. Finally, he does not examine how Jewish tradition will be transmitted in the two-career family. Current fertility trends herald both quantitative and qualitative changes in the Jewish population.

In terms of intermarriage Silberman badly underestimates the dangers intermarriage poses both to Jewish continuity and to communal unity. The logic of his argument that intermarriage will mean a net gain of Jews should lead one to advocate increased intermarriage. More tellingly, if no conversion occurs, it is most questionable whether substantive Jewish content will continue to be transmitted. Children of intermarrieds are unlikely to seek out Jewish mates if they see their parents as successfully intermarried. Impressionistic evidence—at least as persuasive as Silberman's "Items"—points to large numbers of intermarrieds raising their children within a dual-faith framework. One would have to redefine Judaism radically to continue to count these as Jews or to place much hope in the Jewishness of their children. To be sure, evidence does exist that Jews by choice act like most other Jews and frequently enhance the community. Yet, in the absence of conversion, the residue of Jewish identity carried by the Jewish spouse is unlikely to be transmitted to the next generation. Finally, although Silberman downplays the rates of intermarriage, they are clearly high by historical standards. Most tellingly, he cites a 1975 Boston survey to the effect that only 16 percent of Jews aged eighteen to twenty-nine would oppose intermarriage. If Jews are at best neutral on the subject, while the heads of the religious movements unanimously oppose intermarriage, we do have a crisis of norms and values.

Moreover, Silberman fails to gauge how differing attitudes toward intermarriage and conversion threaten to undermine communal unity. He rightly criticizes the Orthodox for their unwillingness to consider possible models of a unified conversion procedure acceptable to all the religious movements, yet fails to acknowledge that the decision by the

Reform and Reconstructionist movements to define the child of a Jewish father and a non-Jewish mother as a Jew heralds a crisis over who is a Jew. The decision informs intermarried couples in which the male is Jewish that their children are Jewish. Yet Conservative and Orthodox Jews agree that such a definition is unacceptable, and they will not accept such individuals as Jews. Silberman casually predicts that Conservative Judaism will soon adopt patrilineality, presumably on the grounds that several Conservative rabbis favor it. For the present, however, the Rabbinical Assembly has overwhelmingly rejected patrilineality as does the incoming chancellor of the Jewish Theological Seminary. A schism in the community seems just around the corner.

Finally, Silberman has little to say about Jewish education. Jewish day schools are thriving, but strangely Silberman chooses to ignore them. Supplementary schools, which continue to attract the bulk of Jewish students, suffer from insufficient contact hours, shortage of qualified personnel, and an overwhelming dropout rate after bar or bat mitzvah. Silberman seems content to observe that about 50 percent of Jewish children receive some Jewish education, without commenting on its quality. Yet clearly, in the open society the least-educated Jews are the most likely to opt to join the larger community. In that sense, the sorry state of Jewish education does herald a "crisis in American Jewry."

To be sure, there are signs of Jewish renewal. Many adults are discovering their Jewish identity for the first time. American Jews have become less self-conscious about their Jewishness and more willing to identify publicly as Jews. Yet we must question the depth and intensity of the renewal when Jews no longer reject intermarriage and are unversed in the traditions, culture, and values—to say nothing of the language—of their people.

Charles Silberman's important new book serves as an excellent introduction to the inner and outer lives of American Jews. One may agree with his basic theme of Jewish renewal and be optimistic about the prospects for Jewish continuity into the next century. Let us acknowledge, however, the serious dangers that Jews confront in terms of Jewish family, literacy, and communal unity.

Anarchism and Judaism:
Jewish Radicals: From Czarist Stetl to London Ghetto

by William Fishman

In recent years an entire literature has developed on the alliance of the Jews with the political Left. Henry Feingold, in his excellent study, *The Politics of Rescue,* examined the ambivalent relationship between the Roosevelt administration and the Jews during the Second World War.[1] Arthur Hertzberg detected the origins of modern anti-Semitism in the liberalism of the enlightenment that tolerated few expressions of cultural pluralism.[2] Similarly Edmund Silberner discovered surprisingly high quotas of anti-Semitic writings among socialist thinkers for whom anti-Semitism ought to have been the monopoly of capitalist bourgeois society.[3] Most recently, the question of anti-Semitism and anti-Zionism current in New Left circles has attracted great attention.[4]

In many ways these books originated from the legacy of the Nazi Holocaust. The horror of Auschwitz provoked discussion on the silence of the liberal world during the tragedy. Significant questions were raised as to the political wisdom of Jews allying with left-wing political parties. The prewar myth that Jews ought naturally to vote liberal to defeat anti-Semitic forces on the Right had now become a highly debatable proposition. In this context of disillusion with the liberal world, post-war historiography veered sharply away from traditional assumptions regarding Jewish political behavior and in itself contributed to the ongoing debate over the directions such political activity ought to pursue. The opposition of the New Left to the State of Israel has recently even further undermined such traditionalist assumptions.

William Fishman examines the case of a particular group of Jews on the Left, the Jewish anarchists of London's East End in the years prior to the outbreak of the First World War. Although the group studied was admittedly peripheral to the Anglo-Jewish community, one can under-

Reprinted from *Gesher,* January 1977.

stand the East End activity as an interesting, if somewhat extreme, case study of the genres of Jewish political liberalism and radicalism. For Fishman the study of such behavior is a "labor of love." He writes with great passion in portraying the careers of Jewish anarchists. His research is pioneering in his excellent use of oral history interviews with surviving anarchists and his utilization of the Anglo-Yiddish press, although the latter is limited to anarchist organs.[5] The book stands as a contribution to Anglo-Jewish history, to socialist Jewish history, and to labor history in general.

The questions Dr. Fishman raises do, however, deserve further analysis. First, one must ask what relationship, if any, is there between Jewish emancipation and Jewish radicalism. Radical political behavior among Jews has by no means been limited to emancipated Jewish communities. Certainly Czarist Russia, as Dr. Fishman describes in his opening chapter, served as the "home base" and "training ground" for leftist Jews. Yet, the phenomenon of Jewish radical politics is in many ways intimately connected to societies which had previously granted civil and political liberties to the Jews.

In one sense such radicalism was fully consonant with the aims of emancipation. Anglo-Jewry constantly denied the existence of a "Jewish vote." If Jews had become fully Englishmen, then it was only logical that Jews be represented in all sectors of the British political spectrum. On a less theoretical plane, however, Jewish radicalism actually constituted a threat to the ideals of emancipation. In England, where emancipation was more delayed but also more complete than in any other European country, the post-emancipation Jewish community deeply believed in the essential morality of English society and institutions. In the eyes of Jewish leadership, anti-Semitism in England was nonexistent even in potentiality. Separatist Jewish institutions, especially Jewish political clubs, were denounced by the Board of Deputies of Anglo-Jews, the leading political institutions. In the eyes of Jewish leadership, anti-Semitism in movements dedicated to the overthrow of Victorian English society constituted a gross violation of the "bargain" of emancipation. Such movements represented as grave a threat to the Anglicization of the Jewish community as did political Zionism and consequently encountered very similar opposition from the "Cousinhood," that network of elitist Jewish families that dominated Anglo-Jewry in the generation following emancipation.[6]

Not all Jews fully shared these assumptions. In the immigrant communities of East London and the provinces, particularly, where anti-Semitism had by no means disappeared, "cells of sedition" were common among those who found their political leadership wanting in sensitivity to the real needs of the community. For such discontented Jews, emancipation had failed to solve the Jewish Question, and alternative solutions were desirable. Much as political Zionism was strongest in the ghetto and in the provinces, so political radicalism made deep inroads in such areas. In this context, one can better appreciate Herzl's appeal to various heads of state, that Zionism would function as a "safe" outlet for the radicalist political tendencies current in their respective Jewries. Perhaps nowhere was this truer than in England, where, as Dr. Fishman indicates in his concluding chapter, the success of political Zionism doomed the Jewish anarchist movement.

Other questions raised by Dr. Fishman during the course of his study involve the how and why of Jewish radicalism. What were the sources of Jewish radicalism? How did Jewish radicals develop their anarchist rhetoric? Why did such men become radicalized? These questions, of course, apply not only to the group in Dr. Fishman's book, but similarly to the more renowned radicals such as Rosa Luxembourg and Leon Trotsky. Some have suggested that Jewish radicalism emanates from the Jewish tradition itself. In other words the universalism of the tradition impels the Jew to adopt ideologies of general humanitarian content. To create the messianic era one must immerse onself in programs aimed at the betterment of society as a whole. That the tradition in itself commands the Jew to be universalistic is, of course, highly questionable. Citations in the spirit of universalism from the literary prophets can easily be countered by parallel citations from Ezra and Nehemiah denoting ethnic particularism. Given the questionableness of the universalism of the tradition, it is even more questionable whether Jewish radicals were influenced by any portion of the tradition at all. Certainly Trotsky and Luxembourg disavowed any such conscious influences of Judaism. Attempts to link the tradition necessarily with reformist or radical politics ignore the reality that more often Jewish radicals have sought to escape their Jewishness rather than confront it. In this respect it is fascinating to observe that the Jewish heroes for London's Jewish anarchists were the Mishnaic and medieval heretics, Elisha ben Avuyah and Hivi Habalki, rather than Isaiah and Jeremiah.

Dr. Fishman suggests that Jewish anarchism, although motivated by personal ideology and only marginally related to Jewish values, appealed to London's East End as a political solution to the Jewish Question in ghetto areas. In other words, the conditions of the immigrants required radical solutions, given the hostility of the Gentile world and the callousness of the indigenous Jewish community. Exactly how political anarchism could practically have solved the Jewish Question in the ghetto is never really explained. Dr. Fishman implies that the Jews gravitated to the Left in response to hostility and pressure from the Right. Significantly, after the passing of the Aliens Act in 1905, which was designed to sharply limit immigration into England and reflected greatly increased criticism and resentment of East End Jewry, Jews apparently voted Liberal in overwhelming majorities as a means of retaliating against the Conservative Party, which had sponsored the Act. Yet, there was indeed a tremendous gulf between voting for the Liberal Party and joining a movement dedicated to remaking society altogether. In this respect we ought continually to recall that very few Jews were actually radicals. The radicals' appeal to the Jewish community was certainly couched in terms of opposition to the political Right. The small numbers of Jews affected by such an appeal truly reflected the more conservative leanings of the majority of the community.

A related question concerns the political wisdom of Jewish radicalism. Whether historians ought to issue judgments on such issues is somewhat debatable, but, as Sir Isaiah Berlin correctly discerned in his landmark essay, "Historical Inevitability,"[8] historians have in the past issued such judgments and undoubtedly will continue to do so in the future. Dr. Fishman is quite sympathetic to the anarchists. In his view, they at times acted misguidedly but were always well-intentioned. He treats acts of violence, physical clashes with Orthodox Jews, and Yom Kippur balls as primarily examples of poor tactics. He apparently misses the destructiveness of such acts. For many of these men Judaism itself was reactionary phenomenon, and the salvation of the world lay in the overthrow of religion *per se*. Moreover, he misses the anti-Semitism common among many of the Gentile allies of the Jewish radicals, possibly because left-wing anti-Semitism in England was generally directed against the richer Jews, although enough prejudice could and did extend to the immigrant community as well. The naive actions of Jews involved in radical politics quite correctly offended Anglo-Jewry as deeply as the anti-Zionism of the New Left offends American Jewry today.

Finally, Dr. Fishman mounts an implicit attack on the "financial aristocracy" of the Anglo-Jewish community, in particular the Jewish members of Parliament who supported restrictionist legislation. Similarly he cites the well-known antipathy of Chief Rabbi Herman Adler to the immigrant Jews. The failures of Anglo-Jewish leadership in relatinship to the newly-arrived immigrants have been well-known since Lloyd Gartner's pioneering study.[9] The picture however ought not be simplified. Certain Jewish M.P.'s, e.g., Lord Rothschild, who served on the Royal Commission on Immigration, passionately defended the immigrants and fought against restriction. The Chief Rabbi acknowledged his failure to relate to the immigrant community and pleaded for a successor who would be more acceptable to East London. The Haham, Moses Gaster, was frequently at odds with the inherent conservatism of the Anglo-Jewish hierarchy. Finally, bneath the Cousinhood a new leadership, was emerging in those years. Coalescing around institutions such as B'nai Brith and forming organs such as the *Jewish Review,* this newer leadership consisted of younger men, Norman Bentwich, Leon Simon, Paul Goodman, Israel Sieff, and others who found allies among the older leadership in Gaster, Chief Rabbi Hertz, and Herbert Bentwich. Together the group aimed at promoting a more consciously Jewish existence in England for all, immigrant and native Jew alike. The revolution these men mounted in 1917 ordained a new order in Anglo-Jewry, in which, Dr. Fishman cogently argues, anarchism seemed strangely anachronistic. The critique of Jewish leadership, voiced so often in our times, frequently portrays such leadership in black and white terminology and ignores the complexities of the particular Jewish communities.

Jewish radicalism continues as a force, albeit peripheral, within the contemporary Jewish scene. At times radical politics can function as a catalyst for the organized community to undertake effective action on certain Jewish problems. At other times radicalism can effectively agitate for reform on issues confronting society as a whole (e.g., Jewish peace groups during the Vietnam War). One cannot, however, overlook the destructive anti-Jewish tendencies of such radicalism. Jewish life ultimately depends on certain frameworks. When Jewish radicalism seeks to uproot such frameworks, Judaism and radicalism cannot coexist.

Notes

1. Henry Feingold, *The Politics of Rescue,* N.Y., 1970.
2. Arthur Hertzberg, *The French Enlightenment and the Jews,* N.Y., 1968.
3. Edmund Silberner, *Western Socialism and the Jewish Question,* (Hebrew), Jerusalem, 1955.
4. For example, Mordechai Chertoff, ed., *The New Left and the Jews,* N.Y., 1971.
5. Compare with Chimen Abramsky's review, *Times Literary Supplement,* June 20, 1975.
6. Chaim Bermant, *The Cousinhood,* London, 1971.
7. A noteworthy example of this reading of the tradition is Arthur Waskow, "How to Bring Maschiach" in Strassfeld, Strassfeld, and Siegel, eds., *The Jewish Catalog,* Philadelphia, 1974.
8. Sir Isaiah Berlin, "Historical Inevitability" in *Four Essays on Liberty,* London, 1969, pp. 41–117.
9. Lloyd Gartner, *The Jewish Immigrant in England* (2nd edition), London, 1973.

From Philanthropy to Activism:
The Political Transformation of American
Zionism in the Holocaust Years 1933–1945

by David Shpiro

As the title of this book suggests, American Zionism underwent a remarkable transformation during the Holocaust years from a body primarily dedicated to fund-raising for practical projects in Palestine to a media-conscious lobby seeking to influence public and governmental opinion. Drawing upon unpublished and newly-released materials, particularly the Roosevelt papers, the author seeks to demonstrate how, after failing to prevent promulgation of the 1939 British White Paper, American Zionism was able to regroup and refocus energies to realize the Zionist vision of a Jewish homeland. In that sense, given the spate of books indicting American Jewry for insufficient resolve during the Holocaust years, Shpiro's book suggests a more dispassionate estimate of American Jewish leadership, or at least its Zionist sectors.

To be sure, American Zionism, in Shpiro's view, suffered from disunity and weaknesses of leadership. Shpiro demonstrates how the Irgun, or "Bergson Boys," succeeded in penetrating the communications barrier concerning the Holocaust precisely because of a vacuum of leadership at senior levels of the Zionist movement. Hadassah, today the largest and most successful of Zionist organizations, split over the question of statehood, with a sizable minority following the lead of Henrietta Szold and Rabbi Judah Magnes in supporting bi-nationalism, policies which gained the approval only of the anti-Zionist American Council for Judaism. Stephen Wise lacked sufficient verve, in Shpiro's view, to break with Britain or defy Roosevelt when necessary. Acknowledging these limitations, Shpiro focuses upon the achievement of the Biltmore Program which committed American Zionism to a maximalist program of Jewish statehood. Where others have faulted American Zionism for focusing on statehood rather than rescue, Shpiro

Reprinted with permission from *Contemporary Jewry,* Volume 15, 1994.

suggests that the drive for statehood transformed the essence of American Zionism from bland non-ideological fund-raising, doing good work that non-Zionists could suport, to the active political and often divisive work of advancing the Zionist agenda in influential circles.

As for rescue activity, Shpiro does underscore the failure of American Zionists, like American Jews generally, to acknowledge the magnitude of the Holocaust tragedy and its uniqueness in human history. As Naomi Cohen has demonstrated concerning the leadership of the American Jewish Committe, so Shpiro suggests of the Zionists, as children of the Enlightenment they failed to comprehend the radical evil embodied in Nazism. This failure, coupled with a general incapacity to influence United States governmental policy, resulted in a fusion of rescue and nation-building into a single program that, in effect, placed Zionist resources in a "statehood alone" initiative, downplaying more immediate efforts at rescue of Jews.

Would alternative policies have proven more successful? Shpiro does not probe sufficiently the alternative directions the Bergson Boys advocated. In any case, it is doubtful that more "militant" actions could ever have captured communal consensus, let alone been capable of modifying governmental policy. Although one might take issue with the particular tactics adopted by Zionist leaders, legitimate disagreement by no means constitutes the moral condemnation of Zionist leadership frequently articulated by extremist circles of Zionism on both Left and Right.

Shpiro, by suggesting a more dispassionate view of what American Zionists did and did not do during the Holocaust years, implicitly calls for more mature and less polemical treatment in Holocaust historiography generally. To be sure, he fails to address the arguments voiced by Elie Wiesel and Rabbi Haskel Lookstein, among others, that regardless of the capacity of American Jews to influence the course of events, the news of the Holocaust should have been "unbearable" for them. What Shpiro does, however, is to document change within the Zionist movement. The equally significant transformations of attitudes within American society towards Hitler warrant a similarly realistic and dispassionate analysis.

British Jewry and the Holocaust

by Richard Bolchover

Although historians and communal leaders continue to debate the role of American Jewry as bystanders during the Holocaust, surprisingly little attention to date has focused upon the parallel case of British Jewry. Britain contained a community of 385,000 Jews, which had placed enormous trust in Britain as guarantor of Jewish equality. Richard Bolchover's important new book will initiate further controversy on whether Jewish leaders effectively exhausted all potential avenues in seeking to rescue European Jewry.

Anglo-Jewry clearly differed from American Jewry in possessing greater unity—symbolized by a single national Jewish newspaper. Moreover, the plight of Jews under Nazism received detailed attention in the British media and garnered the support of sympathetic government officials. To be sure, these apparent opportunities for rescue activity were restricted by governmental sensitivity on the question of Palestine and Jewish anxieties about the emergence of domestic anti-Semitism.

In this context, British Jewry did undertake limited yet praiseworthy rescue initiatives. There was no shortage of public protests and letters. Bolchover singles out the *London Jewish Chronicle* especially for acting responsibly. Similarly he praises the rescue efforts of the Orthodox Aguda faction as both useful and productive.

By contrast, Bolchover argues that the established leadership of Anglo-Jewry—the Chief Rabbi and the Board of Deputies—failed under circumstances which demanded resolute action. Chief Rabbi Hertz equated Nazism with Bolshevism and mistakenly believed that education and rationality would deflect Nazi anti-Semitism. The Board of Deputies, the leading defense organ of the community, scuttled rescue efforts that might undermine its own hegemony within the commu-

Reprinted with the permission of the Jerusalem Center for Public Affairs, from *Jewish Political Studies Review* 7:1–2 (Spring 1995).

nity. For example, the community opposed the creation of a Jewish army, even as it exaggerated its condemnation of the 1944 assassination of Lord Moyne as "among the greatest disasters that befell Jews." Faith in and gratitude to Britain dictated utmost loyalty to Churchill and prevented any domestic lobbying for rescue action. To be sure, Bolchover acknowledges Churchill's heroism in keeping England in the war, yet suggests that the government would have benefitted from domestic pressure to alleviate the plight of international Jewry.

Comparative studies of Anglo and American Jewries are rare in Jewish historiography, and Bolchover's work would have benefitted from appropriate comparisons and contrasts with the American Jewish setting. Both communities shared a common faith in education as the cure for anti-Semitism. Naomi Cohen has written persuasively how the leadership of the American Jewish Committee, in particular, as children of the Enlightenment, could not fathom the demonic nature of Nazi anti-Semitism. Comparatively speaking, Anglo-Jewry actually succeeded in bringing proportionately more Jewish refugees into the British Isles than did their American counterparts.

Is Bolchover's critique, then, unduly harsh? Absent from his work, and regrettably absent as well from similar historical critiques of American Jewish leadership, is analysis of what real leverage Jews could actually have exerted upon governmental policy. Did Anglo-Jewry, for instance, have any real capacity to alter Britain's Palestine policy— probably the only realistic goal of resettlement efforts? The picture Bolchover paints of Anglo-Jewish leadership as weak, fearful of domestic anti-Semitism, and, above all, trapped by its values of faith in education and gratitude to Britain, presupposes that an alternative leadership would in fact have done better. Yet the real story here may be much more a function of Jewish powerlessness during the Nazi era rather than a story of Jewish ineptitude or cowardice. The fact that Zionists and non-Zionists alike—in contrast to sharp and long-standing historical divisions within Anglo-Jewry—united behind the policies of Jewish communal leadership suggests that the opportunities and options for rescue activity may not have been as extensive as Bolchover believes.

In fact, Bolchover locates his heroes among the Jewish counter-establishment. True-blue socialists like Harold Laski or the left-wing publisher Victor Gollancz stand in sharp contrast to the "blandness" of Selig Brodetsky of the Board of Deputies. Rabbi Solomon Shoenfeld of Aguda merits praise for his rescue activities, as do the Revisionist Zionists—precisely for their willingness to challenge existing patterns.

These "counter-establishment" perspectives are important and, indeed, provide balance to accounts written primarily from the viewpoint of mainstream communal leadership. However, before embracing these approaches—whether for America, Britain, or wartime Palestine—we must ask whether indeed these approaches would have been more successful than those that prevailed. The real question is whether Jews enjoyed sufficient leverage and power to alter the course of historical events. To the extent alternate approaches did succeed, e.g., the rescue efforts of the Aguda, their successes may well have been a function precisely of their extremely limited scope. Broadening these efforts may only have guaranteed their failure, given the weakness of Anglo-Jewish political influence in the face of an overarching Allied agenda of prosecuting the war to a successful conclusion. Perhaps, to paraphrase the Israeli historian Yehuda Bauer, the real lesson of the Holocaust is not "never again," but rather "never again should the Jews be so isolated."

Torah and Science:
The Men and Women of Yeshiva

by Jeffrey S. Gurock

During his tenure as Secretary of Education, William J. Bennett frequently urged upon American universities a return to the traditional goals of an undergraduate liberal-arts education: instilling the core values of Western civilization, fostering a critical spirit of inquiry, cultivating an understanding of human nature, nurturing a sense of responsibility for the life of society.

Most of these traditional aims of higher education seem, in theory, compatible with the ideals of Jewish education as well. Jewish texts, too, seek to instill values, to uncover the wellsprings of human behavior, and to train students in critical modes of study and inquiry. But, of course, Jewish education as traditionally understood does not stop there; indeed, it does not even begin there. Rather, it subsumes these pursuits under a larger, more overarching aim—training the mind and heart in service to God and to Jewish religious law.

Are *those* two sides of education, namely, the secular and the religious, compatible? Can they be combined in any meaningful way? This is a question that has bedeviled modern Jewish scholarship on the one hand, and modern Jewish faith on the other. The resulting tension is perhaps most vividly expressed in the institutional history of Yeshiva University, the nation's largest and oldest university under Jewish auspices, which recently celebrated its centennial. In *The Men and Women of Yeshiva,* Jeffrey Gurock affords us a look at that institution's ongoing effort to synthesize traditional Judaism with the values of Western education.

Yeshiva originated as a traditional rabbinical school, its curriculum focusing exclusively on Talmud and Jewish religious law. Over the years, however, the school developed into a broadly conceived university under Orthodox auspices, offering advanced studies in a host of humanistic and scientific disciplines. Today the core is an undergraduate college at which students pursue a dual curriculum of Jewish studies in the morning and secular degree programs in the afternoon and evening. Yeshiva continues to provide rabbinical training, but its primary mandate has become one of educating young Orthodox Jews to function in the world of modern culture while remaining faithful to Jewish tradition.

The academic relationships between these two realms have not always been free of strain. To be sure, Bernard Revel, the university's first president, maintained strongly that Orthodoxy and secular scholarship—by which he meant not only the study of the humanities and sciences but also, perhaps more threateningly, the "scientific" study of Judaism itself—were indeed compatible. Revel, indeed, defied the wishes of many of his Talmud faculty and engaged "modern" scholars to teach Jewish history and Bible. Although in the academic study of Judaism, Yeshiva has never been able to compete successfully with the Conservative movement's Jewish Theological Seminary or, latterly, with American universities, Revel's dream of establishing an institute for scholarly Jewish research has been realized today in the graduate school that bears his name.

It was during the presidency of Samuel Belkin (1943–75) that Yeshiva became a true university. Graduate and professional schools were established in social work, psychology, and medicine, and an undergraduate women's college was founded. Yeshiva also began to reach out to the broader Jewish community, attracting young men and women of Conservative and even occasionally Reform background to its Jewish studies program.

Gurock's best chapters are on the 60s and 70s, when a new source of tension arose. Like their counterparts at secular universities in the 60s, many Yeshiva students in those years campaigned for civil rights and against the Vietnam war. Some volunteered their time to work with ghetto youngsters in the Washington Heights community where the university is located. Yet this was social activism with a difference, informed by debates unique to Yeshiva's Orthodox character.

One such debate was between Rabbis Irving Greenberg of the history department and Aharon Lichtenstein of the Talmud faculty. To

Greenberg, students engaged in the civil-rights and antiwar movements were acting precisely out of the religious values represented by Yeshiva, and thus contributing to the "repair" of society. Lichtenstein did not altogether disagree in theory with Greenberg's line of thought, but argued that the ways of Torah were far more complicated, and more demanding, than what was suggested by the activist liberal social agenda of the 1960s. A different sort of ambivalence marked the position of Joseph B. Soloveitchik, Yeshiva's preeminent faculty member and the dean of the Talmud faculty. While respecting the commitments of the protesting students, Soloveitchik questioned the assumption that this war against Communism was in fact immoral, and he also raised the issue of the possible harmful effect on Israel of a general weakening of America's international posture.

The debate between Greenberg and Lichtenstein/Soloveitchik, though real enough, nevertheless stayed within the framework of certain shared assumptions and beliefs. All three men were proponents of what is known as Modern Orthodoxy, seeking in their various ways to promote that synthesis of "Torah and Science" that is the motto of Yeshiva. Still another central element in the Modern Orthodox ethos can be seen at work in the longstanding commitment of Yeshiva faculty and students to Zionism. Yeshiva's original Teacher's Institute, with its Hebraic curriculum, was an early haven for religious Zionists. Virtually alone in the world of American yeshivas, the university has remained unswervingly faithful to Zionism and the State of Israel, where disproportionate numbers of its alumni have chosen to build their lives.

It must be added, though, that the institution has not been impervious to the more extreme elements of religious Zionism. Long after he had been ostracized by the mainstream Jewish community, for example, Meir Kahane remained one of the most popular and sought-after campus speakers. And there is widespread support at Yeshiva, both among faculty and students, for the Gush Emunim settlers on Israel's West Bank.

If this suggests a rightward religious drift at Yeshiva, other developments similarly add to the impression that the "Torah" side of the balance weighs more heavily than the "Science" side. According to Gurock, members of the Talmud faculty argue routinely that "secular pursuits [are] dangerous on many grounds." Yeshiva students frequently spend one or two years in an Israeli yeshiva studying Talmud exclusively, and only then return to fulfill the most basic liberal-arts requirements.

To complicate matters further, Yeshiva, like many other universities, has been affected by the turn toward professionalism in American higher education. In the 1970s virtually entire humanities departments disappeared or shrank to part-time status while courses in accounting and information science proliferated. Today's undergraduates tend to concentrate entirely in preprofessional areas; rarely in their undergraduate life are they exposed to the classics of Western intellectual history, literature, and political theory, much less compelled to assess their implications for Jewish thought and culture.

So the balance sheet is a mixed one. The institutional success of Yeshiva is undoubted, and it marks the maturation of Orthodoxy on American shores. Those religious Jews who repudiated America as a *"treyfe land,"* and those secularist Jews who dismissed Orthodoxy as an "intellectually bankrupt" tradition, have both been disproved. As Gurock shows, Yeshiva alumni serve with distinction in all walks of life, and they occupy positions of leadership in Jewish communities across the country. Many students at Yeshiva are easily the caliber of students at elite institutions of higher learning elsewhere. And in its current president, Norman Lamm, Yeshiva is fortunate to have an eloquent spokesman for academic excellence and for continued engagement with the broader society and the broader Jewish community.

Yet even as Lamm seeks to define a "centrist Orthodoxy," other voices within the world of Yeshiva now call for increased isolation, or justify retreat into personal or exclusively religious concerns. Whether Yeshiva will continue to uphold, as it once did, the independent value of a liberal education is a question whose answer will affect the very viability of the modern Orthodox synthesis in contemporary America. That answer is by no means clear.

Tradition or Modernity?
Sacred Fragments: Recovering Theology for the Modern Jew

by Neil Gillman

and Torah U'madda

by Norman Lamm

Both of these recent works of modern Jewish thought share much in common. Their authors occupy prominent positions at leading rabbinical seminaries and are addressing rabbis and future rabbis in terms of the contemporary ideological encounter with secularism. Each author also directs himself to the educated lay reader in an attempt to engage synagogue members ideologically. Both works are informed by considerable scholarship and philosophical learning, although neither work amounts to a work of philosophy per se. Each in its own way seeks to redefine programmatically the nature of Jewish identity today. Each author inclines to a traditionalist perspective, articulating the beauties of Jewish tradition for contemporary thinking Jews. Finally, and most importantly, both of these books amount to major restatements of the tensions between Jewish tradition and modern culture—seeking to incoporate the claims of modernity and its ethos of secularism, autonomy and personal conscience, and democratic norms within the rubric of Jewish tradition and to communicate the values of tradition in ways that will be salient to Jews living in the modern world.

Yet, if both works share similar points of departure, they clash sharply over conclusions, definitions, and understandings of Jewish values and identity. These differences far transcend the usual distinctions between Orthodox and Conservative Judaism. Rather, they amount to statements of profound conflict and a parting of the ways over the nature of authority in Jewish tradition. In that sense, to the

Reprinted from *Judaism,* Winter 1993.

extent that each author writes from the perspective of his own movement—Lamm that of Orthodoxy and Gillman that of Conservative Judaism—although neither claims official status as movement spokesman, these books communicate the impression that the gulf between Conservative and Orthodox Judaism has widened considerably.

As president of Yeshiva University, Lamm sets forth to explain the mission and motto of the institution that he heads. Long considered the flagship of Modern Orthodoxy, Yeshiva mandates a dual curriculum of religion and secular studies. In the 1960s, Yeshiva felt little compulsion to justify secular education as a worthy pursuit. On the contrary, its leaders and faculty boldly proclaimed the excitement of synthesis—integrating the best values of Torah and Western culture. This synthesis sharply distinguished itself from both those who rejected secular values entirely, save for vocational purposes, and from those who embraced uncritically all facets of contemporary culture. Rather, Yeshiva sought to develop an integrated Jewish personality—one at home both in the world of the Talmud and in that of Kierkegaard, and struggling to determine what, if any, relationships existed between the two.

However, as Lamm notes in his Preface, the idea of *Torah U'Madda* (Torah and secular knowledge) has come under increasing attack in recent years. The intellectual climate within American Orthodoxy often restricts the desirability of secular education to the strictly utilitarian purposes of enabling one to earn a living. Lamm seeks to engage these right-wing critics of *Torah U'madda* and to restore a sense of mission and excitement to Yeshiva's ideals.

His point of departure is Jewish law, which remains binding as the core aspect of contemporary Jewish identity. To be sure, Lamm understands *halakhah* as, at best, minimum Judaism. However, the halakhic framework is essential for maintaining Jewish tradition and identity in the modern world.

Within that primacy of Torah and *halakhah,* Lamm mounts an eloquent plea for the role and place of secular education. Heavily influenced by Maimonides and the hasidic doctrine of Divine immanence permeating all of Creation, he argues that Torah knowledge includes secular knowledge, which is all a part of the cosmic Divine holiness. Although this argument closely parallels Maimonides' elevation of secular education, or, specifically, the study of general philosophy, into a religious imperative, Lamm is perhaps most brilliant and original in evoking mystical and hasidic sources to address these issues.

Given his defense of secular education within Torah, he proceeds to outline three possibilities for the outcome of the encounter between *Torah* and *Madda*. Following Samson Raphael Hirsch, we should strive for coexistence—with little interaction between these two types of knowledge. Ze'ev Falk argues for a Hegelian synthesis, in which the theory of *Torah* and its antithesis of *Madda* will clash in a higher understanding, or synthesis, of Judaism and modern scholarship. Lamm himself prefers a model of symbiosis in which each world will enhance the other but will stop short of significantly altering its counterpart.

Lamm's program, in short, sets forth an ideological vision of education today at Yeshiva University. Although he concedes that not all will accept this vision of *Madda* as containing value in itself, all will allocate at least an instrumental or utilitarian role for the presence of secular education within Yeshiva's curriculum.

Yet, if this work aims towards a new restatement of the encounter of tradition and modernity, it abandons, in many ways, many of the claims of synthesis set forth by Modern Orthodox exponents. Most strikingly, Lamm ignores all references to contradictions or conflicts between secular knowledge and Torah knowledge. Certainly, for example, one may claim that knowledge of archaeology will enrich our understanding of the Bible. But Lamm offers the serious student of archaeology little or no guidance should archaeological research contradict traditionalist assumptions about Scripture.

More generally, Lamm slights the entire tradition of academic Jewish studies or *Wissenschaft des Judentums*. Although he unabashedly acknowledges its presence and importance, his only advice to the serious Jewish historian is to consider whether knowledge of Torah might enrich the historian's craft—a rather superficial exhortation to the practitioners of *Wissenschaft* that they might benefit from knowledge of Talmud and Midrash—but no guidelines as to whether historicist findings and research can be absorbed by Torah even if they contradict aspects of its literal meaning.

This slighting of academic Jewish studies may explain the most striking omission in Lamm's treatment: the absence of even the slightest reference to Nachman Krochmal, perhaps the most profound exponent of systhesis among modern Jewish thinkers. Krochmal saw his mission as sensitizing contemporary Orthodoxy to the importance of time and historical scholarship. For him, history connoted the essential and critical challenge to traditional faith. In evoking, for his major philosophical work, the Maimonidean title of a modern "Guide for the Perplexed," Krochmal underscored the need for a new synthesis—not between Torah and Greek philosophy but between Torah and historical criticism. This new version of synthesis amounts to a plea for freedom of inquiry and research, coupled with a theology of history which perceives the Divine Spirit as working within history. Krochmal's synthesis, in short, seeks to include historian and believer within a single model while accepting the integrity of both. Regrettably, Lamm's silence on Krochmal underscores a more general bias against permitting secular values to influence traditional Jewish thought, as well as a particular desire to minimize conflict between the world of *Torah* and the world of *Madda.* Although the teachings of *Torah* can profitably be applied to the major ethical and intellectual dilemmas of contemporary times, Lamm allocates little room for the potential influence of secular culture upon the formulation and shaping of *Torah* values.

In short, Lamm mounts an eloquent plea for the role of *Madda* within the world of *Torah.* He aims to persuade Orthodoxy's ideological right-wing both to respect the pursuit of *Madda,* and, programmatically, to accept that the practice of *Torah* and *Madda* need not be alien to the world of *Roshei Yeshivah.* In this latter sense, Lamm's work should be placed in the more general context of Orthodoxy's shift to the ideological Right. In other words, even as Lamm seeks to define a "Centrist" Orthodoxy, other voices within Yeshiva call for increased isolation from the general society and culture. In seeking to placate these voices, he minimizes the intellectual doubts raised by modern science and historical scholarship as well as the excitement and challenge of wrestling with two competing claims or avenues for truth and the effort to find common ground between them. Lamm's ideological redefinition goes so far even as to legitimize the instrumentalist or utilitarian view of secular education, which the author himself denigrates.

To be sure, it may succeed in legitimizing Centrist Orthodoxy for the Orthodox Right. It fails, however, to address the central question of modern Jewish identity: why be Jewish in a world in which the claims of modern culture are so attractive and skepticism towards traditional values is so rampant?

The sociological context, of course, is critical, for Modern Orthodoxy remains an embattled group. It continues to suffer the reproaches of those on the Right who pillory it as a phony or watered-down version of traditional Judaism. Lamm's efforts to maintain Modern Orthodoxy's integrity and vitality therefore clearly merit communal support.

Yet, precisely given this context, Lamm's perception of *Torah U'Madda* appears too limited. Yeshiva's uniqueness lies in its capacity to transcend becoming a yeshivah by day and a college by night. Even Lamm's right-wing critics have long sanctioned evening college courses. Rather, a true synthesis represents a sincere effort to grapple with the challenges of modern culture, to take with equal seriousness the respective claims of tradition and modernity, to explore secular culture for its potential to enhance our understanding of Judaic text and tradition, and to apply Jewish values to contemporary, social and ethical issues. That route, to be sure, is perilous. The claims of modern culture are so powerful that Orthodoxy fears, correctly, for future Jewish continuity. Yet, Yeshiva's distinctiveness lies precisely in its capacity to traverse that exciting, albeit dangerous, path.

If Lamm seeks to claim ground on which *Torah* values permit encounter with general culture, Neil Gillman emphasizes those avenues by which modern Jews may become inspired by *Torah* teachings. Like Lamm, Gillman is concerned with the encounter between tradition and modernity. He, too, is biased in favor of tradition. Unlike Lamm, however, Gillman is compelled to question how Jewish tradition—the "Sacred Fragments"—has been reshaped by modern values.

To be sure, the primary object of *Sacred Fragments* is personal rather than programmatic. Gillman seeks to empower lay readers to develop their own theologies—informed, of course, by millennia of Jewish teachings. The book clearly emanates from encounters over a decade with Conservative synagogue members, and seeks to bridge the gap between the rich Judaic scholarship that prevails at the Jewish

Theological Seminary and the paucity of ideological controversy and Judaic knowledge that prevails within Conservative synagogues. If anything, Gillman's major contribution—both in this book and in his teaching and public lectures—has been to energize Conservative lay leaders and rabbis in the field on the ideological definition of Conversative Judaism, in turn strengthening the ideological salience of the movement to its critical constituencies.

Moreover, many of Gillman's insights will benefit even those most richly versed in Jewish literature and thought. He demonstrates, for example, how deeply Abraham Joshua Heschel was indebted to Yehudah Halevi. Similarly, his chapter on Jewish eschatology must be considered one of the most brilliant treatments of that perplexing topic.

Yet, dominating this virtual catalogue of Jewish theology, is a single startling, and most controversial, thesis. Gillman's starting point is that "Torah is entirely a Midrash"—a myth shattered by the onslaught of modernity, yet portions of which remain sacred and continue to speak to us as modern Jews.

In particular, it is modern critical scholarship which has shattered, for Gillman, our traditionalist myth. He claims that we must choose between a fundamentalist reading of Scripture in which everything remains sacred, and the critical reading, which challenges us to recover the "sacred fragments." Because tradition functions as a myth, it by no means is irrelevant. The rituals and symbols of a myth are often most compelling—*vide* the power of Thanksgiving or the American flag. It does mean, however, that the authority of determining Jewish practice has shifted from the word of God, expressed through the rabbis, to the people of Israel and the community, for, ultimately, their actions will determine what claims a tradition shattered by modern scholarship may still exercise upon us.

By myth, Gillman does not mean fiction or falsehood. He defines myth as a structure—a vehicle by which the community makes sense of its experience. In that sense, the term *midrash* is probably more appropriate and certainly less threatening to the traditionalist reader. What is new is Gillman's willingness to subsume the entire corpus of tradition under the category of myth or *midrash*. Tradition is not binding because it was commanded by God; that, for Gillman, would amount to fundamentalism. Nor is it binding because it represents the historical experience of the Jews—a criterion long favored by Conservative Jewish thinkers. Rather, it is today our challenge as modern Jews to find ways in which tradition can speak to us meaningfully. In other words, can its myths become our myths?

To be sure, Gillman makes no claim to a redefinition of Conservative Judaism. He occupies no official position within the movement save as one trained in it and as a prominent member of the JTS faculty. Therefore, unlike Lamm, he sets forth no institutional programme. Yet, one cannot ignore the implications of this book, as the work of a prominent Conservative theologian in dialogue with Conservative congregations, rabbis, and rabbinical students, for the movement's future.

First, and perhaps foremost, is the question of whether Jewish law remains normative and binding, or is it only part of the myth—some of which remains sacred while other aspects may be discarded. Gillman insists that Judaism remains a halakhic system but maintains that it is the community that will decide for itself what is a mizvah and what is purely optional. Clearly, Gillman's preferences lie with Rosenzweig and Heschel, for whom *halakhah* remained central to modern Jewish identity. Yet, by including *halakhah* within *midrash,* he leaves open the possibility for downgrading its importance the way we might otherwise disregard unreasonable *midrashim.*

For example, we may take three of the most divisive issues on the contemporary Jewish agenda— patrilineal descent, rabbinic officiation at interfaith marriages, and the acceptance of homosexual rabbis. The Reform and Reconstructionist movements have adopted relatively liberal positions on these issues on the grounds that *halakhah* is no longer binding. It exercises a voice rather than a veto. Orthodoxy rejects liberal positions on these issues as violations of Jewish law. Generally, the Conservative movement has sided with the Orthodox on these questions, partly on the grounds of history, and partly on the grounds of *halakhah.* Yet, Gillman rejects the Orthodox position as fundamentalist and locates authority within the community of Conservative Jews. Assuming, as recent research indicates, that the majority of Conservative laity would favor patrilineal descent and, perhaps, rabbinic officiation, Gillman's arguments virtually mandate redefinition of the movement's positions along these more liberal lines. Aside from further blurring distinctions between Conservative and Reform Judaism, such statements would signal the end of any remaining movement claims to represent halakhic Judaism. For, as Rabbi Joel Roth, one of the most perceptive exponents of Conservative Judaism as a halakhic movement, writes,

> [O]nce talk of the absence of a system, or of *a* halachic system rather than *the* halachic system takes hold, . . . they do violence to the halachic system, and break the chain of authentic halachic authority . . . Since the rabbinic period, normative Judaism has been halachic. And it can remain normative only insofar as it remains halachic. If the "defenders of the faith" of our generation think that they meet the challenges of modernity when they advocate ideologies that undermine halacha and the halachic process, they are mistaken. Such ideological stances do not meet the challenges of modernity, they *fail* to meet its challenges.[1]

Significantly, Gillman's position departs from that of Solomon Schechter, a founding architect of Conservative Judaism. Schechter also argued that the community determines norms and standards. Yet, by the term "Catholic Israel," Schechter and his successors meant the community of *committed* Jews. In other words, *halakhah* can evolve only through a process and dialogue with the halakhic community. Gillman, in pronounced contrast, transfers authority to the community *generally,* irrespective of halakhic parameters. Although Gillman repeatedly argues in favor of tradition, his position concerning authority owes more to Mordecai Kaplan than to Schechter.

Equally problematic is the radical pluralism which informs Gillman's work. Myths themselves tend to be highly relativist, for what is salient to one individual may be heresy to another. Gillman leaves us with little guidance as to why we should select one myth at the expense of others. His theme—that "the text can come to mean whatever the community wants it to mean"—challenges us to question what are the limits of pluralism. Are there universal truths to Judaism if Torah is entirely a *midrash?*

This radical pluralism is troubling on two counts. First, Conservative

Judaism has always claimed authenticity in its understanding of Judaism and, therefore, has been critical of the other movements. For Gillman, the difference between Conservative Judaism and the other movements now becomes more a matter of personal taste rather than a conflict over basic values.

Even more telling is Norman Lamm's criticism that "if everything is kosher, then nothing is kosher." As laudable as it may be to include as many individuals and perceptions as possible under a Judaic umbrella, it has been the power of Jewish ideas and values that have made the Jews distinctive as a people. We cannot be all things to all people. Rather, the distinctiveness of Judaic ideas has been precisely the ability to underscore those ideas that we support, and negate those that we reject. Advocates of religious pluralism, to be sure, seek to cast their net widely. Yet, for Gillman, the parameters of the net lie entirely in the hands of the community. We are left, in short, with little sense of what, if any, are the limits of pluralism.

This theme emerges most strikingly in Gillman's chapter on Jewish rituals. There, he clearly aligns Conservatie Judaism with the liberal movements, in pronounced contrast to Orthodoxy. Gillman argues for greater utilization of ritual in personal and communal life. However, in emphasizing the symbolic importance of ritual, he abandons its binding and authoritative quality. At this point, differences between Conservative and Reform Judaism become primarily one of degree rather than of doctrine.

A traditionalist reader who perceives Judaism as halakhic, yet remains influenced by and sensitive to the claims of modern scholarship, will find himself or herself theologically homeless within these books. Both authors purport to address Jews caught between the attractions of tradition and modernity. Neither will satisfy those who align with halakhic teaching but perceive modernity as a source of values with the power to enhance Judaism. Both books compel us to choose between tradition and modernity. A true synthesis of both value systems escapes each author—albeit for different reasons.

Perhaps both authors are only reflecting current sociological realities. Orthodoxy clearly is moving rightward, and Lamm's book represents a retreat from the bold and venturesome vision of synthesis so popular a generation ago. Gillman's work articulates what many Conservative lay people do—what Jacob Staub refers to as "the non-ideological nature of the attachment of so many of its members, who simply don't care, or act as if they don't care, about *halakha.*"[2] These prevailing attitudes of Conservative laity stand in direct contrast to the halakhic norms emanating from the Jewish Theological Seminary. In this sense, Gillman's book supports what many of the movement's left-wing critics, particularly those among the *havurot,* have long advocated—a shift in authority within the movement from rabbi as halakhic decisor to lay leadership as communal builders.

In the sociological sense, then, these works signify the growing distance in the Jewish community between the Orthodox and non-Orthodox. The problem of religious polarization will, doubtless, continue to dominate the Jewish communal agenda. At least as important, however, is the necessity for an ideology that will energize those Jews for whom *halakhah* remains authoritative, yet for whom the claims of modern culture are sufficiently powerful so as to warrant serious consideration not only in their own right but also in their capacity to influence Judaic values. That group, to be sure, may be numerically small. It does, however, have the capacity to serve as a bridge between the movements and to overcome prevailing religious polarization. Moreover, it is precisely as a constituency caught in the dialectic of tradition and modernity that it promises the capacity to mold a distinctive Jewish identity anchored in the authority of Jewish values yet influenced by modern culture, norms, and critiques.

Notes

1. See Joel Roth, "Halakhah and History" in Nina Beth Cardin and David Wolf Silverman, eds., *The Seminary at One Hundred* (New York: The Jewish Theological Seminary and the Rabbinical Assembly, 1987), pp. 287–288.

2. Jacob J. Staub, "Reflections on the Conservative Movement," ibid., p. 302.

Imagining the Jewish Future:
Essays and Response

Edited by David A. Teutsch

As Yogi Berra has observed, "Predictions are very difficult, especially about the future." Nevertheless, the Reconstructionist Rabbinical College convened an impressive gathering of rabbis, social scientists, and social theorists to establish an "Institute for the Jewish Future." This volume reports the fruits of its initial conference challenging the Jewish community to reconceptualize its self-image in light of new and ever-changing conditions and realities.

The overall tone of the book is surprisingly upbeat. In many ways, the authors have been influenced by Charles Silberman's important book, *A Certain People,* although most would agree it was an overly optimistic forecast. Regrettably, Silberman himself did not submit a reconsideration of his thesis in light of the National Jewish Population Study and subsequent communal discussion. In general, the authors celebrate the ethos of diversity in modern culture, find strength in "alternative" Jewish institutions and structures, and articulate a vision of a thriving Jewish community rooted in a pluralist society. Particularly inspiring is the concluding essay by Arnold Eisen seeking to express a religious language of norms, values, and expectations acceptable to liberals, yet running counter to the radical individualism so prevalent in contemporary America. Similarly, Jonathan Woocher takes seriously the challenge of envisioning a future Jewish education sufficiently exciting to make one wish one could actually *return* to the classroom!

Some of the predictions, however, are simply light-headed. Arthur Waskow coolly forecasts a comprehensive Middle East peace by 1994. Arthur Green acknowledges that such a peace will come about only by international imposition and indeed celebrates a single world order capable of controlling population growth by mandating its will. Both authors underrate the continuing importance of tensions with the Third World in the aftermath of the Cold War—much as liberals underesti-

Reprinted with permission from *Contemporary Jewry,* 1992.

mated the importance of tensions with the Soviet Union during the Cold War. Similarly, Egon Mayer looks forward to a Jewish community with far greater numbers because of the inclusion of mixed-married, non-Jews, and "half Jews" (sic) without telling us what, if anything, will remain of Judaic distinctiveness in a world in which boundaries between Jew and Gentile have been so blurred. "Outreach" to these groups presumably will solve the problem of Jewish continuity irrespective of Judaic content and message.

Perhaps most controversial is Martha Ackelsberg's essay denying the existence of Jewish family norms. Her essay, in effect, looks backward to a time when all the alternatives to the family appeared preferable to marriage and parenting. Instead, she seeks to broaden the parameters of family life to include all forms of living arrangements including extramarital sexual relations as long as they are characterized by "mutuality" and "respect." Thankfully, Elliot Dorff rejects this bizarre vision by arguing that it lacks norms and abandons any sense of Judaic ideals.

Yet, the most serious flaws in this volume are of omission rather than commission. Absent is any Israeli perspective on the Jewish future, despite the fact that most of the authors presuppose a continuing Israel-Diaspora relationship. An even more glaring omission is the failure to include any Orthodox thinkers even by way of response to the essays and despite increased evidence of an Orthodox revival.

The editor opens the volume with a plea for pluralism and inclusion. Surprisingly, that view excludes some of the most vibrant and committed sectors of world Jewry today. In the "post-halakhic" world order that the Institute for the Jewish Future celebrates, it appears that nothing can be learned from those engaged in building a Jewish state and those who, with considerable success, articulate and transmit the binding claims of Jewish tradition and values.

To be sure, many of the respondents to these essays acknowledge these problems. In addition to the critique by Dorff, both Martin Raffel and Michael Paley underscore the continuing importance of Modern Orthodoxy in building a creative Jewish future. Nevertheless, the omission of any Orthodox representatives within this volume undermines the editor's claims for pluralism and the politics of inclusion. Regrettably, Yitz Greenberg's jeremiad warning of two Jewish peoples is indeed corroborated by this effort of futurology.

Whither American Jewry?
Community and Polity: The Organizational Dynamics of American Jewry

by Daniel J. Elazar

Portrait of American Jews:
The Last Half of the 20th Century

by Samuel C. Heilman

These new books, by Daniel Elazar and Samuel Heilman respectively, seek to understand American Jewry by placing it within a contextual framework. Elazar's book is a reissue and update of his classic guide to the organizational structure of the American Jewish community. Heilman, best-known as a master of participant observation of American Jewry, here surveys a range of sociological studies to assess the past half century of American Jewish life. Heilman uses a chronological framework to trace patterns of American Jewish mobility, identity, and family life. Elazar has expanded his earlier edition to include recent changes in American Jewish communal life and, in particular, the growing involvement of American Jewry in the world Jewish polity.

In the 1980s, observers were split between survivalists, who bemoaned Jewish assimilation, and transformationists, who saw few dangers to future Jewish vitality. In the latter view, intermarriage, at best, would increase Jewish numbers via conversion, and, at worst, would result in no lossees, for unconverted spouses would raise children within the Jewish faith. Silberman (1985), later supported by the work of Cohen (1988) and Goldscheider (1986), was paradigmatic of this school of thought. Survivalists, particularly Schmelz and DellaPergola (1989), Hertzberg (1989), and Liebman (1989), challenged this view, arguing that a community insufficiently committed to Jewish religion

---

Reprinted with permission from *Contemporary Jewry,* Volume 16, 1996.

held out little hope for Jewish continuity. Among Jewish organizations, the American Jewish Committee noted the presence of both views, but inclined towards the survivalist school of thought perceiving intermarriage as threat and danger rather than opportunity (Bayme and Rosen, 1994).

The release of the 1990 National Jewish Population survey (NJPS), at least in the public perception, loudly proclaimed the dangers of assimilation for future Jewish continuity. Intermarriage had increased significantly, Jewish affiliation had decreased, and at most a minority of mixed-marrieds were making efforts to raise their children Jewishly. In effect, NJPS sent the transformationists into retreat. Cohen, for one, abandoned his earlier optimism concerning American Jewry and confirmed the popular perception of a Jewish community threatened by assimilation and intermarriage (Wertheimer, Liebman and Cohen, 1996). For American Jewry the primary threats and challenges were now internal rather than external.

Heilman's assessment, in particular, gives transformationism an appropriate burial, substituting for it a bipolar view of American Jewry as undergoing the best and the worst of times simultaneously. Never before in Diaspora Jewish history have Jews enjoyed such levels of acceptability. As anti-Semitism declined in post-war America, significant test cases were McCarthyism, the Rosenberg case, and the George Wallace phenomenon, all of which were markedly free of anti-Semitic agitation, Jews encountered fewer and fewer barriers to their full integration in American society. For example, despite comprising a very small percentage within the general population, Jews formed 20 percent of the faculties at elite American universities.

Moreover, the blessings of American cultural pluralism have afforded Jews the complete freedom to develop as Jews. American Jews today enjoy unprecedented opportunities to lead a creative Jewish life, evidenced by the growth of day schools, Jewish scholarship, and the advanced study of Judaic civilization at virtually every American campus of note. Yet, amidst these opportunities lies the depressing reality that only a minority of Jews have availed themselves of them. Greater scholarship of the elite few coexists with the Judaic illiteracy of the masses. As Jews fought to fit into the general culture, Judaic distinctiveness declined. While day schools provide intense educational opportunities for a minority, supplementary schools, catering to the majority, experience a crisis of credibility owing to the paucity of classroom time, poor quality of instruction, and the secondary nature of the enterprise.

Surprisingly, American Jews were slow to recognize these realities. When the American Jewish Committee convened a national conference in 1983 on Jewish population growth to sound the alarm on declining Jewish numbers, the community of Jewish social scientists reacted with disdain, if not scorn. Some argued that numbers do not matter; only quality counted. Others claimed that demographic policies were futile at best, counterproductive at worst. The transformationist school provided considerable solace, claiming Jews have little reason to fear assimilation. Some lay leaders found refuge in anti-Semitism, real or imagined, as a perpetual reminder of their Jewishness. Still others lauded the unprecedented levels of Jewish activism proclaiming Jewish successes in marshaling political support for Israel and Soviet Jewry and defining Jewish renewal through political activism. Orthodox Jews hailed the survival of Orthodoxy despite all the predictions of its disappearance only a generation ago. Historians noted gleefully how *Look Magazine*, with its 1964 cover story "The Vanishing American Jew," had since vanished twice while American Jewry persevered.

These triumphs, however, cannot sustain the Jewish future. External bases such as anti-Semitism or political activism cannot substitute for religious commitment. As for the Orthodox, they have in fact declined numerically, and the much-heralded "returnees to Judaism" comprise at most ten percent of today's Orthodox Jewry.

The real problem of American Jewry is, indeed, symbolized by mixed marriage. Out-marriage is acceptable to over 80 percent of both Jews and Gentiles. The Jew, in short, has become a desirable in-law, and therein lies the symbol of successful Jewish integration into American society.

Yet that very success simultaneously signals an end to Judaic distinctiveness. Many mixed-married Jewish spouses will cease practicing Judaism. Absent conversion of the non-Jewish spouse, Judaism may continue only on the most tenuous of terms. Even the welcome participation of unconverted Gentile spouses in Jewish activities may make it difficult if not impossible for the community to discourage interfaith marriage and may so blur the lines between Jew and Christian as to, in Heilman's (p. 135) words, "be devastating to the cultural integrity of the Jewish people."

American Jewry, in short, is likely to experience significant losses in the decades ahead. Many of those losses are virtually inevitable given the declining commitments to Judaism and increased acceptability of Jews within American society. On a personal level, the losses will be extraordinarily painful, often touching the families of some of the most committed and activist of Jews. On a communal level, the losses will weaken the fabric of Jewish institutional life, which Elazar rightly praises as the most fully developed network of Jewish institutions in Jewish history. Fewer numbers will mean fewer participants and fewer contributors. Contrary to Cohen's (1994) forecast of a Jewish community that will be "leaner and meaner," Heilman argues that in institutional terms, less cannot mean more. Even if the organizational structure is impressive, as Elazar confirms, structures require greater boundaries and clarity of content for a minority culture such as the Jews to remain distinctive.

Elazar's analysis of institutional structure reflects the major changes in Jewish life since the publication of his original edition in the mid-1970s. He demonstrates how the increase in mixed-marriage has affected communal structures. Conversely, the renewal of Orthodoxy has led to greater Orthodox participation in Jewish public affairs on both volunteer and professional levels. However, for Elazar, the major transformation in Jewish life since the 1970s has been the technological revolution enabling global communications and enhancing interdependence between Jewish communities worldwide. As a result, increasingly American Jewry has become intertwined with the world Jewish polity with consequent opportunities to create even more intensively Jewish communal structures. Elazar, however, acknowledges the limited capacity of the community, especially Federation structures built around an ideology of consensus, to ensure Jewish continuity. In an era of freedom of choice and individual autonomy, the organized community can at most "stack the decks" in favor of Jewish choices.

What then of the future? Heilman concludes his assessment on a profoundly pessimistic note, suggesting that immigration to Israel may indeed be the sole vehicle of ensuring Jewish continuity. In effect, he confirms the Zionist analysis of the inevitable withering away of the Diaspora, in this case owing to assimilation rather than to anti-Semitism.

Yet the prognosis may be premature, if not unduly pessimistic. The question remains open as to whether American Jewry has heard the wake-up call of the 1990 NJPS, much less whether it has reacted effectively to it. Some initiatives are being launched to strengthen Jewish life, particularly in local communities, as Jewish Federations slowly change their agendas to meet the internal crisis of continuity. Among Jewish family foundations, Charles R. Bronfman seeks to make Israel experiences accessible to every Jewish teenager, while the Wexner Foundation has sponsored educational programs designed to create new cadres of Jewishly committed professional and lay leadership. Although many are skeptical concerning the capacity of the Jewish community to meet its crisis from within, it is far too early to close the book on American Jewry. Jewish continuity, I believe, will be measured through the future viability of the Conservative and Reform movements, which represent the largest sectors of American Jewry. To the extent these movements preserve their members Judaically, future Jewish continuity is safeguarded. Although some danger signs exist, particularly the tendency towards a bland universalism within Reform Judaism, owing to a well-intentioned desire to attract interfaith couples, both movements are enrolling large numbers of Jews interested in the power of Judaism to provide community and personal meaning. If the Reform and Conservative movements can maintain Judaic distinctiveness, articulate a language of norms, values, commitments, and expectations, and provide opportunities for communal fellowship and spiritual meaning, they will be more rather than less likely to retain their adherents.

This, then, is the policy debate confronting American Jewry, which Heilman too glibly dismisses in favor of *aliyah*. Nevertheless, he, like Elazar, clearly prefers the survivalists to the transformationists. The warning signs are, to be sure, clear. American Jewry faces some painful, yet, at the same time, promising choices. Both Heilman and Elazar seem to favor in-reach strategies, targeting those who have signaled some interest in leading a Jewish life rather than outreach, chasing the unaffiliated who have, in many cases, opted not to lead a Jewish life.

These strategies suggest that some losses are inevitable, but that the continued existence of the community may be secured. Elazar's model of concentric circles of Jews of differing levels of commitment is especially useful. At the core more Jews are engaging Jewishly. At the periphery large numbers are opting out entirely. The middles of Jewish life are in question, those who want Jewish continuity, but lack the content to make it meaningful. The challenge for the Conservative and Reform movement is to retain these middles and bring them closer to the core for whom the rhythms of leading a Jewish life operate on a daily basis.

Some signs exist that the Conservative movement already recognizes this. Conservative Judaism has addressed intermarriage forthrightly, emphasizing intermarriage prevention and conversion to Judaism. Conservative leaders underscore the importance of Jewish norms and religious commitments. Conservative synagogues are striving to redesign themselves as institutional structures enabling Jewish parents to raise Jewish children.

The Reform movement, too, stands at a crossroad. Some Reform leaders emphasize programs of Judaic literacy and increased religious commitment. The recent controversial decision by the Union of American Hebrew Congregations to deny Jewish education to those receiving instruction in another faith signals the need for greater demarcation between Jew and Gentile. To be sure, the pervasiveness of mixed marriage within Reform ranks raises the specter of a Judaism so diluted of its distinctiveness as to be meaningless. The current debate within the Reform movement over rabbinic officiation at mixed marriages signals the divide over these issues between traditionalists and universalists.

The answers must lie, I believe, in serious Judaism. Well-educated, serious, and literate Conservative and Reform Jews are most unlikely to assimilate. For that reason, Jewish communal resources ought be increasingly directed towards strengthening those movements and their current members. In turn, and for the same reason, the critical importance of pluralism in Jewish life must be underscored. Orthodox leaders would do well to recognize that the primary threats to Jewish identity emanate from religious indifference rather than from religious pluralism.

In short, American Jewry has succeeded in advancing its agenda of securing a home in America. The question for its future is whether it has the will to build a Judaically authentic culture sufficiently compelling to articulate a language of norms, commitments, expectations, and demands of its adherents, alongside its place in the broader American society, a duality that the unique experience of America affords.

Failure to articulate such a language will connote an end to Judaic distinctiveness, and a sad commentary that the impressive structures so brilliantly analzyed by Elazar cannot survive absent the members and serious Jewish content that Heilman insists, correctly, are necessary.

References

Bayme, Steven and Gladys Rosen (eds.). 1994. *The Jewish Family and Jewish Continuity.* Hoboken: KTAV and the American Jewish Committee.

Cohen, Steven M. 1988. *American Assimilation or Jewish Revival.* Bloomington and Indianapolis: Indiana University Press.

———. 1994. "Why Intermarriage Might Not Threaten Jewish Continuity." *Moment* 19 (December): 54–57, 89, 95.

Goldscheider, Calvin. 1986. *Jewish Continuity and Change.* Bloomington: Indiana University Press.

Hertzberg, Arthur. 1989. *The Jews in America.* New York: Simon and Schuster.

Liebman, Charles. 1989. "The Quality of American Jewish Life: A Grim Outlook." In *Facing the Future: Essays on Contemporary Jewish Life,* edited by Steven Bayme. New York: KTAV and the American Jewish Committee: 50–71.

Schmelz, Uziel O. and Sergio DellaPergola. 1989. "Basic Trends in American Jewish Demography." Pp. 72–111 in *Facing the Future: Essays on Contemporary Jewish Life,* edited by Steven Bayme. New York: KTAV and the American Jewish Committee.

Silberman, Charles. 1985. *A Certain People.* New York: Summit Books.

Wertheimer, Jack, Charles Liebman, and Steven M. Cohen. 1996. "How to Save American Jews." *Commentary* 101 (January): 47–51.

Three-Part Strategy for Intermarriage:
It All Begins With a Date.
Preserving Jewishness in Your Family

by Alan Silverstein

Intermarriage symbolizes the dilemma of contemporary American Jewry. It suggests both the acceptibility of Jews in American society and, conversely, the crisis Jews now confront of ensuring their own future continuity. As a result, communal debate has centered around appropriate responses to intermarriage, including conversion to Judaism and outreach to mixed-marrieds and their families.

Some argue that intermarriage is now inevitable and efforts to prevent it are futile at best and harmful at worst. Therefore, these advocates urge a new focus upon outreach and inclusion.

Conversely, others argue that abandoning prevention efforts and becoming neutral toward mixed-marriages will itself increase the incidence of intermarriage by declaring its acceptibility and, on the level of Jewish values, constitute an unconscionable abandonment of Jewish tradition and historical perspective.

Moreover, these advocates warn that intensified efforts at outreach may waste limited communal resources and may, albeit with the best of intentions, create a climate within the community in which it becomes difficult if not impossible to discourage interfaith marriage.

Liberal Jews are often inclined to the former position and traditionalists to the latter although, to be sure, there are many exceptions to this generalization as well as considerable overlap between the two groups.

Within this communal debate, the "swing vote" lies primarily within the Conservative movement, and, in this sense, these two volumes by Rabbi Alan Silverstein, president of the Rabbinical Assembly, constitute an official movement position of Conservative Judaism and its leading institutions.

The volumes comprise a project of the leadership council of Conser-

Reprinted with permission from the *Jewish Advocate*, November 10–16, 1995.

vative Judaism and are introduced by the executive vice president of the United Synagogue and the chancellor of the Jewish Theological Seminary. Both volumes focus on a three-part policy of intermarriage prevention, conversion of the non-Jewish spouse where intermarriage has occurred, and continued outreach to mixed-marrieds and their families so as to maintain the possibility of conversion to Judaism. Taken together, the volumes align the Conservative movement with the traditionalist camp advocating continued resistance to intermarriage.

This Conservative approach is distinctive in many ways. First, Silverstein underscores the position adopted by United Synagogue Youth requiring officers of the Conservative youth movement to refrain from interdating. Moreover, Silverstein articulates Conservative Judaism's sustained opposition to patrilineal descent as a criterion for defining Jewishness, despite much-heralded predictions that Conservative Judaism would soon follow the lead of the liberal movements in embracing the principle of patrilineality. Perhaps most importantly, Silverstein insists upon the importance of conversion as the primary antidote to the reality of mixed-marriage.

These positions hardly are popular among the rank and file of the Jewish community generally or its readership. Expressing opposition to mixed-marriage and insisting upon conversion as a response risk alienating the mixed-marrieds as a potential constituency. Silverstein is not prepared to permit sociological reality to dictate Judaic principle. He does not see intermarriage as an opportunity when, in truth, it poses serious risks to the Jewish future.

Yet Silverstein succeeds in expressing these positions in ways concerned Jews everywhere will find welcome. He clarifies many seemingly obscure yet significant issues such as why Jews oppose "messianic Judaism" as a potential solution for mixed married couples wishing to celebrate both faiths. He explains why divorce rates among mixed-marrieds far exceed the rates for in-marrieds. One of his best chapters explains all the reasons for leading a Jewish life today. His appendices provide highly useful bibliographies and guides to program resources.

Most importantly, Silverstein urges parents to speak up in defense of their beliefs. Silence may postpone problems and buy some degree of family peace but will not ensure the Jewish future.

Rather parental responsibility lies in teaching children to choose Jewish social environments, to build Jewish families, and to lead rich and intensive Jewish lives. He urges that Jewish youth defer dating if there are no Jews to date and to choose colleges and universities at least partly on the criteria of Jewish population density on campus and richness and availability of campus Jewish life.

To be sure, there are problems with these manuals. Silverstein is probably overly optimistic about perserving Jewishness in the mixed-marriage home, when, absent conversion, 90 percent of current mixed-marrieds are most unlikely to have Jewish grandchildren. Similarly, in urging parents to resist mixed-marriage, he understates how dissonant such resistance is with American currents of universalism and romantic love. In addition, the volumes are marred by unnecessary repetitions. The generally optimistic tone of these volumes does offer considerable hope, but that optimism may be rooted more in wishful thinking than in current realities.

Yet one ought not understate their significance, both in terms of their content and in their expressing the official position of American Judaism's largest religious stream.

Thus far, the Jewish community has made little headway on its much-touted "Jewish continuity agenda." Although the rhetoric has changed, "business as usual," with some important exceptions, prevails. Jewish continuity advocates have failed thus far to alter significantly communal priorities and articulate normative statements of Jewish values, commitments, expectations and obligations.

Jewish leaders want Jewish continuity but seemingly are unable and unwilling to pay the price for it—a price measured in cultural and religious commitments to leading a Jewish life that are at times dissonant with otherwise desirable components of American society generally.

For these reasons, Silverstein's volumes are invaluable both to Jewish parents seeking a language to transmit Judaism in the home and to Jewish leaders trying to formulate a Jewish continuity agenda. For both types of readers, his message is simple yet salient: There can be no Jewish continuity absent serious commitment to Judaism.

The "normative" strategy enriches the current debate over Jewish continuity. First, it insists upon Judaic content rather than a general language of inclusivity. Secondly, it advocates limited outreach to mixed-marrieds, but only when targeted to mixed-marrieds interested in leading a Jewish life and carefully designed so as to perserve the messages of endogamy and Jewish in-marriage.

Perhaps most movingly, Silverstein describes how it has been precisely his intensive involvement in outreach to mixed-marrieds that has convinced him of the necessity to concentrate efforts on intermarriage prevention and "inreach" to enrich the core of the Jewish future. Coming from the president of Conservative Judaism's Rabbinical Assembly, the "swing vote" in the Jewish continuity debate between traditionalists and liberals, that message is doubly welcome.

Jewish Power:
Inside the Jewish Establishment

by J. J. Goldberg

J. J. Goldberg's analysis of American Jewry is certain to elicit strong reactions. Some will be put off by the book's very title. Indeed, as Goldberg demonstrates, Jews have often felt uncomfortable about public discussion of Jewish power and influence. Others will criticize the book's political slant—Bill Clinton is termed the "most pro-Jewish President in history," while Richard Nixon remains an unrepentant anti-Semite. Still others will react defensively to the author's maverick thesis that Jewish organizations fail to represent grass-roots Jewish constituencies.

Yet readers who ignore this book because they disagree with its hypotheses will be missing a great deal. For one thing, Goldberg provides a good read—a splendid *tour d'horizon* of the organized American Jewish community. As one of the most experienced of journalists covering the American Jewish scene, he provides good vignettes of leading personalities and a useful guide to the behind-the-scenes workings of Jewish communal organizations. For Goldberg, the sources of Jewish influence in American society have rested primarily on money and the power of ideas rather than on numbers of Jews.

Goldberg's strength lies in his capacity to bring to life well-known but often poorly understood incidents. Thus he explains Rabbi Alexander Schindler's decision to embrace Prime Minister Menahem Begin. Schindler, a leader of Reform Judaism, might have been expected to reject Begin's hard-line policies. However, he felt Begin, in contrast to his predecessor, passionately cared about world Jewry. By embracing Begin shortly after his victory in the May 1977 Israeli elections, Schindler legitimized the Likud leadership in the eyes of American Jewry and the Carter administration. Jewish access to Washington

Reprinted with permission from the *Jewish Book World,* Vol. 14, No. 3, Winter 1996.

sources of power would serve Israel well in subsequent years at difficult moments in the American-Israeli relationship.

Similarly, Goldberg illuminates the much-debated role of Jews in the media. Unquestionably, many Jews occupy critical positions in the communications industry. Rarely, however, have these been committed or involved members of the Jewish community. Paradoxically, therefore, in Jewish eyes the media often have been hostile to Jewish interests, while to the general society Jewish names predominate in the industry.

This dual perspective on Jewish influence permeates Goldberg's entire analysis. American Jews often feel besieged in an unfriendly world. Gentiles, by contrast, envy Jewish influence and access to power. Both groups fail to recognize sufficiently that in a democracy minority groups can realize their ends only to the extent that their ideas are consonant with the prevailing values of the general society. Therefore, the key to Jewish power lies in the capacity of Jews to persuade American society of the desirability of Jewish political goals.

A good case in point is Goldberg's treatment of President Roosevelt and the Jews. Goldberg dismisses Jewish disappointment with Roosevelt, noting that Roosevelt's greatness lay in moving America from isolationism to interventionism. Specific measures intended to rescue Jews, no matter how strongly urged by American Jewry, could hold few hopes for success given their dissonance with the culture of the time. Postwar exercises in Roosevelt-bashing often have ignored his constructive leadership in bringing America into confrontation with Nazi Germany, especially given the political context of an isolationist American society.

Conversely, Goldberg details the remarkable decline in anti-Semitism in post-war America. For example, at the height of the Rosenberg case in the 1950s, only 5 percent of Americans identified Jews with Communists. Yet American Jews continued to perceive themselves as highly vulnerable. International silence during the crisis of May 1967 reawakened the myth of Jewish isolation. A series of books on the Holocaust underscored America's abandonment of the Jews. This myth of the Jews standing alone colored much of American Jewish political culture, particularly the movement to free Soviet Jewry and the self-identification of American Jews. Thus, Goldberg quotes a prominent Jewish leader that the opening of the United States Holocaust Memorial Museum constituted his proudest moment as an American Jew—a rather sad commentary on the meaning of being Jewish in contemporary America.

Therefore, Goldberg urges Jews to confront the reality of an American society that welcomes Jewish participation. Nor does he fear Jewish disappearance via assimilation, relying as he does upon estimates of intermarriage rates of below 40 percent. Rather he argues that the most critical danger facing the Jewish community is that Jews are losing interest in what the community is doing on their behalf. However, in dismissing reported intermarriage rates in excess of 50 percent, Goldberg understates the relationship between declining commitment to Judaism and declining Jewish influence.

Orthodox Jews, of course, constitute an exception to this trend. Yet American Orthodoxy fairs poorly in Goldberg's analysis. He treats Orthodox Jewry as monolithic in its opposition to the Middle East peace process, ignoring the third of American Orthodox Jews who favored the peace policies of Israel's Labor government. For Goldberg, American Orthodoxy originated among "fundamentalist Russian immigrants" who rejected accommodation to American culture. Surprisingly he has nothing to say of Modern Orthodox communal professionals working within secular Jewish organizations, who often help transform the Jewish identity and ethos of communal agencies.

Goldberg's chapter on black-Jewish relations is likely to garner the most attention. He argues that militants on both sides inflamed tensions while silencing moderates. Correctly, he criticizes both black and Jewish leadership for consistently insisting upon their status as victims. His argument fails, however, for its lapses into moral equivalence. In his view, Jewish racism constitutes the mirror image of black anti-Semitism. Contrary to Goldberg, however, Jews have consistently repudiated the racism of Meir Kahane—while, in contrast, black leaders found it far more difficult to marginalize Louis Farrakhan. Moreover, Goldberg at times distorts historical reality so as to balance his argument for militancy on both sides. Thus he claims that Israel demanded the ouster of UN Ambassador Andrew Young, when in fact Young was dismissed because he had violated the policies of his own State Department in 1979 in initiating contacts with the PLO and subsequently failing to inform his superiors. Similarly, Goldberg claims that it was wrong for Jews to label the 1991 Crown Heights disturbances as a "pogrom," for he argues the term refers only to government-sponsored actions. In fact, historians today generally agree that the Russian pogroms of the 1880s, unlike their counterparts twenty years later, were generally *not* government-inspired. Nevertheless, they clearly were pogroms. Lastly, Goldberg evokes Jewish opposition to the mayoral campaign of David Dinkins as evidence for Jewish racism, ignoring the well-founded doubts many non-racist Jews had concerning Dinkins' qualifications for the office.

These are, of course, trees within a larger forest. Readers must confront Goldberg's central thesis—the absence of democracy and true representation in organized Jewish life. In Goldberg's view, Jewish organizations, increasingly led by activist and committed Jews, are losing touch with their constituents. Rather than provide leadership, Jewish organizations invite apathy and disaffiliation.

Goldberg utilizes the case of convicted spy Jonathan Pollard as a prime example. Jewish organizations adopted Pollard's brief allegedly in response to grass-roots sentiment. Yet a survey of Jewish public opinion at the time revealed that only 22 percent of respondents wanted Jewish organizations to argue for a reduction in Pollard's sentence.

For Goldberg, this is no aberration. He maintains that since 1967 a determined minority of Zionists, Orthodox Jews, and neo-conservatives repeatedly have opted for "defensive nationalism" rather than reflect the more liberal views of the Jewish community generally. This narrow coalition, best evidenced at the Conference of Presidents, resulted in the virtual absence of communal support for the policies of Prime Minister Rabin, despite overwhelming popular and grass-roots support for the peace process he initiated.

The analysis, however, will not hold. First, if a narrow coalition of Orthodox Jews, Zionists, and neoconservatives have truly captured communal leadership, it is strange that the domestic Jewish agenda so frequently echoes the pronouncements of liberal politicians opposed by precisely those three groupings. Secondly, Jewish organizations do not make claims to speak on behalf of the community generally. They do claim to speak on behalf of their members. Democracy in the Jewish community therefore means representation of affiliated Jews, much as barely a majority of Americans actually vote in presidential elections, and far fewer do so in congressional and local elections.

Lastly, Goldberg's hopes for change rest on the proposed merger of the Council of Jewish Federations (CJF) and the United Jewish Appeal (UJA). To his credit, he explains why the proposed merger matters, for it facilitates a centralized national leadership reflective of grass-roots needs in the communities. Yet he fails to ask whether strengthening the ideology of consensus so prevalent in the work of Jewish Federations might only increase the boredom and paucity of ideological debate that invite further erosion and disaffiliation. Actually, as Goldberg notes, the CJF resisted public debate on the peace process, preferring to endorse the policies of the Israeli government of the day.

J. J. Goldberg has written a thought-provoking book. The Jewish community needs to be challenged by independent and tough-minded commentators. Whether one finds Goldberg's criticisms compelling, or one believes, as I do, that he misfires, the community can only benefit from the intense scrutiny and keen eye he brings to reporting the conduct of Jewish communal affairs.

Struggles in the Promised Land:
Towards a History of Black-Jewish Relations in the United States

by Jack Salzman and Cornel West, eds.

This newly-published collection of essays on black-Jewish relations provides a perspective on the past and at least a glimpse of the future. The contributors address historical aspects of relations between Jews and blacks and usually conclude their remarks with a forecast or prescriptive comment on future relationships. In that sense, the work is appropriately subtitled "towards a history" implying that the essays collectively provide building blocks for a history yet to be written.

As might be expected in such a collection, the quality of the essays is varied. Some are, indeed, brilliant; others must be considered highly valuable. Particularly noteworthy is David Goldenberg's examination of rabbinic sources in which he exempts rabbinic tradition from the charge of racism. By contrast, Goldenberg locates within Islam the identification of blacks with slavery. Similarly, David Brion Davis, perhaps the preeminent historian of slavery, finds the role of the Jew in the slave trade to be infinitesimal. To be sure, Jason Silverman acknowledges that most southern Jews did support slavery. However, Silverman argues that the numbers of Jews in the South were simply too negligible to be of much consequence as slave owners. Collectively, these essays correctly expose the lie of Jewish predominance within black slavery.

Other essays are most welcome for their realism and hard-headedness concerning black-Jewish relations. Several authors, nobably black intellectuals, correctly demythologize the black-Jewish alliance and place it within the context of group interests. Patricia Williams and Clayborne Carson are particularly successful in identifying the basis of a productive relationship as anchored in shared interests rather than idealized images of one another. Among the Jewish contributors, Mi-

Reprinted with permission from *Jewish Book World*, Fall 1997.

chael Walzer cogently argues that the battle against anti-Semitism within the black community must be the first step in any efforts at reconstruction of black-Jewish alliance.

By contrast, other essays in this collection noticeably lack this hard-headed realism. Several authors commit factual errors. Thus the reader will be surprised to discover that Martin Peretz of the *New Republic* is characterized as "a leading Jewish neo-conservative" because he finds that the problems of the inner cities relate to culture and family as well as to employment. Howard Stern, the outrageous talk-show host, is misleadingly identified as a Jew—he actually defines himself as a "half-Jew." Michael Lerner of *Tikkun* magazine is wrongly credited with the quip, "Jews earn like Episcopalians but vote like Puerto Ricans," a statement originally coined by Milton Himmelfarb of the American Jewish Committee. Most importantly, supporters of the Union of American Hebrew Congregations and the National Council of Jewish Women will be surprised to learn that a Jewish intellectual credits their organizations as advocating quotas—an assertion that is simply untrue.

These, to be sure, are mere trees within a large forest, and it is the forest that is most questionable. For one thing, the editors never fully explain why existing histories of black-Jewish relations are inadequate. Most noticeably, the recent and widely-discussed narrative by Murray Friedman, *What Went Wrong? The Creation and Collapse of the Black-Jewish Alliance* (Free Press, 1995) is treated only casually. Friedman, to be sure, is a neo-conservative, and the failure to engage his work underscores a deeper failure in the selection of contributors—virtually all of whom emanate from the progressive Left, and certainly none represent the perspectives of Jewish neo-conservatives. Among African-Americans, it would have been especially desirable to hear the voices of Glenn Loury, Shelby Steele, and Tom Sowell—senior scholars with pronounced views on the subject. Notwithstanding the rhetoric of diversity and pluralism, the editors in fact included a rather narrow range of contributors.

This ideological slant becomes most evident in the wistfulness that underlies some of the essays. Some contributors look to a coalition on the Left and believe that Jews and blacks could return to the halcyon days of the civil rights coalition if only one or two obstacles could be cleared away. Thus, Paul Buhle and Robin Kelley describe a New York City hospital workers' union as a "shining light of black-Jewish-Latino solidarity" despite the union's support for the legal defense of the Black Panthers and its protest against Israeli occupation of the West Bank—clearly divisive issues for both Jews and blacks. Gary Rubin asks the Jewish community to pay less attention to statements critical of Israel by black leaders and instead focus more on grass-roots sentiment where Israel is a far less salient issue—as if elite opinion possesses only marginal significance. Lastly, Letty Pogrebin urges Jews and blacks to unite for together they comprise "fifteen percent of the population and much of its moral conscience" as if a paradigm of shared suffering entitles groups to exclusive claims of moral virtue.

Strikingly and significantly, the wistfulness of these comments is virtually shattered by the candid concluding essay of Cornel West in which he states that he "was never a Zionist" and that "only a secular democratic state—with no special Jewish character can secure Jewish survival." In the decade since the heyday of the civil rights alliance, Zionism and pro-Israelism have become central to the minds, hearts and identity of American Jews. The Jewish people is exercised by the relationship with Israel and the struggle over how to define the Jewishness of the Jewish State. Only the most extreme of Jewish intellectuals would agree with West's evocation of a secular democratic state devoid of Jewish content. Although often lionized by American Jewish audiences for his eloquence, West offers compelling testimony as to why the agendas of these two peoples are so different and why relations between them have fallen upon such difficult times.

The Vanishing American Jew:
In Search of Jewish Identity
for the Next Century

by Alan Dershowitz

In 1964 *Look* magazine published a cover story entitled "The Vanishing American Jew." In the three decades since, *Look* magazine has vanished twice, but American Jewry continues.

Nevertheless, there has been no shortage of jeremiads concerning Jewish disappearance. Alan Dershowitz's book is the latest in a long line of forebodings about assimilation. Dershowitz does offer, however, a new focus: Concerned that the myths that inspired his generation to lead a Jewish life do not speak to younger Jews today, he searches for new bases on which to construct Jewish identity. In that respect, he moves far beyond his earlier work, *Chutzpah*, in which he located anti-Semitism under virtually every nook and cranny. In contrast, in this book, the real story of American Jewry is that the Jews are, indeed, accepted and even welcomed in American society. Here Dershowitz addresses today's young Jews, for whom the phenomenon of American anti-Semitism is simply not their reality.

Indeed, the best part of Dershowitz's book is his diagnosis of American Jewry. To be a Jew in American society connotes an asset rather than a debit. To be sure, anti-Semitism continues, but, to America's credit, has been marginalized in American society. Holocaust denial, Louis Farrakhan, and the Ku Klux Klan hardly represent mainstream America today. Far more revealing is that Justice Stephen Breyer could be appointed to the United States Supreme Court without comment as to his Jewishness. For Dershowitz, the Clinton administration symbolizes the end of discrimination against Jews in America. One generation after the Holocaust, Jews can hardly afford complacency. Yet Dershowitz correctly identifies the need for a new Jewish agenda—one that will

Reprinted with permission from *Jewish Book World*, Fall 1997.

build upon positive Jewish identity rather than focus upon Jewish fears of external enemies.

The problem lies in the vision of the Jewish world according to Dershowitz. Often he relies upon shrill, exaggerated, and unreliable cries of Jewish disappearance and Orthodox triumphalism. By contrast, he overlooks significant research and data indicating that while the losses to American Jewry will undoubtedly be severe, the currently existing bases of Jewish life are sufficiently powerful to sustain American Jewry at its core—a core that is far larger than ultra-Orthodoxy and, in many ways, far more committed to leading an intensive Jewish life than previous generations had ever imagined. For example, Dershowitz is convinced that Jews who marry Jews today do so by accident, ignoring the sincere convictions of many Jews that leading a Jewish life is so precious that they wish to share it with one similarly identified. Both trends—renewal and assimilation—are happening simultaneously. Dershowitz, unfortunately, notices only the latter.

Similarly Dershowitz fears that the Christian Right will transform America into a theocracy. To be sure, Jews have parted company with many components of the social vision of the Christian Right. Moreover, Dershowitz correctly criticizes American Jews for all too often framing their Jewish identity as the negation of Christianity. Yet in exaggerating the vision of the Christian Right to create a theocratic America—in the face of over two centuries of separation between church and state—Dershowitz appears guilty of expressing precisely the Jewish paranoia he rightly urges Jewish leadership to abandon. Surely a Jewish community that is at home in America can overcome inordinate fears of Christianity and learn to disagree on social and theological grounds while working together with other religious leaders to combat unbridled secularism. And therein lies Dershowitz's greatest problem—his spirited defense of secular Judaism and his naive belief that secular Jewish identity may sustain American Jewry. Correctly Dershowitz urges secular Jews to become Jewishly literate—to open up the Jewish library and thereby to join the debate over meaningful Jewish identity. However, he ignores the sorry record of secular Jewishness in sustaining Jewish identity over more than two generations. For example, where today are the heirs of Bundists conversant in Yiddish literature? Strangely, Dershowitz ascribes the failures of Jewish education today to the monopoly of religious educators, an analysis which undervalues the incredible accomplishments of religious education in Jewish day schools within all the movements of American Judaism. Conversely, Dershowitz overstates the successes of Jewish education under secular auspices. In downplaying the real evidence for Jewish renewal, he appears oblivious to the fact that much of that renewal has been religious in nature.

Dershowitz's attack upon religious leadership is most pronounced in his treatment of mixed-marriage. He calls rabbis to account for refusing to perform mixed-marriages, again ignoring research data indicating that rabbinic officiation or non-officiation has little impact on the subsequent Jewishness of the mixed-married family. Rather Dershowitz advocates a fundamentally new attitude towards mixed marriage in which the Jewish community no longer perceives it as a danger to be contained but as an inevitable reality of American society. Again, he appears shrill in arguing that the only ways of combating mixed-marriage are retreating to the ghetto and rejecting modern culture. Serious Jewish education, creating environments that are richly Jewish, and attending universities with large numbers of Jewish students will by no means guarantee Jewish in-marriage, but they do increase the odds—without retreating to the ghetto that Dershowitz rightly decries.

Moreover, Dershowitz appears to understand little of the dynamics of mixed-marriage itself. His radical pronouncement that "we must anticipate the end of the Jewish people as we know it precisely to become the masters of our own destiny"—i.e., abandon efforts to counter mixed-marriage in order to create a new Jewish identity—poses serious risks to Judaic cultural distinctiveness and to preserving traditional Jewish values. The new attitude Dershowitz advocates may well make it difficult if not impossible to discourage interfaith marriage.

Dershowitz doesn't address the real capacity of the Jewish community to address the needs and desires of the mixed-married population. Many mixed-marrieds have accepted the American ideal that two faiths are better than one and wish Jewish communal assistance in dual-faith parenting. In the well-intentioned desire to reach out to this population,

American Jewry risks diluting its core values and cultural distinctiveness and, I may add, its religious heritage.

Dershowitz's call for a more open, inclusive, and secular Jewish community ultimately blurs the boundaries between Jew and Gentile. For example, at his *seder* he emphasizes ecumenical aspects of Passover and downplays distinctive and ethnic components. One may disagree, as I do, with his assumptions concerning how attractive such a Jewish identity will be. However, even more problematical is that a minority such as the Jews cannot survive without distinctive boundaries. In the more open, inclusive Judaism Dershowitz desires, there will be few reasons for marrying other Jews, and Jewish identity will surely be diluted into a vague universalism lacking both distinctive practices and ties to Jewish peoplehood.

Surprisingly, that scenario has already been outlined in the popular television series *Star Trek*. The vision of a Federation that retains many Jewish ideas—progress, optimism, equality, and tolerance of diversity—is articulated by the producers and actors. Yet the Federation remains a universe in which Judaism has become extinct and no contemporary Jews exist. Should one advocate such a universe in the name of preserving Jewish continuity? Excessive *chutzpah* does not make one correct.

Finding the Middle Ground:
Tradition Renewed

by Jack Wertheimer

Long considered a beacon of academic Jewish studies and flagship institution of Conservative Judaism, the Jewish Theological Seminary has compiled an impressive record of distinguished faculty and alumni, ideological leadership on public policy issues, and serious scholarship in the tradition of the "Science of Judaism." Moreover, Seminary scholars have been remarkably candid in their self-criticism and appraisal of Conservative Jewish thought and practice.

Thus it comes as no surprise that in two magisterial volumes— *Tradition Renewed: A History of the Jewish Theological Seminary of America*—Jack Wertheimer, Seminary provost and preeminent historian of the movement, has compiled a fascinating set of studies assessing the Seminary's impact on the Conservative movement and, by extension, on the American Jewish community. (Volume I is titled "The Making of an Institution of Higher Learning," and Volume II is titled "Beyond the Academy.")

From its earliest days, JTS, established in 1886, felt compelled to distinguish itself ideologically from both the Orthodox and the Reform camps. Initially, the distance was greater from Reform, which Solomon Schechter regarded as primarily a way station toward assimilation. Both Schechter and his successor, Cyrus Adler, regarded themselves as more Orthodox than Reform and hoped that JTS would project a face of Orthodoxy engaged with rather than isolated from modern culture. For example, until the 1960s, biblical criticism was limited at JTS to the latter books of the Bible rather than the Pentateuch itself. Until the 1950s, Yeshiva University served as the primary undergraduate feeder school for JTS, and YU alumni frequently comprised as much as 30 percent of the JTS rabbinical school student body. Saul Lieberman, the Seminary's foremost Talmudist, initiated discussions in the 1950s with

Reprinted from the *Jewish Week of New York,* May 29, 1998.

Yeshiva's Joseph B. Soloveitchik in an effort to establish a joint *beit din* for the Jewish community.

JTS by no means limited its focus to the Jewish community. Chancellor Louis Finkelstein focused on interfaith work, building bridges between scholarship and the spiritual needs of post-war America. Rather than supply a voice for the Conservative movement alone, Finkelstein wished for the Seminary to serve as the voice of Judaism in an America increasingly thirsting for spiritual leadership. Finkelstein's critics, in fact, argued that the chancellor's broader focus on American Jewry generally was ignoring the real needs of the Conservative movement itself. Ironically, it was left to Gerson Cohen, a scholar's scholar, to restore the Seminary to its roots in Conservative Judaism.

As Jonathan Sarna here demonstrates, two traditions of scholarship coexisted within the Seminary's walls. An elite tradition of critical and textual scholarship, represented by, among others, Louis Ginzberg, Lieberman, and Cohen himself, has been accompanied by a tradition of scholarship on popular and timely issues addressed to the broader community. By stressing both traditions, JTS enhanced the quality of Jewish scholarship in America and provided a distinctive Conservative voice of social commentary on issues of the day.

Among the latter, of course, was the debate over women's ordination, perhaps the defining issue in postwar Conservative Judaism. Beth Wagner's study, "Politics of Women's Ordination," cogently analyzes the internal discord over the prospect of women as Conservative rabbis. In retrospect, the debate exposed deep contradictions within the ideology of Conservative Judaism. Could the movement regard itself as halakhic, or did *halakha*, following Mordecai Kaplan, possess a voice rather than a veto? If women could count in a minyan, as they could after 1975, on what basis might they be excluded from the rabbinate? For that matter, the debate over women's ordination is currently being replayed in a debate over ordaining gays and lesbians, an issue which similarly has divided the movement between halakhists and post-halakhists.

Nor has the relationship with Israel been devoid of tension. Gerson Cohen actually wished to be remembered for solidifying the Seminary's presence in Israel and mandating a year of study in Israel for all rabbinical students. In fact, today no less than 10 percent of the membership of the Rabbinical Assembly resides in Israel. However, Louis Finkelstein, like Schechter, was noticeably ambivalent about political Zionism, even as JTS students in the 1940s joined hands with counterparts at Yeshiva University and Hebrew Union College in protest against the anti-Zionist American Council for Judaism and demanded that *Hatikvah* be recited at JTS commencement ceremonies. Similarly, while Hebrew was venerated at the Seminary's Teacher's Institute, Professor Lieberman opposed the recitation of Hallel with a blessing on Israeli Independence Day.

The last decade, of necessity treated only briefly in these volumes, has witnessed the sharpening of two trends—increased distance from Orthodoxy and explicit protest at the absence of religious pluralism in Israel. Significantly, at the onset of his tenure, Seminary Chancellor Ismar Schorsch warned that alignment with Reform would undermine the credibility of Conservative Judaism in Israel because of Reform Judaism's liberal stances on patrilineal descent and rabbinic officiation at mixed marriages. Politically, however, the presence of a common adversary in the chief rabbinate in Israel has done wonders to bring Reform and Conservative closer much as, a century ago, the arrival of *haskala,* or Jewish enlightenment, in Eastern Europe quelled the bitter debates between hasidim and their deeply Orthodox critics, the *mitnagdim.* Most recently, Chancellor Schorsch's unqualified condemnation of the chief rabbinate, failing to distinguish between current practices of its incumbents and the office itself, has alienated many Modern Orthodox Jews, otherwise sympathetic to Seminary efforts to revitalize Jewish tradition in a modern context.

Putting down these volumes leaves the reader in awe of JTS as an academic center of scholarship and as training grounds for Conservative Jewish leaders. The volumes themselves testify to that dual self-perception of scholarly excellence and ideological leadership. JTS has benefited from a plurality of ideological voices. Alone among seminaries, JTS in the 1960s sponsored a course on differing Jewish theologies featuring faculty drawn from the intellectual leadership of all the religious movements in dialogue with one another. Indeed, the diversity between Abraham Joshua Heschel and Mordecai Kaplan, or Saul Lieberman and Seymour Siegel, enriched JTS in ways not at all present in either Hebrew Union College or Yeshiva University, which, by comparison, were more uniform in outlook.

The volumes, to be sure, contain omissions. One wishes for some analysis of Conservative rabbis in the field—JTS alumni charged with transmitting the Torah they studied at JTS to constituencies often indifferent to those texts.

Yet the primary legacy of these volumes is that JTS has found its distinctive voice. In some respects more traditional than Reform, in others more liberal than Orthodox, JTS strives to preserve the Jewish center. At a time of greater polarization between Jews, and as the Seminary witnesses its own internal and external battles over homosexuality, religious pluralism, and Jewish continuity, it has become increasingly difficult to preserve the middle ground. Yet precisely at a time when the gulf between Jews is widening, the distinctive voices of centrist groupings are all the more necessary to bridge divides and maintain lines of communication within the Jewish people. For all of our sakes, let's hope the voices of the center prevail.

Chasidim Do More Than Dance:
The Religious Thought of Hasidim

by Norman Lamm

No group in today's Jewish community is as poorly understood as the somewhat esoteric hasidim. Often depicted in the media as isolationist and even racist, hasidim rarely receive the nuanced treatment they merit. Certainly few Jews, let alone Gentiles, can say much more concerning Lubavitch than their messianic belief in a deceased rebbe or more of Satmar than their aggressive anti-Zionism.

Dr. Norman Lamm, president of Yeshiva University, has undertaken a much-needed corrective to these common stereotypes by focusing upon the intellectual and theological teachings of hasidism, many of which are far more profound than popular images suggest. That Lamm has continued, throughout his 25-year presidency, to author works of Judaic scholarship, testifies both to his own incredible productivity and his capacity to articulate the beauties of Judaic heritage for popular and scholarly audiences alike.

Indeed, *The Religious Thought of Hasidim* (Yeshiva University Press) provides the reader access to a rich intellectual culture encompassing hasidic beliefs, doctrines, and religious teachings.

Contrary to Martin Buber, among others, Lamm argues for continuity of hasidic thought with traditional Judaism. For example, he traces the intellectual roots of Lubavitch, expressed in the teachings of the Tanya, to traditionalist notions of the soul and its respective drives toward good and evil. As might be expected, he underscores hasidism's preference for faith over reason, that man's greatest accomplishment lay in trust in God, in direct contrast to the modern temperament which emphasizes the triumph of secularist reason as arbiter of faith and even in contrast to Moses Maimonides, who defined man's highest good as intellectual cognition of the Deity.

Conversely, Lamm is by no means reticent at examining hasidism's

Reprinted from the *Jewish Week of New York,* April 21, 2000.

innovations. He notes how hasidism anticipated Freudian depth psychology by considering the potential of evil to elevate man. In particular, he demonstrates the remarkable belief of some hasidim that the exile of the Jews presented an opportunity for proselytization—a doctrine by no means devoid of contemporary relevance.

At the core of the book are the central hasidic doctrines of worship through joy, immanence of God, clinging to the Almighty, and the role of the tzaddik or rebbe. By emphasizing God's presence as permeating all of creation, hasidism democratized religion in making God accessible to all. Given God's immanence, it would only be proper to assume a state of rejoicing in God's presence, thus restoring a badly needed dimension of happiness and celebration to East European Jewish life. Clinging to God, or *devekut,* represented perhaps the most innovative of hasidic doctrines, suggesting that the human soul could literally adhere to God rather than the more traditional rabbinic emphasis on study and imitations of God's ways through ethical and religious behaviors.

Lamm is not oblivious to potential dangers within these doctrines. The role of the tzaddik or rebbe invites a cult of personality once belief in individual infallibility is permitted. Lubavitch messianism, with its unprecedented theme of a dead messiah, departs radically from traditionalist rabbinic views of messianism, which preserved the messianic idea of hope and restoration while actively discouraging messianic movements as wasteful at best and destructive at worst.

Lastly, Lamm candidly admits that hasidism feared feminine sexuality and therefore assigned women an inferior role. The much-renowned Maid of Ludmir, the exception that literally proved the rule, had to renounce feminine identity in order to function as hasidic leader.

This book is addressed both to the general reader interested in a reference guide to hasidic thought and to the serious student eager to pursue a course of study on hasidism. The book, in fact, originated in courses Lamm taught at Yeshiva University in the 1960s on hasidism and mysticism. As a student in those early years, I delighted in those courses and can safely promise today's reader that then, as now, the work was demanding but the rewards far exceeded the effort.

Across the Great Divide:
Jewish or Israeli? Israelis and the Jewish Tradition

by David Hartman

Few among contemporary Jewish thinkers have more carefully and thoroughly probed the theological implications of Israel's rebirth and the return of Jews to sovereignty and statehood than David Hartman. Since his *aliyah* over three decades ago, Rabbi Hartman consistently has imagined Israel as an historic opportunity to implement the covenant of Sinai and to become a "holy people." In recent years his efforts to expose secular Israelis to the beauties of Judaic heritage have borne significant fruit, especially through the teacher-training initiatives of the Shalom Hartman Institute.

In this brief, compelling, and eminently readable new volume, originally delivered as lectures at Yale University, Hartman summarizes both the philosophic foundations and the programmatic directions of his work within Israel society. His starting point is that religious and secular Zionists alike must rethink their hypotheses. Religious Zionism erred by supremacizing the sanctity of land in the aftermath of the 1967 war. Secular Zionists erred in defining Jewish identity exclusively through the principle of peoplehood, closing the door to continued engagement with Jewish teaching and heritage as the domain of an entrenched Orthodoxy. Hartman urges both sides to return to the spirit of Maimonides—engagement of Jews with universal reason while discouraging messianic activism and expectation.

This centrist position of moderation in politics accompanied by a Jewish identity rooted in tradition and Jewish learning is currently threatened from multiple directions. Ultra-Orthodoxy claims exclusive reliance upon Torah, denigrating the concrete achievements of secular Israel. Religious Zionism embraces the Jewish state in quasi-mythical and messianic terms, excluding the possibility of diplomacy and nego-

Reprinted from the *Jewish Week of New York,* June 29, 2001.

tiations based upon territorial compromise. Conversely, on the Left, the inroads of post-Zionism and the quest for normalcy threaten to attenuate the Jewish foundations of Israel and its highly "abnormal" claims upon world Jewry as an international Jewish people. Similarly, the new archaeology, ironically currently popular within some elite rabbinical circles, undermines the foundational narratives of the Bible as historical bulwarks of Jewish solidarity.

The end result is a crisis of Jewish identity and a broadening gulf within the Jewish people. To be sure, in Hartman's view, secular Jewish identity has, in some measure, been sustained in Israel even as it has failed in the Diaspora. However, he believes that increasing numbers of Israelis have recently acknowledged the limits of secularism, especially in light of the Holocaust embodying a radical evil, and wish to reengage Judaic tradition. Hartman believes that making the library of Jewish texts accessible to all will both address the crisis of Jewish identity and restore a fragmented Jewish unity.

Implementing such a program entails embracing the accomplishments of an Israeli secularism that affirmed Jewish peoplehood and rejected assimilation. For these reasons, Joseph B. Soloveitchik, the dean of American Orthodoxy, assigned covenental significance to secular Israel as battling on behalf of the collective destiny of the Jewish people—a "covenant of shared fate." Similarly, Rav Kook, dean of religious Zionism, included secular Zionism as part of the cosmic redemption of the Jewish people.

Neither Kook nor Soloveitchik, however, assigned existential value to secular Israeli identity. Neither can be described as pluralist. Both sought to include rather than exclude, yet both derided secular Zionism as having ultimate value even as they conceded its usefulness.

Hartman's position, by contrast, is more daring and controversial. Unlike Kook and Soloveitchik, he remains quite skeptical of the ultimate triumph of Jewish religious renewal. The dangers of assimilation in the Diaspora and attenuated Jewishness within Israeli society, for him, are all too real. Therefore, he is not be content with a "live and let live" social contract with the secular camp. Rather he advocates a vigorous and open-ended engagement with Judaic tradition—a dialogue without any assumptions either of Jewish tradition being archaic or of the ultimate return or *teshuva* of the secularists. The crucial debate, for Hartman, is not over the authority of *halakha* but rather over the centrality of Jewish text and learning to Jewish identity. By inviting all Jews to reconnect with Torah, he hopes to rehabilitate the meaning of a Torah-covenental community.

Orthodox and liberals alike find this position threatening. The Chief Rabbinate dismisses Hartman's defense of pluralism as validating non-Orthodox approaches and undermining an Orthodox monopoly. Post-Zionist and "ultra-secular" elites value his ethos of pluralism and tolerance but prefer a society rooted in the values of Western liberalism and individualism to one that is grounded in Torah. Moreover, Hartman offers no clear prescription of ultimate destination. His objective is to reengage the Jewish people upon a journey of Judaic study rather than predict the nature of its final resting place.

Hartman's vision is truly inspirational. Precisely by taking Israel seriously as a theological and covenental opportunity, he provides meaning to the value of Jewish peoplehood. All too often, both in our history and in our contemporary reality, we have defined peoplehood as encompassing all those who are threatened because of their Jewishness. Hartman creates an alternative vision of peoplehood that is far nobler—as heirs to shared texts and as possessors of a golden opportunity to create a covenantal community. Whether the Jewish people can rise to that vision or will remain locked in its external and internal conflicts will be the critical question for the twenty-first century.

LETTERS TO THE EDITOR

Letters to the editor have provided yet another opportunity to impact upon public climate of opinion. Some of these brief letters engage controversial issues—e.g., the rejection of pluralism among the Orthodox Right or the controversy over New York City's gay synagogue and the Israel Day Parade. Others provide additional information or analysis to trends, e.g., what is happening inside American Jewry's religious movements.

ArtScroll and Scholarship

To the Editor of *Tradition:*

Dr. Barry Levy's provocative and controversial review of the Art-Scroll series has aroused considerable comment in the pages of *Tradition.* Much of the criticism of Dr. Levy's review, however, centers upon his style rather than the substance of his analysis. Permit me to add several comments for consideration in discussing the ArtScroll series.

1. The Question of Language

In high school, my classmates struggled to read and understand the classic commentaries in their original Hebrew. The task was difficult, fraught with error, time-consuming, yet in the long run most rewarding. Our instructors aimed to instill in us a desire to study the commentators and to appreciate their wisdom. Perhaps we did not cover as much ground as we might have accomplished reading English translations, but certainly we emerged with the ability to read Ramban, Abarbanel and the others.

The ArtScroll series, frequently used today in yeshivah day schools, subverts this purpose. It serves as a "trot," a made-easy translation that removes from the student the challenge and the responsibility of learning how to master traditional commentators. The selectivity of the translations attempts to eliminate the complexities and doubts raised by many of the classic commentaries. Instructors who utilize the ArtScroll series rather than encourage students to undertake study of commentators on their own are raising serious questions about the direction of Jewish education.

2. The Question of Ideology

Dr. Levy's analogy to a pig may be in poor taste, but the substance of his comments must be considered rather than his style, In fact, the

ArtScroll looks "modern." Its illustrations are beautiful. It is neatly bound (a minor miracle in the publication of *seforim*). The style is both attractive and lucid.

Yet the contents of ArtScroll are anything but modern. Not only does it not take modern scholarship and modern science seriously, it pretends that they simply do not exist. Consider, for example, the ArtScroll volume on the Book of Esther. The historical introduction sets forth a chronology in which the Declaration of Cyrus occurred in the year 370 B.C.E. The author does not deem it even worth mentioning that historians are of the unanimous opinion that the Declaration occurred many years earlier, approximately 537 B.C.E. This is no mere question of dates. What is at stake is the response of the modern Orthodox Jew to a conflict of assumptions between historical scholarship that places the Persian period as lasting over 200 years and a traditionalist reading of history which assumes the period lasted only 52 years.

One could multiply the examples in which ArtScroll manages to ignore or dismiss as irrelevant the findings and source materials of modern scholarship. Does modern Orthodoxy wish to educate its people towards functioning as modern men and women in the social and business realms, or as individuals isolated and sheltered from the ideas and values of modern culture? One has every right to challenge historical scholarship. However, to omit and ignore the serious questions raised by historians in an historical essay amounts to intellectual dishonesty. Moreover, by ignoring historical scholarship, ArtScroll is implicitly confessing that all attempts to harmonize and synthesize traditional theology with modern historical analysis are inherently impossible.

Permit me again to recall my experience in yeshivah high school. During my junior and senior years an East European *rosh yeshivah,* who had himself never undergone a college education, assigned several term papers concerning questions such as the account of creation in Genesis compared with the doctrine of evolution and a comparison of the Joseph sequence of stories in Genesis with Thomas Mann's epic *Joseph and His Brothers.* The intellectual adventure in studying both traditional commentaries and modern scholarship—literary, scientific and historical—formed some of the highlights of my day school education. In contrast, the ArtScroll series pretends that one may study sacred texts with no references whatsoever to historical method, literary criticism, or scientific scholarship.

3. *Modern Orthodoxy's Self-Definition*

Correspondents to *Tradition* have emphasized the reality of the Art-Scroll phenomenon—people do read it, and it has become a significant dimension of Orthodox education. In many ways this phenomenon symbolizes Orthodoxy's general rightward drift. Recently a student of mine, wearing blue jeans and a knitted *kipah,* questioned my assumption that Modern Orthodoxy was defensible. He suggested abandoning the ideal of synthesis and rejecting all secular culture except for professional and vocational purposes. I will not suggest that ArtScroll created my student. I do suggest that much as ArtScroll has adopted the forms of modernity (illustration, proper binding, effective use of the English language) and rejected the content of modernity, so my blue-jeans clad student and countless others of his peers are defining Modern Orthodoxy as modern purely in form and not at all in content.

Whether or not these developments are fortunate or unfortunate is a matter of personal values and ideology. Yet the social reality of Art-Scroll connotes that Modern Orthodoxy and right-wing Orthodoxy have virtually coalesced. If this means the demise of the ideals of *Torah U'Mada* in favor of a compartmentalized Orthodoxy whose members are quite sophisticated in their professional enterprises yet close their minds to modern scholarship when they think Jewishly, then we must pay the price of acknowledging that Orthodoxy and modernity are indeed incompatible. That *Tradition*'s correspondents have all reacted so negatively to Dr. Levy's review indicates their personal confession of Modern Orthodoxy's failure to develop its own ideology. To maintain independence and integrity, Modern Orthodox leadership must now formulate an ideology of intellectual synthesis between tradition and modernity. That route is perilous and fraught with danger. Far more dangerous, however, are the directions implied by those who celebrate ArtScroll as the most significant publishing event in the history of American Orthodoxy.

In the previous generation of American Orthodoxy, the Hertz commentary became the most popular English language exposition of

Scripture. Hertz's work, although flawed and now frequently outdated, provided a sincere effort to come to grips with modern scholarship. What is necessary now is a revised and updated version of Hertz—not ArtScroll's feeble efforts to pretend that modern scholarship does not exist.

On Gays in the Parade

To the Editor of the *Jewish Week:*

In recent weeks the Jewish community has been sorely divided and often polarized over questions of homosexuality and its public presence within Jewish communal institutions and events. Public disputes have centered upon, although they have by no means been limited to, the question of the right of a gay synagogue to march in the Salute to Israel Parade.

Advocates of gay rights uphold principles of equal rights for all and the need to include homosexuals within the Jewish community. Conversely, their opponents seek to circumscribe homosexual behavior, often citing Jewish tradition as justification. Charges and counter-charges of "gay-bashing" and "moral perversity" further polarize the issue and stifle expressions of legitimate disagreement and dissent.

Homosexuals, like members of any other minority group, deserve preservation of rights and liberties. There can be no equivocation on this point. But there is a clear difference between toleration of homosexual behavior and its articulation as a communal norm. Jewish ethics clearly uphold heterosexual marriage as the norm for society. That message, unfortunately, often is blurred in the context of debating gay rights.

Homosexual orientation ought rightly be protected. Gay-bashing serves no social purpose and is morally odious. Yet the moral relativism inherent in declaring homosexuality as an "alternate lifestyle" is similarly unacceptable. We must find ways to articulate societal preferences for heterosexual marriage while at the same time upholding the civil rights of individuals. Gay rights activists ought rightly be challenged to articulate a message that underscores rather than detracts from social norms of heterosexual marriage. Homosexuality is an orientation that we protect, not one that we prefer. Judaism is by no means homophobic, nor is it morally relativist.

Reprinted with permission from the *Jewish Week of New York,* April 23–29, 1993.

Engaging the Debate on Pluralism

To the Editor of *The Jewish Sentinel:*

Rabbi Avi Shafran's rejoinder (Jan. 27) to my column on American Orthodoxy (Dec. 23) misreads both my intentions and thrust, and suggests that I am guilty of a "canard" befitting historical and contemporary anti-Semites.

Rabbi Shafran, director of public affairs of Agudath Israel, neglects to note that the column was adapted from an address to the national convention of the Orthodox Union at a session entitled "How Others See Us." Two past presidents of the OU responded to my comments and urged, as I did, greater cooperation with rather than separatism from the non-Orthodox community. That Rabbi Shafran takes exception to my remarks should occasion no surprise, for Agudath Israel historically has opposed Orthodox participation in communal bodies such as the Commission on Jewish Continuity that incorporate representatives from all sectors of the community. That refusal to participate communicates—as I noted—dismissal of large sectors of American Jewry. In contrast, I argued that the voices of Orthodoxy need to be heard and are generally welcomed in communal forums.

One more serious difference relates to my defense of Jewish pluralism, which, he suggests, is a "sanitized name" for a phenomenon that threatens the entire Jewish people. My historical and theological disagreements with Rabbi Shafran probably are far too extensive for a newspaper exchange. Suffice to say, however, that I reject religious relativism, in which all expressions of Judaism have equal validity, and I identify personally—proudly, I may add—as a practicing Modern Orthodox Jew. In defending pluralism, however, I suggest that different Jews require different avenues and points of connectedness to their heritage. Communal interests lie in broadening those points of entry and access. Our objective ought be creating a community in which people care sufficiently to engage in intellectual battle over the meaning of the Torah and its teachings rather than remaining indifferent to them.

Reprinted from *The Jewish Sentinel,* February 3–9, 1995 (New York).

As Rabbi Shafran admits, we suffer primarily from assimilation and Judaic illiteracy. For that reason, the entire Jewish community, including the Orthodox, ought be supportive of efforts designed to encourage Jews to reconnect with their heritage. Which programs are in fact successful, the appropriateness of particular target populations for initiatives, and the relative scale of priorities within the community are all debatable. My point was that the Orthodox should engage that debate rather than dismiss it.

Jewish Continuity

To the Editor of *Commentary:*

Jack Wertheimer, Charles S. Liebman, and Steven M. Cohen, in "How to Save American Jews," deserve great credit for restoring the Jewish continuity debate to where it appropriately belongs—the realm of values, culture, and normative commitments to leading a Jewish life. There can, in short, be no Jewish continuity absent serious commitment to Judaism.

The authors correctly diagnose the reason why the Jewish community has thus far been unable to develop a meaningful agenda and strategy to secure the future quality of American Jewish life—the well-intentioned but misguided desire to target a broad and inclusive consensus that ultimately is so bland as to be essentially meaningless. Indeed, it is perhaps a point of no small irony that the ideology of consensus that has served American Jewry well in marshaling support for Israel and defending against anti-Semitism may very well be counterproductive in trying to inspire commitments to leading a meaningful and creative Jewish life.

Rather than aim for broad consensus, American Jewry would do well to recognize that some losses are, sad to say, inevitable, given the degree of Jewish acceptance in American society coupled with declining commitments to Judaism.

The solution must lie in serious Judaism. The most important battlefield in the fight for Jewish continuity, I believe, will be the Conservative and Reform religious movements. Serious, well-educated, and literate Conservative and Reform Jews are most unlikely to assimilate. For that reason, Jewish communal resources ought to be increasingly directed toward strenthening those movements and their members. In turn, and for the same reason, the critical importance of pluralism in Jewish religious life must be underscored. Orthodox leaders would do well to recognize that the primary threats to Jewish identity emanate from religious indifference rather than from religious pluralism. Steps recently taken by the Reform movement to enhance Jewish literacy and to deny Jewish education to children being raised even partially as Christians merit the approbation of Orthodox Jewry.

American Jewry has succeeded in advancing its agenda of securing a home in America. The question for its future is whether it has the will to build a Jewishly authentic culture sufficiently compelling to articulate a language of norms, commitments, expectations, and the demands of its adherents, alongside its place in the broader American society—a duality that this unique country makes possible. Failure to articulate such a language connotes an end to Jewish distinctiveness—a future scenario perhaps best forecast by the popular science-fiction series, *Star Trek.*

Conservative Judaism

Clifford E. Librach's prognosis for Conservative Judaism, albeit compelling in some respects, wrongly undermines those within the movement who, at considerable personal risk, have struggled to maintain its distinctive norms and ethos and its unique blend of Jewish tradition and modern American culture. Over a decade ago, the creedal statement of Conservative Judaism, *Emet V'emuna,* argued that, with the important exception of including women in the rabbinate and liturgical functions, the standards of Jewish tradition and history must continue to prevail within the movement. Since that time, Conservative leadership has successfully and consistently resisted efforts to dilute these standards on questions of mixed marriages, homosexuality, and patrilineal descent.

Within the past year, Rabbi William Lebeau, the vice chancellor and dean of the Jewish Theological Seminary's rabbinical school, articulated traditional norms of sexuality for rabbinical students in a public letter to the student body. JTS provost Jack Wertheimer has consistently argued, in these pages and elsewhere, for a Conservative language of commitments and demands—even if these run counter to many of the prevailing currents of American culture. Longstanding academic policy at JTS has placed expectations upon faculty to uphold traditional Jewish norms and practices, including that spouses be Jews. Instead of too glibly predicting the dilution of Conservative Judaism into theological blandness (or worse), external critics like Rabbi Librach would do better to endorse these efforts by Conservative leaders to maintain a distinctively Jewish ethos.

If Rabbi Librach is so pessimistic about current trends within Conservative Judaism—and presumably he has similar fears for the future of Reform Judaism—why, one must ask, does he not pursue the logic of his convictions and adopt Orthodox Judaism? He suggests an answer to this question when he singles out for praise certain trends toward greater Jewish learning and religiosity within his own Reform movement. By remaining within, and working to encourage these trends, Rabbi Librach offers a model for how Reform Judaism may continue to help preserve the Jewish future. Do not similar efforts within Conservative Judaism warrant his support and encouragement?

Intermarriage

To the Editor of *Commentary:*

Jack Wertheimer offers a compelling case that the Jewish community's will to resist mixed marriage is in danger of collapse. In an American culture that so overwhelmingly endorses interfaith marriage, the Jews will stand virtually alone if they are to mount a counterargument.

Fortunately, the situation may not be as bleak as Mr. Wertheimer describes. Officially, all the religious streams within Judaism continue to resist mixed marriage. The Conservative movement recently resolved that those employed in "role-model" positions (rabbis, educators, cantors, etc.) in its institutions ought to have Jewish spouses. Even more surprisingly, the movement's youth organization has urged its officers to refrain from dating non-Jews. The Reform movement, too, has formally opposed admitting children raised partially in another faith to its educational institutions, and has refused to approve rabbinic officiation at interfaith unions.

To be sure, there are those who counsel communal neutrality, in a well-intentioned effort to bring families back into the fold. The American Jewish Committee, though supportive of reaching out to interfaith couples, believes that we cannot afford such neutrality. Rather, we must underscore the contemporary vitality of both Judaism and Jewish peoplehood, and communicate that Jewish ideals are best realized through being shared with Jewish spouses and in the raising of Jewish children. For millennia, Judaism has survived precisely due to its ability to swim against the tide and articulate countercultural messages. Jack Wertheimer's essay eloquently makes the case that we should continue to do so.